A CENTURY OF
CONSUMER PROTECTION

Wayne L. Pines

EDITOR

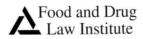

ISBN-10   1-885259-90-5

ISBN-13   978-1-885259-90-5

FDLI is a nonprofit, educational organization founded in 1949. Its mission is to advance the public health by providing a neutral forum for critical examination of the laws, regulations, and policies related to drugs, medical devices, other healthcare technologies, and foods.

FDLI's role is strictly educational. FDLI provides a neutral forum for the exchange of views on legal and regulatory problems and issues, but does not lobby. Our activities benefit attorneys; corporate officials; regulatory affairs professionals; research, quality control, manufacturing, and marketing personnel; government officials; and consumer organizations.

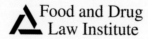
Food and Drug
Law Institute

For additional information or to order copies of this publication, contact:

Customer Service Department
Food and Drug Law Institute
1000 Vermont Avenue, NW, Suite 200
Washington, D.C. 20005-4903

Call (800) 956-6293 or (202) 371-1420
Fax: (202) 371-0649
www.fdli.org

FDA: A Century of Consumer Protection

Contents

And more…

At left, the Bureau of Chemistry building, 1910. At right, FDA's new building in White Oak, Maryland, a century later.

Preface

Andrew C. von Eschenbach, MD
Acting Commissioner of Food and Drugs

On a sweltering Saturday in June 1906, President Theodore Roosevelt made a trip down the Washington Mall to the U.S. Capitol, where he signed into law nearly 100 pieces of legislation passed by Congress in the waning days of its session. One of those bills, which had been voted out of conference committee just the day before, instructed the government to prevent "the manufacture, sale, or transportation of adulterated or misbranded or poisonous or deleterious foods, drugs, medicines, and liquors…." Its vision wasn't fully realized for years to come; however, the federal Food and Drugs Act placed into American law the protection of the nation's most vital and lifesaving commodities.

The new law added regulatory functions to the scientific mission of the Bureau of Chemistry, an office of the Department of Agriculture that, in the years immediately after the Civil War, had been staffed by a single chemist. In 1930, the burgeoning Bureau of Chemistry took on the name by which it is known to this day. And that institution, the Food and Drug Administration, is recognized—in the twenty-first century—as the world's "gold standard" of safety and security. FDA extends a blanket of protection over food safety and labeling; the effectiveness of human and animal drugs and human vaccines; blood used for transfusions; medical devices, from simple scalpels to high-tech imaging devices; tissues used for transplantation; radiation-emitting equipment like X-ray machines and microwave ovens; and cosmetics. Without a doubt, it's been quite a century.

With nearly 10,000 employees and regulatory responsibilities encompassing a quarter of the American economy, FDA can no longer be termed small. Nor can its accomplishments. In recent years, FDA's contributions have helped bring revolutionary advances to heart patients, such as coronary stents, implantable defibrillators, and minimally invasive bypass surgery. Advanced diagnostics, facilitated by FDA, are saving thousands of lives by enabling detection of cancer at a time when it's more treatable. Antiretroviral drugs have brought new hope to victims of HIV infection and AIDS. The United States continues to set global benchmarks for the safety of its food and the efficacy of its vaccines—whether for people or animals. Indeed, the FDA impacts every American life. And its future will be nothing less than to lead a new era of biomedical science.

From a modern perspective, it seems nearly unimaginable to contemplate that for centuries—before there was an FDA or even a United States—what we knew of biology and disease was largely what we could detect with our five senses, principally what we could see or touch. Diseases could be witnessed and chronicled, but rarely treated. Close to a century ago, science began to fully harness the power of the microscope. With that advance, life's processes began to reveal themselves at the cellular level. Bacteria, viruses, and tumors became visible. The existence of many diseases and conditions could be conclusively proved—even if the capacity to help patients remained largely elusive.

But in the last decade or so, biomedical science has experienced its most-pronounced growth in history: Cutting-edge technologies have fueled a molecular view of life. That exponential advance, including the decoding of the human and several animal genomes, is tantamount to nothing less than a metamorphosis. The worlds of science and medicine being constructed today are no more like the past than a butterfly is to a caterpillar. We are learning that diseases are not events, but processes that begin long before something we can see, touch, or feel. Indeed, molecular discoveries are rapidly leading to an era of personalized medicine, when we will intervene ever earlier, delivering the right treatment to the right patient at the right time, with predictable, right outcomes.

FDA will be the bridge to the development required by that future, connecting the promise of discoveries to the delivery of each advance, guiding new interventions through the critical path of development, so that the fruits of progress will be available to patients and the public. The FDA of our next century will utilize the latest information technology and techniques to facilitate lifesaving and life-enhancing interventions, delivered quickly and affordably, with all of the safety and security Americans rightly expect. The molecular metamorphosis will affect us all.

A modernized system of discovery, development, and delivery will require FDA's regulatory mechanisms and its system of clinical trials to keep pace. Empirical tests based on trial and error will yield to mechanistic explanations of why a drug does or doesn't work. Genomics, for one, will allow doctors and scientists to predict, using genetic markers, who will respond to a new medicine, who might suffer a side effect, or who might experience no beneficial effect. This new world will require new ways of thinking and a new openness to collaborations. To grasp every potential advance, FDA will need to work with partners, including the National Institutes of Health, the Centers for Medicare and Medicaid Services, the Centers for Disease Control and Prevention, the Agency for Healthcare Research and Quality, academia, and industry.

The molecular era will lead to improved methods of developing and producing vaccines, and will make certain that immunization remains at the forefront of disease control. The sciences of medical device development, radiological health, and veterinary medicine will continue bringing impressive improvements. Our food will be safer and even more wholesome, setting global standards for protection from contamination, even as the FDA accelerates the public's knowledge of nutrition and continues to drive down the number of food-related hospitalizations in the United States. With FDA's work, we will be a healthier America.

One hundred years of success is worthy of celebration. FDA stands tall because of each dedicated staff member. In the FDA's second century, we will build on a strong foundation to create a science-led regulatory agency dedicated to improving and enhancing health. Our second century will be based on new opportunities, but grounded in even-greater responsibility.

This is a time to celebrate the past—and to be exuberant about our future. Whether it is freedom from the suffering and death due to disease or generations of healthier infants, FDA must use its proud legacy to ensure a future more impressive than its past, and deliver that promise to all Americans. At its core, the FDA is about people. None of its accomplishments would be possible without the work of chemists, physicians, engineers, dentists, pharmacologists, nutritionists, veterinarians, nurses, attorneys, physiologists, technicians, administrators, and office professionals. Thank you for all of the hours and efforts you so generously offer every day.

Introduction

Wayne L. Pines

I was having lunch with Rich Cooper to discuss the outline of this book, and asked him for ideas about titles. After discussing the obvious ones, Rich came up with a novel one: "We Are 'They.'" The notion, Rich explained, is that the cover of the book would have a cartoon of two people talking in a grocery store. One points to the ingredient list on a box and says, "I can't even pronounce all these things. How do I know they won't kill me?" The other replies, "If those things would hurt you, *they* wouldn't let them be in there." Rich said he had heard Al Gottlieb, a career FDA employee, describe the cartoon at a dinner honoring two other career employees for thirty years of service to the agency.

The title, "We Are 'They,'" would convey the idea that "we"—the people of the Food and Drug Administration—are the ones who are looking out for the public by helping to assure the safety and when appropriate the effectiveness of the products they use every day. In the end, we did not use that title. As you can see, we went with a more conventional, descriptive title for this book, which marks the 100th anniversary of the enactment of the Pure Food and Drugs Act of 1906. But, I remain persuaded that, although "We Are 'They'" requires some thought to grasp, it would have been an apt title for this book. The underlying message is that FDA over its century of history is an agency whose work consumers take for granted. We, those who have worked at FDA, are the anonymous people on whom the public relies for basic product safety.

When our work is successful, it goes unnoticed by a public that takes safety for granted. FDA makes its biggest news with its failures. All that is as it should be. One of the important services FDA provides is that consumers generally don't have to worry about the safety of their foods, medical products, and cosmetics.

———————————◼———————————

This book came about as a consequence of a lunch meeting in October 2002 with Jerry Halperin and Mark Novitch. Jerry, former Deputy Director of the Bureau of Drugs at FDA and former Executive Director of the U. S. Pharmacopeia, was then (as now) President of the Food and Drug Law Institute (FDLI). Mark, a former FDA Deputy Commissioner and on two lengthy occasions Acting Commissioner, was then semi-retired and serving as FDLI's chairman.

Mark and I had discussed many times doing a book about the centennial, and invited Jerry to lunch in the Doubletree Hotel on Rockville Pike near FDA's headquarters to discuss whether FDLI would publish it. Jerry said he would pursue it with his board, and so FDLI came to be the publisher of this book.

When we started considering how it would be organized, we realized that there were many options. How best to capture 100 years of the world's most prestigious consumer protection and scientific regulatory agency? To answer this question, on May 2, 2003, FDLI invited all living former commissioners, deputy commissioners, general counsels and center (bureau) directors to a meeting to discuss their interest in the book and how best to approach the topic. The meeting was remarkably well attended—an all-star cast of FDA leadership for the previous thirty years. The group was enthusiastic about the idea of a centennial book. From that meeting and a subsequent one emerged a general outline, which later was refined. Authors for the chapters volunteered or were recommended, and we were off and running. The product, of course, is this volume.

The group decided that this should not be a chronological history of FDA. The history had been told in other books, and FDA's own website has an extensive series of articles and photos about FDA's history. There was no purpose in merely recounting the past and citing every milestone. Nor should it be a legal history, even though the book was to be published by an institute whose members are largely from law firms or the legal divisions of companies, and many of the authors happen to be lawyers. Instead, we designed a book that sought mainly to explain the consequences of food and drug regulation in the century since the enactment of the Pure Food and Drugs Act. We decided that the chapter authors would present, from their own viewpoints, not just a history, but rather a perspective, a point of view. They all had been personally involved in one way or another in the subject they were writing about. They have lived through the recent times and have intimate knowledge of the subjects of their chapters.

We also wanted to focus on individual episodes in FDA's history—there are so many to choose from—that would illustrate how the agency functions day to day. Vignettes that give an inside glimpse and perhaps stimulate memories among those who lived through the same times. Interspersed among the chapters are those vignettes, captured from a variety of sources.

We discussed at great length the intended audience for this book. Was it the general public, whose knowledge of FDA is derived from news articles? Was it to be addressed to the present and past employees of FDA? Since the book probably would have focused, rather than general, distribution, we decided that we would write it for someone who is generally familiar with FDA, but who may not know in detail its history and the full scope of its regulatory responsibilities and accomplishments.

Finally, we wanted to present this perspective in part through photographs and other graphics. Suzanne White Junod, an FDA historian, volunteered to draw from the agency's vast archives a selection of photographs that would illustrate the story of FDA's century. And so we moved forward, always keeping in mind that the most important theme that the planning group wanted the book to emphasize was, "What does it all mean?" What has been the influence, the impact, the legacy of FDA's first century of regulation of foods and medical products for the people of the United States and the world?

Telling the story of FDA during the century inevitably meant understanding how the food, drug, medical device, and cosmetics industries developed and grew. Indeed, the changes in those industries and the products they developed have been remarkable. The development during the nineteenth and twentieth centuries of better and more transportable food production methods changed forever how and what Americans eat. The development of pharmaceuticals, biologicals, and medical devices, especially in the last half of the twentieth century, changed healthcare forever, and was a major factor in extending the human life span from an average of forty-nine years in 1901 to more than seventy-seven years by the end of the century.

At the same time, of course, we experienced unprecedented changes in every other industry, and in our way of life. The changes achieved in the twentieth century—whether in communication, transportation, medicine, or a host of other areas—were unlike any previously experienced by humankind. In just sixty-six years, we went from the Wright brothers at Kitty Hawk to Neil Armstrong on the Moon! In the twentieth century, the United States became electrified; the automobile replaced the horse and buggy; superhighways and the telecommunications revolution connected us as never before; television, radio, and the Internet became universal; household appliances changed our home lives and the role of women; elevators and air conditioning created new patterns of urban living and enabled large-scale settlement of hotter regions. The list is endless.

In the industries FDA regulated during the twentieth century, refrigeration and freezing transformed agriculture from local to global, while pesticides and mechanized vehicles changed how farmers grew food. In the world of medicine, the century saw the development of vaccines for tuberculosis, yellow fever, hepatitis, polio, and childhood diseases such as measles and chicken pox. Antibiotics cured infectious diseases, insulin enabled diabetics to lead a normal life, psychotropic drugs enabled people with mental illness to function, and we learned to extend the lives of, and sometimes even cure, patients suffering from cancer and other killing diseases. Anesthesia vastly improved surgery, and implants enabled us to replace body parts. X-rays, discovered before the turn of the last century, made possible scientifically-based disease diagnosis. This list, too, could go on endlessly; and a list of the same length could legitimately mention entirely different advances.

FDA's role was to respond and shape these developments—to assess them; to ensure their effectiveness, safety, and proper labeling; and to oversee their introduction to the public. FDA not only set the standards for effectiveness and safety; more often than not, it also provided the stimulus for the regulated industries to raise their own standards still higher. By setting uniform national standards for food production, FDA helped assure that foods made far from where we live are safe to eat, so safe that all of us really do take food safety for granted. By setting standards for clinical trials and pharmaceutical development, FDA played a central role in assuring that the medicines we take are safe and effective and that the medical devices we use will work properly. Similarly, our cosmetics are safe, and the drugs used to treat animals are safe and effective.

The twentieth century transformed the products regulated by FDA, and FDA acted to ensure that those transformed products were appropriate for use. This volume seeks to explain the connections between FDA, its laws and its people, and the amazing advancements of this past century.

———————————■———————————

We start with the people of FDA. The agency is a conglomerate of thousands, with many types of specialized training who work together to protect the public and to advance the public health. They are a remarkably diverse group who serve a common mission. Many of the people who joined FDA during its first century stayed their entire career, thirty years or more, working for a federal salary when the expertise they gained had far greater financial value in the private sector. It is a testament to FDA and its mission that so many chose and continue to choose to stay for their entire career.

Other than Harvey W. Wiley, universally regarded as the father of the Pure Food and Drugs Act of 1906, no single person's achievements are prominently featured in this book. Certainly, recognition is appropriate for the men (and one woman) who have served as commissioner. Their photos are posted on FDA's history website. Certainly, Dr. Frances Kelsey, the woman who was credited with preventing thalidomide from being approved in the United States, thereby preventing birth defects, deserves recognition (her story is told in the section on drug regulation). Countless others at the agency have made important contributions, but with far less public recognition. Some of these unheralded heroes are featured in the vignettes.

———————————■———————————

As FDA enters its second century, some fundamental definitions integral to an understanding of the agency remain open to debate. For example, there is a perpetual debate within FDA as to whether it is predominantly a scientific agency or a law enforcement agency. Of course it is both—a scientific agency with law enforcement powers, and a law enforcement agency whose decisions are based on science. Which comes first, the law or the science? Law and science are inseparable in FDA's world. That is true now and always has been. Decisions are collaborative among those who understand the relevant science, those who understand the legal mandate (and its limits), and those who deal every day in the practicalities of enforcement.

Another perpetual question is how FDA should relate to the regulated industries. Critics of FDA describe the relationship as too cozy, but officials of regulated companies complain about their inability to influence the agency's priorities and decisions. The relationship has always been described as "arm's length"—which means that, even though the agency must deal with regulated companies daily, it must never develop relationships that undermine its ability to enforce the law with appropriate vigor by taking action against products that threaten the health and well-being of consumers, and by taking action against companies and individuals as circumstances warrant. Within FDA, the institutionalization of the decision-making process, whereby no single person makes a decision without consultation and collaboration with colleagues, helps maintain equilibrium in the relationship with industry. As we enter FDA's second century, that relationship continues to be adjusted to meet new challenges.

FDA's first inspector badge under U.S. Department of Agriculture jurisdiction, and FDA's current inspector badge as a component of the Department of Health and Human Services and the Public Health Service.

———————————■———————————

Originally this book was to have included a chapter on the future of FDA and of the industries and products it regulates. Peter Barton Hutt, a former FDA Chief Counsel and author of one of the chapters, thought that trying to predict the future, given how quickly the world is changing, has limited value. The risk in writing such a chapter is that readers of this book will see how narrow and naive we were in 2006 when thinking about the century ahead—imagine what an author in 1906 would have predicted about the century we just lived through. We don't know what the next century holds for FDA and the products it regulates. It is safe to say that there will be treatments for diseases that thus far have proved baffling. True, Americans in 2006 generally live much longer than Americans did a century ago, but not everyone shares in this longevity, and we have yet to understand the biological basis for many diseases. In the next century, medical progress will continue, perhaps not at the rate that occurred in the twentieth century, but perhaps so.

We are today, in 2006, on the verge of individualized medicine, the ability to alleviate or cure diseases with therapies specifically designed for individual patients. We are developing new medical devices that can be used to make life easier, but more importantly can keep people alive and active longer—in hospitals and outside them. We are marketing foods that can be produced less expensively and have a longer shelf life.

As we look to the future, regulation will become even more global than it is now. For the past century, FDA has set a standard, and retains unique expertise whose value crosses political borders. The gap between U. S. regulation and regulation in other countries undoubtedly has narrowed, and how, in the next century, countries can work even more closely to achieve uniformity remains to be seen.

But, perhaps the greatest challenge we Americans face in 2006 is not part of FDA's mandate— how to pay for all the medical advances FDA approves, and how to bring them to more people worldwide. As new products extend and enhance life, our society must figure out how to deal with the sequelae. The FDA must keep up with and anticipate the latest advances and be prepared to review and approve them promptly while not compromising the basic mission of protecting consumers from harm and deception. That's a balancing act FDA is accustomed to, and whose challenge it will meet, as it has for 100 years.

Harvey Wiley at his desk on his last day in office, 1912.

LIKE FATHER, LIKE SON.

EARLY CHAPTERS IN THE LIFE OF DR. WILEY'S BABY.

Thanks to...

This book has been a labor of love for so many people.

Trying to capture 100 years of FDA history and contributions is a daunting goal. What we tried to achieve with this book is a snapshot and perspective of how FDA came to be what it is, beginning with the 1906 Pure Food and Drugs Act, and what it has accomplished over its century.

I will leave it to the readers, and to future FDA watchers, to assess how successfully we have been able to achieve that goal.

There are many people to thank for enabling this book to be published.

I originally discussed this book with Dr. Mark Novitch, who agreed there should be a centennial book and that FDLI was an appropriate publisher. Jerome A. Halperin, President and CEO of the Food and Drug Law Institute, brought it to his Board for endorsement.

The book itself was planned by FDA's former commissioners, deputy commissioners, and general counsels. Many attended an initial planning meeting to discuss the conceptual approach to the book, and then another meeting to select the authors of the major chapters.

The idea for the book was endorsed by both the FDA and by the FDA Alumni Association.

The book was written by some of the busiest people around. Special thanks go to the authors of the eleven major chapters, who did the research needed to bring FDA's century into clear focus.

The book was designed by Costa Bugg and Jeff May and copy edited by Winfield Swanson.

Two people deserve special mention:

At FDLI, Rita Fullem coordinated the logistics of the book from start to finish. She was there every step of the way, to make sure that things got done.

At FDA, historian Suzanne White Junod did so much—she wrote a number of sidebars, identified most of the photos and wrote the captions, and served as a sounding board throughout.

This book would not be what it is without Rita and Suzanne. Double bouquets for them. Make that triple.

Inevitably, there are many more omissions than inclusions in this book. For every sidebar, another ten or more could have been substituted, with equal merit. There was an endless pool of potential subjects and authors. If the omissions are fatal, I plead guilty.

Finally, this book was financially supported by individuals, companies, and law firms with a commitment to FDA. By subsidizing the printing, their contributions enabled us to include many expensive-to-process photos and illustrations, and, at the same time, to produce a more affordable book. Their generosity made it possible for us to proceed with confidence from the outset, and to produce what I hope readers believe is a high-quality book.

Many, many thanks to the following for their financial support:

Arnold and Porter LLP
Bausch and Lomb
BD (Becton, Dickinson and Company)
The Coca-Cola Company
Consumer Healthcare Products Association
Covington & Burling
GlaxoSmithKline
Jerome A. Halperin
Hogan & Hartson LLP

Hyman, Phelps and McNamara, P.C.
Medtronic, Inc.
Merck & Co., Inc.
Mark and Louise Novitch
Novo Nordisk, Inc.
Olsson, Frank & Weeda, P.C.
Patton Boggs, LLP
Wayne L. Pines
Wyeth

A final personal note: In 1981 when FDA celebrated the seventy-fifth anniversary of the Pure Food and Drugs Act, I was responsible for FDA's very modest celebratory activities. We could not afford a book; instead, a special issue of FDA Consumer was dedicated to the anniversary. The cover was an illustration of Harvey Wiley. I recall wondering at the time whether I would still be involved with FDA when the 100th anniversary of the Act came around, and whether I would be able to contribute to the celebration. I now know. I regard it as an honor to have been able to edit this book, and I thank all who made it possible.

Wayne L. Pines
Chevy Chase, Maryland
January 2006

Historical Milestones

Compiled by Suzanne White Junod

Following are some selected milestones in the development and regulation of products under FDA's jurisdiction:

1820 – Eleven physicians meet in Washington, D.C., to establish the U.S. Pharmacopeia, the first compendium of standard drugs for the United States.

1848 – Drug Importation Act passed by Congress requires U.S. Customs Service inspection to stop entry of adulterated drugs from overseas. A. Wright produces the first X-ray in the U.S. at Yale University.

1897 – Tea Importation Act passed by Congress providing for quality inspections of imported tea.

1898 – Association of Official Agricultural Chemists (now AOAC International) establishes a Committee on Food Standards headed by Harvey Wiley. States begin incorporating these standards into their food statutes.

1899 – Discovered by German chemist Felix Hoffman in 1897, aspirin is first marketed.

1900 – New York City's first large electric sign for the Heinz Company posted on the site of the present flatiron building. Food processing had become a major U.S. industry.

1901 – Scientific understanding of blood groups and improved storage methods makes possible the first blood transfusions.

1902 – The Biologics Control Act is passed to ensure purity and safety of serums, vaccines, and similar products used to prevent or treat diseases in humans.

1903 – The Bureau of Chemistry begins its "hygienic table studies," which soon became know to the public as the "Poison Squad studies."

1904 – Pure food crusaders set up a booth at the St. Louis Exposition, displaying dyes extracted from familiar processed foods that were used to color swatches of wool and silk. This exhibit prompted the General Federation of Women's Clubs, the National Consumers' League, and the American Medical Association to join forces in support of passage of a federal statute.

1905 – Samuel Hopkins Adams concludes his muckraking series on the patent medicine industry entitled "The Great American Fraud."

1906 – January – Upton Sinclair's Socialist novel, *The Jungle* was published; July 30 – President Theodore Roosevelt signs the 1906 Pure Food and Drugs Act and the Meat Inspection Act into law

1907 – Forty regulations for enforcement of the new law went into effect along with the law on January 1, 1907. First certified color regulations, requested by manufacturers and users, list seven colors found suitable for use in foods.

1908 – Synthesis of the first sulfonamide, sulfanilamide.

1910 – Marie Curie publishes her *Treatise on Radiography*.

1911 – The Supreme Court rules that the 1906 Pure Food and Drugs Act does not prohibit false therapeutic claims but only false and misleading statements about the ingredients or identity of a drug.

1912 – The Sherley Amendment prohibits labeling medicines with false therapeutic claims intended to defraud the consumer. Harvey Wiley retires from federal service.

1913 – Gould Net Weight amendment requires food package contents to be "plainly and conspicuously marked on the outside of the package in terms of weight, measure or numerical count.

1914 – The Supreme Court issues its first ruling on food additives, finding that for bleached flour with nitrite residues to be banned from foods, the government must show a relationship between the chemical additive and the harm it allegedly caused in humans. The Harrison Narcotic Act requires prescriptions for products exceeding allowable limits of narcotics and imposes record-keeping requirements for physicians and pharmacists who dispense narcotic drugs.

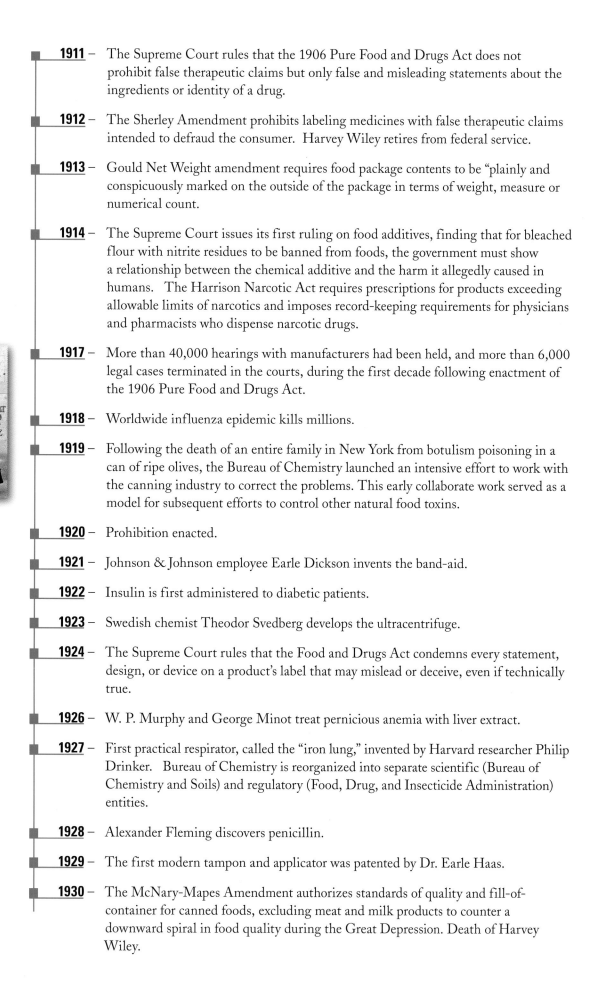

1917 – More than 40,000 hearings with manufacturers had been held, and more than 6,000 legal cases terminated in the courts, during the first decade following enactment of the 1906 Pure Food and Drugs Act.

1918 – Worldwide influenza epidemic kills millions.

1919 – Following the death of an entire family in New York from botulism poisoning in a can of ripe olives, the Bureau of Chemistry launched an intensive effort to work with the canning industry to correct the problems. This early collaborate work served as a model for subsequent efforts to control other natural food toxins.

1920 – Prohibition enacted.

1921 – Johnson & Johnson employee Earle Dickson invents the band-aid.

1922 – Insulin is first administered to diabetic patients.

1923 – Swedish chemist Theodor Svedberg develops the ultracentrifuge.

1924 – The Supreme Court rules that the Food and Drugs Act condemns every statement, design, or device on a product's label that may mislead or deceive, even if technically true.

1926 – W. P. Murphy and George Minot treat pernicious anemia with liver extract.

1927 – First practical respirator, called the "iron lung," invented by Harvard researcher Philip Drinker. Bureau of Chemistry is reorganized into separate scientific (Bureau of Chemistry and Soils) and regulatory (Food, Drug, and Insecticide Administration) entities.

1928 – Alexander Fleming discovers penicillin.

1929 – The first modern tampon and applicator was patented by Dr. Earle Haas.

1930 – The McNary-Mapes Amendment authorizes standards of quality and fill-of-container for canned foods, excluding meat and milk products to counter a downward spiral in food quality during the Great Depression. Death of Harvey Wiley.

1931 – Agricultural appropriations act becomes effective, changing Food, Drug, and Insecticide Administration into the Food and Drug Administration. Electron microscope invented in Germany.

1932 – Engineer Harry Jennings builds the first folding, tubular steel wheelchair.

1933 – FDA begins the process of replacing the 1906 Pure Food and Drugs Act with a new federal statute with the blessing of the White House secured through "Brain Truster" Rexford Tugwell, Secretary of Agriculture. The first bill is introduced into the Senate, launching a five-year legislative battle.

1934 – February 19, 1934 – Senator Royal Copeland introduced S2800, a revision of the original food and drug bill. He prefaced his introduction by saying, "I thought I had had all the troubles one could have in this life, but in all my experience I have never had so many worries and so much trouble as I have had in connection with this bill."

1935 – Vitamin C is the first vitamin to be artificially synthesized.

1936 – FDA Information Officer Ruth de Forest Lamb publishes The American Chamber of Horrors as a private citizen, documenting the need for a new federal food and drug statute.

1937 – Elixir Sulfanilamide, containing the poisonous solvent diethylene glycol, kills 107 persons, dramatizing the need to establish drug safety before marketing. The first heart-lung machine is built by physician John Heysham Gibbon. The first blood bank opened in Chicago.

1938 – Food, Drug, and Cosmetic Act is enacted, extending control to cosmetics and therapeutic devices, requiring new drugs to be shown safe before marketing, authorizing standards for foods, factory inspections, and adding remedy of court injunctions to previous penalties of seizure and prosecution.

1939 – Charles Drew's system for storing blood plasma revolutionizes medicine.

1940 – FDA transferred from the Department of Agriculture to the Federal Security Agency. Walter G. Campbell appointed as the first Commissioner of Food and Drugs.

1941 – Insulin Amendment requires FDA to test and certify purity and potency of this lifesaving drug for diabetics.

1942 – First use of chemotherapy as a treatment for cancer. First successful clinical use of penicillin in the United States.

1943 – In *U.S. v. Dotterweich*, the Supreme Court rules that the responsible officials of a corporation, as well as the corporation itself, may be prosecuted for violations. It need not be proved that the officials intended, or even knew of, the violations. Publication by Papanicolaou of monograph, *Diagnosis of Uterine Cancer by the Vaginal Smear*, leads to the Pap test.

1944 – Public Health Service Act is passed, covering a broad spectrum of health concerns, including regulation of biological products and control of communicable diseases.

1945 – Penicillin Amendment requires FDA testing and certification of safety and effectiveness of all penicillin products. Later amendments extended this requirement to all antibiotics. In 1983, the requirement was abolished.

1946 – FDA scientists contend with increasingly complicated analytical techniques for the new organic insecticides, including DDT, and begin to express concerns about their safety for civilian use.

1947 – FDA disrupts wartime use of deleterious substances being used as food preservatives (monochloracetic acid and quaternary ammonium compounds) in foods.

1948 – Miller Amendment affirms that the federal Food, Drug, and Cosmetic Act applies to goods regulated by the agency that have been transported from one state to another and have reached the consumer. First artificial heart pump developed at Yale.

1949 – FDA publishes guidance to industry for the first time, "Procedures for the Appraisal of the Toxicity of Chemicals in Food," came to be known as the "black book."

1950 – House Select Committee to Investigate the Use of Chemicals in Food Products (Delaney Committee) opens hearings on the safety of chemicals in foods and cosmetics, laying the foundation for the 1954 Miller Pesticide Amendment, the 1958 Food Additives Amendment, and the 1960 Color Additives Amendment. John Hopps invents the first cardiac pacemaker. Oleomargarine Act requires prominent labeling of colored oleomargarine to distinguish it from butter.

1951 – Durham-Humphrey Amendment defines the kinds of drugs that cannot be safely used without medical supervision and restricts their sale to prescription by a licensed practitioner. Vitamin B6 determined to be essential to human nutrition.

1952 – The Supreme Court rules that the factory inspection provision of the 1938 Food Drug and Cosmetic Act is too vague to be enforced as criminal law. FDA consumer consultants are appointed in each field district to maintain communications with consumers. Jonas Salk creates first polio vaccine.

1953 – Federal Security Agency becomes the Department of Health, Education, and Welfare (HEW). Factory Inspection Amendment clarifies law and requires FDA to give manufacturers written reports of conditions observed during inspections and analyses of factory samples. James Watson and Francis Crick unravel the mystery of the human genetic coding called DNA.

1954 – Miller Pesticide Amendment spells out procedures for setting safety limits for pesticide residues on raw agricultural commodities. First large-scale radiological examination of food carried out by FDA when it received reports that tuna suspected of being radioactive was being imported from Japan following atomic blasts in the Pacific. FDA begins around the clock monitoring.

1955 – Lloyd Conover patents tetracycline, which became the most prescribed broad spectrum antibiotic in the United States. FDA conducts tests on the effects of atomic explosion on foodstuffs in cooperation with the Federal Civil Defense Administration.

1957 – Rachel Fuller Brown and Elizabeth Hazen patent Nystatin, the first useful antifungal antibiotic.

1958 – FDA approves Enovid to treat menstrual disorders.

1960 – FDA approves Enovid for use as an oral contraceptive.

1961 – Thalidomide is found to have caused birth defects. FDA's Dr. Frances Kelsey keeps drug off the market in the United States.

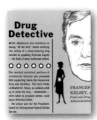

1962 – Congress enacts the Drug Amendments, requiring manufacturers to prove the efficacy of their products before marketing them.

1963 – Baruch Blumberg discovers antigen that detected the presence of hepatitis B in blood samples. After blood banks began using the test in 1971, hepatitis B after blood transfusions decreased by 25%. President John F. Kennedy proclaims the Consumer Bill of Rights in a message to Congress. Included are the right to safety, the right to be informed, the right to choose, and the right to be heard. Dr. Michael DeBakey first uses an artificial heart. Major reorganization of FDA as per recommendations of the Second Citizens' Advisory Committee

1964 – FDA sanctions the use of gamma rays from cobalt 60 radiation to sterilize insect eggs in wheat and wheat products since tests showed no radioactivity and no nutritional loss in the final wheat.

1965 – President Lyndon Johnson, in his health message to Congress noted: "Modernization of the Federal Food, Drug, and Cosmetic Act is imperative if our health protection program is to keep pace with the technological and industrial advances of recent years."

1966 – Dr. James Lee Goddard became the first "outside" appointee as Commissioner of Food and Drug. FDA contracts with the National Academy of Sciences/National Research Council to evaluate the effectiveness of 4,000 drugs approved on the basis of safety alone between 1938 and 1962.

1967 – South African surgeon Dr. Christian Barnard performs the first heart transplant operation.

1968 – FDA's Bureau of Drug Abuse Control and the Treasury Department's Bureau of Narcotics are transferred to the Department of Justice to form the Bureau of Narcotics and Dangerous Drugs (BNDD). FDA forms Drug Efficacy Study Implementation (DESI) to implement recommendations of the National Academy of Sciences investigation of effectiveness of drugs first marketed between 1938 and 1962. Animal Drug Amendments make approval of animal drugs and medicated feeds more efficient.

1969 – FDA begins administering several former Public Health Service programs including sanitation programs for milk, shellfish, food service and interstate travel facilities, and for preventing poisoning and accidents. White House Conference on Food, Nutrition, and Health recommends systematic review of GRAS substances in light of FDA ban on the artificial sweetener cyclamate. President Nixon orders FDA to review its GRAS list.

1970 – Court of Appeals upholds enforcement of the 1962 Drug Amendments by ruling that commercial success alone does not constitute substantial evidence of drug safety and efficacy. FDA requires the first patient package insert, for oral contraceptives.

1971 – Bureau of Radiological Health transferred to FDA. National Center for Toxicological Research is established in the biological facilities of the Pine Bluff Arsenal in Arkansas.

1972 – Regulation of biologics, including serums, vaccines, and blood products, is transferred from NIH to FDA. Over-the-Counter Drug Review begins.

1973 – Supreme Court upholds the 1962 drug effectiveness law and endorses FDA action to control entire classes of products by regulations rather than rely only on time-consuming litigation. Stanley Cohen and Herbert Boyer invent technique for DNA cloning, allowing genes to be transplanted between different biological species. An outbreak of botulism from underprocessed soup leads to the enactment of low-acid canned foods regulations. Consumer Product Safety Commission is created by Congress, taking over several programs pioneered by FDA including those regulating caustic poisons and hazardous substance labeling.

1974 – FDA establishes Freedom of Information policy designed to insure the protection of "trade secrets" under the 1938 Act, and allow public scrutiny of FDA's actions and activities.

1975 – Robert S. Ledley patented the diagnostic x-ray system known as CAT scan.

1976 – Medical Device Amendments passed to ensure safety and effectiveness of medical devices, including diagnostic products. Vitamins and Minerals Amendments stop FDA from establishing standards limiting potency of vitamins and minerals in food supplements or regulating them as drugs based solely on potency.

1977 – Saccharin Study and Labeling Act prohibited FDA from banning saccharin, but required a warning label stating that it had been found to cause cancer in laboratory animals. FDA initiates Bioresearch Monitoring Program as an agency-wide initiative to ensure the quality and integrity of the data submitted to FDA and providing for the protection of human subjects in clinical trials. NIH reports that for the first time, a life-threatening viral infection – herpes encephalitis—had been successfully treated with a drug.

1978 – World's first "test-tube" baby born in England.

1979 – Three Mile Island nuclear emergency occurs on March 28, 1970. FDA contracted with firms to quickly prepare and package enough doses of potassium iodide to protect those threatened with thyroid cancer if exposed to radiation.

1980 – Infant Formula Act establishes special FDA controls to ensure necessary nutritional content and safety.

1981 – FDA and the Department of Health and Human Services (HHS) revise regulations for human subject protections.

1983 – Orphan Drug Act enables FDA to promote research and marketing of drugs needed for rare diseases.

1984 – Drug Price Competition and Patent Term Restoration Act expedites the availability of less costly generic drugs by permitting FDA to approve generic versions of brand-name drugs without repeating research. Brand name drugs secure patent extensions.

1985 – AIDS blood test approved by FDA.

1986 – Childhood Vaccine Act requires patient information on vaccines, gives FDA authority to recall biologics, and authorizes civil penalties.

1987 – Investigational drug regulations revised to expand access to experimental drugs for patients with serious diseases that have no alternative therapies.

SACCHARIN

1988 – Food and Drug Administration Act of 1988 officially establishes FDA as an agency of the Department of Health and Human Services (HHS) with a Commissioner of Food and Drugs appointed by the President with the advice and consent of the Senate. Prescription Drug Marketing Act bans the diversion of prescription drugs from legitimate commercial channels, requires drug wholesalers to be licensed by the states, restricts reimportation from other countries, and bans the sale, trade or purchase of drug samples, as well as the counterfeiting of drug coupons. Generic Animal Drug and Patent Term Restoration Act extends to veterinary products benefits given to human drugs under the 1984 Drug Price Competition and Patent Term Restoration Act.

1990 – Anabolic Steroid Act of 1990 identifies anabolic steroids as a class of drugs and specifies over two dozen items as controlled substances. Nutrition Labeling and Education Act requires all packaged foods to bear nutrition labeling and all health claims for foods to be consistent with terms defined by HHS. The law preempts state requirements, and, for the first time, authorizes some health claims for foods. The food ingredient panel, serving sizes, and terms such as "low fat" and "light" are standardized. Safe Medical Devices Act requires nursing homes, hospitals, and other facilities to report to FDA incidents that suggest that a medical device problem. Manufacturers are required to conduct post-market surveillance on permanently implanted devices whose failure might cause serious harm or death, and to establish methods for tracing and locating patients depending on such devices. The act authorizes FDA to order device product recalls and other actions.

1992 – Generic Drug Enforcement Act imposes debarment and other penalties for illegal acts involving abbreviated drug applications. Prescription Drug User Fee Act requires drug and biologics manufacturers to pay fees for product applications and supplements, and other services. The act also requires FDA to use these funds to hire more reviewers to assess applications. Mammography Quality Standards Act requires mammography facilities to be accredited and federally certified.

1994 – Dietary Supplement Health and Education Act establishes specific labeling requirements, provides a regulatory framework, and authorizes FDA to promulgate good manufacturing practice regulations for dietary supplements. FDA announces it could consider regulating nicotine in cigarettes as a drug. Uruguay Round Agreements Act extends the patent terms of U.S. drugs from seventeen to twenty years. Animal Medicinal Drug Use Clarification Act allows veterinarians to prescribe extra-label use of veterinary drugs for animals under specific circumstances. In addition, the legislation allows licensed veterinarians to prescribe human drugs for use in animals under certain conditions.

1995 – FDA declares cigarettes to be "drug delivery devices." Restrictions are proposed on marketing and sales to reduce smoking by young people.

1996 – Federal Tea Tasters Repeal Act repeals the Tea Importation Act of 1897. Saccharin Notice Repeal Act repeals the saccharin notice requirements. Animal Drug Availability Act adds flexibility to animal drug approval process. Food Quality Protection Act eliminates application of the Delaney Clause to pesticides.

1997 – Food and Drug Administration Modernization Act reauthorizes the Prescription Drug User Fee Act of 1992 and mandates the most wide-ranging reforms in agency practices since 1938, including measures to accelerate review of devices, regulate advertising of unapproved uses of approved drugs and devices, and regulate health claims for foods.

1998 – FDA promulgates the Pediatric Rule, a regulation that requires manufacturers of selected new and extant drug and biological products to conduct studies to assess their safety and efficacy in children. Mammography Quality Standards Reauthorization Act continues 1992 Act until 2002. First phase to consolidate FDA laboratories nationwide from nineteen facilities to nine by 2014 includes dedication of the first of five new regional laboratories.

1999 – Clinicaltrials.gov is founded to provide the public with updated information on enrollment in federally and privately supported clinical research, thereby expanding patient access to studies of promising therapies. A final rule mandates that all over-the-counter drug labels must contain data in a standardized format.

2000 – The Supreme Court rules 5-4 that FDA does not have authority to regulate tobacco as a drug. FDA revokes its rule, issued in 1996, that restricted the sale and distribution of cigarettes and smokeless tobacco products to children and adolescents.

2002 – The Best Pharmaceuticals for Children Act continues the exclusivity provisions for pediatric drugs as mandated under the Food and Drug Administration Modernization Act of 1997. In the wake of the events of September 11, 2001, the Public Health Security and Bioterrorism Preparedness and Response Act of 2002 is designed to improve the country's ability to prevent and respond to public health emergencies; provisions include a requirement that FDA issue regulations to enhance controls over imported and domestically produced commodities. Under the Medical Device User Fee and Modernization Act, fees are assessed sponsors of medical device applications. The Office of Combination Products is formed within the Office of the Commissioner, as mandated under the Medical Device User Fee and Modernization Act.

2003 – The Medicare Prescription Drug Improvement and Modernization Act requires, among other things, a study of how current and emerging technologies can be utilized to make essential information about prescription drugs available to the blind and visually impaired. The Animal Drug User Fee Act permits FDA to collect subsidies for the review of certain animal drug applications. FDA is given clear authority under the Pediatric Research Equity Act to require that sponsors conduct clinical research into pediatric applications for new drugs and biological products.

2004 – Project BioShield Act of 2004 authorizes FDA to expedite its review treatments against chemical, biological, and nuclear agents that may be used in a terrorist attack. Food Allergen Labeling and Consumer Protection Act requires the labeling of any food that contains a protein derived from foods that account for the vast majority of food allergies. FDA bans dietary supplements containing ephedrine alkaloids.

2005 – Formation of the Drug Safety Board is announced, consisting of FDA staff and representatives from the National Institutes of Health and the Veterans Administration, to deal with drug safety issues across several therapeutic categories.

2006 – FDA celebrates the 100th anniversary of the Pure Food and Drugs Act.

The 1906 Pure Food and Drugs Act was often referred to as the "Wiley Act" in tribute to the Bureau of Chemistry's Chief Chemist, Dr. Harvey Washington Wiley. Nicknamed the "crusading chemist," he was a populist hero in the mind of the public, although industry often held a different view of his alleged "virtues." His popularity, however, was such that few were willing to even contemplate changes in the original "Wiley Act" until after his death in 1930. Wiley himself, who left government service in 1912, did not perceive the law's many shortcomings which hampered its effective enforcement, arguing that the law simply was not being enforced the way he and Congress had intended.

The Struggle for the 1906 Act

Richard M. Cooper

. . . Tiddy was toying with a light breakfast an' idly turnin' over th' pages iv the new book [Upton Sinclair's The Jungle] with both hands. Suddenly he rose fr'm th' table an' cryin': "I'm pizened," begun throwin' sausages out iv th' window. Th' ninth wan sthruck Sinitor Biv'ridge on th' head an' made him a blond. It bounced off, exploded.... Sinitor Biv'ridge rushed in, thinkin' that th' Prisidint was bein' assassynated be his devoted followers in th' Sinit, an' discovered Tiddy engaged in a hand-to-hand conflict with a potted ham. Th' Sinitor fr'm Injyanny, with a few well-directed wurruds, put out th' fuse an' rendered th' missile harmless. Since thin th' Prisidint, like th' rest of us, has become a viggytaryan....

"They ought to make thim ate their own meat," said Mr. Hennessy, warmly.

"I suggested that," said Mr. Dooley, "but Hogan says they'd fall back on th' Constitution. He says th' Constitution f'rbids crool an' unusual punishmints."
—Finley Peter Dunne (1906).[1]

AMERICA EMERGED FROM the Civil War a single nation politically, with a predominant national government. It was the railroads, aided by the telegraph and telephone, however, that created the possibility of American national economic markets continental in scope. These technological marvels led to falling prices for transportation and communication, and thus to new opportunities and incentives for commerce—and fraud—over long distances, and in turn to the Pure Food and Drugs Act of 1906.[2]

The transcontinental railroads, completed after the Civil War, made possible the rapid and cheap transport of food from farms to processing plants, and from both to distant cities. Railroad track mileage increased from 35,000 in 1865 to 193,000 in 1900.[3] Some cities, thus supplied with the means to feed large numbers of workers and their families, became industrial metropolises, whose factories mass-produced products for regional, national, and international markets.[4]

In the 1870s, for the first time in American history, agricultural workers constituted less than half the workforce.[5] From 1870 to 1900, the overall U.S. population increased ninety-one percent,[6] but the agricultural workforce increased only fifty-nine percent.[7] Nevertheless, that relatively decreasing workforce could feed a growing population and also provide increasing exports[8] due to huge increases in agricultural productivity (in 1880, 152 man-hours were needed to produce 100 bushels of wheat; in 1900, only 108 were needed)[9] and also due to greatly increased farmland. Thanks to the railroads and innovations in farm equipment and communications, more American acreage was brought under cultivation during 1870–1900 than during 1607–1870.[10]

Indeed, agricultural production was so robust that, despite increasing population and exports, agricultural commodity prices fell fifty percent during 1866–1900.[11] That long-term decline, aggravated by economic depressions in the 1870s and 1890s, caused very hard times for farmers, and, together with other grievances, generated long-lasting resentment against the railroads, financiers, food-processing companies, and urban interests generally. Especially in the West, this resentment contributed to support for federal regulation of the economy, including legislation to ensure the purity of food and drugs. In several Plains states, in particular, "deep-rooted sentiments of sectional frustration and inferiority nurtured the pure-food crusade."[12]

The growth of huge cities packed with industrial workers and their families (millions of them immigrants), who did not grow their own food, created a demand for food from distant locations. In the past, the few national markets had been mediated by regional and local suppliers, who had some responsibility for the quality of products they delivered to consumers. After the Civil War, national food companies developed to meet the greatly increased urban demand with prepackaged products, whose inherent quality did not depend on regional or local suppliers. The railroads connected those companies with consumers.

Thus, for example, before the War, canned foods were handicraft, luxury items (with high spoilage rates); during the War, there was large demand for canned military rations; and, by 1870, 30 million cans of food a year were being processed.[13] Refrigerated cars, introduced in the mid 1870s, made it economical to ship processed meat products from the Chicago packing plants to Washington, D.C., for consumption by President Roosevelt and others.

The broad emergence, in the 1880s, of branded, nationally distributed products[14] necessitated the creation of standardized manufacturing systems to ensure that product quality would be consistent from package to package. Having achieved such control over quality, successful national manufacturers would be expected to seek to strengthen that advantage through legal prohibitions against their less well-organized competitors.

The emergence of such national companies was facilitated by the development of the modern large, hierarchical business corporation, with separate departments for operations, finance, marketing, and so on. The railroads had initiated that organizational structure.[15] The telegraph and, later, the telephone facilitated communications and, thus, centralized control over geographically dispersed activities.

High and rising literacy (thanks to increased availability of public education), innovations in the technology of publication, and reduced postage rates fostered the emergence of mass-circulation magazines. Metropolitan daily newspapers also expanded—from 971 in 1870 to 2,226 in 1900.[16]

These publications helped shape popular taste, and offered greatly expanded opportunities for advertising to introduce new, branded products (including fraudulent ones) with standardized content and packaging, and to serve generally the new national markets. In 1900, advertising expenditures in the United States were ten times what they had been in 1865.[17]

After the turn of the century, the magazines also became important organs for social, economic, and political criticism. Sensational exposés of fraudulent consumer products sold magazines, thereby attracting advertisers[18] and creating public demand for reform.

It was "a pushing, competitive, bourgeois world."[19] It was also becoming a consumer society, as annual earnings per worker rose from 1876 to 1915, and the average workweek in factories declined from sixty-six hours in 1850 to fifty-five in 1914.[20] More goods and services were available, and people had more money to buy them and more time to enjoy them.[21] Once advertisers conceptualized people as consumers, people began to think of themselves as consumers. As it came to be widely recognized that consumers

This cartoon shows a cross-section of a refrigerated train car, which runs "coast to coast." Such advances changed the basic dynamic of food production and led to the need for federal regulation. (Courtesy of Armour Co.)

of foods and drugs were being badly served by many food processors and drug manufacturers, individuals and organized groups identified a consumer interest in reform legislation, which they would advance in the political process.

The new technologies of food distribution permitted a lengthy time between production and consumption, and thereby increased the possibilities of spoilage and contamination, while creating incentives to prevent or hide them. Chemical preservatives offered one method of prevention, but there was little knowledge of their short-term or long-term effects on health. Where spoilage or contamination had occurred or might occur, fraudulent means could be applied to conceal it.

Working-class people spent forty to fifty percent of their income on food, and so were very price-sensitive.[22] Consequently, price competition among food processors generally was fierce, and control of costs and avoidance of waste were critical to survival. The result was powerful incentives to exploit the new opportunities for adulteration and misbranding.[23]

Adulteration helped food suppliers keep prices low.[24] Although no broad quantifications are reliable, many types of fraud apparently were widespread—e.g., skimming cream from whole milk; adding

Milk was one of the most heavily adulterated products in urban America at the turn of the century; it was frequently watered down and preserved with formaldehyde. The formaldehyde was clearly dangerous to health, and both the federal and state governments cracked down on its use.

coloring agents to improve the appearance and mask the rotting of processed foods; substituting cheaper for more expensive substances in coffee, tea, edible oils, and spices.[25] Unsanitary conditions in food processing facilities were common, and toxic substances were detected, e.g., lead in confectionary colors. In the late 1870s, adulteration of milk and controversy over sugar drew public attention to problems in the food supply.[26]

A common factor in nearly all the significant forms of adulteration and fraudulent labeling was the inability of even careful consumers to detect product problems before purchase or, commonly, even after purchase. The face-to-face, neighborly relationships that had encouraged honesty and fair dealing between producers and consumers in rural areas and small towns generally did not exist in urban areas, and were becoming less common throughout the country. As long as adulteration and fraud could go undetected while costs decreased and sales increased, perpetrators could be successful against competitors who did not employ such a strategy.[27] This undetectability, together with press reports about adulteration and fraud, generated consumer concern.[28] Manufacturers of legitimate products, including new products likely to encounter consumers' suspicion, thus had an incentive to support legislation that would drive out their unscrupulous competitors (and, perhaps, even some scrupulous competitors) and raise consumer confidence in the food supply.

New, less expensive food substances and products, made possible by technological progress, were not universally welcomed. Some threatened established products through competition on the merits or by being fraudulently substituted for them or mixed with them. Oleomargarine (made from animal fats) was invented in 1869 in France, and by the 1870s threatened American dairy interests, which obtained anti-oleo legislation in numerous states by 1887 and also succeeded, in 1886, in obtaining the first federal law regulating a domestic food product.[29] Artificial glucose, a sugar substitute made from vegetable starches, was a threat to producers of honey, molasses, and maple syrup. Alum-based baking powder threatened producers of established cream-of-tartar baking powder. The efforts of producers of established products to obtain legislation to stifle or at least impair competition from newer and cheaper products were a persistent component of the struggle for pure food and drugs legislation.

There was also some genuine confusion as to what constituted objectionable adulteration. In 1879, Samuel W. Johnson, a professor of chemistry at Yale, initiator of the system of state agricultural experiment stations, and past president of the American Chemical Society, stated that

> certain additions to food that
> were originally fraudulent and
> gross adulterations, having been
> practiced without complaint for
> a long time, have acquired the
> sanction of use which exempts
> them from the charge of

falsification or even makes them fairly respectable.[30]

Like the food industry, the drug industry underwent a profound transformation after the Civil War. Before the War, the professions of medicine and pharmacy had begun to separate, as more highly trained physicians lobbied for state statutes to bar pharmacists from diagnosing. In turn, better educated pharmacists sought to eliminate competition from grocers and other uneducated formulators and dispensers of "patent" medicines.[31] For example, the American Pharmaceutical Association argued that the low prices of patent medicines, which cost little to manufacture, led to pharmacists adulterating legitimate drugs in an attempt to compete.[32]

Physicians' and pharmacists' attacks on each other, coupled with newspaper attacks on incompetents in both professions, generated public concern about drugs.[33] Such attacks and concerns had ample basis, for neither medicine nor pharmacy had a firm scientific basis.[34] Only a few of the hundreds of drugs used in the nineteenth century would be considered useful today—e.g., "digitalis, morphine, quinine, diphtheria antitoxin, aspirin, and ether."[35] Oliver Wendell Holmes, Sr., professor of anatomy at Harvard Medical School, commented out of frustration : "if the whole *materia*

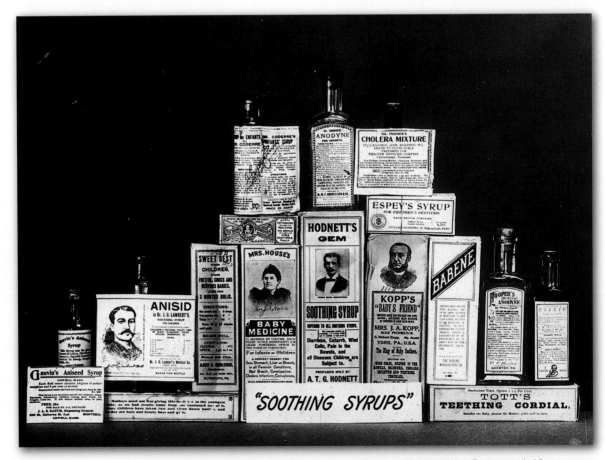

Opposition to the addictive "soothing syrups" helped galvanize public support for passage of the 1906 Act. Recommended for "teething" babies and colicky infants, many of these products contained morphine sulfate or other opium derivatives. Some were certainly effective in reducing pain, but others were imitations with no effective active ingredients. Which was the lesser evil? The 1906 Act specified eleven "dangerous" ingredients, including morphine, which, if present in the product, had to be listed on the label. If not present, it could not be listed on the label. It was not until 1917 that legislation limited the availability of these addictive ingredients.

medica, as now used, could be sunk to the bottom of the sea, it would be all the better for mankind—and all the worse for the fishes."[36]

After the War, both physicians and pharmacists were becoming sellers of drugs. Before 1861, there were only ten U.S. drug manufacturers; by 1880, there were almost 100. Manufactured drugs—standardized by sophisticated manufacturers, prepackaged, and labeled with directions for use—could be sold by grocers as well as physicians and pharmacists. In 1882, the United States Pharmacopeia (USP) initiated the publication of tests for determining the identity and quality of many drugs.[37] A survey in 1882-1883 found that forty-one percent of drugs tested were below USP standards.[38]

There was explosive growth in the manufacturing of patent medicines. It was made possible by the primitive state of chemistry; lack of scientific medical theory and training; the anarchy that accompanied the emergence of a new country with few legal precedents for regulation and a jealous tradition of separating individual, local, and federal rights; and a belief in the "inalienable rights to life, liberty, and quackery."[39] Not until medicine found a scientific basis could there be an effective critique of quack medicines.

By the 1880s, patent medicines constituted a majority of the drugs sold in the United States.[40] As Americans became accustomed to revolutionary technological progress, they accepted false claims that similar progress had been achieved in healthcare.[41] In the late 1880s, a product called "Microbe Killer" exploited misunderstanding of the discoveries of Koch and Pasteur, and promised to cure all diseases; in 1890, seventeen factories were producing it.[42]

In 1893, 104 companies—more than half patent-medicine manufacturers— spent in excess of $50,000 for national promotions.[43] About a million dollars a year each was spent on advertising for Lydia E. Pinkham's Vegetable Compound and Scott's Emulsion.[44] Medical journals as well as newspapers depended on revenue generated through patent medicine advertising.[45] Many nostrums contained opium or one of its derivatives (codeine, paragoric, laudanum) or alcohol;[46] e.g. Hostetter's Bitters in 1883 contained 64% water, 32% alcohol, and 4% herbal oils and extracts.[47] Such products relieved pain, but often at the cost of addiction and other serious adverse effects.

These economic and social transformations were brought about by powerful forces, and how to respond to their negative consequences was far from clear in the last third of the nineteenth century. Was a remedy to be found in voluntary actions or in government? The American tradition of rugged individualism favored voluntary action. If governmental action was called for, should it be at the state or federal level? It was well-established legal doctrine that protection of public health and welfare was part of the "police power" of the states.[48] Should government at some level take ownership of the huge new national companies, break them up into smaller units, or merely regulate them? If the answer was regulation, what form should it take, and who should administer it? History provided scant precedent.

As to foods and drugs, no definitive answer was forthcoming until 1906. What took so long? Enactment of general food and drugs legislation depended on the overcoming of formidable cultural, ideological, and institutional obstacles, as well as the normal political obstacles to any complex major regulatory legislation.

A central legacy of the American Revolution was (and is) distrust of government, especially central government, and particularly its Executive Branch. The grievances listed in the Declaration of Independence were attributed not to colonial governments, nor to the Parliament, but to the King. In the Constitution, the only mention of "the executive departments" is the provision in Article II, section 2, that the President "may require the opinion, in writing, of the principal officer in each…, upon

Lydia Pinkham was one of the best known (and widely vilified) patent medicine preparations on the market in the late nineteenth and early twentieth centuries. The alcohol content of the "Vegetable Compound" was similar to that of sherry. When the White House gave FDA leaders permission in 1933 to draft a new law to replace the "Wiley Act," FDA officials assembled an exhibit to illustrate the old law's shortcomings. Eleanor Roosevelt visited, and a reporter accompanying her dubbed the exhibit an "American Chamber of Horrors." Chief Information Officer Ruth de Forest Lamb wrote a book by that title, which provided even more evidence of the failures of the 1906 statute. This panel illustrated for viewers the fact that patent medicines were still on the market and thriving in the midst of a nationwide economic depression. The fact that little but the labeling on Lydia's product had changed in the ensuing decades surprised many would-be supporters of the 1938 Food, Drug, and Cosmetic Act.

any subject relating to the duties of their respective offices...."[49] The Constitution has no concept of large, powerful, complex, federal bureaucracies creatively and energetically addressing major national problems. Such problems were to be addressed by legislation enacted by the states or by the Congress, and implemented by the courts. Government was to be by laws, not by men (or women).

For more than a century after the ratification of the Constitution, American political culture reflected not the Hamiltonian vision of a strong, vigorous federal government, but, rather, the Jeffersonian vision of a federal government of limited powers and activities presiding over a predominantly agrarian society of sovereign states and largely self-reliant individuals, who wanted government off their backs.[50] The Hamiltonian vision was revived only when the capitalist forces unleashed by the Revolution and magnified by the Civil War finally transformed the economy and the society in the last third of the nineteenth century. The Pure Food and Drugs Act was one of the earliest markers of that revival.

In 1835, de Tocqueville noted that "the King of France has eleven times as many places at his disposal as the President, although the population of France is not much more than one and one-half times that of the Union."[51] From 1816 to 1908, U.S. population and total employment in the Executive Branch outside the Post Office and the War and Navy Departments were as follows:

Year	Population[52]	Executive Branch Employees (Civ. ex P.O.)[53]
1816	8,659,000	948
1831	13,321,000	1926
1861	32,351,000	4891
1871	40,938,000	12,276
1881	51,542,000	21,961
1891	64,361.000	34,834
1901	77,585,000	50,340
1908	88,709,000	97,910

The nineteenth century federal civilian bureaucracy was not merely small.[54] It was also turned out of office *en masse* when political party control of the White House changed. Andrew Jackson's administration (1829-1837) institutionalized the spoils system, under which federal employment was a temporary reward for party loyalty. The general result was that the Executive Branch offered no careers to the talented and public-spirited, and Executive Branch employees were widely viewed in the society as beholden to corrupt political machines.[55] "The Custom House," the introduction to *The Scarlet Letter*, published in 1850, describes in the Salem Customs House on a typical day:

> a row of venerable figures, sitting
> in old-fashioned chairs, which
> were tipped on their hind legs
> back against the wall. Oftentimes
> they were asleep, but occasionally
> might be heard talking together,
> in voices between speech and a
> snore, and with that lack of energy
> that distinguishes the occupants of
> alms-houses, and all other human
> beings who depend for subsistence
> on charity, on monopolized labor,

or any thing else but their own independent exertions. These old gentlemen—seated, like Matthew, at the receipt of custom, but not very liable to be summoned thence, like him, for apostolic errands— were Custom-House officers.[56]

Federal employees were not a group to whom one instinctively would look for solutions to the national problems created by the economic transformations of the last third of the nineteenth century.[57] As Robert Wiebe has observed, during the latter decades of the nineteenth century, the federal government did little and did it poorly.[58] Much of what it did, it also did corruptly. In the 1870s and 1880s, major activities of the national government— support for the railroads, policy toward Native Americans, excise taxes on alcohol, and the post office—were tainted by major scandals.[59]

Civil Service reform did not come until the Pendleton Act of 1883,[60] and was not fully implemented until years later,[61] though the Department of Agriculture, by 1889, was one of the earliest departments to be brought under it.[62] Even as of 1906, there were very few examples of successful problem-solving by the federal civilian bureaucracy.

The prevailing economic ideology during the last third of the nineteenth century was hostile to any governmental intervention in the economy. Social Darwinism, developed in England principally by Herbert Spencer, applied biological Darwinism to society, with a prescriptive gloss. Society—particularly,

the economy—was conceptualized as a "struggle for existence" (Darwin's phrase[63]), for "the survival of the fittest" (Spencer's phrase[64])—subject to laws of nature. Left to itself, that struggle, through delicate, complex, self-correcting mechanisms, inevitably produced unending progress: ever-improving competitors, products, and services, as inferior ones lost out and were cast aside or destroyed. In society, as in nature, any resulting hardship and suffering were the unavoidable price of progress. As Andrew Carnegie put it, "While the law [of competition] may be sometimes hard for the individual, it is best for the race, because it insures the survival of the fittest in every department."[65]

Those who lost out in the struggle—the poor, the unemployed, those unable to protect themselves from injury at work or from illness caused by adulterated or fraudulent products—were "unfit." The remedy was individual self-improvement, not governmental action. Any governmental effort to aid the "unfit" (i.e., any "reform") would disturb the self-correcting mechanism and thereby retard progress, without ultimately alleviating hardship and suffering. Drawing on classical economics and contemporary theories in geology, biology, and physics, Spencer developed a comprehensive philosophy in defense of limited government and *laissez faire*.[66]

Richard Hofstadter has commented that, "[i]n some respects the United States during the last three decades of the nineteenth and at the beginning of the twentieth century was *the* Darwinian country," and that Spencer was "far more popular" here than in England.[67] From 1869 to 1901, America's gross national product, in 1929 prices, nearly quadrupled, and *per capita* more than doubled.[68] That economic growth, together with minimal governance, appeared to confirm the social utility of *laissez faire*. To attempt regulation of any economic activity would be to jeopardize that activity's continued provision of benefits to society.

Spencer's works sold well in America, and influenced a generation of intellectuals from the 1870s to the 1890s. His theories were disseminated by William Graham Sumner at Yale, who fused them with the American ethic of rugged individualism;

and they became the common coin of leading businessmen and politicians, who characterized themselves as the victors in Darwinian struggles. For example, Sen. George Hearst of California, a mining tycoon, observed that "the members of the Senate are the survivors of the fittest."[69] Commenting on Spencer in 1895, Oliver Wendell Holmes, Jr., expressed doubt that "any writer of English except Darwin has done so much to affect our whole way of thinking about the universe."[70] Social Darwinism was the validating philosophy of success in America.[71]

Nevertheless, social Darwinism failed as an adequate vision of society and as a prescription for public policy; and its influence began a terminal decline in

The term "clerk" covered a wide range of administrative (as opposed to scientific) positions in the turn-of-the-century civil service. These are clerks in the Interstate Office of the Division of Chemistry circa 1910.

the 1890s. The dislocations caused by rapid industrialization after the Civil War, economic depressions in the 1870s and 1890s, and the emergence of huge business corporations that dominated national life and government at all levels were widely viewed as grievous problems; and they stirred up broad demands for governmental intervention, which ultimately proved irresistible.

William James's pragmatism, Lester Ward's sociology, the social gospel, socialism, Richard Ely's and other young academic economists' attacks on *laissez faire*, and other intellectual movements rejected the political fatalism of social Darwinism. For its strong individualism, they substituted recognition of collective interests and the value of collective action.[72] They encouraged a more instrumental view of human institutions, and fostered purposeful efforts to solve perceived social and economic problems.[73] These intellectual trends were amplified by applied social science, which was already being reflected in such diverse forms as Taylorism (scientific industrial management), the new field of public relations, city planning, conservation, and birth control.[74]

The final rejection of social Darwinism as a basis for governmental policy, however, took time. In 1905, the Supreme Court, relying on an unyielding doctrine of freedom of contract, characterized a New York law that would limit the working hours of bakers to ten per day and sixty per week, as "a meddlesome interference … with the rights of the individual," and

held it invalid.[75] In that case, Justice Holmes characterized social Darwinism as "an economic theory which a large part of the country does not entertain." "The Fourteenth Amendment," he thought it relevant to assert, "does not enact Mr. Herbert Spencer's *Social Statics*." He argued, however, in dissent.[76]

Movie poster from *The Jungle*. The book, published in 1905, was Sinclair's socialist novel depicting the wretched plight of the workers in Packingtown. Nauseating scenes of the meatpacking process itself led Sinclair to observe that he had "aimed for America's heart, and hit her in the stomach instead." National meat sales dropped by one third. Theodore Roosevelt sent in supposedly "undercover" investigators of his own, but by the time they arrived in Chicago, their cover had already been blown. Surprisingly then, even forewarned, the meatpackers did not clean up their acts, and the investigators substantiated the gist, if not the particulars, of Sinclair's portrayal of conditions inside the packing plants. Roosevelt needed little persuasion to sign the 1906 Meat Inspection Act into law. The law, unlike the 1906 Pure Food and Drugs Act, provided for continuous inspection of meats within the packing plants.

American constitutionalism conceived of people as voters; social Darwinism conceived of them as producers. There was no politically relevant concept of people as economic consumers, with interests and rights to be vindicated through political processes. Although consumers were, in fact, the beneficiaries of long-established laws requiring honesty in weights and measures and other commercial matters and could seek redress in the courts, there were no organized groups of consumers seeking to advance their own interests.

In America, the great political movements of the last third of the nineteenth century—agrarianism; populism; the emergence of labor unions; movements for free silver, women's suffrage, and temperance—largely by-passed consumers. Early in the McKinley Administration (1897-1901), the young Louis Brandeis, at a House hearing, testified in support of low tariffs "on behalf of those who, I believe, form a far larger part of the people of this country than any who have found representation here … [t]he consumers …." He was laughed at.[77] The first national consumers' group, The National Consumers' League, whose initial purpose was to mobilize the economic power of women as consumers to bring about better working conditions for women and children (i.e., as producers), was not formed until 1899.[78] Even Upton Sinclair's *The Jungle* (1906) was intended to arouse indignation on behalf of packing-plant workers, not on behalf of consumers. The book was dedicated "To the Workingmen of America."[79] "I aimed

at the public's heart," Sinclair later wrote, "and by accident I hit it in the stomach."[80]

One group that did receive political attention as "consumers" of a service was those who shipped goods by railroad.

Upton Sinclair

Farmers and others, particularly in the West, in their capacity as producers, were utterly dependent on railroads for transportation of their products to distant markets. In the 1890s, most railroads belonged to six systems, four controlled by J.P. Morgan; the other two, by Kuhn, Loeb & Co.[81] Without effective competition or regulation, railroads charged monopoly prices and discriminated in pricing, to the great benefit of some and the correspondingly great detriment of others. Strong agitation for regulation of railroads led in 1887 to enactment of the Interstate Commerce Act (ICA),[82] but in several decisions in the late 1890s the Supreme Court emasculated the statute,[83] until the ICA exemplified regulatory failure. There was no remedy until Theodore Roosevelt secured the enactment of the Hepburn Act in 1906.[84]

American popular democratic culture was not easily accepting of claims of professional expertise, particularly in healthcare. Americans, James Harvey Young has written, "wanted no restrictions on their right to choose the method by which they would be treated."[85] Battles over many types of occupational licensing reflected public hostility to claims of expertise and privilege.[86]

The first American medical schools, medical societies, and medical licensing laws were created in the mid-eighteenth century, but lack of a scientific basis for medicine until the late nineteenth century led to the proliferation of competing unscientific medical theories and the absence of a reliable basis for licensure. Licensing was widely viewed as a mark of privilege, not a certification of competence. In the wake of Jacksonian democracy, very few states enforced a medical licensing law.[87] The press and the public accepted pluralism in medicine as in religion.[88]

Only the arrival in America of scientific medicine brought about the creation of a relatively unified, publicly respected, and therefore strong American medical profession. In 1876, Pasteur and Koch discovered that specific microorganisms cause specific diseases. Thereafter, European scientists identified the sources of specific diseases, and Americans identified important parasites. The spread of the new scientific medicine then gradually substituted for folk and quack remedies.[89]

In the 1870s, the social status of physicians was not higher than that of the general run of their patients.[90] Thus, even when physicians had something useful to add to public discussions about problems with food and drugs, there was no particular reason for politicians to defer to them. The American Medical Association (AMA) was founded in 1846, but the profession was internally divided and the AMA remained weak until it was reorganized in 1901.[91] Only thereafter did it become a significant voice for food and drugs legislation.

At the national level, there were serious institutional obstacles to enactment of food and drugs legislation, or any other reform legislation. For many years, the government was divided. From 1860 through 1908, the Republican Party lost presidential elections only in 1884 and 1892. The Democrats controlled the House most of the time from 1874 through 1894. During that period, the Republicans controlled the presidency and both Houses only in 1889–1891; the Democrats, only in 1893–1894. In 1894, the Republicans won control of both Houses, and kept it for the next sixteen years. After the traumatic election of 1896, they also controlled the White House through the elections of 1912. William McKinley's decisive victory over William Jennings Bryan in 1896 was, however, a victory of national business interests over populist reformers.

From 1865 to 1900, Congress—imbued with social Darwinism and dominated by business interests and local political machines—had little interest in regulating any economic activity or, indeed, in legislating to address any national problems. Until ratification of the Seventeenth Amendment in 1913, U.S. senators were selected by state legislatures, many of which were controlled by local machines. Hence, Congress produced few economically significant laws other than tariffs and subsidies. Appropriations bills consumed two-thirds of each session.[92] Due to excise taxes on alcohol and high tariffs supported by Republican orthodoxy, the federal budget was in a surplus every year from 1866 to 1893, even without an income tax.[93]

The record of effective economic reform legislation was sparse. The Civil Service Reform Act of 1883 was a significant response to a serious problem (it was occasioned by the assassination of President James A. Garfield by a self-described disappointed office-seeker). The Interstate Commerce Act of 1887, however, failed to address the central grievance against the railroads: their totally unrestrained power over rates. The Sherman Antitrust Act of 1890[94] initially was used mostly against unions.[95] Any attempted use against businesses, was gutted in 1895 by the Supreme Court in the *E.C. Knight* case, which held that the act did not apply to a monopoly in manufacturing.[96]

House Speaker Thomas Reed, as depicted in a contemporary cartoon.

The House of Representatives was characterized by strong party loyalty and rules that permitted endless obstruction by the minority. In the fifty-first Congress in 1890, Republican Speaker Thomas Reed of Maine, over tumultuous opposition, revolutionized the House procedure as to quorums and then the House rules, in order to prevent obstruction. Reed's rules greatly strengthened the power of the Speaker. After the Democrats took control of the House by a landslide in the elections of 1890, the fifty-second Congress in 1891 rejected Reed's new rules. After their majority was sharply reduced in the elections of 1892, however, the fifty-third Congress in 1893 restored the rules. Thereafter, the rules stayed, and the majority party was able to push legislation through the House.

In 1899, Reed resigned. The next strong Speaker was Joseph Cannon of Illinois, who became Speaker in 1903. He was "gregarious, lovable, cigar-chewing, unabashedly tyrannical—despised reformers of both parties, saw no need to change the status quo, and would regard Roosevelt's policies as Republican party heresies."[97] Although the House was now capable of legislating, enactment of reform legislation would not be easy.

James Madison characterized the Senate as "an anchor against popular fluctuations."[98] During the late nineteenth and early twentieth centuries, so it was. Robert Caro has written:

> To a degree perhaps unequaled in any other period of American history, the Gilded Age was

the era in which the Senate was the preeminent force in the government of the United States… [a]nd it was during this era that the government was, as the historian John Garraty puts it, "singularly divorced from what now seem the meaningful issues of the day"—divorced to a degree perhaps unequaled in any other period of American history.[99]

For most of the period from 1880 through 1906, the Senate was controlled by Republicans, and during the latter part of that period was dominated by a small group of Republicans who met for poker and conversation, and called themselves the Philosophers' Club. Their philosophy was to keep government out of the way of business.

One member of the club was Nelson W. Aldrich of Rhode Island, who during Roosevelt's presidency was the effective leader of the Senate. He started as a delivery boy, made a modest fortune as a wholesale grocer, went to the Senate in 1881, and became a millionaire. His daughter married John D. Rockefeller, Jr. He was a strong supporter of unregulated private enterprise and, for example, opposed the Interstate Commerce bill. The Senate, led by Aldrich, was unlikely to be receptive to food and drugs legislation.

From Andrew Johnson through William McKinley, during the reign of social Darwinism, no president championed reform. There was no real possibility of serious reform at the federal level until the ascendancy of Theodore Roosevelt to the presidency, upon the assassination of McKinley in 1901.

The earliest widespread efforts to bring about pure food and drugs legislation occurred at the state level. In 1879, George Angell, a retired Boston lawyer who had founded several societies to prevent cruelty to animals, publicized in many newspapers sensational claims of widespread food adulteration. Although not well-supported, the reports stimulated a national debate about the extent of adulteration,[100] and undermined confidence in existing protections of public health.[101]

Nelson W. Aldrich

E.R. Squibb

That same year, in New York, Dr. E. R. Squibb presented a "Rough Draft of a Proposed Law to Prevent the Adulteration of Food and Medicine and to Create a State Board of Health." Squibb's draft included a clear definition of adulteration, made intent irrelevant, provided for governmental rather than private enforcement, and authorized severe penalties. The bill lacked a mechanism for product-by-product standards, was technically deficient in many respects, and received little attention.[102]

In the early 1880s, the leading advocate of anti-adulteration legislation was Francis B. Thurber. He had built up and headed the nation's largest wholesale grocery firm (which also was a manufacturer), was a leading member of New York City's Chamber of Commerce and numerous other organizations, and owned the *American Grocer*, a leading trade publication. Thurber's company was one of the largest distributors of glucose, and for a time had the American patent rights to oleomargarine.[103] He was also a leader in the anti-monopoly movement directed against the railroads.

Thurber's reform activities flowed from the view that, "if we would preserve the principles upon which our Government is founded, there must somewhere be lodged a superior power to protect the people."[104] In 1881, while social Darwinism still reigned, Thurber said in a speech: "The time for *laissez faire* policy is past. Our civilization is constantly growing more complex and the forces which now control it must themselves be controlled and directed or disastrous collisions will surely result."[105]

In response to Angell and others who raised public concerns about the food supply, Thurber championed a law, based on an English model, that would restrict only "harmful" adulteration and would require disclosure of harmless additives on the label. Michael Okun has summed up the approach of Thurber and like-minded business leaders:

> Thurber wanted to empower responsible professional sanitarians to hound the corrupt business competitors, yet leave space for the normal give and take of everyday trade while silencing the anxieties of a consuming public that had been aroused by men such as Angell and by the exaggerations—and the revelations—of the press.[106]

This approach on the part of business interests is a persistent theme through the entire history of food and drugs legislation. A similarly persistent theme is the desire of organized professionals to achieve their own goals in such legislation through temporary alliances with business leaders like Thurber.

Private groups and members of Congress in 1880–1881 developed a variety of legislative proposals to address the concerns Angell and others had raised. Great Britain supplied a precedent for combining food and drugs in a single anti-adulteration law, which unavoidably brought to bear together a broad array of interest groups.[107]

Many of the controversial issues that later would have to be resolved before enactment of the 1906 Act surfaced then. What is "adulteration?" Are substances such as oleomargarine and synthetic glucose adulterants or merely cheaper foods? Are economic adulterations "accepted by long usage in the market" to be accepted by law or prohibited? For example, is it adulteration to add flour and flavoring to mustard because pure mustard is too strong for public taste? Should standards for specific foods be set forth in a statute or developed in some other way? What role should "experts" (including organized private groups of chemists, pharmacists, or physicians) have in the elaboration and administration of the law?

Should a federal law prohibit fraud as well as physical harm? Should prohibitions be limited to "knowing" violations? Should enforcement be directed against manufacturers, importers, wholesalers, or retailers—or all, or only some of those categories? Should a statute authorize private lawsuits for violations, or should all enforcement be by the government? Should the law cover drugs; if so, should the USP (controlled by the American Pharmaceutical Association, founded in 1852) be officially recognized as the sole authority on drug formulations within its scope, and thus the standard for determining adulteration of such drugs? Should the law cover patent medicines? Should it cover liquor?

This burst of discussion and activity in the early 1880s quickly led to enactment of general food adulteration laws in New Jersey, New York, and Massachusetts. Many other states already had adulteration laws addressed to specific kinds of foods, especially oleomargarine. During the next two decades, nearly every state enacted pure food and dairy laws.[108]

In general, the state laws regulated labeling, authorized regulators to test samples, and provided for punishment in cases of adulteration.[109] One key to an effective regulatory program was an analytical chemistry laboratory. Because consumers could not detect many subtle types of adulteration or fraud, testing of samples by competent and trustworthy laboratories was necessary. Thus, government laboratories potentially had a comparative advantage over consumers

and over private-sector laboratories if they could develop public confidence in their competence and probity.[110] Over time, many state laboratories did. Thus, they established the crucial precedent that independent scientific expertise, including such expertise in a government agency, had a useful role in the regulation of food and drugs.

Most of the state laws defined adulteration as the adding of impurities to a product without disclosure on its label. Thus, these laws did not protect manufacturers of "pure" products from all competition, but only from dishonest competition. Economist Marc Law has found that "consumption of commonly adulterated foods was higher in States with pure food laws," and that this conclusion is "consistent with the hypothesis that pure food regulation reduced information costs about the quality of certain food products."[111] Manufacturers of legitimate products whose sales were helped by such laws might well be expected to support a similar national law.

Many state laws, however, were substantively inadequate, and were inadequately enforced. There also was a lack of clarity as to the location of the line between a state's police power and the limits on that power imposed by the Commerce Clause of the U.S. Constitution.[112] Some state food laws were responsive to local producers seeking protection against out-of-state producers and against new products made possible by technological innovation (e.g., dairy farmers seeking protection against oleomargarine).[113]

Even effective state laws, however, were an inadequate and economically inefficient means of solving the problems created by national products in national markets. They were inadequate because they could not directly reach out-of-state manufacturers, but only in-state wholesalers and retailers, who were not the most attractive targets for state legislators and prosecutors. Presumably due to their political influence, enforcement generally was lax. State laws also were inefficient. For large national manufacturers, compliance with different state laws was costly.[114] Hence, efforts to achieve federal legislation were simultaneous with efforts in the states, and continued after the limitations of state laws became clear.

The precedents at the federal level for legislation relating to foods and drugs were uninspiring. The Drug Importation Act of 1848[115] had been prompted by concerns about adulteration of drugs imported for troops in the Mexican War.[116] Because imports were the major source of drugs in America in 1848,[117] the law could be viewed as protectionist. It did not apply to domestic products, but gave semi-official status to the USP and other pharmacopoeias, a feature later incorporated into the 1906 Act.[118] Over time, the 1848 Act was not vigorously enforced.[119]

Also in 1848, Congress had appropriated $1,000 for the first federal study of agricultural products used for food.[120] The appropriation was prompted not by concern about what Americans ate, but about the effect of the reputation of American agricultural products on exports.[121]

The first bill to provide federal regulation of food generally (though not drugs) was introduced by Rep. Hendrick B. Wright of Pennsylvania in 1879. It received little press attention, and died in committee. Also in 1879, Rep. Richard T. Beale of Virginia, a former Confederate general, introduced a food-adulteration bill, which, as amended, was reported by the House Committee on Manufactures in 1880. The committee report stated:

> The rapid advance of chemical science has opened a wide doorway for compounding mixtures so nearly resembling nature's products that the senses are impotent to detect the difference. Human cupidity eagerly grasps the chances offered to turn a dishonest penny, and its greed for money becomes callous to human suffering. Not only are substances of less value commingled with those of greater, but such as are injurious to health, and we have no doubt often destructive of life, are freely used in manufacturing and preparing for consumption the necessaries and luxuries of life.[122]

The reported bill prohibited fraudulent as well as harmful adulteration. Beale's original bill had been attacked on the ground that Congress lacked constitutional power to regulate the sale of food or drink within a state.[123] The reported bill was limited to the District of Columbia, the territories, and interstate trade;[124] but it failed, nonetheless.

Seeking an alternative to the Beale bill, the National Board of Trade (NBT) in 1880–1881 conducted a contest for the best essay and draft bill relating to food adulteration. Thurber provided the prize money. The chairman of the prize committee was John Shaw Billings, the leading figure in the National Board of Health (NBH), created by Congress in 1879 to address yellow fever. The winning entry (drafted by G. W. Wigner, a member of the British Society of Public Analysts) defined types of "adulteration;" prohibited offers to sell, as well as selling, adulterated food; and did not require guilty knowledge. Nevertheless, the organizers of the competition and the prize committee considered it unsuitable because they preferred that the initial legislation in this field be "tentative and educational in character."[125] Billings drafted a bill that covered "foods" and "drugs" (both broadly defined), included definitions of types of "adulteration" (from Wigner's draft) that survived into the 1906 Act, and gave the enforcement role to the NBH except for imports; the Treasury's authority over imported drugs under the 1848 law would be extended to imported foods, but with a significant role for the NBH. The bill was endorsed unanimously by the NBT at its convention in December 1880, and in January 1881 was introduced in the forty-sixth Congress by Rep. Joseph R. Hawley of Connecticut.[126] It died in committee.[127] The bill was re-introduced in the House

in the forty-seventh Congress and referred to the Commerce Committee. Angell vigorously opposed the NBT-NBH bill as inadequate. Chairman Roswell G. Horr of Michigan apparently wanted to include liquor in the bill,[128] but the bill that emerged from his committee was limited to imported drugs. The committee thought domestic commerce a matter for the states.[129]

The NBT-NBH legislative effort had failed. For more than two decades thereafter, no session of Congress lacked

A recently discovered album dated 1910 contains photos of all Bureau of Chemistry labs at that time as well as this portrait of Harvey Wiley. An oil painting based on this photo is on display at the Wiley Building in College Park, Maryland. The painting was pronounced illegal shortly after it arrived for the dedication of FDA's downtown building, known as FOB-8, in the 1960s. Department rules apparently did not deem officials below Cabinet Secretary of sufficient rank to merit such an honor. Though originally threatened with prosecution, in the end, the responsible official was merely reprimanded.

Staff of the Bureau of Chemistry in the Department of Agriculture in 1885, shortly after Wiley's arrival in Washington. Left to right: A.C. Knorr (a chemist who later invented the Knorr tube); C.A. Dugan, a laboratory helper; C.A. Crampton, a chemist who later went to the Treasury Department; Harvey Wiley, Chief Chemist; C. Trescott, a specialist on nitrogen content and one of Wiley's closest friends; and Miles Fuller, an assistant who was associated with Wiley in an early Washington, D.C. area real estate development [Somerset, Maryland].

a broad food adulteration bill,[130] but none was enacted until 1906.

Enter Harvey Washington Wiley. He was born in a log cabin in Indiana in 1844. His father was a farmer and schoolmaster. Wiley fought briefly for the Union in the Civil War, obtained a medical degree, was a professor of chemistry at Purdue, and in 1883 became Chief of the Division of Chemistry in the U.S. Department of Agriculture, where he remained until 1912.[131] Although a Republican, he survived both of Grover Cleveland's Democratic administrations. Mark Sullivan, an investigative journalist, has described him:

On the platform the forcefulness and originality of his utterances gained from the impressiveness of his appearance: his large head capping the pedestal of broad shoulders and immense chest, his salient nose shaped like the bow of an ice-breaker, and his piercing eyes, compelled attention. He had a keen instinct for the dramatic.[132]

Wiley's division (it became a bureau in 1901[133]) was based on a discipline— chemistry. He gave it a mission, raised its importance, and achieved for it a high measure of independence, by focusing it on a national problem—food adulteration. In

This is the earliest known photo of Harvey Wiley as Chief Chemist in the Department of Agriculture after he came to Washington D.C. from Purdue University. Denied the presidency of that university reportedly because he was "too young, too jovial, and a bachelor, besides," Wiley was offered the position because of his expertise in sugar chemistry. The U.S. trade deficit at the time was largely due to imported sugar, and the Department of Agriculture was trying to develop a domestic sugar source. Wiley is third from left.

1887, the division published the first part of Bulletin 13, a series of major reports on adulteration in various categories of food,[134] which extended over sixteen years to ten parts containing 1,400 pages.[135] Bulletin 13 was moderate and credible; and it helped Wiley and the division develop a reputation for reliable, non-partisan science.[136] From 1889 on, the division's appropriations—and its activities and output—increased.[137]

In 1888, the House Agriculture Committee reported a food adulteration bill sponsored by Rep. William H. F. Lee, son of Robert E. Lee. The committee report specified that the Department of Agriculture was to enforce the bill because adulteration harms food producers, who were that department's

concern, and because the department's chemists had made "considerable progress in the examination and analysis of foods and food adulterants."[138] Thus, by 1888, Wiley's Division of Chemistry had begun to build, in a critical constituency, the reputation for distinctive relevant expertise that was the foundation for all his later efforts to achieve enactment of a food and drugs law.

In 1889, Wiley commissioned the publication of Bulletin 25, a *Popular Treatise on the Extent and Character of Food Adulteration*, to demonstrate the need for federal legislation. The gist of the treatise was that fraud was widespread (evident in perhaps fifteen percent of the food supply); that most adulteration did not injure health, though some did, and sometimes

Harvey Wiley's secretary recalled years later that, when her boss came to work in his "top hat and tails," it usually meant that he was going to give a speech to a women's group or other gathering that day. Wiley's "stump" speeches were remarkably effective in winning support for passage of the 1906 Act.

fatally; but that economic adulteration harmed everyone, especially the uneducated, the poor, and farmers (whose export sales were harmed). This was a moderate view of the problem, supported by the available scientific literature, some of it produced by the Division of Chemistry. With that view, Wiley, over many years, was able to build a broad coalition to support remedial legislation.

In 1890, the first meat-inspection law was enacted.[139] It was prompted by a perceived need to address European concerns about exported American meat.[140] The law separated the regulation of meat from that of other foods, which involved a more complex mix of conflicting interests.[141]

In 1892, the Senate passed a general food and drugs bill sponsored by Sen. Algernon S. Paddock of Nebraska, Chairman of the Agriculture Committee. The bill was supported by "[t]housands of petitions from urban boards of trade, state legislatures, the National Farmer's Alliance, the National Colored Farmers' Alliance, women's leagues, and individual citizens."[142] Thus, already there was broad, diverse public support. In a pattern that would continue until 1906 and beyond, Wiley helped in the drafting of the bill, and provided technical information in aid of enactment. The role of Wiley, a bureaucrat, in shaping, and even drafting major parts of such major legislation was unprecedented; it reflected the importance of technical expertise in the development of new types of legislation,

and it expanded the influence of Executive Branch officials having such expertise.[143]

In defending the enforcement role of the Division of Chemistry in the debate, Paddock evidenced another critical aspect of the division's reputation: the division was "as nearly nonpartisan in its work as such an institution can be under our system, … purely a scientific force."[144] Before passage, Paddock accepted an amendment providing for seizure and condemnation of adulterated products as a remedy in addition to criminal penalties.[145] In the House, cottonseed interests (concerned about enforcement against use of cottonseed oil in lard) and food manufacturing interests prevented the bill from coming to a vote.[146]

In 1897, Rep. Marriott Brosius of Pennsylvania, a Civil War hero, introduced a revised version of the Paddock bill. It included cosmetics, defined "drug" more broadly, and deleted the limitation of enforcement to "knowing" violations. It also would have authorized the Secretary of Agriculture to have the Association of Official Agricultural Chemists (AOAC, an association of state agricultural chemists founded in 1884 by Wiley and others) establish food standards, similar to USP standards for drugs, which would be enforceable in court. The bill failed.

During the 1890s, pure food and drug bills were introduced, but rejected, often, Wiley reported in his autobiography, with ridicule.[147] Comprehensive food and drugs bills drew comprehensive opposition, on general ideological grounds and from more particularly interested parties, including

A PERSPECTIVE ON DR. WILEY

Wiley led a dual life. A majority of his colleagues, both in the federal government and in the state agencies, disliked and distrusted him intensely. Meanwhile, the media and the public canonized him as a crusading hero.

At the Association of Food and Drug Officials (AFDO) meeting following his abrupt retirement from the USDA in 1912, a resolution honoring him was explicitly rejected by a roll-call vote. Two of the three USDA representatives voted against the resolution. The next year, the new FDA Commissioner, Dr. Carl L. Alsberg, pledged a new era of cooperation between federal and state officials and deplored Wiley's confrontational approach:

> The Wiley administration of the food laws was at sword points all the time with a large part of the food control officials, with the result that little was accomplished toward uniform legislation based on scientific truths.

On scientific matters, Wiley was seriously deficient. He argued that any chemical that is harmful in large amounts must be harmful in small amounts, and therefore should be banned. He rejected the dose/response paradigm, well-known to scientists at that time. He therefore advocated banning such common food substances as sodium benzoate, bleached flour, caffeine, and saccharin—all of which remain on the market today and are regarded as safe. The Secretary of Agriculture's two committees prevented him from carrying out his views, and the Supreme Court decision in 1914 in the *Lexington Mill* case explicitly rejected his position. His policy on food toxicology was thus completely and irretrievably wrong.

—Peter Barton Hutt

manufacturers of chemical preservatives, food processors who used preservatives, manufacturers of patent medicines, and so-called "rectifiers" of whiskey, who blended alcohol with colors and flavors. Efforts by manufacturers of cream-of-tartar baking powder to gain a competitive advantage over manufacturers of alum-based baking powder also contributed to the legislative stalemate.[148]

Most southern members of Congress opposed pure food and drugs legislation. The South was more rural than the rest of the country, and so felt less need for the legislation. The legislation was a threat to some southern economic interests, including cottonseed producers, distillers, brewers, and patent-medicine manufacturers. Federal regulatory legislation also conflicted with doctrines of states' rights.

Nevertheless, evidence of problems continued to accumulate. An 1893 Division of Chemistry report on canned vegetables raised concerns about lead and tin used in canning, and copper and zinc salts used to preserve the color of canned green vegetables.[149] In 1894, there was an incident of exploding cans of insufficiently cooked peas.[150] Following the Spanish-American War in 1898, controversy over so-called "embalmed" beef raised highly publicized concerns about the quality of refrigerated and canned beef provided to the troops. One critic of the beef was Theodore Roosevelt, who reported that it was universally viewed "from the generals down to the privates" as "a bad ration."[151] After two official inquiries, however, it turned out that the beef had not contained poisonous preservatives, but had been of the lowest quality, though no worse than canned beef sold to civilians.[152] In 1900, the Senate Committee on Manufactures, chaired by William E. Mason of Illinois, published a massive report of fifty-one days of hearings on food adulteration.[153] Wiley served, in effect, as staff to the committee, and also testified.[154] Subsequent congressional reports further documented the adulteration of foods.[155]

In response to publicity about food adulteration and concerns about patent medicines, a grassroots movement for reform legislation developed. Women's health protection associations organized to deal with concerns about urban slaughterhouses.[156] The Women's Christian Temperance Union (WCTU), founded in 1874, viewed patent medicines containing alcohol, opium, cocaine, morphine, and other substances of abuse as sources of addiction. A growing problem in the 1880s was drug abuse among women, initiated most frequently by medical use. Men turned to alcohol; women, to socially accepted "medicinal" drugs.[157] The WCTU considered substance abuse and food adulteration related evils, and it viewed poor nutrition as a source of intemperance. WCTU groups agitated for state laws to control patent medicines and ensure the purity of foods.[158]

In the mid-1890s, the WCTU broadened its mission from achieving the prohibition of alcohol to include obtaining federal pure food and drugs legislation. The WCTU brought to the national struggle for the legislation experience gained at the state level from efforts to obtain enactment and enforcement of a variety of laws relating to temperance. From 1895, the WCTU's national Department of Legislation was led by Margaret Dye Ellis, wife of Sen. J. H. Ellis of New Jersey. By 1900, the WCTU had 500,000 members (no men).[159] Ultimately, however, its championship of prohibition alienated enough other people that other groups supplanted the WCTU in the leadership of the grassroots movement.

A convention, called the National Pure Food and Drug Congress, met in Washington, D.C. early in 1898. The main organizer was Alexander Wedderburn, head of the Virginia State Grange; Wiley was chairman of the Congress's advisory committee. The Congress brought together 300 delegates representative of the broad coalition of diverse groups supporting pure food and drugs legislation—federal and state government agencies, farm groups, professional societies, food processors, grocers, women's groups, and others. President McKinley received delegates at the White House.

A major focus of the National Pure Food and Drug Congress was to agree on a revised version of the Brosius bill, which had died in committee. With compromises, the legislative committee reached agreement on a bill drafted by an AOAC committee chaired by Wiley, which was introduced in both Houses in 1898.[160] The Congress solidified links among the groups supporting legislation. It was the first time pure-food and pure-drug activists had joined forces.[161] It gave public legitimacy to their efforts, and established Wiley as their leader.[162] Follow-on congresses were held in 1899 and 1900, but conflicts among business groups prevented consensus. At the 1900 Congress, an effort was made to exclude Wiley as chief enforcer. He opposed further congresses, and none was held. James Harvey Young has noted that, thereafter, efforts to achieve compromise on a bill focused on the real Congress.[163]

On September 6, 1901, President McKinley was shot by an anarchist; he died eight days later, and was succeeded by Theodore Roosevelt. Roosevelt had been made McKinley's running mate in 1900, with misgivings on both sides, to solve a Republican political problem in New York. Roosevelt had an aristocratic disdain for mere plutocrats.[164] He had expressed his basic approach to the great economic and political issues of the day when he was governor of New York:

> [T]hese representatives of enormous corporate wealth have themselves been responsible for a portion of the conditions against which Bryanism is in ignorant revolt. I do not believe that it is wise or safe for us as a party to take refuge in mere negation and to say that there are no evils to be corrected. It seems to me that our attitude should be one of correcting the evils and thereby showing that, whereas the Populists, Socialists,

and others really do not correct the evils at all … we Republicans hold the just balance and set ourselves as resolutely against improper corporate influence on the one hand as against demagogy and mob rule on the other…. I think it is in the long run the only wise attitude….[165]

Roosevelt viewed large national corporations (and unions) as inevitable, and also economically beneficial if, through regulation, their activities were subordinated to the public interest.[166] His accession to the Presidency created new possibilities for reform. Wiley got off to a bad start with TR by testifying against a reduction in sugar tariffs, which TR favored.[167] Roosevelt was very sensitive to currents of public opinion,[168] and philosophically open to regulation of business,[169] however; and eventually he played a critical role in the enactment of the pure food and drugs law.

In the late fall of 1901, contaminated diphtheria antitoxin killed thirteen children in St. Louis and nine in Camden, New Jersey. Wide publicity about these incidents easily led to enactment of the Biologics Act of 1902.[170] The manufacturers of biological products were new and small, and many were in the public sector; none opposed the bill.[171]

The House passed a food and drugs bill in the fifty-seventh Congress (1901–1902), but the Senate did not bring it to a vote. Even after House passage and after deleting the most controversial provisions, Sen. Porter McCumber of North Dakota, who had succeeded Mason as chairman of

THE PEOPLE WHO ATE POISONS

It's hard to imagine people volunteering to eat "poison," but that very courageous act was influential in the enactment of the 1906 Act. The famous "Poison Squad" studies or the "hygienic table studies," as Harvey Wiley preferred to call them, were a crucial prelude to enactment of the 1906 Act. As discussions of a pending federal food and drugs law began to revolve around questions about the safety and suitability of many early preserving chemicals, Congress granted the Bureau of Chemistry $2,000 to test these preservatives on human subjects.

A dozen young men were recruited for each panel, and each panel tested a single preservative. Volunteers were fed high-quality meals with doses of the preservative under study gradually increased until effects were evident. Wiley himself often dined with the men.

Sanctioned by Congress, implemented by Bureau Scientist F. C. Weber, and overseen by Wiley, these experiments made the daily papers, especially when the tabloids learned that the men's motto was "only the brave dare eat the fare." The overall results of the study were scientifically questionable, since the Bureau used no "control" group and Wiley took to giving the men preservatives in capsules after they began avoiding the butter laced with borax.

With the slogan "only the brave dare eat the fare," Dr. Wiley's Poison Squad became, according to him, "the most famous boardinghouse in America."

One of the lesser known photos of the "Poison Squad" and its cooks. The man on the left was William Carter, who later became a pharmaceutical chemist and retired from the Food and Drug Administration in 1943.

But the staid Bureau of Chemistry scientists learned a totally unanticipated lesson from their studies. They watched in amazement as the public, lackadaisical at best for nearly two decades, was suddenly drawn into debates over food safety; and reporters, anxious to get a story, began interviewing the cook through a basement window. Wiley provided the press with information himself, and clearly was aware of how the media were advancing his cause. The "Poison Squad" became so well known, it even was mentioned at minstrel shows.

Alarmed at the adverse effects he witnessed from large doses of the preservatives, Wiley became equally concerned about the cumulative effects of many small doses in the daily diet. Without the scientific advances in toxicology that would enable him to show that small quantities of such preservatives were safe, he took the position that it would be impossible to control the number of such substances in the daily diet, and that they should be disallowed in the food supply. This rigid position set the stage for many debates with industry after the 1906 law was enacted.

There seemed to be no lingering effects on the health of the volunteers of the "Poison Squad." The last volunteer to die was ninety-four when he died in 1979.

—Suzanne White Junod

the Committee on Manufactures, could not secure a Senate floor vote on the bill.[172]

At Wiley's request, Congress in 1902 appropriated funds for the Bureau of Chemistry "to investigate the character of proposed food preservatives and coloring matters, to determine their relation to digestion and to health, and to establish the principles which should guide their use."[173] Wiley recruited a group of twelve young men, mostly from the Department of Agriculture, to eat a prescribed diet containing borax, and he observed the results. There was no control group or blinding and little statistical analysis; only short-term effects were observed, and most of those were subjective. Wiley described his rationale:

> I wanted young robust fellows, with maximum resistance to deleterious effects of adulterated foods. If they should show signs of injury after they were fed such substances for a period of time, the deduction would naturally follow that children and older persons, more susceptible than they, would be greater sufferers from similar causes.… I allowed no experiment to be carried to the point of danger to health.[174]

When Wiley published his results in 1904, he reported that ingestion of borax led to decline in appetite, occasional stomach discomfort and pain, headache, and inability to work. Similar experiments were done with other young men and other preservatives, some of which elicited more pronounced effects. Wiley concluded that chemical preservatives should be banned from processed foods, though they might be supplied, like salt and pepper, for consumers to use as they pleased.[175] George Rothwell Brown of *The Washington Post* called the young men Wiley's "Poison Squad."[176] The experiments were not much as science, but they were great politics.[177] The Poison Squad attracted widespread publicity, and even became the subject of a song.[178] By 1905, "Dr. Wiley" was a household name.[179]

From 1899, Wiley also administered authorities granted to the Secretary of Agriculture to exclude imported foods that were dangerous to health and, starting in 1903, those that were falsely labeled as to the place of manufacture.[180] Wiley set high standards for imports, but was lenient to first offenders, especially for misbranding. No importers challenged him, and the United States ceased to be a dumping ground for substandard foreign foods.[181] Wiley's effective use of regulatory authority earned him opposition from some food processors and whiskey rectifiers,[182] but also demonstrated another dimension of his competence.

After his election in 1904, TR proposed much reform legislation in his December 1904 message to the second session of the fifty-eighth Congress. None of it passed.[183]

In the fifty-eighth Congress, Weldon B. Heyburn of Idaho, a first-term Senator, succeeded Porter McCumber as chairman of the Committee on Manufactures. He had grown up in Pennsylvania, studied civil and mining engineering, metallurgy, and geology, and received a law degree from the University of Pennsylvania. He eventually settled in Idaho, where he practiced law and invested in mining. He generally opposed progressive legislation, but strongly supported a pure food and drugs law. In explaining that support, he recounted the story of a friend who had spent half his pension on fraudulently advertised patent medicines.[184] He was very clear that "the object of this bill is not to protect the

Weldon B. Heyburn

dealer. It is to protect the persons who consume the articles. It is against the dealer that we are seeking to protect the purchaser, the consumer."[185] Heyburn's influence was reflected in the inclusion of patent medicines in the legislation, over strong opposition from the patent medicine industry. To achieve enactment, McCumber, who had included them in his bill in the fifty-seventh Congress, was willing to exclude them; so, too, was Wiley in 1904; Heyburn was not.[186] The fifty-eighth Congress repeated the pattern of the fifty-seventh: the House passed the bill, but efforts to obtain a floor vote in the Senate failed. The reform movement, however, was gaining strength.

The General Federation of Women's Clubs (GFWC, founded in 1890), and the National Consumers League (NCL), both with national reach through local chapters, provided organized support for pure food and drugs legislation (NCL starting in 1904). In 1904, the GFWC had more than 500,000 members.[187] Although women could not vote, they lectured, wrote newspaper articles, wrote and distributed pamphlets, held mass meetings, called on legislators and sent them letters, telegrams, and petitions, and otherwise agitated for the legislation. In response to a proposal from the GFWC's Alice Lakey, NCL in 1905 created the Pure Food Committee, headed by Lakey, which constituted a network of activists for pure food and drugs legislation, with connections to physicians, public health officials, journalists, and others. Lakey, an ally of Wiley, spoke for the cause to women's groups throughout the United States.[188] Thus, the movement for food and drugs legislation attracted new organizations and pressure groups not affiliated with any political party.

Mass-circulation magazines began to present sensational exposés of segments of the food and drug industries. Starting in February 1905 and continuing throughout the year, *Everybody's* published a monthly article by Charles Edward Russell on the beef trust. The *Ladies Home Journal*, in 1904–1905, exposed fraud associated with patent medicines.[189] Among other things, the manufacturer of Lydia E. Pinkham's Vegetable Compound was sending what purported to be personal responses to women's private letters from Lydia herself; but Mark Sullivan found Lydia's grave in Lynn, Massachusetts, and the *Journal* published a photograph of her 1883 tombstone.[190] Sullivan also obtained copies of advertising contracts between patent-medicine manufacturers and newspapers, which contained the "red clause," a provision in red ink that the contract would be void if the state where the newspaper was located enacted any law prohibiting or restricting the manufacture or sale of patent medicines. Sullivan's article appeared in *Collier's* in November 1905.[191]

From October 1905 into February 1906, *Colliers* also published a series of articles by Samuel Hopkins Adams on patent medicines, under the title "The Great American Fraud." Also in 1905, *World's Work* published two articles by Edward Lowry on "The Senate Plot against Pure Food." The articles described Senators as defending interests engaged in fraudulent labeling.[192] There were also drug exposés in 1905–1906 in *Popular Science Monthly*, the *Nation*, and *Outlook*.[193]

In February 1906, Henry Beach Needham published in *World's Work* "Senate of Special Interests," which linked Senators Aldrich's opposition to pure food and drugs legislation to his ties to the wholesale grocery business.[194] In a series in *Cosmopolitan*, beginning in March 1906, David Graham Phillips, in "The Treason of the Senate," exposed connections between wealthy Senators and large corporations, and attacked particularly Sen. Aldrich and TR's friend, Sen. Henry Cabot Lodge of Massachusetts.[195] It was Phillips's work that TR, in a speech on April 14, 1906, denounced as "muckraking,"[196] a term he drew from John Bunyan's *The Pilgrim's Progress*. Phillips had been a college roommate of Sen. Albert Beveridge of Indiana, who would

play a significant role in the enactment of the meat inspection law of 1906.[197]

The muckrakers in the mass-circulation magazines were a sharp contrast to mainstream newspapers and magazines, which, in general, published large quantities of patent-medicine advertising

Samuel Hopkins Adams

and, accordingly, were not vigorous champions for pure food and drugs legislation. Even most medical journals, including the *Journal of the American Medical Association*, accepted patent-medicine advertising.[198] *The New York Times*, however, reported on medical frauds and the dangers of patent medicines, and supported strong legislation.[199]

In February 1905, Roosevelt received a delegation seeking to persuade him to support pure food and drugs legislation. The delegates were: Robert M. Allen, Food Commissioner of Kentucky and secretary of the National Association of State Dairy and Food Commissioners;[200]

Albert Beveridge

Horace Ankeney, Ohio Pure Food Commissioner; J. B. Nobel, Connecticut Food Commissioner; A. B. Fallinger, representing the National Association of Retail Grocers; Alice Lakey; and Sebastian Mueller from H. J. Heinz Company.[201] (Heinz was a processor of high-quality foods generally without

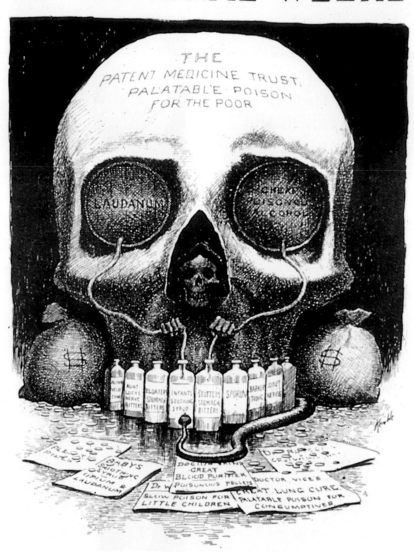

Collier's Magazine was one of the "muckraking" magazines that exposed the dangerous nature of many medicine preparations at the turn of the century. This frontispiece, drawn by E. W. Kemble, was memorable both for its imagery and for its assessment of most patent medicines as "palatable poisons for the poor." Such publicity helped garner support around the country and in Congress for enactment of the 1906 Pure Food and Drugs Act.

It required over twenty-five years to enact federal food and drugs legislation in the form of the 1906 Pure Food and Drugs Act, but towards the end of the national debate, it became obvious that politics rather than principle was delaying a final vote on the food and drug bill in the Senate, as lampooned in this early cartoon.

preservatives.[202]) Roosevelt said he would study the matter, and asked them to return in the fall. In the summer of 1905, William Frear, Food Commissioner of Pennsylvania and an ally of Wiley, wrote to TR to urge him to include a call for pure food and drugs legislation in his annual message to Congress. Secretary of Agriculture James Wilson supported the request. TR consulted with Wiley; Ira Remsen, an eminent chemist and president of the Johns Hopkins University; and his personal physician, Samuel W. Lambert. During the remaining months of 1905, letters and petitions to Congress continued, as did the onslaught of muckraking articles.

The delegation, joined by Dr. Charles Reed of the AMA, met with the President again on November 16.[203] TR told them his message to Congress in December would recommend legislation. It did:

> I recommend that a law be enacted to regulate interstate commerce in misbranded and adulterated food, drinks, and drugs. Such law would protect legitimate manufacture and commerce, and would tend to secure the health and welfare of the consuming public. Traffic in foodstuffs which have been debased or adulterated so as to injure health

or to deceive purchasers should be forbidden.[204]

Although he had been in office for four years, Roosevelt had not championed the legislation. His December message was a critical victory for the pure food and drugs movement. Presumably, he was responding to the force of public opinion, built during two decades by Wiley and others and strengthened by the muckrakers. There were two sets of further prerequisites for enactment, however.

First, it was necessary to neutralize the influence of those opposed in principle— on grounds of the Constitution, states' rights, *laissez faire*, or the alliance between the Republican Party and large business firms.[205] Those so opposed included leading members of Congress, among them Sen. Aldrich and Speaker Cannon. Many senators had significant constituents who opposed the bill, had other ties to food or drug businesses opposed to it, or had ties to other businesses opposed to federal regulation altogether.[206] Most of the congressional leaders of the final battle for the law represented agricultural states west of the Mississippi. Since their states had little industry (and few food processors or drug manufacturers), they incurred little political risk in supporting the legislation.[207] They did not control Congress, however.

Second, to create a bill acceptable to the various power centers in Congress, it was necessary to work out detailed practical compromises on key issues. From 1879 to June 30, 1906, 190 bills relating to pure food and drugs had been introduced.[208]

President Theodore Roosevelt was one of the nation's "larger than life" Presidents. Far from being a man "of the times," he virtually created his own times, which included forging a coalition of progressive and conservative supporters to help implement pragmatic solutions and compromises involving many pressing problems of the industrial era. H.J. Heinz is reported to have helped persuade Roosevelt to sign the Pure Food and Drugs Act in 1906 by demonstrating to him the adulteration found in his beloved brand of whiskey.

Few had been enacted, and none of those broadly regulated domestically produced foods or drugs in interstate commerce. It was easier to enact narrow legislation relating to one product, such as to protect dairy interests against oleomargarine[209] or filled cheese;[210] to regulate foreign-made products offered for import;[211] to regulate exports at the request of the exporters;[212] to control goods sold in the District of Columbia, in contrast to those sold in interstate commerce;[213] and to regulate a limited class of products as to which a public health disaster had removed all opposition to regulation.[214] It also was easier to prohibit false labeling of place of origin than other kinds of fraud.[215]

Public pressure determined that there would be some kind of pure food and drugs law, but other forces determined its content. Within the scope of the emerging legislation, businesses struggled to weaken regulatory controls on themselves (generally, by trying to eliminate or diminish the role of the

Department of Agriculture and Wiley's Bureau of Chemistry, a result Wiley, of course, opposed) and to gain advantages against their competitors.[216] Thus, with the broad ideological struggles, were interwoven other struggles that engaged a complex mix of political, economic, and bureaucratic interests.

The principal issues for compromise included: the locus of standard-setting and enforcement authority; whether the legislation would cover patent medicines and liquor; whether it would prohibit only "knowing" violations; whether it would require ingredient labeling. There also were controversies as to specific products (e.g., whiskey, baking powder), whose manufacturers sought advantage over one another.

The congressional opposition in principle was overcome by at least four sets of forces. First, actual experience with the industrial economy and general intellectual and cultural trends eroded the attraction of social Darwinism and *laissez faire*. Second, Wiley and other federal and state officials, particularly state agricultural chemists,[217] made the case for this particular kind of law with analyses, data, strong testimony at congressional hearings, effective publicity, and prudent use of the powers they already had been given; and Wiley won the confidence of, and assisted, key committee chairmen and others. Third, grassroots activist groups, in coalition with Wiley, kept up pressure on Congress and the President. Fourth, the muckrakers created a climate of scandal, to which the politicians had to respond.[218] In addition,

Wiley avoided stirring up opposition from the working class and the poor by designing the legislation generally to preserve the option to sell and buy cheap substitute foods properly labeled.[219]

In the struggle for the law, the final and most influential piece of muckraking was Upton Sinclair's novel, *The Jungle*, which exposed horrific conditions in the meatpacking industry. The book's publisher, Doubleday Page, extensively promoted it;[220] and it was an immediate sensation: 25,000 copies were sold in the first 45 days after its publication on February 16, 1906.[221] By the summer, it was the number one best seller.[222]

TR read it (as Finley Peter Dunn noted in our opening quotation),[223] and sent his own representatives, Charles P. Neill and James B. Reynolds, to Chicago to verify Sinclair's description. He later used their report to pressure Congress to enact both a meat inspection law and a pure food and drugs law. The public and Congress viewed the two laws as parts of one package.[224] The book was published, however, only three days before the Senate debate began, and only five days before it passed the Senate, which had been the major obstacle to enactment.[225] Therefore, its actual impact almost surely was in increasing the pressure (including the pressure from TR) on the House.

An example of the many detailed compromises necessary to achieve enactment is provided by whiskey. The American bourbon industry consisted of manufacturers of straight whiskey (mainly in Kentucky, Pennsylvania, Maryland, and

Virginia) and manufacturers of blended or rectified whiskey (mainly in Illinois, Indiana, and Ohio). Rectified whiskey was cheaper and outsold straight whiskey. Rectifiers opposed any legislation that would require their labels to disclose ingredients. The WCTU and other temperance advocates demanded inclusion of whiskey in the legislation. Wiley viewed rectified whiskey as adulterated, and he opposed exemptions for particular kinds of food, such as whiskey. With his support, however, the enacted legislation provided, in effect, that ingredient labeling was not required, and that whiskey that contained no added poisonous or deleterious ingredients and that was labeled as a blend would not be deemed adulterated or misbranded.[226]

Heyburn introduced his bill on December 6, 1905, and it was reported from committee on December 14. During the next several weeks, despite making compromises on a range of issues, Heyburn was unable to obtain a floor vote. In mid-February, Roosevelt personally appealed to Aldrich to permit a vote. Aldrich agreed (it is unclear why) and told Beveridge to tell Heyburn that, if he wanted consideration of his bill, there would be no objection. Heyburn was suspicious, but Beveridge pressed him, and Heyburn proceeded.[227]

Further compromises were accepted on the Senate floor—including an amendment sought by Sen. Lodge (and drafted by Wiley[228]) to protect use of a preservative by the Massachusetts codfish industry,[229] and one sought by drug

manufacturers to permit less than full compliance with standards of the U. S. Pharamcopeia or National Formulary.[230] An amendment to clarify that the drug misbranding provisions applied only to false claims about ingredients, not to false therapeutic claims, was rejected when Heyburn and McCumber explained that those provisions did not reach therapeutic claims.[231] An industry-supported substitute bill proposed by Sen. Hernando DeSoto Money of Mississippi was rejected. Finally, the Senate passed the Heyburn bill on February 21 by a vote of 63 to 4, with 22 (including Aldrich) not voting.[232] The four voting nay were all Southerners.[233]

In the House, the leading proponents of pure food and drugs legislation were William P. Hepburn of Iowa and James R. Mann of Illinois, Chairman of the Committee on Interstate and Foreign Commerce and a close friend of Speaker Cannon.[234] Their initial bill

James R. Mann

in 1906 was stronger in some respects than the Senate bill. The Senate bill left standard-setting to the courts; the House bill authorized the Secretary of Agriculture to set standards having the force of law. The House bill required all mixtures, including liquors, to disclose ingredients. It also did not limit prosecutable violations to those committed knowingly; it did not, however, cover patent medicines.[235]

The House Commerce Committee held hearings on the bill during the second half of February.[236] The committee reported a revised bill on March 7 as a substitute for the Senate bill. It covered patent medicines;[237] but, in a compromise with Wiley's opponents, the bill granted regulatory authority to the Secretary of the Treasury and the Secretary of Commerce and Labor, as well as to the Secretary of Agriculture.[238] In a compromise with state food commissioners, the Secretary of Agriculture was authorized to consult with

IN THE HANDS OF HIS PHILANTHROPIC FRIENDS.

Uncle Sam Trusts – The public in the early twentieth century remained skeptical of the federal government (Uncle Sam's) ability to act independent of "big" interests. One of the reasons that Theodore Roosevelt's "Progressive" administration was so admired was his ability to show that the government could and would act independently on issues to further truly national interests.

the National Association of State Dairy and Food Departments as well as with the AOAC.[239] Imprisonment was limited to perpetrators of knowing violations. Nevertheless, floor consideration was delayed. "[T]he friends of the bill observed a disconcerting sign: the professional lobbyists, carrying their packed grips out of Washington hotels on their way home."[240] A Republican leader told a journalist that, under pressure from business interests, the House leadership had decided to let the bill die;[241] Mann denied the story,[242] but Wiley despaired.[243]

On May 27, TR wrote to Cannon that he "earnestly favor[ed]" enactment of a pure food and drugs bill. On June 4, *The Times* reported that Republican legislators feared that Cannon's obstruction would cost them the fall elections.[244] The next day, *The Times* reported a statement from Cannon's office that he favored the bill, with amendments, but could not obtain passage in the House.[245] A *Times* editorial on June 8 disputed that assessment.[246]

Since its publication in February, *The Jungle* had generated further attacks on the meatpackers. On May 21, Sen. Beveridge introduced a meat inspection bill as a rider to an appropriations bill. On May 25, it passed the Senate without dissent.[247] The packers focused their opposition on the House. TR sought to pressure the industry and its supporters by threatening to release the (still unwritten) Neill-Reynolds report on the Chicago packinghouses. Sinclair, knowing that the report would support his allegations and seeking public vindication, leaked to *The Times* supportive comments

A "QUAINT" LAW

More than a century after the Boston Tea Party of 1773, America passed its own Tea Act, not in protest but for protection against inferior teas judged "little better than hay or catnip," which were being "dumped" in America. The original law was passed in 1882 and strengthened in an 1897 amendment by establishment of a National Board of Tea Experts to create uniform standards for imported tea. The board met once a year to sample tea varieties submitted by importers. One standard tea from each variety was chosen; and samples were distributed to importers, dealers, and tea inspectors to serve as a uniform basis for comparison.

In 1902, the Supreme Court upheld the Tea Act's authority to outlaw the importation of substandard teas by upholding quality standards for tea. The ruling galvanized the less scrupulous elements of the food industry in their opposition to a federal food and drugs act. Worried that food standards set by the government might outlaw certain controversial foods and ingredients, this group lobbied influential senators. They succeeded in eliminating appropriations for food standards research and deleting standards provisions from the draft food and drugs bill. Thus, the 1906 Pure Food and Drugs Act recognized the U.S. Pharmacopeia and National Formulary as standards authorities for the nation's drug supply, but provided no such standards for foods. Federal food standards were not established until the 1938 Act.

The Tea Board met every year for 99 years, except during World War II when tea was rationed. FDA maintained a tea laboratory with professional tea tasters exercising their judgment as to the quality of the tea by spending their days brewing cups of tea, tasting a mouthful, and spitting it out. Congress abolished the program in 1996, one year shy of its 100th anniversary.

Although the tea industry, itself, had paid for the Tea Board's services since the 1950s, several administrations attempted to portray it as a quaint example of the useless proliferation of government advisory committees, and vowed to have the Board abolished. The task proved a little more difficult than expected. Early attempts to curtail the committee failed because the White House misunderstood that the Board was supported in law rather than by regulation. In 1996, Congress itself repealed the original Tea Act.

—**Suzanne White Junod**

FDA "Tea Taster" Hutchinson preparing tea for sampling to compare with "standard" teas in each category. Note the use of eighteenth century style handle-less porcelain cups.

to him by Neill and Reynolds.[248] On May 28, the lead article in *The Times* reported that Neill had met with Speaker Cannon, described the conditions in the Chicago meatpacking plants, and thereby convinced him to support the Beveridge bill; the front-page headline was: "Report on Meat Converts Cannon/Speaker Horrified by the Revelations."[249] TR ordered Neill and Reynolds to write their report in forty-eight hours.[250] On June 4, he publicly released the first section of the report. In his accompanying message to Congress, he called the conditions described "revolting," and threatened to withhold Department of Agriculture inspection labels on canned meat for export unless the Beveridge bill was passed.[251] After TR rejected a bill much weaker than the Beveridge bill, and Cannon helped work out a compromise satisfactory to TR, the House on June 19 passed a revised version of Beveridge's meat-inspection bill. After further controversy, the Senate yielded to the House version.[252]

The pressure on House members for consideration of the pure food and drugs bill included newspaper editorials and telegrams from physicians and women.[253] Perhaps, as Mark Sullivan has suggested, the aggregate of disclosures about meat, patent medicines, and food generally, and the controversy over whiskey made TR's demand for action "invincible."[254] Finally, Cannon permitted floor consideration of the pure food and drugs bill. The crucial procedural vote was won by supporters 143 to 72 on June 20.[255] Debate began on June 21. On June 23, the House passed the bill 241 to 17, with 6 voting "present" and

112 not voting. Those voting against it were predominantly Southern Democrats. Necessary compromises between the Senate and House bills were quickly achieved in the Conference Committee. The limitation of prosecutable violations to those committed knowingly, present in both bills, vanished without comment.[256] Both Houses accepted the Conference bill on June 29. On June 30, TR signed the pure food and drugs bill and the meat inspection bill at the Capitol.

"How does a general feel who wins a great battle and brings a final end to hostilities?" Wiley asked in his autobiography. "I presume I felt that way on the last day of June, 1906."[257] Mark Sullivan noted that the enactment was

EQUAL OPPORTUNITY PREVAILS

In 1895, in an era in which it was difficult for a woman to obtain a PhD in a scientific field, Mary Engles Pennington received her PhD from the University of Pennsylvania. Faced with a lack of opportunity, she formed her own company, Philadelphia Clinical Laboratory, conducting bacteriological analyses. Among other work, she began efforts to clean up the ice cream supply peddled to young children by opting to educate state farmers rather than prosecute them.

This work drew the attention of Harvey Wiley, who in 1905 contracted Pennington to work on cold storage problems. In 1906, after the statute was passed, Pennington took the Civil Service exam and Wiley submitted her name to Department of Agriculture officials as M. E. Pennington to disguise the fact that she was a woman. Once his ruse was discovered, he successfully argued that the law did not allow him to refuse to hire her just because she was female. She had, after all, drawn the top score on the Civil Service exam!

Mary Engles Pennington was the first female lab chief in the Department of Agriculture. Harvey Wiley hired her as chief of the Cold Laboratory where she and her colleagues revolutionized the transport and preservation of "cold storage" foods such as eggs.

While Wiley and others were busy enforcing the 1906 Act through court actions, Pennington steadfastly refused to appear in court or allow her staff to testify. Her sole focus was on research. Her work on the "cold chain" helped revolutionize the transport of cold foods. Keeping foods cold kept their bacterial counts low, and thereby made them safer for consumers and more profitable for businesses.

Pennington left the Bureau of Chemistry in 1919 and subsequently developed an interest in the new frozen foods that dominated the late years of her professional life.

—**Suzanne White Junod**

Harvey Wiley thought benzoate of soda as a preservative was harmful; Ira Remsen and his researchers concluded that, in small doses, the preservative was "perfectly safe and natural." At stake was how early food additives were to be regulated. The Supreme Court ruled that, in order for Wiley and the bureaucrats to prevail, they had to show some adverse relation to health resulting from use. The result was a virtual standoff on benzoate. Some catsup manufacturers continued to use 1/10 of 1% in their products until passage of the 1938 Food, Drug, and Cosmetic Act, knowing that the government would not act against such a small amount of the preservative. The first food standards issued under the new food standard provisions in the 1938 law were for tomato products, however, and they prohibited use of benzoate in catsup. Later, however, benzoate was put onto the GRAS (generally recognized as safe) list. Today if you see "1/10 of 1% benzoate of soda as a preservative" on a product label, that disclosure reflects the early history under the 1906 Act.

also the first national victory for organized women over organized liquor.[258] It would not be the last.

Many factors contributed to the final enactment of the bill—too many to be discussed or even listed here. But, a few are of particular interest. The role of *The Jungle* and other works of the muckrakers in increasing public concerns about foods and drugs and in precipitating a legislative response to those concerns was analogous to the role played later by other crises in bringing about major changes in food and drug law. The principal examples are the Elixir Sulfanilamide crisis, which led to the enactment of the Federal Food,

Denver Post, August 1909—Another take on the benzoate debate. Remsen's report was at odds with Wiley's conclusions, based on his Poison Squad studies; and the standoff had widespread remifications for other early preserving chemicals, including saccharin, studied by the Poison Squad. Ira Remsen was the inventor of saccharin.

Drug, and Cosmetic Act of 1938, and the thalidomide crisis in Europe, which led to the Drug Amendments of 1962.[259]

Enactment of the 1906 Act was facilitated by change in constitutional law. *Champion v. Ames* in 1903 upheld the national anti-lottery law, and thereby strengthened the potential for use of the Commerce Clause to regulate articles moving in interstate commerce.[260]

Robert Crunden has characterized the Pure Food and Drugs Act as "an archetype of how moral indignation could lead to progressive legislation."[261] Long before the muckrakers, Wiley had approached the problems of food and drug adulteration and misbranding as fundamentally moral problems—problems of dishonesty. Whereas both the Biologics Act of 1902[262] and the Meat Inspection Act of 1906[263] required governmental inspection before the regulated products could be marketed, the Pure Food and Drugs Act did not. Wiley's predominant solution was a requirement of honest labeling, together with limited prohibitions of hazards to health, backed by *post hoc* enforcement in the courts. By emphasizing honesty in labeling as the principal regulatory requirement, he appeared very moderate because he could appeal to traditional legal condemnations of fraud.

The 1906 Act was an aid to competition in a free market, principally through a governmentally enforced prohibition of false labeling. Choices about what products would be produced and consumed were "left entirely in the hands of private producers and consumers."[264] As to drugs, the law did not require disclosure, except of narcotics and alcohol; but it did require that all disclosures made be true.[265] Consumers would need to accommodate to the market by reading labels.

Despite the difficulties he had from time to time with Agriculture Secretary James Wilson, who served from 1897 until 1913, Wiley was very fortunate to be in the Department of Agriculture (USDA).

> By 1890 the Department of Agriculture was the strongest voice for scientific policymaking in the federal government, if not the entire nation. While constrained politically, the USDA had broken ideologically from the parties and had distinguished itself from the agrarian revolt. It occupied a unique space in turn-of-century national politics.[266]
>
> From 1900 onward, the USDA established a reputation *par excellence* as the principal scientific agency of American government. It also became an authority in the policymaking process, an unrivaled supplier of drafts and amendments for Congress and the President. The department's officials did not merely participate in the legislative process. They directed the course and the terms of significant bills, transforming their organization into a firm gatekeeper of farm legislation in the United States.[267] The USDA's continued success was reflected not only in Wiley's work, but also in the department's work in plant science, in forestry conservation under Gifford Pinchot, and in transforming itself from a disseminator of seeds into a disseminator of agricultural knowledge.[268]

Wiley had able colleagues.

Over the years, Wiley's Bureau of Chemistry, together with state agencies, and greatly aided by the muckrakers, persuaded the public that there were serious problems with food and drugs. The bureau also established a reputation for competent, honest, credible, creative, energetic, and effective analysis and action in pursuit of the public welfare, and thereby persuaded the key actors in Congress that entrusting it with regulatory power was the principal component of the solution to those problems.[269] As a consequence of this reputation, Wiley's staff grew from 20 in 1897 to 50 in 1902 and to 110 in 1906.[270]

During more than twenty years, Wiley personally established relationships with key members of Congress, state officials, leaders of the relevant professions, business leaders, and grassroots groups.[271] He thus brought together a diverse coalition, which enabled him to champion the legislation without regard to the preferences of his nominal political superiors, and to create and preserve an extraordinary independence in negotiating necessary

compromises.[272] He also used publicity masterfully to educate the public and build support for legislation.

Wiley created for himself a position of such authority and popular support that, in championing the cause of pure food and drugs legislation, he was able to escape many of the normal political constraints on Executive Branch officials. Coppin and High observe that TR "is reported to have told one dissatisfied businessman who wanted Wiley dismissed, 'You don't understand, Sir, that Dr. Wiley has the grandest political machine in the country.'"[273] In the battle for pure food and drugs legislation, Wiley, in what has been

Roosevelt's signing into law of the 1906 Pure Food and Drugs Act was viewed as "something worthwhile" for the people by this Denver cartoonist. Similar sentiments were widespread following enactment of the popular law.

called bureaucratic entrepreneurship,[274] used that machine to obtain legislation that, *inter alia*, would secure the leading role for his bureau. Wiley was thus one of the first federal senior civil servants with substantial political independence; others would follow.

The Act can be viewed as an experiment in bureaucratic management through regulation of two economic sectors—foods and drugs—as a way to end the chaos in which competition unconstrained by considerations of honesty or the public health served consumers inadequately.[275] The law was also an example of government catching up with business: as the scale of national businesses transcended the ability of states to address adulteration and misbranding, it became necessary to organize the federal government to take the lead in addressing them. This need led to a new conception of government, of which the Bureau of Chemistry was a model: a group of professionally qualified civil servants continuously monitoring and intervening in an economic sector to protect people dependent on that sector.[276]

Many business motivations for support of the legislation were not anticompetitive: promotion of trust and confidence in American processed foods to foster domestic sales and exports;[277] maximization of the realization of economies of scale, which were impeded by varying state packaging and labeling laws; avoidance of having to compete against fraudulent products. The pure food and drugs law can fairly be viewed as a part of a broad movement toward rationalization of the national economy—acceptance of large national business corporations as a beneficial part of the economy, and the establishment of a political and legal framework that provided a relatively high degree of stability and predictability for the benefit of those corporations, while meeting the most urgent needs of their customers. Thereby, the law protected the regulated firms against more radical measures, such as a populist antitrust policy of breaking up large concentrations of economic power, or even nationalization. Business interests may also have felt reasonably comfortable even with a new regulatory law to be administered by Harvey Wiley because his political superiors in the administration and Congress were all Republicans (though TR could not always be relied on).[278]

Some scholars have argued, however, that the 1906 Act is best understood as an example of the use (or "capture") of a regulatory process by businesses to achieve anticompetitive effects, such as control over entry, suppression of competing products, and shared rules of behavior that have the effect of raising prices.[279] Certainly, such motivations were among those that led some businesses to support the legislation; and regulatory legislation commonly has such effects. It would be misleading, however, to characterize the 1906 Act overall as an example of capture. The enacted law addressed problems of adulteration and misbranding of food and drugs that were widely considered serious by grassroots and professional organizations, federal and state public health officials, and the press—who collectively moved the political establishment to act. The Act was a response to what Keller has characterized as the widely accepted "view that the state bore some minimal responsibility for the safety and well-being of its citizens."[280] Like much other reform legislation, it "rested on traditional conceptions of public power and was constantly circumscribed by an ingrained hostility to the active state."[281]

Although Harvey Wiley had fixed views (and consequent blind spots) on some issues, made tactical alliances with some business groups in their battles against competitors, charted a somewhat shifting course through the multitude of interest groups engaged in the legislative process, and sought to shape the legislation so as to increase his own power,[282] there can be no serious doubt that his overriding desire was to secure legislation that would effectively address the perceived problems of food and drug adulteration and misbranding (with the principal emphasis on food) as they were understood at the time. The 1906 Act—Wiley's law—did just that, and set the nation on a course toward increasingly effective regulation of food and drugs in later years.

In 1998, as part of its "Celebrate the Century" stamp series marking the new Millennium, the U.S. Postal Service chose this image from FDA's collection of turn-of-the-century images to illustrate and commemorate the enactment of the landmark 1906 Pure Food and Drugs Act. The 1906 Act was one of a dozen or so cultural, social and political events chosen by a national commission to represent highlights from the period 1900–1910 in American history. This is, therefore, the official commemorative stamp for FDA's Centennial. This first day "cover" with Harvey Wiley's picture pays tribute to the fact that the first commemorative stamp issued by the Post Office in tribute to the 1906 Act was a three cent stamp issued in 1956 to mark the fiftieth anniversary of the Pure Food and Drugs Act.

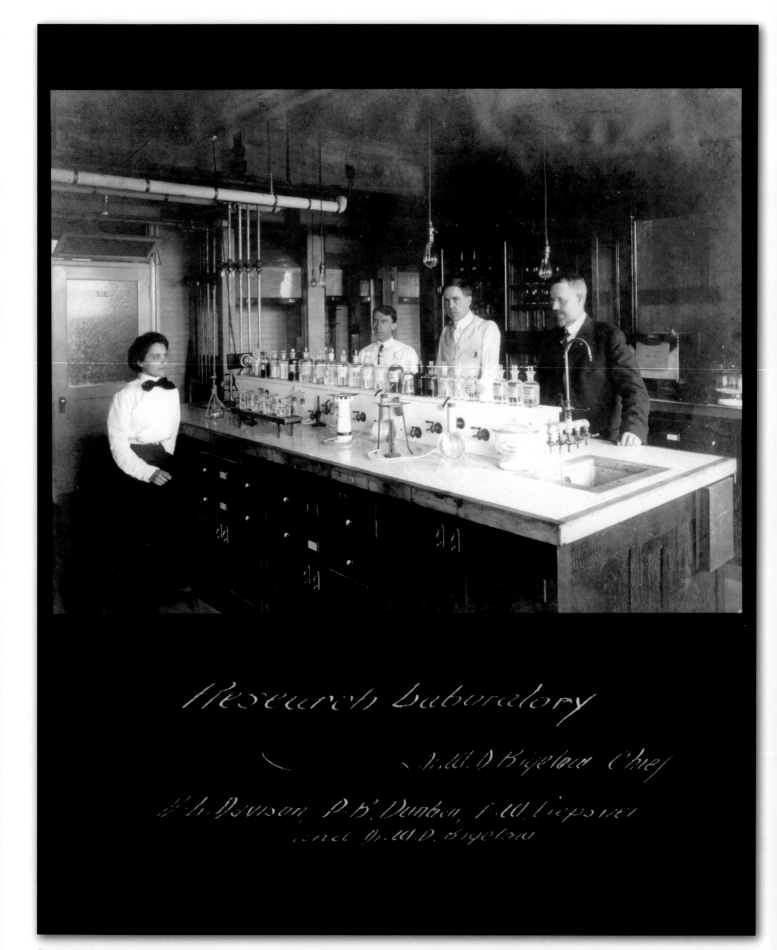

Research Laboratory

M. W. D. Bigelow Chief

L. h. Davison, P. B. Dunbar, F. W. Liepsner and M. W. D. Bigelow

Research Laboratory in the Bureau of Chemistry, 1910. The seated woman is L. Davison, an early PhD chemist from the University of Pennsylvania. Davison later married the man across from her in this photo—Paul. B. Dunbar, future Commissioner of Food and Drugs. Paul Dunbar's desk today is used by FDA's oral historians in the FDA History Office.

The Mission and the Institution: Ever Changing Yet Eternally the Same

**Anthony A. Celeste &
Arthur N. Levine**

THE FDA THAT STANDS TODAY as the world's leading consumer protection agency evolved over the twentieth century from a tiny agency charged with implementing the 1906 Act to one that has managed new responsibilities and new challenges. FDA's mission statement declares that it is responsible for "protecting the public health by assuring the safety, efficacy, and security of human and veterinary drugs, biological products, medical devices, our nation's food supply, cosmetics, and products that emit radiation." Over the years, the concept of advancing the public health, rather than just protecting it, has become an integral part of the mission: FDA's mission statement also says that the agency is responsible for "advancing the public health by helping to speed innovations that make medicines and foods more effective, safer, and more affordable; and helping the public get the accurate, science-based information they need to use medicines and foods to improve their health."

The evolution of FDA from strictly an enforcement agency to a consumer protection and public health promotion agency has been the result of several influences, many of them reflecting congressional judgment about what products FDA should regulate and how. Altogether, FDA as an institution, and the way FDA has approached its regulatory obligations, has been molded by the laws Congress has authorized FDA to enforce, by the evolution in science and technology reflected in the products it regulates, and by changes in American society.

The evolution of FDA as an institution can be traced through the agency's primary functions. Through the years, the extent to which FDA has relied on these functions to various degrees, and modified its way of performing them, has defined FDA's institutional identity. The influences on FDA—like the products FDA regulates—have become more numerous and complex over time. Various constituencies have had an impact on FDA's institutional identity and on the exercise of its regulatory functions—Congress, the regulated industry, consumers, health care professionals, trade associations and advocacy groups, the media, other regulatory authorities, and supervisory elements of the Executive Branch of government. Nonetheless, FDA's institutional identity has reflected substantially internal forces, predominantly the philosophy of FDA's leadership and senior staff.

One fundamental aspect of FDA as an institution has remained essentially the same for 100 years—its emphasis on consumer protection through law enforcement. The agency's law enforcement function took root in the last two decades of the nineteenth century under the guidance of Harvey W. Wiley, the chief chemist of the U.S. Department of Agriculture's (USDA's) Bureau of Chemistry, and first found legislative expression in the Pure Food and Drugs Act of 1906. The 1906 Act codified the primary enforcement practices of Dr. Wiley's bureau—the collection and testing of "specimens" of foods and drugs to discover evidence of unsafe products or unsupported product claims, the seizure of adulterated and misbranded products, and the criminal prosecution of those who violated the law. The structure of the 1906 Act, and the imprint of Dr. Wiley's tenure on its enforcement, when he served as the head of what later became the FDA, forged the foundational element of FDA's institutional identity as a science-based law enforcement agency. This identity was supported by:

- a dedicated inspection cadre;
- an "arms-length" approach to the companies that made regulated products; and
- a strong commitment to consumer protection.

The central role of law enforcement in FDA's institutional identity took root

The 1906 Pure Food and Drugs Act created the position of the federal food and drugs inspector. In spite of the objections of many Southern senators who complained that the law was merely "a Trojan horse with a bellyful of inspectors," the early inspectors hired to implement the 1906 Act were a talented group. When they first reported for duty at the Bureau of Chemistry, Harvey Wiley himself was overheard to say that he was "damned if he knew what to do with them," but they soon became an organized and respected part of the organization. Acting as the eyes and ears of the agency out in the marketplace, they were able to help industry comply with the new law and the food and drug supply of the United States was revolutionized between 1906 and 1916. This photo was donated by one of Wiley's assistants, Fred B. Linton, and is a photo of the first Bureau of Inspectors Convention, held in Buffalo, NY, 1909.

FDA's Organizational History

In his 1837 annual report, Patent Commissioner Henry L. Ellsworth recommended a national agency for the encouragement of agriculture. Congress responded in 1839 with an appropriation of $1,000 to the Commissioner of Patents for "the collection of agricultural statistics, and for other agricultural purposes." From then on, the Patent Office collected and reported agricultural statistics, sponsored or conducted chemical investigations on agricultural matters, monitored agricultural developments, and reported on all of these in its annual reports. Beginning in 1849, a separate report was made by the Patent Commissioner to Congress on agricultural matters. An Agricultural Division was established in the Patent Office and a chemical laboratory was created in that Division.

In 1846, Professor Lewis C. Beck, MD, of Rutgers College and Albany Medical College, published the first American treatise on adulteration of food and drugs. Two years later, at the request of Patent Commissioner Edmund Burke, Congress appropriated $1,000 for the Commissioner of Patents to conduct chemical analyses of "vegetable substances produced and used for the food of man and animals in the United States." Commissioner Burke recruited Dr. Beck to do this work for the Patent Office. Dr. Beck submitted his *Report on the Breadstuffs of the United States* in 1849 and a second report in 1850.

When Congress created the USDA in 1862, it included authorization to employ chemists. The Agricultural Division of the Patent Office, including its chemical laboratory, was transferred to the new department, and the USDA occupied the office space in the basement of the Patent Office that previously had belonged to that division. The first Commissioner of Agriculture, Isaac Newton, immediately established the Chemical Division from the former Patent Office chemical laboratory, which became the Division of Chemistry in 1890; the Bureau of Chemistry in 1901; the Food, Drug, and Insecticide Administration in 1927; and the FDA in 1930. The FDA was transferred from the USDA to the Federal Security Agency in 1940 and to the Department of Health, Education, and Welfare in 1953, which became the Department of Health and Human Services in 1979.

The following have served as Chemist / Chief Chemist / Chief / Commissioner since 1862:

Charles Mayer Wetherill	(1862–1864)	George P. Larrick	(1954–1965)
Henri Erni	(1864–1866)	James L. Goddard	(1966–1968)
Thomas Antisell	(1866–1871)	Herbert L. Ley, Jr.	(1968–1969)
Ryland T. Brown	(1872–1873)	Charles C. Edwards	(1969–1973)
William McMurtrie	(1873–1878)	Alexander M. Schmidt	(1973–1976)
Peter Collier	(1878–1883)	Donald Kennedy	(1977–1979)
Harvey W. Wiley	(1883–1912)	Jere E. Goyan	(1979–1981)
Carl L. Alsberg	(1912–1921)	Arthur Hull Hayes, Jr.	(1981–1983)
Walter G. Campbell	(1921–1923)	Frank E. Young	(1984–1989)
C. A. Browne	(1923–1927)	David A. Kessler	(1990–1997)
Walter G. Campbell	(1927–1944)	Jane E. Henney	(1998–2001)
Paul B. Dunbar	(1944–1951)	Mark B. McClellan	(2003–2004)
Charles W. Crawford	(1951–1954)	Lester M. Crawford	(2005)

—**Peter Barton Hutt**

because of the lengthy tenure, continuity, and shared philosophy of the heads of the organization during its first fifty years. Dr. Wiley was the first person responsible for enforcement of the 1906 Act. He served as chief for five years, from 1907 to 1912. The next chief, Carl Alsberg, served from 1912 to 1921. One of the most influential leaders of what would become the FDA joined the bureau in 1907, the year Dr. Wiley became chief. This was Walter R. Campbell. Mr. Campbell shared Dr. Wiley's views about the central role of enforcement. He served as the acting chief beginning in 1921, was responsible for enforcement of the 1906 Act in several capacities and headed the organization—renamed the Food and Drug Administration in 1930—through its various structural re-designations, and the passage of the Federal Food, Drug, and Cosmetic Act in 1938, which he was instrumental in shaping.

Even after the passage of the 1938 Act dramatically expanded FDA's regulatory jurisdiction, the original culture of FDA continued to reflect the philosophy of Dr. Wiley and of Mr. Campbell, who headed FDA during the first six years after passage of the 1938 Act. Dr. Paul Dunbar, FDA commissioner from 1944 to 1951, had served as Mr. Campbell's special assistant as early as 1915; Charles W. Crawford, FDA commissioner from 1951 to 1954, was the administrative assistant to Mr. Campbell in 1917; and George P. Larrick, commissioner from 1954–1965 was Mr. Campbell's special assistant in 1928.

Enforcement of the 1906 Act relied on a small number of inspectors and chemists, supported by an administrative staff; a total that ranged between 300 and 700 during the life of the 1906 Act. These resources were heavily concentrated on testing suspect products, removing "violative" products from the market, and

Federal food and drugs inspectors were a new breed of civil servant. To illustrate their varied and diverse work, FDA created a slide show illustrating "A Day in the Life of A Food and Drug Inspector," which featured Inspector John Earnshaw making inspections in and around the Baltimore area around 1912. Here, Earnshaw is inspecting a coffee roasting plant.

prosecuting those responsible for the production and shipment of violative products. In 1919, more than 1,050 recommendations for seizure were made; in 1920, the number exceeded 1,400. In those two years, more than 1,900 criminal cases were recommended. In the year before the passage of the 1938 Act, the FDA analyzed more than 63,000 samples of foods and drugs and recommended seizure or prosecution for more than 2,200 of them.

The passage of the 1938 Act established, in rudimentary form and scope, the primary functions of FDA, even as they exist today. First, the Act conferred upon the FDA authority to approve products before their being marketed. Under the 1938 Act, new drugs could be marketed only after demonstrating to the FDA that they were safe for use. In the early 1940s, Congress amended the Act to require FDA to certify the suitability of insulin and penicillin products before they could be sold.

Second, the 1938 Act also provided FDA with standard-setting functions, particularly the power to set standards for food, and with its basic authority for rulemaking. FDA was authorized to promulgate rules "for the efficient enforcement of the Act." Third, the Act set the stage for the exercise of FDA's public communication functions by explicitly authorizing FDA to issue publicity and public warnings. Finally, the 1938 Act expanded the scope of FDA's enforcement authority by applying the adulteration and misbranding provisions

to medical devices and by establishing requirements to preclude the adulteration and misbranding of cosmetics. In addition, the new law granted FDA the power to inspect manufacturers, producers, and storage warehouses of FDA-regulated products. Thus, by 1938, Congress had provided FDA with at least some form of all of its major functions—product review and approval, standard setting, rulemaking, education and communication, and law enforcement over foods, drugs, medical devices, and cosmetics.

Soon after the passage of the 1938 Act, responsibility to enforce the Act was transferred from the USDA to the Federal Security Agency. Then, in 1953, the Federal Security Agency was transferred into the Department of Health, Education, and Welfare (now the Department of Health and Human Services [DHHS]). Thus, what had been USDA's Bureau of Chemistry just before the passage of the 1906 Act, and had been renamed the Food and Drug Administration eight years before passage of the 1938 Act, emerged in the last half of the twentieth century as a part of DHHS.

Beginning in the 1940s, all District Offices of FDA reported to a headquarters Division of Field Operations. In 1968, FDA established a Bureau of Compliance to centralize and coordinate enforcement activity throughout the country and created the position of regional director to provide administrative and policy guidance to the various District Offices. From that point, FDA's field force—the eyes and ears of the agency—took on the structure it would have for the next quarter century, with Regional Offices (5), District Offices (19), and numerous resident posts and import offices (149) throughout the United States. These offices, supported by three specialized laboratories, all report to the Associate Commissioner for Regulatory Affairs (formerly the head of the Bureau of Compliance). It has been said that someone from FDA's field force works within two hours' driving time of ninety percent of the people comprising the entire U.S. population.

Through all the structural changes, and well into the 1950s, FDA was still very much the same organization it had been in 1938. FDA's staff numbered fewer than 900 for several years after the passage of the 1938 Act, and FDA was still a relatively small federal agency of some 1,200 employees with an operating budget of about $5 million at the beginning of the 1960s. The agency's product-approval activities were limited to the safety of new drugs and the safety and potency of insulin and penicillin. The agency had not significantly pursued its standard-setting function, nor had it begun to actively utilize its rulemaking function. Public education and communication to the regulated industry were secondary features of FDA's regulatory regime; the agency issued its first guidance to industry only in 1949. From 1938 through the 1950s, FDA continued to focus its energies on law enforcement as the primary means of fostering compliance with the laws for which the agency had responsibility. Although the 1938 Act provided FDA with authority to pursue injunctions against companies, FDA's enforcement activities continued to rely heavily on

Inspector John Earnshaw inspecting coffee packing operations, circa 1912. These early photos of Earnshaw are valuable, not just to illustrate food and drug regulatory work in the early days under enforcement of the 1906 Act, but also to illustrate turn-of-the-century work life in America.

the seizure of adulterated or misbranded products and on criminal prosecutions. In 1944, FDA recommended nearly 2,150 seizures and more than 280 criminal cases. In 1949, FDA recommended approximately 1,840 seizures and 350 criminal cases.

Charged with regulating a large number of manufacturing and storage facilities, but with limited resources, FDA also began to rely on voluntary product recalls whereby companies would avoid seizures and fulfill corporate commitments to product quality and protection of the public. Later, in the 1980s and 1990s, Congress provided FDA with new authorities to assess civil money penalties in certain program areas, to order mandatory recalls of biologicals and dangerous medical devices and to debar individuals from participating in drug development activities.

During the 1980s and 1990s, FDA began to significantly alter its enforcement profile. It increased its use of warning letters to promote compliance with its regulatory requirements, simultaneously recommending dramatically fewer product seizures. The few injunctions initiated each year focused on large companies, which FDA hoped would elicit a large deterrent effect. Routine criminal prosecutions substantially decreased, replaced by aggressively developed criminal cases against persons engaging in fraud in FDA-regulated areas. These cases did not necessarily involve charges of violation of the Food, Drug, and Cosmetic Act itself, but relied increasingly on charges under the fraud provisions in

the U. S. criminal code. The resurgence of a strong and visible FDA presence in criminal law enforcement resulted primarily from the creation in 1991 of the Office of Criminal Investigations, which investigates and develops cases involving fraud and intentional violations of law. Thus, FDA was at first, and has remained, a law enforcement institution. The interplay between the enforcement function and FDA's other primary functions continued to shape FDA's institutional identity in the second half of the agency's 100 years of protecting the public health.

In the 1960s and before, Congress, responding to growing public concerns regarding scientific and technical advances in food manufacturing and the development of new drug products, expanded the scope of FDA's authority, enabling it to develop its standard-setting, rulemaking, and product-approval functions. In 1951, Congress passed the Durham-Humphrey Amendment defining those drugs that could not be used without medical supervision and establishing the requirement for a prescription for such drugs. In 1958, Congress passed the Food Additives Amendment and, in 1960, the Color Additives Amendment, both significantly increasing FDA's responsibilities for review and approval of chemical substances. In 1962, Congress passed the Drug Amendments, expanding FDA's review and approval authority to the effectiveness of drugs, and establishing that drugs not manufactured in compliance with current good manufacturing practices are considered adulterated. The Drug Amendments of 1962 shaped FDA's regulatory approach to pharmaceutical development and production for the next forty years. All of these congressional enactments, and others, dramatically expanded FDA's regulatory mission.

These new laws were not self-executing. Rather, the significant expansion of FDA's regulatory jurisdiction merely provided an outline of legal parameters. FDA was required to set standards and develop interpretive rules and regulations. Thus,

among many other initiatives, in the 1960s, the agency promulgated its first adverse event reporting regulations, comprehensive current good manufacturing practice regulations for drugs, and, in the early 1970s, rules for thousands of previously unregulated blood banks. During these years, FDA also developed procedural regulations establishing processes for formal and documented interactions between FDA and citizens and the regulated industry. These initiatives further expanded FDA's regulatory responsibilities.

YES, VIRGINIA, THERE HAVE BEEN SCANDALS

FDA's historical legacy is rich in scandal. Even the public record (many official records remain closed and unavailable) reveals substantial evidence of agency indiscretion.

The first FDA scandal focused on none other than FDA Commissioner Harvey W. Wiley himself. He was accused—along with Assistant Commissioner W. D. Bigelow and Chief of the Drug Laboratory L. F. Kebler—of paying a scientific consultant an amount that exceeded the Attorney General's explicitly determined maximum salary for a classified scientific investigator. Undoubtedly because of the well-documented resentment of Wiley within USDA, the USDA Committee on Personnel determined that Wiley and Bigelow should be given an opportunity to resign and that Kebler's position should be reduced. The Secretary of Agriculture submitted this report to President Taft, who in turn requested a review by the Attorney General. The Attorney General, who also disliked Wiley, concurred with the recommendations of the USDA Personnel Committee. Nonetheless, President Taft gave the three defendants a new opportunity to review the record and fully respond, reviewed the entire record, and determined that Wiley was not a party to the decision and was acting in accord with prior USDA precedent. Thus, the charges against Wiley were dismissed completely and the Secretary of Agriculture was directed only to issue a reprimand to Bigelow and Kebler. A concurrent investigation by a House committee, released the following year, also exonerated Wiley. Nonetheless, Wiley resigned a few weeks later, recognizing that his position within USDA was increasingly tenuous.

The next great FDA scandal became public in 1959, when an article in the *Saturday Review* charged that Dr. Henry Welch, Director of the FDA Division of Antibiotics, had an improper relationship with the pharmaceutical industry. After a congressional investigation, Dr. Welch retired. Secretary of Health, Education, and Welfare Arthur S. Flemming requested the National Academy of Sciences (NAS) to review the scientific decisions under Welch's tenure and established a special investigation to deal with the relationship between FDA employees and the pharmaceutical industry. The NAS issued a three-page report in 1960 concluding that the FDA scientific decisions were acceptable. The internal department investigation resulted in a report recommending controls on the access of industry representatives to FDA, thus providing the first of many recommendations over the past four decades on the relationship of FDA to the regulated industry.

In August 1974, several employees of the FDA Bureau of Drugs testified, in a hearing conducted by Senator Edward M. Kennedy, that FDA was dominated by the pharmaceutical industry and was

To address the agency's new product-review, rulemaking, and standard-setting obligations, FDA finally began to experience a significant growth in staff. From 1960 to 1970, the number of FDA employees grew from approximately 1,700 to 4,200, and by 1980, to more than 7,600. Similarly, FDA's 1960 budget of approximately $14 million dramatically expanded to over $300 million by 1980. Nevertheless, FDA continued to lack all the resources to do the job mandated by the frequent and numerous legislative changes enacted over the years. In

part because of its resource limitations and the resource-intensive nature of individual enforcement cases, FDA in the 1970s turned to establishing regulatory requirements and promoting compliance through rulemaking.

FDA's reliance on "notice and comment rulemaking" was based on its "authority to promulgate regulations for the efficient enforcement" of the law. At first, this legislative grant of general rulemaking authority was regarded as conferring only the power to issue "interpretative" rules subject to judicial review in enforcement

inadequately protecting the public against unsafe and ineffective new drugs. FDA Commissioner Alexander M. Schmidt conducted a full investigation and issued a lengthy report in October 1975 that found no basis for the accusations made at the August 1974 Senate hearings. In the interim, Secretary of Health, Education, and Welfare F. David Mathews appointed his own Review Panel on New Drug Regulation, which conducted a separate investigation and issued its own lengthy reports in May 1977. These reports concluded that the system of new drug regulation was fundamentally sound and that FDA was neither for nor against industry in its review and approval of new drugs, but that the system needed substantial improvement. Although the Review Panel found that FDA had not been dominated by the pharmaceutical industry, it did find some improper procedural steps with respect to individual bureau employees. It also found improper action by Senator Kennedy in conducting his August 1974 hearings.

During 1988–1989, Representative John Dingell conducted hearings that ultimately determined that: (1) some employees of the FDA Division of Generic Drugs had accepted illegal gratuities from generic drug manufacturers; (2) some generic drug manufacturers had conducted and submitted bioavailability and bioequivalent studies using the pioneer drug rather than their own generic products; and (3) there were significant discrepancies in the testing and manufacture of some generic drugs. Agency employees and responsible officials of the implicated manufacturers were prosecuted, the suspect products were recalled and approval of their abbreviated NDAs were withdrawn, and FDA undertook investigations of manufacturing facilities and testing of products to verify the quality and clinical effectiveness of the generic drug supply. Ultimately, five FDA employees were convicted of bribery or perjury, and many more generic drug officials and companies were convicted. As a result of this scandal, FDA Commissioner Frank E. Young was reassigned within the Department of Health and Human Services even though he was not personally involved and could not possibly have prevented it.

Each of these scandals had a substantial impact on FDA regulation of food and drugs. In two instances, the commissioner himself left the agency. In two other instances, the close working relationship between the regulated industry and FDA that is essential for an efficient and effective pre-marketing approval system in the regulation of drugs was substantially disrupted. The agency suffered greatly, both internally and in the eyes of the public, in each of these episodes.

—Peter Barton Hutt

actions. Later, the courts came to regard rules established under the Act as legally binding requirements with the force and effect of law. By the mid-1970s, FDA appeared to be utilizing its rulemaking authority to support a substantial amount of the agency's significant compliance efforts. FDA's heavy reliance on rulemaking and the issuance of guidance documents also reflected a shift in its enforcement approach. Rulemaking was, to a substantial degree, based on the philosophy that the regulated industry would comply with FDA's interpretation of the law if that interpretation was clearly articulated, and an opportunity for comment had been provided before proposed rules were made final. Thus, in the 1970s, FDA began to pursue "voluntary" compliance before violations might occur, moving away from resource-intensive individual law enforcement actions.

FDA regulatory processes realigned as rulemaking became its predominant form of regulation. For example, FDA established standardized procedures for its decision-making processes. In addition, the agency's adjudicatory process evolved into a highly structured procedure designed to avoid formal legal hearings in all but the most intractable cases. As an alternative to formal hearings conducted by an administrative law judge, FDA introduced new hearing forums whose presiding officers are scientists and agency officials.

The scope of FDA's regulatory responsibilities continued to grow. In 1968, FDA took on the responsibility for enforcement of the Radiation Control for Health and Safety Act, bringing within FDA's jurisdiction products as diverse as microwave ovens, an ever-expanding number of radiation-emitting medical diagnostic products, and eventually wireless telephones. In 1972, FDA assumed responsibility for the licensing and regulation of biological products.

Finally, through the 1976 Medical Device Amendments, FDA was charged with product review and marketing clearance for medical devices. Consequently, in the early 1970s, FDA was reorganized along product lines with the creation of the Bureaus of Radiological Health, Biologics, and Medical Devices. FDA's obligations for the review of numerous food additives, as well as the review and approval of biological products and medical devices, and the implementation of its review of drugs for effectiveness, further realigned the balance of FDA operations. Product review and approval began to take a more central role in FDA's regulatory operations, and as the role expanded, it fostered a gradual shift in the agency's approach to product reviews.

For most of the 1960s and 1970s, while FDA's primary product review function centered on drugs, the agency was extremely cautious in assessing product approvals. This caution was part of the legacy of FDA's experience with thalidomide, a drug that was approved in Europe but subsequently discovered to cause physical abnormalities in some children born to women who had taken it during pregnancy. Before the adverse consequences of thalidomide were known, FDA's drugs center had reservations about the safety of thalidomide and had not approved the drug. President Kennedy awarded the Medal of Honor to the medical officer who refused to approve thalidomide, Dr. Frances Kelsey, who became a national hero.

That event became a symbol of FDA as the world's "gold standard" in product review. Against this background, FDA began to review market applications and notifications for medical devices, many of which involved new engineering technologies that offered to dramatically increase the health of patients who might benefit from these devices. The new devices center was more receptive to these innovative products and approached product review decisions more flexibly. One consequence was a greater degree of engagement with manufacturers of medical devices.

Two initiatives significantly affected FDA's product review and approval function and signaled a shift toward increased reliance on outside experts and advisory committees. One was FDA's contract in 1966 with the National Academy of Sciences to evaluate the effectiveness of some 4,000 drugs approved on the basis of safety alone between 1938 and 1962. The project, known as the Drug Efficacy Study Implementation (DESI), took about three years, although final implementation of the review would take many decades. The implementation relied on a combination

of FDA's standard-setting, rulemaking, and law enforcement functions. The DESI program, which resulted in the removal of some 300 drugs from the American market, represented a significant step in FDA's reliance on outside experts' scientific assessment.

The second major initiative, begun in 1972, was the Over-the-Counter (OTC) Drug Review and the establishment of a monograph system to regulate drugs sold without a prescription. Through this program, FDA conducted a retrospective review of the safety, effectiveness, and labeling of OTC drug products. Like the DESI program, the OTC review relied heavily on outside scientific and technical assistance, and again brought together standard-setting, rulemaking, and law enforcement functions.

FDA was also influenced by the consumer movement in the United States in the 1960s and 1970s. This movement spawned a variety of consumer protection legislation—the Federal Hazardous Substances Act, the Consumer Product Safety Act, the Environmental Protection Act, the Drug Abuse Control Amendments, the Child Protection Act, the Poison Prevention Packaging Act, and the Fair Packaging and Labeling Act. To enforce the Federal Caustic Poison Act and the Federal Hazardous Substances Act, FDA created the Bureau of Product Safety. This bureau was transferred to the Consumer Product Safety Commission when the Consumer Product Safety Act was passed in 1972. A similar pattern was followed in FDA's creation of a Bureau of

Drug Abuse Control to enforce the Drug Abuse Control Amendments, a bureau that became part of the Drug Enforcement Agency in 1970 when the Comprehensive Drug Abuse Prevention and Control Act was passed. At the same time, FDA retained certain authorities over some environmental and trade regulation issues, and exercised concurrent regulatory jurisdiction with other federal agencies in some areas and a coordinating role in others.

Coupled with the consumer movement of the 1960s was an awakening in the extent to which Americans were taking a more active role in their own health. Gradually, the societal empowerment of consumers began to be reflected in FDA policies. FDA greatly enhanced its public communication function, symbolized perhaps by the naming of its official magazine *FDA Consumer*. It also began to approve the switch of drugs from prescription to over-the-counter use, endorsed patient package inserts for prescription drugs, loosened its enforcement programs concerning vitamin supplements, and opened its deliberative processes to consumer and patient advocacy groups.

In the 1970s, FDA promulgated regulations and established policies in response to two federal statutes designed to make federal regulatory decisions more transparent and inclusive. FDA's Freedom of Information Act regulations were among the most expansive among any federal agency, resulting in tens of thousands of requests each year. FDA's policies implementing the Advisory Committee Act developed into a broad and comprehensive mandate for numerous sitting and ad hoc committees to provide ongoing recommendations on a variety of product approval decisions on drugs, medical devices, and biological products.

DESIGNATION AND LOCATION OF FDA IN THE FEDERAL GOVERNMENT

Year	Designation and Location	Statute
1839	Patent Office, Department of State	5 Stat. 353, 354 (1839)
1849	Chemical Laboratory of the Agricultural Division in the Patent Office, Department of the Interior	9 Stat. 395 (1849)
1862	Chemical Division, Department of Agriculture	12 Stat. 387 (1862)
1889	Chemical Division, USDA	25 Stat. 659 (1889)
1890	Division of Chemistry, USDA	26 Stat. 282, 283 (1890)
1901	Bureau of Chemistry, USDA	31 Stat. 922, 930 (1901)
1927	Food and Drug Insecticide Administration, USDA	44 Stat. 976, 1002 (1927)
1930	Food and Drug Administration, USDA	46 Stat. 392, 422 (1930)
1940	FDA, Federal Security Agency	54 Stat. 1234, 1237 (1940)
1953	FDA, Department of Health, Education, and Welfare	67 Stat. 631, 632 (1953)
1979	FDA, Department of Health and Human Services	93 Stat. 668, 695 (1979)

In the 1970s, other factors also began to emerge in defining FDA's institutional identity. These included what FDA employees sometimes refer to as "political" phenomena: first, an increase in the number of political appointees in high-level agency positions, and a decline in the number of traditional agency careerists; second, an increased level of review of FDA decisions at higher levels of government, such as the Department of Health and Human Services and the Office of Management and Budget. These are generally viewed as related phenomena, perhaps because of the relatively short tenure of the Commissioners of Food and Drugs beginning in the late 1970s and the perception that increasingly the commissioners had ties to the administration and were less likely to resist pressure from superiors in the federal hierarchy.

The 1980s and 1990s brought another shift in FDA's regulatory approach, as the agency dramatically increased its public education and industry communication functions, a shift that corresponded to an increase in FDA's engagement with the regulated industry, consumer and patient advocacy groups, and trade associations. During this period, FDA substantially increased its issuance of informal guidelines, known as guidances, where previously it would have engaged in formal rulemaking. Although these guidance documents are not legally binding on either the regulated industry or the agency itself, by expressing FDA's thinking on a subject, they in effect establish regulatory expectations if not de facto standards. In that way, FDA substantially, though not completely, uses its education and communication functions to further compliance in ways previously achieved through the rulemaking and standard-setting functions.

Probably the greatest change since the 1970s in FDA as an institution was the geometric increase in FDA's interaction with its various constituencies through, for example, press releases, guidances on a wide variety of topics, and meetings with "stakeholders" and representatives of regulated industries on a company-by-company basis. These communications were facilitated through use of the Internet and establishment of a website where FDA can post announcements, publications, and other documents to provide timely information to consumers, health care and regulatory professionals, and the industry. FDA's era of iterative engagement responded to, and in turn has resulted in, a more informed public and has advanced consumer empowerment in all health-related issues.

At the same time, the agency's traditional enforcement and consumer protection efforts have continued, exemplified by the 1982 case in Chicago of tampering with Tylenol capsules. This incident resulted in seven deaths, the recall of all Tylenol capsules, the passage of the Federal Anti-Tampering Act, the promulgation of new packaging regulations for all over-the-counter drug products, and the establishment in 1989 of the FDA Forensic Center. Although

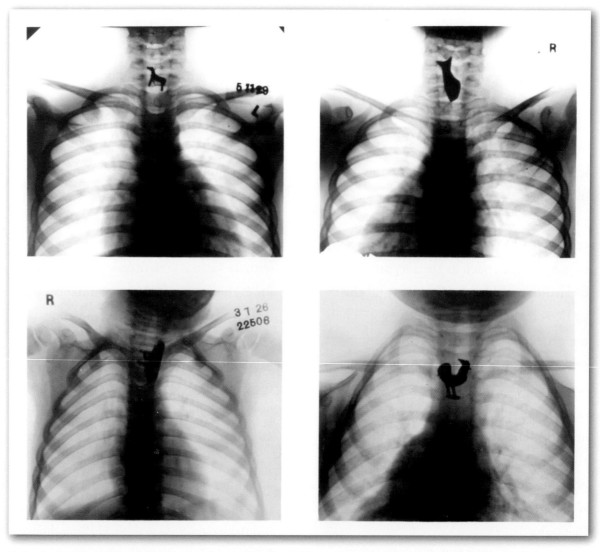

During the Great Depression, confections were frequently sold to children with lead trinkets or coin "prizes" embedded in them. These early high-dose/high contrast x-rays clearly show the lead trinkets embedded in childrens' throats and explains why the 1938 Act prohibits embedding trinkets in candy.

in the early years the center was used to detect and trace contamination in FDA-regulated products, it developed techniques to screen for more than 250 of the most toxic poisons commonly present in FDA-regulated products, and to detect counterfeit drugs.

For most of its history, FDA was unconcerned about the economic consequences of its compliance actions or about competitive issues, and, indeed, consistently resisted opportunities to become involved in competitive issues. Notwithstanding, one form of FDA

regulation that emerged in the 1980s required the agency to become involved in competitive and economic issues, namely, the development of mechanisms to make it easier for generic drugs to get on the market. Thereafter, congressional interest in providing a statutory framework for reviewing generic drugs and protecting the marketing rights of the research-based pharmaceutical companies led to the passage in 1984 of the Drug Price Competition and Patent Term Restoration Act, known as the Hatch-Waxman

THE ROLE OF PRODUCT DISASTERS

Sad, but true, Congress and the media focus on sensational stories of failure, not on routine daily success. A single product disaster is likely to be highlighted in congressional hearings and media inquiries. Nevertheless, it is these sensational product disasters, and the major publicity that attends them, that have accounted for many of our most important food and drug laws, for example:

• Vaccine Act of 1813: fraudulent sale of ineffective products represented as smallpox vaccine.

• Import Drug Act of 1848: adulterated drugs imported for use of American troops in Mexico.

• Biologics Act of 1902: death of children in St. Louis from contaminated biological product.

• Pure Food and Drugs Act of 1906: gross insanitation in the meat industry.

• Federal Food, Drug, and Cosmetic Act: death of more than 100 people from poisonous Elixir Sulfanilamide.

• Drug Amendments of 1962: deformed children caused by thalidomide.

• Medical Device Amendments of 1976: serious harm caused by the Dalkon Shield.

• Safe Medical Devices Act of 1990: harm caused by unsafe medical devices.

One wonders how our federal statute would have evolved absent these well-publicized product disasters.

Although Congress has passed many food and drug laws without an attendant crisis, it is readily apparent that legislation that has often been most important in establishing national policy on food and drug regulation was created in the aftermath of a major product disaster. As is often true under these conditions, the legislation has been shaped as much by public emotion as by rational policy design, so that congressional analysis and legislative history have often been insufficient to guide FDA, the regulated industry, and the courts in the intended meaning and application of the resulting statutory language.

—Peter Barton Hutt

Amendments, which helped create the generic drugs industry.

Legislation that required FDA to address competitive issues contributed to the beginning of an era of FDA coordination with other federal agencies that were responsible for medical product competition, pricing, and federal reimbursement—an era that would grow exponentially in the early years of the twenty-first century.

In the 1990s, Congress began to address two issues associated with FDA's product review and approval functions—the timeliness of these reviews and agency resources available to conduct them. Faced with increasing responsibilities, but the same-sized staff, FDA sought approval to charge for the review of a marketing application for a drug or biological product, intending to use the fee to hire needed staff. In 1992, Congress passed the Prescription Drug User Fee Act (PDUFA), reauthorized by the Food and Drug Administration Modernization Act of 1997 and by the Public Health Security and Bioterrorism Preparedness and Response Act of 2002. The program has been very successful. In 1992 (prior to the enactment of PDUFA), FDA dedicated approximately 1,280 staff-years to the review of human drug applications. By 2003, PDUFA fees and appropriations paid for an additional 1,200 staff-years, essentially doubling FDA's resources to review such applications. The new approach required FDA to establish strict deadlines for completing the review of human drug applications, which enabled the process to be managed more efficiently and with greater certainty. The vast majority of drug applications are reviewed

in six to ten months, a far cry from the time when applications could take as long as three years.

In 2002, Congress authorized user fees for devices in the Medical Device User Fee and Modernization Act of 2002 (MDUFA), enabling FDA to reduce the time for marketing approval for devices. Likewise, the Animal Drug User Fee Act of 2003 permitted user fees to help defer the cost of the review of new animal drug applications. User fees contributed to the further shift of FDA resources from the field organization to headquarters that had

SPINOFFS FROM FDA

It has been said that FDA oversees twenty-five percent of the consumer's dollar. Much of that responsibility can be attributed to two major laws, the 1906 Pure Food and Drugs Act and the 1938 Food, Drug, and Cosmetic Act. In addition, assignments have been added throughout the past century. For example, just from 1969 to 1972, oversight of sanitation programs for milk, shellfish, and interstate travel, authority over radiation-emitting consumer products and biological medicines, and still other jurisdictions were transferred to FDA.

Many other programs were moved from FDA to other entities during the last century, often because of larger reorganizations. In 1940, for example, jurisdiction over two long-standing programs was transferred from FDA. The Naval Stores Act, which set and enforced grades for turpentine and rosin, had been assigned to FDA since its passage in March 1923. The Insecticide and Fungicide Act prohibited interstate traffic in adulterated or misbranded lead arsenates and other products identified in the Act. The Insecticide and Fungicide Board had overseen it from the time it became law in 1910, but in 1927, oversight of that Act was assigned to FDA—and even became incorporated, albeit briefly, in the name of the agency as the Food, Drug, and Insecticide Administration (FDIA). When FDA moved into the new Federal Security Agency in 1940, both functions remained in the Department of Agriculture. The same year the agency was assigned the Insecticide and Fungicide Act, Congress passed the Caustic Poison Act to regulate warning labels and antidotes for corrosive acids, alkalis, and other dangerous substances. FDIA was given responsibility for regulating these products, too. That function remained in FDA for forty-five years.

One program lasted longer in FDA than any other before Congress removed an important provision of its enabling legislation, though both the Executive and Legislative branches had tried for decades to end it. The Tea Act of 1897, amended twice by 1920, mandated that tea imports abide by standards of purity and quality set by the Secretary of Agriculture, based on the recommendations of a Board of Tea Experts appointed by the Secretary. Oversight remained in FDA and its predecessors until the Federal Tea Tasters Repeal Act of 1996, which eliminated the federal board. Regulation of tea itself is still under FDA.

From the 1940s until the 1960s, FDA spent more time interdicting illegally distributed amphetamines and barbiturates than all other drug enforcement work combined. Major sources for these drugs included truck stops, beauty salons, cafés, and over-the-counter sales in pharmacies. By the 1960s, hallucinogenic substances also were gaining in popularity. The Drug Abuse Control Amendments of

begun at the height of FDA's rulemaking era. They also underscored Congress' and FDA's commitment to enabling quicker availability of technical advances in medicine. Even without congressional action, FDA developed regulations and policies to support expedited review of new drug applications and other product reviews.

Advances in science and technology in the 1980s and 1990s dramatically expanded the range and type of products for which FDA assumed regulatory responsibility. These included the use of embedded software in FDA-regulated products, microparticle drug products, laser-guided implanted devices, gene-based therapies, genetically modified foods, non-invasive diagnostic equipment, in vitro fertilization, and human cloning. Much of the growth in biomedical research and development has been devoted to new areas of product development, including genomics, proteomics, imaging and informational technologies. While Congress continued to pass product- or

1965 established a graded schedule of controls for drugs with abuse potential, and gave FDA increased authority over drugs that fell into the schedules. To regulate such products, FDA created the Bureau of Drug Abuse Control; in 1968, an Executive Order of the President transferred it to the Justice Department, the long-time regulator of traffic in narcotics. Thus, the Bureau of Narcotics and Dangerous Drugs was formed. That program merged with two others in 1973 to form the Drug Enforcement Administration. Nevertheless, regulation of the medical use of scheduled drugs still remains with FDA.

Pesticide regulation, despite the provisions of the Insecticide and Fungicide Act, was a major FDA activity since passage of the 1906 law, but a major component of this effort, the setting of tolerances for pesticides, was transferred to the Environmental Protection Agency when that institution was created in 1970.

It takes more than safety packaging.

In 1970, Congress enacted the Poison Prevention Packaging Act to require safety packaging for household products that could be injurious to children. The Food and Drug Administration's Bureau of Product Safety is enforcing this law.

But safety packaging will work only if you, the consumer, let it.

Don't forget to store potentially hazardous substances out of children's reach. A locked cabinet or high shelf is appropriate.

Keep close watch on young children.

And when safety packaging is available, get it and use it. Preventing accidental poisonings is your responsibility as well as ours.

An FDA product safety poster, 1972.

Three years later, the Consumer Product Safety Commission (CPSC) was created to strengthen protections against a broad array of commodities; theretofore, legislation often focused on specific hazards, and several agencies were involved in regulating consumer products. Among the programs CPSC inherited from FDA were oversight of caustic poisons that dated back to the 1920s, and responsibility for carrying out provisions of two acts from the 1960s, the Hazardous Substances Labeling Act and the Child Protection and Toy Safety Act.

Some programs have come and gone within FDA during the past 100 years. However, the product areas identified in the 1906 Act and those added in 1938—foods, human and animal drugs, medical devices, and cosmetics—have always remained an essential part of the agency's regulatory mission.

—John P. Swann

issue-specific legislation (e.g., nutrition labeling, dietary supplements, infant formula), relatively few technological advances resulted in new legislation. For the most part, FDA was required to develop new regulatory approaches to deal with the explosion of new products and new technologies. In some instances, FDA lagged far behind industry in understanding the new products and thus

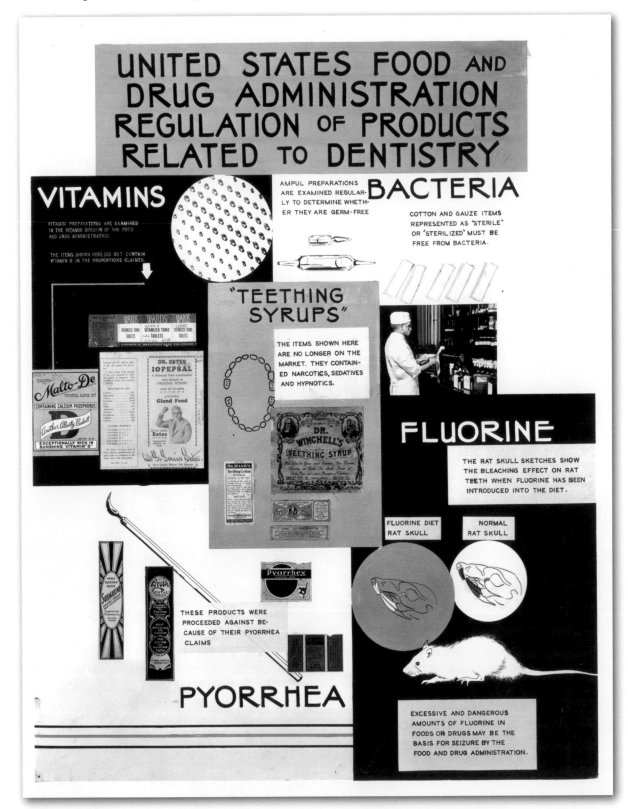

One of the most enduring regulatory "habits" of FDA— dating from before its formal inception—is the collection and creation of exhibits. Exhibits for Congress, consumers, trade associations, and conventions are still an important way for FDA to get out its public health messages.

being able to efficiently regulate them. In recognition of the need to stay current with technical advances, in the 1990s, FDA instituted a number of programs and cooperative agreements with experts in academia and industry, and engaged in more frequent scientific exchange with companies developing new products.

Congress continued to give FDA significant regulatory responsibilities to address public health issues. In 1992, breast cancer was the second leading cause of mortality among American women. The most effective technique for early detection of breast cancer is mammography, and the effectiveness of mammography is directly related to the quality of mammography procedures. In response to concerns that many providers were using mammography procedures of insufficient quality, Congress enacted the Mammography Quality Standards Act (MQSA) of 1992. The Act required certification and annual inspection of all mammography facilities. Because there were so many facilities to be inspected and certified, FDA contracted with a number of states to conduct the inspection and certification program. Such FDA delegation to and reliance on state health officials became more common in the 1990s as FDA resources became strained by the ever-increasing scope of its public health obligations.

Regulation of new technologies, as well as regulation of more conventional products developed to treat AIDS, cancer, new infectious diseases, "orphan" diseases, and diseases associated with aging,

altered FDA's traditional relationships with healthcare practitioners, research institutions, patient and consumer advocates, legislative reform and public policy organizations, and individual citizens. To deal with these new constituencies, FDA found ways to take advantage of resources beyond those that FDA could directly support. By 1995, FDA's budget was $900 million and its staff numbered 9,500. The outside resources included: quasi-governmental or third-party reviewing organizations; cooperative agreements with states, other federal agencies, and foreign governmental organizations whose responsibilities parallel FDA's; professional trade associations; and the regulated industry itself.

All of these FDA constituencies played a large role in shaping FDA as an institution at the end of the twentieth century. Congress repeatedly expanded, defined, and revised FDA's statutory mission—the original 1938 Act was amended more than sixty times since its promulgation. Consumers and consumer advocate groups made their voices heard in FDA policy decisions, and FDA expanded and modernized its communication functions to provide formal and informal opportunities for interested persons to contribute to FDA's assessment of healthcare issues. In the process, the agency redefined its relationship with healthcare professionals, who are increasingly more active in expressing their perspective on policy decisions affecting the products that they use, administer, and prescribe.

The explosion of FDA education and communication functions paralleled an expansion in the advertising and promotional activities by FDA-regulated companies, which have grown steadily since the 1960s. Concomitant with this growth has been the amount of advertising aimed directly at consumers and practitioners. Generally, FDA has encouraged the industry to improve the quality and usefulness of these promotional activities while seeking to prevent undue influence by companies over prescribing decisions and medical education.

As it entered the twenty-first century, FDA could be defined as a science-based regulatory agency. The balance between voluntary compliance and law enforcement, which long defined the ebb and flow of FDA operations, has become muted by FDA's broader engagement with a wide range of stakeholders. Nevertheless, FDA's basic functions remain:

- Product review and approval, which, by the end of the twentieth century, had become facilitated by pre-application meetings, FDA review of product development protocols, and more frequent dialogue between the agency and applicants;
- Standard setting, but with more reference to international standards and non-government standard-setting entities;
- Rulemaking, but only in instances of inadequate adherence to informal agency guidances and other regulatory expectations;
- Education and communication, turning the former into an open dialogue with consumers, practitioners, and experts while turning the latter into opportunities to set informal, de facto regulatory requirements and to supplement FDA resources through communications with a wide range of entities outside of FDA; and
- Law enforcement, still the ever-present stick, with emphasis on fraudulent practices, promoting voluntary compliance through various means, and expanding enforcement coverage through cooperative regulatory initiatives with federal and state authorities and foreign governments.

As the new century opened, FDA regulated more than 150,000 products, including 3,000 investigational new drugs under development. FDA monitored the manufacture, distribution, storage, and sale of $1 trillion of consumer healthcare products, at a cost to taxpayers of about $3 per person per year. As the new century opened, FDA's budget exceeded $1 billion dollars, and its staff stood at slightly fewer than 10,000.

In a way, FDA's institutional identity of the twenty-first century began in the mid-1990s as FDA sought to expand its regulatory jurisdiction in an area affecting one of the nation's most significant public health issues. In 1994, FDA set in motion an initiative to address the public health problems associated with smoking. FDA developed a legal theory that tobacco products were medical devices used to deliver the addictive drug nicotine. The stated goal of the FDA plan was to reduce minors' use of tobacco. FDA's assertion of regulatory jurisdiction was carried forward using outside experts, public health alliances, a sophisticated communication plan, and engagement with interested parties in Congress and the public. In August 1996, FDA published a final rule governing the promotion, labeling, and accessibility of tobacco products. Tobacco manufacturers, retailers, and advertisers challenged the rule in court, and in March 2000, the United States Supreme Court ruled that Congress had not given FDA the authority to regulate tobacco products as customarily marketed.

The tragic events of September 11, 2001, again reshaped FDA. The terrorist attacks on the Pentagon and the World Trade Center led to the passage of the Public Health Security and Bioterrorism Preparedness and Response Act of 2002. It imposed on FDA the responsibility: to protect the security and safety of the food and drug supply; to register all foreign food establishments that export products to the United States; to receive notification of all imported food products prior to entry into the country; and to assist in the development of products to treat and control biological and toxic agents. These activities resulted in a sizeable increase in FDA's budget and resources.

In August 2003, FDA issued a Strategic Action Plan for Protecting and Advancing America's Health. The plan reflects evolving institutional identity of FDA at the outset of the twenty-first century. The plan begins with the observation that "FDA's mission has become much more complicated. Public

FDA's REGULATORY SCIENCE UNDERPINNING

FDA has always needed, and has always had, a strong and credible science base to support its decision-making process. While most of the science is developed by the regulated industries or by academic researchers, there is a distinct need for FDA itself to have the internal capability to set research priorities and to focus on the unique scientific needs of a regulatory agency.

The National Center for Toxicological Research (NCTR) is a focal point within FDA for regulatory science. NCTR's mission is to conduct peer-reviewed scientific research that supports and anticipates FDA's current and future regulatory needs. "This research is aimed at understanding critical biological events in the expression of toxicity and at developing methods to improve assessment of human exposure, susceptibility and risk," according to NCTR's own definition of its mission.

Between Little Rock and Pine Bluff, in Jefferson, Arkansas, NCTR's campus occupies almost 500 acres and thirty-five buildings with more than one million square feet of floor space, which includes state-of-the-art research laboratories and support facilities.

NCTR conducts its work by entering into financial partnerships with other government agencies such as the Environmental Protection Agency; through Collaborative Research and Development Agreements with nongovernmental organizations, nonprofit organizations, and private companies; and through informal agreements to work collaboratively on projects of mutual interest. NCTR's programs span all categories of products FDA regulates. Its scientists possess internal expertise that is invaluable when decisions must be made regarding the health effects of FDA-regulated products.

—Wayne L. Pines

health protection now includes addressing unprecedented challenges … that are more sophisticated and complex than those of the last century." The plan consists of five elements.

The first, "Efficient Risk Management: The Most Public Health Bang for Our Regulatory Buck," focused on the use of science-based risk management in agency regulatory activities, "so that the agency's limited resources can provide the most health promotion and protection at the least cost for the public." The primary objectives of this element include providing a "timely, high quality, cost-effective process for review of new technologies/pre-market submissions" and "cost-effective oversight of industry manufacturing, processing and distribution to reduce risk."

The second element, "Empowering Consumers: Improving Health Through

THE INFLUENCERS

As the nation's foremost health regulatory agency, FDA gets lots of advice and requests from others (outside regulated industry, which of course must deal with FDA daily). Four of the most consistently influential sources have been congressional oversight committees, activists from the consumer community, the scientific community, and the news media.

Congressional oversight committees frequently hold hearings on FDA matters. The intensity of the hearings depends on many variables—the political leanings of the congressmen and of the administration in the White House, the interests of the committee chairmen and most particularly of their staff, and the kinds of issues that arise. FDA senior officials spend dozens of days each year testifying before Congress, each appearance requiring substantial staff work and preparation. FDA witnesses are at the mercy of the congressmen and senators, but the process, while sometimes painful, can lead to needed legislative changes and useful insights.

The consumer community has generated many supporters of FDA and a handful of critics, but in the last three decades of FDA's first 100 years, three have had significant influence—Sidney Wolfe, Michael Jacobson, and Abbey Meyers. Wolfe, a physician, focuses on the drug and medical devices area, while Jacobson, a PhD microbiologist, focuses on food issues. Meyers, who describes herself as a housewife from Connecticut, has been the catalyst behind policies involving orphan drugs.

Wolfe created in the early 1970s the Health Research Group, whose role is to monitor the government's health regulatory activities and identify issues. He has been super-critical of FDA for virtually all of this time, periodically sending letters to the commissioner asking for action against products he regards as unsafe.

Jacobson works with a lighter touch through his Center for Science in the Public Interest. He too identifies food issues he believes FDA needs to address.

Both Wolfe and Jacobson clearly have had significant influence over FDA decision-making, generally for specific products but on larger policy issues. They differ from other advocates, such as Linda Golodner of the National Consumers League, who is more supportive of FDA but focuses almost exclusively on broad policy.

Meyers became involved with FDA while seeking a treatment for one of her children. Her work led to the enactment of the Orphan Drug Act of 1983, which provided incentives for the development of orphan products—medical products intended for relatively few patients. She then founded the National Organization for Rare Disorders, which brings together dozens of small organizations dedicated to the treatment of diseases affecting few people.

Better Information," was designed to enable consumers "to make smarter decisions by getting them better information to weigh the benefits and risks of FDA-regulated products." The objectives of this element include helping to ensure that industry communications convey "the degree of scientific uncertainty associated with such product messages," and improving and increasing FDA-initiated health benefit/risk information.

The third element focuses on "Improving Patient and Consumer Safety" by reducing risks associated with FDA-regulated products through an enhanced ability to quickly identify risks associated with FDA-regulated products, increased capacity to accurately analyze risks associated with medical products, dietary supplements, and foods, and taking "appropriate actions to communicate risks and correct problems

The scientific and medical community has a very large influence on FDA through service on advisory committees and as consultants, by issuing reports on matters regulated by FDA, by participating in scientific conferences and meetings where opinion leaders in that community share views with FDA scientists and medical personnel, and by educating a large proportion of FDA's decision-makers. The community, whether through its organizations or as individuals, is not shy about telling FDA what it thinks about its decisions and directions, and has been especially helpful in supporting the need for good science to support sound regulation.

The news media help set the agenda for Congress and the consumer community. To some extent, both the congressional oversight committees and the consumer advocates select their issues and gauge their successes by media coverage. When he was General Counsel at FDA, Peter Barton Hutt once said he would read carefully the morning papers to see what was on FDA's agenda for the day. That obviously was intended as an overstatement, but, on some of the major crises FDA has managed, the relationship with the media is critical.

From FDA's standpoint, dealing with these outside influencers often is a challenge, and success often means that an issue is managed before it gets into the media. But the reality is that the outside influencers serve a valuable purpose: they help identify flaws in judgment or process, they help FDA set priorities, and most importantly they continually remind the agency that it will be judged by how well its achieves its mission of protecting and enhancing public health. They are not always right—it's hard to assess their success rate in identifying real issues and in truly protecting the public health—but they always must be reckoned with.

Other parts of government, of course, also influence FDA—the courts, the White House, the Office of Management and Budget, FDA's parent Department of Health and Human Services, the Centers for Disease Control and Prevention, the National Institutes of Health, the Department of Justice, and the individual state departments of health and consumer protection. All have close, often daily relationships, with FDA.

Those who have worked at the FDA know that it functions in a "fish bowl;" any memo, any action, is potentially public and subject to critical scrutiny. At the end of the day, although the public nature of the system increases anxiety and sometimes frustration, it clearly has made for a better system of regulation.

—**Wayne L. Pines**

THE INTERACTORS

FDA interacts with a diverse universe of groups: voluntary health organizations, consumer and professional associations, and the manufacturers of medical products, food, and nutritionals. Each group, at varying levels of sophistication and resource allocation, represents its membership's interests before the agency. These interactions take many forms, formal—such as written correspondence commenting on legal, scientific, or policy standards—or informal—as one-on-one meetings where outside interests can inform agency personnel of new innovations in the marketplace. The results of these discussions can lead to partnerships, research agreements, or educational opportunities for both the agency and the outside party. Below is a sampling—by no means comprehensive list—of groups actively engaged with the agency to promote and protect their members' interests.

—Nancy Bradish Myers

Industry Trade Associations:

Advanced Medical Technology Association (AdvaMed): a trade association representing manufacturers of healthcare technology, including medical devices, diagnostic products, and health care information systems.

American Association of Tissue Banks: a scientific, peer-group organization founded to facilitate the provision of transplantable cells and tissues of uniform high quality in quantities sufficient to meet national needs.

American Clinical Laboratory Association (ACLA): an association representing the interests of national and regional clinical laboratories on key issues of common concern, including federal and state regulatory policies.

American Herbal Products Association (AHPA): the national trade association representing the herbal products industry, an industry comprised of growers, processors, manufacturers, and marketers of herbal products.

American Meat Institute (AMI): the national trade association representing companies that process seventy percent of U.S. meat and poultry and their suppliers throughout America.

American Pet Products Manufacturers Association (APPMA): a trade association made up of nearly 850 pet-product manufacturers, their representatives, importers, and livestock suppliers.

Animal Health Institute (AHI): a trade association representing the manufacturers of animal health products including the pharmaceuticals, vaccines, and feed additives used in food production and medicines for pets.

Association of Food Industries (AFI): a trade association serving the food import trade. AFI is committed to developing programs that facilitate the business of its member companies, encourage free and fair trade and foster compliance with U. S. laws and regulations for the food industry.

Association of Health Insurance Plans (AHIP): a national association representing nearly 1,300 health insurance companies.

Biotechnology Industry Organization (BIO): a trade association representing medical, agricultural, and industrial biotechnology companies.

Blue Cross Blue Shield Association (BCBSA): the trade association for the forty Blue Cross and Blue Shield Plans, which offer health insurance and managed care services.

Consumer Healthcare Products Association (CHPA): a trade association representing the leading manufacturers and distributors of nonprescription, over-the-counter medicines and nutritional supplements.

Cosmetic, Toiletry, and Fragrance Association (CTFA): a trade association representing the personal care products industry.

Council for Responsible Nutrition (CRN): a trade association representing ingredient suppliers and manufacturers in the dietary supplement industry.

Fresh Product Association of the Americas: an association with a mission to develop and promote trade between growers and shippers in Mexico and other foreign countries, and receivers throughout the United States and Canada.

Generic Pharmaceutical Association (GPhA): a trade association representing the manufacturers and distributors of finished generic pharmaceutical products, manufacturers and distributors of bulk active pharmaceutical chemicals, and suppliers of services to the generic pharmaceutical industry.

Grocery Manufacturers of America (GMA): a trade association representing the interests of the food, beverage, and consumer products industry.

International Dairy Foods Association (IDFA): an association created to promote positive domestic and international dairy policies.

Medical Device Manufacturers of America (MDMA): a trade association that represents independent manufacturers of medical devices, diagnostic products, and healthcare information systems.

National Cattlemen's Beef Association: a marketing organization and trade association for America's 1 million cattle farmers and ranchers.

National Chicken Council (NCC): a trade association representing the U.S. chicken industry, including chicken producers and processors, poultry distributors, and allied industry firms.

National Confectioners Association (NCA): a trade association representing the confection industry.

National Electrical Manufacturers Association (NEMA): an organization focused on the standardization of electrical equipment.

National Food Processors Association (NFPA): a trade association of the food and beverage industry and representing them on scientific and public policy issues.

National Grain and Feed Association: a trade association that represents and provides services for grain, feed, and grain-related commercial businesses.

National Health Lawyers Association: an educational organization devoted to legal issues in the healthcare field.

National Pork Producers Council (NPPC): an organization that conducts public policy outreach on behalf of its forty-four affiliated state association members.

National Renderers Association: a trade association whose members focus on transforming waste from the meat industry into useable products for animal feeds and technical use.

Orthopedic Surgical Manufacturers Association (OSMA): an association representing companies that manufacture medical devices used in orthopedic surgical procedures, such as implants, instruments, equipment, and associated products.

Pharmaceutical Research and Manufacturers of America (PhRMA): an industry association that represents the leading research-based pharmaceutical and biotechnology companies in the United States.

Plasma Protein Therapeutics Association: an association of source plasma collectors and producers of plasma-based and recombinant biological therapeutics.

United Fresh Fruit and Vegetable Association: a trade association representing growers, shippers, processors, brokers, wholesalers, and distributors of produce.

United States Pharmacopeia (USP): a science-based public health organization that serves as a public standards-setting authority for prescription and over-the-counter medicines, dietary supplements, and other healthcare products manufactured and sold in the United States.

Professional/Consumer Organizations:

American Association of Retired Persons (AARP): association of retired persons that advocates the interests of those fifty years of age or older.

American Association of Blood Banks: a group representing the interests of those concerned with transfusion medicine and related biological therapies.

American Cancer Society: a voluntary health organization dedicated to cancer prevention and research.

American Heart Association: a voluntary health agency dedicated to cardiovascular diseases and stroke.

American Medical Association (AMA): the nation's largest physicians' professional association.

American Public Health Association (APHA): the oldest and largest organization of public health professionals.

American Society of Gene Therapy (ASGT): a professional organization representing researchers and scientists in gene therapy and related fields.

American Society of Microbiology: a professional society for the microbiological sciences.

Association of American Feed Control Officials: an association of officials who enforce the laws regulating animal feeds or livestock remedies.

Association of Official Analytical Chemists International (AOAC): a scientific association committed to worldwide confidence in analytical results.

Association of Food and Drug Officials (AFDO): an association of state and local food and drug officials who work closely with FDA on a variety of issues.

Center for Science in the Public Interest: a group that advocates for food policy, including nutrition, food safety, and alcohol policy.

Consumer Federation of America (CFA): an advocacy group that works on consumer-related issues.

Drug Information Association (DIA): an organization that facilitates the exchange and dissemination of healthcare information.

Friends of Cancer Research: a non-profit organization established to raise awareness and provide public education on cancer research.

National Egg Regulatory Officials (NERO): an egg industry group that encourages uniformity in quality assurance.

National Health Council: a member organization made up of voluntary health agencies, professional and membership associations, and non-profit organizations with an interest in health, business, and industry.

National Medical Association (NMA): a medical association of physicians of African descent that serves as the collective voice of physicians and patients of African descent.

National Nutritional Foods Association: the nation's largest and oldest non-profit organization dedicated to the natural products industry that includes foods, dietary supplements, and health/beauty aids.

National Organization for Rare Disorders (NORD): a federation of voluntary health organizations dedicated to helping people with rare "orphan" diseases and assisting the organizations that serve them.

National Women's Health Network: an organization concerned with women's health issues.

Public Citizen: a non-profit consumer advocacy founded to represent consumer interests.

Regulatory Affairs Professional Society (RAPS): a member organization for regulatory affairs professionals.

associated with medical products, dietary supplements and foods."

The fourth element, "Protecting America from Terrorism," was designed to strengthen FDA's capability to identify, prepare for, and respond to terrorist threats and incidents.

Finally, the plan calls for a "More Effective Regulation through a Stronger Workforce." To ensure "a world-class professional workforce, effective and efficient operations, and adequate resources to accomplish the agency's mission," FDA's plan calls for ensuring effective "communication and working relationships with key external stakeholders to enhance U.S. and global health outcomes."

FDA's twenty-first century initiative reflects FDA's new approach to regulation, its objective being to promote a risk-management approach to drug manufacturing and quality assurance.

FDA's strategy focuses on developing and using technologically-based guidance to industry to promote voluntary compliance; using the latest innovations in production, inspection, and regulatory techniques; integrating risk-management in product design, development, application, and manufacture; encouraging international harmonization of advanced techniques; and cooperating with outside experts and the industry to define common goals. FDA's website regularly reports progress of the initiative.

FDA's food program also incorporates a risk management approach. Because food-borne disease remains a major public health problem, FDA established a program to provide a timely, high-quality, cost-effective process for the review of new technologies and oversight of manufacturing to assure the safety of foods and cosmetics.

FDA's Major Initiatives, 2006

A century after the enactment of the Pure Food and Drugs Act of 1906, FDA set forth its major initiatives as it entered a new century. This is from the FDA's website:

The twenty-first century has presented FDA with unprecedented challenges. To accomplish its mission of promoting and protecting the public health, the agency will need to be innovative and resourceful in the years ahead. To help guide the agency as it moves forward, FDA has created a blueprint that maps out five critical challenges facing the agency and how they can be accomplished. These major initiatives will help the agency use twenty-first century knowledge to bring medical products and foods safely to the greatest number of people:

Efficient Risk Management—Searching for new and better ways to reduce risks to public health

Better Informed Consumers—Helping consumers get truthful information about products they use so they can make informed decisions

Patient and Consumer Safety—Preventing adverse events involving FDA-regulated products

Counterterrorism—Responding quickly to terrorist acts and enhancing food security

A Strong FDA—Maintaining a strong science base to support FDA's risk management responsibilities.

In 2004, FDA issued a report, *Innovation or Stagnation?—Challenge and Opportunity on the Critical Path to New Medical Products*, which examines the critical steps in medical product development. Because the applied sciences needed for medical product development have not kept pace with advances in basic science, FDA called for a new focus on modernizing the tools that applied biomedical researchers and product developers use to assess the safety and effectiveness of potential new products, and the manufacturing tools necessary for high-quality mass production of cutting-edge therapies. The report describes the need for FDA—together with academia, patient groups, industry, and other government agencies—to embark on an aggressive, collaborative research effort to generate performance standards and predictive tools that will better, faster, and more certainly answer concerns about the safety and effectiveness of investigational products.

Collaborative and cooperative efforts appeared pre-eminent as FDA began the twenty-first century. And such efforts were not limited to the product review and approval process, but applied equally to FDA's engagement on product pricing issues with the Centers for Medicaid and Medicare Services and FDA's enforcement initiatives with the Securities and Exchange Commission and the Federal Trade Commission, both designed to enhance the agencies' mutual obligations to ensure accurate communication to citizens and investors.

Meanwhile, FDA's century-long focus on compliance remains, but the agency's means to achieve it, at the centennial of the 1906 Act, have revised how FDA exercises its basic functions. Accordingly,

FDA Alumni Organize

In 2001, nearly a century after the enactment of the 1906 Act, a small group of former employees gathered to form what became the FDA Alumni Association (FDAAA). At the time, FDA personnel staff estimated that some 50,000 people had worked for FDA or its predecessor agencies. Whether this number is accurate, no one knows for sure, but the camaraderie among people who have worked for the FDA generated enthusiastic support for the organization.

The FDAAA, incorporated in Maryland in 2003 as a non-profit organization, had more than 600 members by 2005, mostly from the Washington, D.C. area, but including members from around the country and the world. Current FDA employees may join as associate members.

The association established a memorandum of understanding with FDA in 2003, offering to collaborate on appropriate projects. The association also recommends awardees for FDA Alumni of the Year, and is an official participant in the agency's centennial celebration. The organization's own award, named after Harvey Wiley, honors distinguished contributions. The first two awardees were former Congressman Paul Rogers (D-FL), once known as "Mr. Health" on Capitol Hill, and Abbey Meyers, founder of the National Organization for Rare Disorders.

The FDAAA enables alumni to gather at educational forums, featuring speakers discussing current FDA topics. As FDA enters its second century, the FDAAA seeks new opportunities to support the agency and help former employees maintain valuable contacts with their colleagues.

—Wayne L. Pines

Chief Inspector George P. Larrick (later Commissioner) assembled the famous "Chamber of Horrors," an exhibit which effectively illustrated many of the shortcomings of the 1906 Pure Food and Drugs Act. A reporter accompanying Eleanor Roosevelt to see the exhibit dubbed it an "American Chamber of Horrors," and FDA's Chief Education Officer, Ruth de Forest Lamb, wrote a book by the same name providing details on the dangerous and mislabeled products in the exhibit. The exhibit helped secure eventual passage of the 1938 Food, Drug, and Cosmetic Act.

FDA Comes of Age:
A Century of Change

Peter Barton Hutt

FOOD AND DRUG REGULATION as it existed 100 years ago bears little relation to what occurs today. The principles and objectives of regulation remain the same, but the statutes and their implementation and enforcement have changed dramatically. This transformation of U. S. food and drug law can be found in every element of current regulatory programs.

In implementing and enforcing the laws Congress assigned to FDA, the agency must rely on a wide variety of processes and procedures. Some have evolved naturally based on need, others have been codified in formal regulations. None of the laws enforced by FDA is self-executing. Congress usually writes laws very broadly. Thus, FDA has spent the past century determining, and then making public, procedural and substantive policy statements designed to facilitate its administration of the organic statute.

The 1906 Act required the Secretary of the Treasury, the Secretary of Agriculture, and the Secretary of Commerce and Labor to make uniform rules and regulations to carry out the provisions of that Act. Public meetings were held to obtain the views of the regulated industry and the public before final regulations were issued. Those regulations were in fact adopted less than four months after enactment of the statute, and they remained virtually unchanged throughout the entire life of the 1906 Act.

In addition to these fundamental operating procedures, FDA also sought to issue announcements designed to deal with specific food- and drug-labeling and safety matters. These were made available in the form of Food Inspection Decisions (FIDs) through 1913 and as Service and Regulatory Announcements (SRAs) beginning in 1914. The first 39 FIDs were in fact issued before enactment of the 1906 Act, as part of a government program to provide guidance to state regulatory agencies to foster uniform national regulation. Beginning in October 1906, many FIDs and SRAs were issued to provide operational rules for enforcement of the new law.

At that time, the Bureau of Chemistry was one of a very few agencies charged with administration of a federal regulatory statute. With the growth of administrative agencies under the New Deal, however, Congress realized that it was essential to establish a uniform place where all federal regulations would be published and thus made publicly available. Congress therefore created, in 1935, the *Federal Register* for this purpose.

Following enactment of the 1938 Food, Drug, and Cosmetic Act, FDA once again promulgated general regulations, many of them covering the same subjects as the regulations adopted in 1906. This time, however, they were published in the Federal Register. The 1938 Act provided for two types of regulations: Section 701(a) provided for regulations for the efficient enforcement of the Act; Section 701(e) provided for regulations to implement specific substantive provisions of the statute—food standards, special dietary food regulations, emergency permits for control of food pathogens, environmental contaminants in food, drug assays, habit-forming drugs, drug stability packaging and labeling, and coal tar colors in food, drugs, and cosmetics. The regulated industry had persuaded Congress that these were of sufficient importance to require formal rulemaking on an evidentiary record following a public administrative hearing.

Until the early 1970s, it was thought that the first of these two sections permitted only procedural regulations and statements of policy, and that the second provision resulted in the only regulations that could be enforced as legal requirements. In the early 1970s, however, the courts confirmed FDA's interpretation that regulations promulgated under the first provision also resulted in binding legal requirements.

FDA found it necessary under the 1938 Act to issue the same type of statements of policy or interpretation that it had issued

FDA was at the forefront of work in the 1910s through 30s to help establish and enforce legal limits on arsenate and lead pesticide residues on Western fruit, particularly apples. At this station, FDA inspectors in the "show me" state demanded that truck drivers bringing apples into the state of Missouri do the same, either submitting the apples for testing or providing evidence that they were in compliance with the legal residue limits.

BURTON J. HOWARD AND HIS REVOLUTIONARY MOLD COUNT

Burton J. Howard using a spectrophotometer in his laboratory, circa 1915.

Burton J. Howard was the early Bureau of Chemistry's Renaissance man. Officially the Chief of the Microchemical Laboratory, he was also a talented photographer, scientist, and researcher. During the course of his career in the Bureau of Chemistry, he secured two patents. One was for a "ruling apparatus" and the other for "processes for the removal of maggots from blueberries," and both were dedicated to the "people of the United States."

Following passage of the 1906 Act, it was difficult to convince juries and even judges that a high bacterial count alone should condemn products such as catsup and eggs, especially when a threat to public health had been neither alleged nor proven. A judge in 1910 lamented that the 1906 Act had been drafted using common rather than scientific language and therefore had no reference to the "minute microscopic creatures that had become of great importance within a comparatively few years," but rather referred to food that juries and judges themselves might find "filthy, decomposed, or putrid."

In 1911, Howard authored a circular describing a new method for detecting decomposed tomato products microscopically. Almost casually, he noted that the new method required a certain level of expertise. Two drops of tomato product were put on a slide under the microscope. Each drop was then divided into twenty-five fields and the molds in each field were counted. The overall count was calculated to show the percentage of mold in the sample.

The so-called Howard mold count revolutionized the canned food industry, and the courts themselves increasingly held that the filth in foods that could not be seen was at least as reprehensible as the filth that could be seen.

—**Suzanne White Junod**

in the form of FIDs and SRAs under the 1906 Act. Between 1938 and 1946, FDA issued these in the form of letters to industry. Those of general applicability and importance were then made public as Trade Correspondence (TC), numbered sequentially, for guidance to the regulated industry.

By 1946, however, it was again clear to Congress that the growth of administrative law in the United States required a more systematic approach to the issuance of agency policy statements and regulations. Congress therefore enacted the Administrative Procedure Act (APA), which established requirements for agency adoption of its policy positions in the form of informal statements of policy or formal regulations. FDA abandoned the use of Trade Correspondence (although it has continued to correspond with the regulated industry) and has followed the requirements of the APA ever since.

One of the major reasons for the use of rulemaking to replace individual court enforcement actions in the early 1970s was to achieve greater fairness and consistency in application of the law. Use of court enforcement, while clearly a permissible course of action, is inherently selective and can lead to the perception, and perhaps at times the reality, of invidious discrimination. Establishment of policy by promulgation of regulations, in contrast, assures that all affected companies have equal notice of FDA requirements and an equal opportunity for compliance.

As the size of FDA increased, the need for internal understanding, as

well as external communication, of FDA requirements also increased. FDA therefore determined that, where new programs were begun or new requirements were instituted, they should be preceded by the promulgation of regulations to fully inform both FDA employees and the general public about the nature of the new program or requirement. Rather than interpret the statute through court enforcement action, FDA began to interpret the law through the promulgation of regulations.

Instead of simply adopting a program through internal memoranda, as it did for the Drug Efficacy Study Implementation

WHY NOT AN INDEPENDENT FDA?

Established under the chairmanship of former President Herbert Hoover in 1947, the Commission on Organization of the Executive Branch of Government was popularly known as the Hoover Commission. President Truman believed in an activist government, but even though there was public support for an independent FDA, as depicted in this cartoon, such a scenerio does not appear to have been seriously contemplated. Today, in 2006, there is no serious discussion of FDA independence from its parent department.

(DESI) program, FDA implemented the later Over-the-Counter (OTC) Drug Review and Biological Products Review through detailed procedural regulations. FDA promulgated dozens of regulations governing such diverse matters as nutrition labeling, safety substantiation for cosmetics, the regulation of *in vitro* diagnostic products, and good laboratory practice for nonclinical laboratory studies, to name just a few.

Prior to the 1970s, it was common practice simply to propose a regulation, obtain public comment, and then publish a final regulation, without an explanation of the reasons for the proposal or why the changes recommended by the public comment were or were not accepted in the final regulations. FDA pioneered the use of explanatory preambles to both the proposed and the final regulations. The preamble to the proposal laid out, in detail, the need for the proposed regulation, any documentation appropriate for its specific provisions, and an analysis of its intended interpretation and implementation. The preamble to the final regulation responded to each type of comment, stating the reasons it was accepted or rejected. To this day, these preambles have educated FDA employees, the regulated industry, and the general public about the important work of the agency.

USP AND FDA

The relationship of the FDA and the U. S. Pharmacopeia (USP) formally began in 1906 with the recognition of USP and the National Formulary as official sources of standards for judging the adulteration of drugs. This special relationship between a governmental and a private body necessitated that the two organizations work closely over the years.

Starting in 1910, with Harvey Wiley serving as USP Convention President while also serving as Chief of the Bureau of Chemistry, many FDA and USP employees and scientists have served in joint roles on USP, FDA, or joint expert committees. Following the publication of an Office of Technology Assessment Report in 1974 criticizing both FDA regulatory practices and USP standards for failing to adequately assure the bioequivalency of drug products, a formal liaison mechanism was established between the two bodies. This resulted in progress through improved compendial monographs, modernization of antibiotic standards, eventual elimination of the certification process, and numerous improvements in product packaging and labeling.

FDA and USP have also cooperated in areas other than the development of drug quality standards. For example, in 1971, FDA and USP initiated a program by which pharmacists could report problems with products. FDA also participated in the USP Drug Information (DI) program to develop authoritative information describing for both health professionals and patients the appropriate use of medications.

Although the importance of the FDA and USP as a source of standards has somewhat diminished with the introduction of the new drug and abbreviated new drug approval processes, the USP and National Formulary remain important and useful tools in assuring drug quality. Even though this complex synergistic relationship imposed by Congress sometimes has resulted in cooperation, competition, or even conflict between FDA and USP officials over the years, there is no doubt that it has served the American people well and improved the public health far beyond what either organization could have achieved separately.

—**Joseph G. Valentino**

THE IPECAC MYSTERY

In the 1970s, the Centers for Disease Control and Prevention and FDA began receiving reports from doctors and parents that certain brands of syrup of ipecac were not working; they were not causing children who had accidentally swallowed poison to vomit and expel the poison. FDA began an investigation to determine why syrup of ipecac made from a particular supplier of bulk ipecac was not having its desired emetic effect. FDA's investigation was initially frustrated because samples of the supplier's ipecac showed that the bulk ipecac had the labeled potency.

The mystery was solved when FDA laboratory experts recognized that the established test for the presence of ipecac did not in fact specifically measure ipecac, but measured the presence of a certain alkaloid that was usually presumed to be ipecac when the product being tested was labeled as ipecac. One substance that has amounts of this alkaloid at about the same level as ipecac is ephedrine.

FDA renewed its investigation of the supplier and discovered large amounts of ephedrine at the supplier's facility. The president of the supplier company explained that he was conducting research on ephedrine and writing all of his research notes in a small notebook. FDA demanded to see the notebook. When the day came for the company president to produce the notebook, he produced instead a sworn statement claiming that when he was on a catwalk above the large machines that grind ipecac root into the bulk ipecac powder, he lost his grip on the notebook and it tumbled into the grinding machine.

Given that explanation, it was not surprising that within a few days, the company president pleaded guilty to adulterating his bulk ipecac by substituting large amounts of ephedrine. (The government did not amend the charges to add a different form of adulteration—the presence of shredded pages of a research notebook among the bulk ipecac material.)

Notwithstanding the potentially life-threatening consequence of the company's adulteration of ipecac by the substitution of an ingredient that would not cause a poison victim to vomit the poison, the federal judge imposed only a fine on the company president and did not send him to jail.

—Arthur N. Levine

Several events that occurred in the mid-1970s led FDA to the conclusion that it should promulgate regulations governing all of its administrative procedures. As the agency issued more and more substantive regulations, there was a greater need for administrative procedures to govern the rulemaking process. The effect of premarket approval for an increasingly large number of products regulated by the agency also required procedural regulations to govern this process. The regulated industry sought guidance from FDA on a wide variety of issues, requiring standard procedures to handle these matters. The Freedom of Information Act and the Federal Advisory Committee Act also required the promulgation of regulations to ensure that FDA would implement them in a uniform and fair way. Finally, with an agency of more than 6,000 employees throughout the country, it was essential to have written rules that could be followed by everyone to ensure a uniform approach within the agency.

FDA therefore undertook to reduce all of its administrative practice and procedure to written regulations, an approach that no other government agency had tried. Comprehensive regulations were proposed in 1975 and promulgated in final form during 1976-1977. As a result of these regulations, FDA has achieved a more consistent approach to implementation of the 1938 Act than would otherwise have been possible.

Because of the increasing burdens imposed by regulatory agencies on industry, Congress has responded with corresponding requirements for all federal agencies to justify their rulemaking. FDA has been required to cope in its rulemaking process with additional requirements under such statutes as the National Environmental Policy Act, the Regulatory Flexibility Act, and the

Paperwork Reduction Act, and regulatory reform Executive Orders issued by the President. During the same time, internal requirements for review of FDA rulemaking by the Department of Health and Human Services and the Office of Management and Budget has further increased the time and resources needed for the promulgation of regulations. As these requirements for the promulgation of regulations have increased, the number of regulations promulgated by FDA has decreased correspondingly. Issues that previously might have been resolved through regulations of the type promulgated by FDA during the 1970s

ORIGINS OF THE ORPHAN DRUG ACT

In the late 1970s, I was a simple housewife from Connecticut with children who have a rare genetic disorder. My oldest son was severely impacted, and we tried many medications to no avail. Finally he was put on an investigational drug, and it worked.

But a few months later the manufacturer decided to stop development of the compound. I did not know at the time that the decision was based solely on economic—not medical—reasoning. The drug was being developed for a prevalent disease and it was not effective for that condition. The manufacturer didn't care that it worked for my son's disease because the market was too small to be sufficiently profitable.

In other words, it was an "orphan drug."

Since I had no answers as to why we couldn't get the drug, I phoned the FDA. Eventually I spoke to a woman in the neuropharmacology division and asked why development of the drug was being stopped. In particular, I wanted to know if my son was in danger; for example, did FDA find out that it caused a serious side effect such as cancer and therefore ordered the sponsor to discontinue the clinical trials?

The woman on the phone said, "I can't talk to you until I speak to a Freedom of Information Officer," and she promised to call me back. A few hours later she did call me back. She said, "I spoke to the Freedom of Information Officer, and he said I cannot talk to you."

Needless to say, I hung up the phone in disbelief. That phone conversation, however, was the very beginning of a battle that culminated in passage of the Orphan Drug Act of 1983. I spoke with numerous rare disease support groups who felt the orphan drug dilemma needed to be solved, and that coalition evolved into the National Organization for Rare Disorders (NORD) dedicated to the identification, treatment, and cure of rare diseases through programs of education, advocacy, research, and services for patients and families.

—**Abbey S. Meyers**

THE START OF *FDA CONSUMER*

I had many memorable meetings with the many FDA commissioners with whom I worked, but none more memorable than my very first meeting after joining FDA in 1972. I was hired as Director of Consumer Education and Information. At the time, FDA had no consumer education program, but it did have a magazine called *FDA Papers*, which was written for the regulated industries.

Commissioner Charles Edwards summoned me to his office soon after I arrived. I knew him well because I had been a reporter for *The Pink Sheet* and had covered him. Now I sat in his office as an employee. The meeting lasted less than five minutes, including pleasantries. Dr. Edwards wanted me to achieve two goals: create a consumer education program and figure out what to do with *FDA Papers*—"Kill it or change it," he said. He added something to the effect that he would leave it to me to decide, and added, "Let me know if you have any problems doing what you need to do."

I remember those quotes verbatim. I recall reflecting at the time on Dr. Edwards' management style—set your goals clearly, let the staff figure out how to do it, and bring me problems if you have any.

My intention in joining FDA was to do something different with *FDA Papers*, and so within a few months we had refocused it toward the consumer and renamed it *FDA Consumer* to reflect its new orientation. The transformation of the magazine reflected a new era for FDA—reaching out directly to the consumer. Shortly thereafter, FDA hired a new consumer liaison to build bridges to the consumer community, and the agency has never looked back. Thirty years later, *FDA Consumer* remains an important voice for FDA to the public.

—Wayne L. Pines

---

increasingly have been handled by more informal approaches.

The FDA procedural regulations had already laid the groundwork for a new and less onerous approach. Those regulations provided for the adoption of informal guidelines without the need for publication in the Federal Register with a lengthy preamble and time for public comment. Guidelines represent policy that is acceptable to FDA but that is nonetheless not binding upon the public. Thus, they provide the same useful information to the regulated industry as the FIDs and SRAs under the 1906 Act and the TCs under the early days of the 1938 Act, but without the full procedural requirements for substantive rulemaking mandated by the APA.

In the early 1990s, the use of guidelines by FDA, largely to implement the premarket approval requirements under the 1938 Act, skyrocketed. Some courts found that these informal statements of policy were poorly disguised regulations, and invalidated, or refused to enforce, substantive guidelines implemented by FDA as though they were regulations. Because of greatly expanded use of guidelines in lieu of regulations, FDA had to reconsider the role of guidelines in the administration of the 1938 Act and what requirements should be imposed on their use. Reconciling regulations and guidelines will be an important objective of FDA.

Advisory Committees

From its very beginning, FDA and its predecessor agencies have had a long tradition of using advisory committees. The oldest advisory committee connected with FDA was the Board of Tea Experts. This Board met yearly to establish tea standards under the authority of the Tea Act of 1897 (which superseded the earlier Tea Act of 1883). Only in 1996 was that venerable statute repealed and the Board disbanded. The tea program had long stood the test of time.

Another early comittee was the Food Standards Committee. For a number of years before enactment of the 1906 Act, the government was authorized by appropriations legislation to investigate the adulteration of food and drugs. In accordance with this authority, it not only conducted chemical investigations but also established informal standards for pure food and drug products to assist the states in enforcing state and local food and drug laws. The appropriations legislation for 1902 for the first time explicitly authorized the Bureau of Chemistry, in collaboration with the Association of Official Agricultural Chemists and such other experts as may be deemed necessary:

...to establish standards of purity for food products and to determine what are regarded as adulterations therein, for the guidance of the officials of the various States and of the courts of justice... .

First Food Standards Committee. From left: E.H. Jenkins, H.A. Weber, William Frear, Harvey Wiley, and M.A. Scovell

To implement this provision, in 1902 FDA established a Food Standards Committee, comprised entirely of state food and drug law officials. The committee continued to exist for decades.

The loss of the Food Standards Committee, when Congress enacted the Federal Advisory Committee Act, was an unnecessary and unfortunate setback in the cause of national uniformity in food and drug regulatory efforts.

Establishment of the first FDA scientific advisory committee of independent academic experts in February 1908—the Referee Board of Consulting Scientific Experts—was accompanied by substantial controversy. It took one opinion of the Attorney General to decide that the Referee Board was lawfully constituted, a second opinion to determine the compensation of the Referee Board, and a third opinion to decide that reports of the Referee Board were advisory in nature and not binding upon FDA. Following a critical report by a congressional committee, the Referee Board was terminated in mid-1915, and no further scientific advisory committees were used by FDA under the 1906 Act.

After enactment of the Drug Amendments of 1962, however, FDA again found itself in need of expert advice, both internally and externally. Internally, the agency established advisory committees of outside academic experts to obtain independent medical and scientific advice on implementation of the requirements for approval of new drugs under the new statute in 1963 and for

specific advice on oral contraceptives in 1965. This modest beginning led to the establishment in the early 1970s of a large number of scientific advisory committees, covering individual pharmacological categories of drugs and devices. FDA's reviews of the safety and effectiveness of all nonprescription drugs and all biological products licensed between 1902 and 1972 under the Biologics Act of 1902 were also accomplished through standing scientific advisory committees. FDA thus substantially increased its access to scientific expertise and greatly enhanced the stature of its decisions.

Externally, the agency turned to two well-recognized scientific organizations to conduct major reviews for which the agency did not have the capacity. To review all of the new drugs for which a new drug application (NDA) had become effective under the 1938 Act between 1938 and 1962, FDA contracted with the National Academy of Sciences (NAS). Between 1966 and 1968, the NAS convened thirty panels of experts in specific drug categories and completed the requested review. The NAS reports covered approximately 4,000 different drug formulations.

Following FDA's removal of cyclamate from the FDA list of generally recognized as safe (GRAS) food substances, President Nixon ordered FDA to review the safety of all of the food substances included on the FDA GRAS list. To accomplish this, FDA contracted with the Federation of American Societies for Experimental Biology (FASEB). Using committees of scientific experts, FASEB reviewed more than 400 GRAS substances and submitted its reports to FDA between 1972 and 1982.

The success of these advisory committees, to supplement FDA's own scientific staff, was recognized in the Medical Device Amendments of 1976. Scientific advisory committees became an integral part of the consideration of class III medical devices, which require premarket approval. Other statutory advisory committees include the Device Good Manufacturing Practice Advisory Committee, the Technical Electronic Product Radiation Safety Standards Committee, and the color additive advisory committees.

From the precedent set in 1908 with the appointment of the Referee Board, which consisted of the leading scientists of that era, FDA progressed to an agency-wide system of expert advisory committees on which it could rely heavily for scientific and medical advice. Following enactment of the Federal Advisory Committee Act in 1972, all proceedings of an advisory committee were required to be open to the public, with rare exception. Because of its frequent use of advisory committees, FDA was the first federal agency to issue

---

AOAC AND FDA

Assuring FDA's objective of worldwide confidence in analytical results is central to achieving the mission of FDA. AOAC International has worked closely with FDA throughout its entire history to achieve that objective. AOAC International is a 121-year-old scientific association, which began in 1884 as the Association of Official Agricultural Chemists, operating from the Bureau of Chemistry of the U.S. Department of Agriculture. It was transferred to FDA after the passage of the Federal Food, Drug, and Cosmetic Act of 1938.

Established by Dr. Harvey W. Wiley and state chemists who enforced fertilizer labeling laws, it took on the responsibility of approving only those methods of analysis that gave the same results in the hands of different chemists in different laboratories. This principle of validating methods of analysis was then expanded to animal feeds, human foods and drugs, pesticides, and other commodities that were regulated by state and federal authorities. It has become central to the regulatory process.

The AOAC was also responsible for other important advances in analytical chemistry. When the Bureau of Chemistry laboratory director, Dr. Lyman Kebler, started in 1903, he found that the reagents used by the laboratory were misbranded and adulterated! He turned to the AOAC for a national study of the quality of chemical reagents. The AOAC created the Committee on Testing of Chemical Reagents with Dr. Kebler as its head. This collaboration of laboratories around the country resulted in setting standards of quality for laboratory reagents. This activity was later taken over by the American Chemical Society, whose specifications are still the mark of quality. AOAC's work has given FDA, as well as other federal and international agencies, methods that law courts have come to rely upon as trusted and reproducible.

AOAC became a private professional organization in 1985. But the relationship and collaboration between AOAC and FDA has remained strong, especially as FDA needs shifted to more challenging fields, such as microbiology, dietary supplements, and genetically modified organisms. All of these emerging problems required validated methods of analysis. AOAC has served, as it had for the previous century, as a partner with FDA in advancing the methods needed to protect the public health.

—**Walter Benson & William Horwitz**

comprehensive regulations governing applicable procedures.

Statutory Mandates

The history of food and drug regulation over the past century is largely the history of the development of science, not the enactment of statutory provisions. The 1938 Act contained broad statutory mandates that are meaningless without the infusion of scientific knowledge that permits the development of specific operational rules. One example will suffice. Parliament enacted a statute for all of England in 1266 that prohibited food "that is not wholesome for Man's Body." This law continued in effect throughout England for more than 600 years. The U.S. law prohibits the addition to food of "any poisonous or deleterious substance which may render it injurious to health." There is no discernable difference between these two statutory provisions, enacted centuries apart. It is only the extraordinary increase in scientific knowledge since 1266 that allows our modern regulatory agencies to achieve a level of public protection that was unavailable when the English statute was enacted 740 years ago.

From its very origin, FDA has been at the forefront of regulatory science. It was FDA and the state agencies that organized the Association of Official Agricultural Chemists (AOAC) to promote the development of accurate and reliable analytical methods to detect the

---

I MET THE PRESIDENT BECAUSE OF WORDPERFECT 6.1

In the mid-1990s, the biggest project at FDA was the tobacco rule. In 1994, Commissioner David Kessler initiated an investigation to determine whether the nicotine in tobacco was a drug subject to FDA's jurisdiction. Subsequently, he directed his staff to develop a proposed regulation that would deter youth access to tobacco and ensure that tobacco advertising did not target children.

In early 1995, the agency was briefing the leadership of the Department of Health and Human Services (DHHS) to obtain approval of the details of the regulation. Meanwhile, the Commissioner and I, the agency's Deputy Commissioner for Policy, met with Abner Mikva, White House Counsel and former Chief Judge of the D.C. Circuit, concerning the legal issue of whether FDA could declare jurisdiction over tobacco products. Judge Mikva referred the issue to Walter Dellinger, then head of the Office of Legal Counsel at the Department of Justice. Ultimately, DHHS Secretary Donna Shalala cleared the proposed rule, and Mr. Dellinger agreed that FDA had legal authority to assert jurisdiction, although he correctly predicted that the issue would be decided in a closely divided decision of the U. S. Supreme Court.

We then participated in three grueling meetings in the office of the White House Chief of Staff. In addition to the Chief of Staff, Leon Panetta, the meetings were attended by most of the top White House officials, other than the President and Vice President, including Harold Ickes, Erskine Bowles, George Stephanopoulos, Doug Sosnick, and Judge Mikva.

Once the White House cleared the rule, it was decided that President Clinton would make the announcement on August 11, 1995. This required my presence in Washington right in the middle of a two-week family vacation that I had purposely planned for the usually quiet month of August. FDA prepared a briefing package for the President, and, after approval by the officials at DHHS, I took the materials to a White House staffer who worked in the Old Executive Office Building for final editing and clearance.

At FDA, the materials had been prepared with a computer that used WordPerfect 6.1, but the White House computer had an earlier, incompatible version of WordPerfect

Button distributed by tobacco manufacturers to farmers opposing FDA regulation of cigarettes as a "nicotine delivery device."

adulteration and misbranding of food and drugs. Throughout the past century, both state and regulatory scientists have been in the forefront of scientific inquiry into improved methods of implementing our food and drug laws.

Development of some of the most important principles of toxicology can be attributed to FDA. The contributions that FDA has made in this area have been little recognized and even less appreciated. For example, faced with the Elixir Sulfanilamide disaster in the fall of 1937, scientists in the FDA Division of Pharmacology were determined to turn that tragedy into a benefit for society. It was impossible, of course, ever to conduct a true toxicity feeding study in humans at sufficiently high doses to learn anything about the relationship between toxicity in animals and toxicity in humans. But the Elixir Sulfanilamide presented, for the first and perhaps only time, the opportunity to obtain an actual LD_{50} in humans as well as in animals.

FDA scientists obtained the dose taken by 100 people, as well as the dose consumed by others who did not die. They then conducted the animal experiments that would have prevented this tragedy, to determine the range of lethal doses in a variety of animal models. They discovered a roughly ten-fold variation in the lethal dose both among humans and among animals. Multiplying these two factors by ten during the 1940s, they gradually

and we could not open the file! After a few phone calls, we determined that the only computer in the White House equipped with WordPerfect 6.1 was located in the small lobby between the offices of the President's Chief of Staff and the Deputy Chief of Staff. We were joined there by Chris Cerf, an attorney in the White House Counsel's office.

As we worked on the briefing package, the President and Mr. Panetta emerged from the Chief of Staff's office. As the President was telling Mr. Panetta to call former President Carter and former Surgeon General C. Everett Koop (obviously in anticipation of the tobacco announcement), they walked by us, and Chris introduced me to the President. We talked for about five minutes, and it was clear that he was both enthusiastic about the tobacco initiative and knowledgeable about its details. For my part, I knew my meeting with the President was due solely to the superiority of FDA computer software over that used in the White House.

The next morning, the rule was placed on the public record at the Federal Register at 8:45 a.m. At 9:00 a.m., the tobacco industry sued FDA in North Carolina. The President announced the rule at a press conference later that morning. Although the White House staff had complimented the quality of the briefing materials we had prepared, the President's responses to questions significantly improved on them, which he probably read only a few minutes before the press conference.

The announcement of the proposed rule was a landmark event, and we knew that completing work on the final rule would be a monumental task. As might be expected, the industry inundated FDA with comments (purportedly more than any agency had ever received in a rulemaking proceeding). During the months-long development of the final rule, I received numerous press calls. Most of the reporters were interested in one question: When would the agency issue the final rule? I always responded that I had planned a family vacation during the last two weeks of August, 1996, and, because of that planned vacation, I was confident that the rule would be issued during the second half of August. The final rule was issued on August 28, 1996. Never have I more regretted being right.

—**William B. Schultz**

derived the now well-accepted rule of toxicology that a safe human dose may be determined by dividing the lowest no-observed-effect level (NOEL) in animals by a safety factor of 100. The importance of this investigation and analysis cannot be overstated. For centuries, there had been no operational definition of human safety. Only the extraordinary insight and initiative of these FDA scientists led to a rule of product safety that has been employed daily throughout the world for more than five decades. During the 1940s and 1950s, indeed, under the leadership of Arnold J. Lehman, M.D., FDA scientists were regarded as the unquestioned world experts in the field of consumer product toxicology.

A comparable event occurred in the early 1970s. For decades, academic scientists had postulated methods of quantifying the risk of human exposure to carcinogens. In mid-1972, FDA for the first time learned that when diethylstilbestrol (DES) was administered to cattle to promote growth, residues of this carcinogen could be found in the meat supply even after a lengthy period of withdrawal. This produced a crisis in regulatory policy. It became clear that any carcinogen fed to a food-producing animal would ultimately be found in the resulting food at some level, if a sufficiently sensitive detection method became available. FDA debated how to proceed in light of this new information. Scientists in the FDA Bureau of Veterinary Medicine proposed the use of a specific method of quantitative risk assessment and carried the matter

forward for adoption by the agency. This was the first use of quantitative risk assessment by any government agency. Today, quantitative risk assessment has been adopted and is applied routinely throughout the world as the accepted method for evaluating carcinogenic risk. Once again, it was the work of dedicated FDA scientists that resulted in this extraordinary development.

FDA has long struggled with its identity as a "regulatory" or "law enforcement" agency, on the one hand, or as a "science" agency, on the other hand. This was crystallized in the famous exchange between FDA Commissioner Charles C. Edwards and Representative L. H. Fountain (D-NC) in 1970. Fountain contended that FDA is a regulatory agency. Edwards countered that it is a scientific agency with regulatory responsibilities. Fountain responded that it is a regulatory agency with scientific responsibility. Edwards tried to have the last word in calling it a scientific regulatory agency, but Fountain forced him to concede that it is first and foremost a regulatory agency. The debate continues to this day over the true role of science in the agency, and the extent to which scientific research by agency personnel should be limited to purely regulatory issues or should extend into broader areas of inquiry. This issue became more pronounced with the transfer to FDA of the Radiation Control for Safety and Health Act in 1971, the National Center for Toxicological Research in 1971, and the Biologics Act of 1902 in 1972. The role of science

TOP COURT CASES FOR FDA

FDA is almost always involved in litigation, and many court decisions over the years have had significant consequences for the course of FDA regulation. Here is a list of arbitrarily selected, major court decisions that have affected FDA:

United States v. Lexington Mill & Elevator (1914). Interpreting the 1906 Food and Drugs Act, the Supreme Court established the basic principle that the safety of a food that contains an added chemical is to be judged not by the chemical's toxicity in the abstract, but by the risk posed by the food itself. At the same time, the court held that to prove the food was adulterated, one need only demonstrate a possibility of harm.

United States v. Dotterweich (1943) and *United States v. Park* (1975). Both held that, to establish criminal liability, the government need not prove a defendant's intent to violate the law, nor even his knowledge of the specific violation, but only that he was responsible for the business at issue and had the power to stop the violation.

Weinberger v. Bentex Pharmaceuticals (1973). The Supreme Court upheld FDA's primary jurisdiction, i.e., its paramount authority to determine whether a product falls within its jurisdiction and whether it satisfies the requirements of the Food, Drug, and Cosmetic Act. This was one of four cases decided in the agency's favor on the same day, confirming the agency's implementation of the 1962 Drug Amendments.

Abbott Laboratories v. Gardner (1967). The Supreme Court rejected the government's argument that an FDA regulation could be judicially reviewed only when the agency sued to enforce it; but, in the process, the court laid the foundation under section 701(a) of the Act for FDA's authority to adopt regulations having the force of law.

National Ass'n. of Pharmaceutical Mfgrs. v. FDA (1981). This case squarely confronted and rejected claims that section 701(a) of the Act did not give FDA authority to adopt substantive regulations with the force of law, thus confirming the agency's most important power.

United States v. An Article of Drug... "Bacto-Unidisk" (1969). The court upheld FDA's expansive interpretation of the Act's "drug" definition to encompass an *in vitro* diagnostic product. The court's opinion firmly endorsed FDA's public health protection role and, in the process, prompted Congress to enact the 1976 Medical Device Amendments.

Kordel v. United States (1948). This case upheld FDA's broad interpretation of the Act's definition of "labeling" to include all printed materials displayed or distributed in association with a product and thus made effective its jurisdiction over product claims.

American Pharmaceutical Ass'n. v. Weinberger (1974). FDA cannot limit distribution of an approved drug to specific hospitals or pharmacies. The decision appeared to confirm that the agency could not interfere with the right of physicians to prescribe any drug FDA had found safe and effective. It led, indirectly, to Congress' authorization of broader restrictions over the distribution and use of medical devices.

United States v. Evers (1981). This decision confirmed the right of physicians to prescribe approved drugs "off label," i.e., for conditions other than those FDA has found safe and effective.

United States v. Rutherford (1979). The Supreme Court held that the Food, Drug, and Cosmetic Act requirements of safety and effectiveness apply to all drugs, and do not allow for exceptions for products marketed to persons suffering from fatal illnesses, such as cancer.

Thompson v. Western States (2002). The Supreme Court struck down, as inconsistent with the First Amendment's guarantee of free speech, FDA's restrictions on advertising by pharmacists who offer compounding services. The court thereby signaled its agreement with two lower courts that FDA's authority to regulate the content of product labels and product advertising was subject to constitutional constraints.

—Richard A. Merrill

FDA GOES INTERNET

Just as the Internet radically changed how we get information, it changed the way the public, the professions, and all others get information about FDA. Electronic access to FDA information began with the agency's electronic bulletin board service (BBS) in 1979. But it was taken to a much higher level in March 1995 with the launch of the FDA website, <www.fda.gov>.

The site began with just a handful of pages prepared by the Office of Public Affairs. We were thrilled to find that between 50 and 100 people accessed the site daily during its first weeks of operation. Soon every FDA center developed its own site and was linked to the FDA home page. (FDA's Center for Food Safety and Applied Nutrition actually had already launched a site of its own in December 1994.)

Now, eleven years later, the FDA website comprises more than half a million pages and forty databases. It attracts more than 150,000 people a day and some 2.5 million unique visitors every month. Visitors from 214 countries make use of the FDA site, and not only the ones you'd expect—such as Japan, China and Germany—but also people from places such as Iran, Cuba, Iraq, Vatican City, and North Korea. In all, more than a fourth of our visitors are from other countries.

The FDA website is the most comprehensive source of information about all of the agency's activities. There is information on product approvals, enforcement actions, recalls, counterterrorism, and much, much more. Moreover, the site is interactive. Visitors can:

• report adverse reactions and other problems with FDA-regulated products,

• report websites that may be selling prescription drugs or other medical products illegally,

• subscribe to FDA Consumer magazine or any of some twenty e-mail lists on various FDA topics,

• comment on proposed regulations, or

• ask questions or lodge complaints.

And, of course, the site is a major part of FDA's Centennial celebration, offering an online panorama of the agency's proud history (<www.fda.gov/centennial>). Moreover, the site has earned numerous awards, most recently from the World Wide Web Health Awards competition.

—William M. Rados

in each of these three areas was even stronger than in the traditional FDA areas of food, drugs, medical devices, and cosmetics. In the intervening decades, FDA sought to preserve the science base it had inherited in each of these three areas, while changing their focus to concentrate more directly on regulatory matters. It remains a delicate balance, and one that will continue to provoke strong feelings on both sides in the future.

Freedom of Information

The work of FDA before and after the enactment of the 1906 Act seldom raised issues of secrecy or openness. FDA was all too willing to publicize its investigations into the adulteration of food and drugs, both when it was pushing for national legislation and after the 1906 Act became law. Under the 1906 Act, FDA had neither records inspection nor premarket approval power. Thus, there were few, if any, documents reflecting industry trade secrets within the agency's files.

Following enactment of the 1938 Act, however, the situation changed dramatically. Recognizing that FDA would begin to accumulate industry trade secret information as a result of its new authority, Congress included a provision in the statute explicitly prohibiting FDA from releasing any of this information. FDA for many years took the position that none of the information contained in its files was required to be disclosed to the public, and that it could exercise discretion in deciding what documents would be released. Following enactment of the Freedom of Information Act in 1966, however, FDA was forced to change this approach. From the position of retaining virtually all records as confidential, FDA reversed itself and made most of its records available for public disclosure upon request.

The same issue was presented by the use of advisory committees. Initially, FDA allowed its advisory committees to conduct their deliberations behind closed doors. With enactment of the Federal Advisory Committee Act, this reversed. Since then it has been the rare exception when an FDA advisory committee conducted its deliberations in private. Private deliberation occurs only when trade secret information is involved. Nonetheless, the central issue of trade secrets remains.

FDA has grappled with this issue for the past quarter century, through promulgation of regulations and litigation, but many important issues remain unresolved. FDA must reconcile several competing statutory provisions, each reflecting a slightly different policy and using slightly different terminology. The agency must balance the right of citizens to see government records against the right of citizens to retain the confidentiality of trade secrets and other related business information that has substantial commercial value. Without question, this area will remain in the forefront of FDA controversies for many years to come.

Enforcement

Under the 1906 Act, any violation constituted a misdemeanor, punishable by fine, imprisonment, or both. Violative products were also subject to seizure. The 1938 Act expanded FDA's enforcement power. In addition to criminal liability and seizure, FDA was authorized to obtain a judicial injunction against any violation of the statute. FDA was also authorized to issue a written administrative notice or warning for minor violations in lieu of formal court proceedings, to conduct factory inspection, and to issue publicity and other public information.

Being dissatisfied with the enforcement powers specifically included within the 1938 Act, FDA sought to expand these powers both through administrative action and through new legislation. On the administrative level, FDA expanded its statutory authority to issue a suitable written notice or warning to include requests for recall and regulatory or warning letters for any type of statutory violation. It also adopted the policy of declining to conduct premarket approval of products when the applicant has been found to be in violation of the statute.

On the legislative level, FDA has sought new statutory authority both to make its job in implementing the statute easier and to impose additional penalties for violation. It has, for example, sought increased records inspection. Congress has granted this authority for prescription drugs, nonprescription drugs, and restricted medical devices but has denied it for all other FDA-regulated products. FDA has also sought authority to impose administrative orders requiring detention, recalls, civil penalties, and the production of documents under a subpoena. All but the last of these additional authorities were granted for medical devices only. Additionally, FDA has been granted administrative detention power specifically for meat, poultry, and eggs, but not for any other FDA-regulated products.

Debarment of companies and individuals and temporary denial or suspension of approval of abbreviated new drug applications were authorized in 1992 under the Generic Drug Enforcement Act of 1992. Legislation to grant broad new enforcement powers for all FDA-regulated products has been strongly opposed by the regulated industry.

Some states have been granted enforcement power that Congress has not provided for FDA. In particular, many states have administrative detention authority that allows state officials to "red tag" a product, thus preventing its movement or use for any purpose. FDA has on occasion requested a state to take such action while a federal seizure is being prepared. This represents an area where regulatory officials and the regulated industry have disagreed for a full century and are not likely to agree in the future. Everyone agrees that the law should be fully and fairly implemented, but that is where the matter ends. The regulated industry believes that existing FDA powers represent the strongest enforcement authority ever granted to an administrative agency. FDA believes that, if given greater administrative enforcement powers, it could implement the statute more efficiently and effectively.

FDA Enforcement Statistics

Activity	1939	1951	1963	1976	1989	1994	2003
Criminal prosecution	626	347	248	43	16	8	1
Seizure	1861	1341	1049	317	144	98	25
Injunction	0	4	30	39	13	16	22
Regulatory/warning letters	N.A.	N.A.	N.A.	982	370	1594	545
Recalls	0	54	101	837	2183	3236	4627
Factory inspections	N.A.	13,357	35,539	39,870	17,740	15,179	22,543
Import inspections	16,352	39,942	30,985	71,643	102,617	93,323	139,310
Samples	39,746	40,853	103,166	57,495	71,932	22,502	15,590
Personnel	565	1000	3210	6683	7395	9370	10,327
Appropriations/budget ($ millions)	2.226	5.467	29.065	201.805	487.344	934	1,381.08

Under the 1906 Act, FDA enforced the statute almost exclusively through seizure actions and criminal prosecution. Very few regulations or other forms of policy statement were issued. New law was made through court interpretation and informal policy statements issued as FIDs and SRAs, not through agency rulemaking. This pattern of enforcement continued under the 1938 Act, but was profoundly affected by changes in statutory authority and FDA policy. First, as the 1938 Act was amended to require premarket approval for regulated products, FDA enforced the statute informally through administrative decisions as part of the approval process rather than by formal court action. Second, as FDA realized that informal administrative sanctions, such as regulatory/warning letters and recall requests, were more efficient and effective, these informal actions also displaced formal court enforcement. Third, when FDA began to issue more and more of its policy in the form of regulations in the early 1970s, and later guidelines in the early 1990s, violations by industry substantially decreased and thus the need for either informal or formal enforcement was diminished. As a result of all of these developments, FDA enforcement statistics under the 1938 Act show an extraordinary shift from formal court action to informal administrative action.

Congress and FDA

The relation of any federal agency with Congress is tenuous. Congress has two functions with respect to a regulatory program. First, it creates the agency and authorizes the program. Second, it conducts oversight to determine any weakness or limitations and to recommend changes in both legislative and administrative policy. During the first half of its existence, FDA was subjected to relatively little oversight from congressional committees. Until the late 1950s, most congressional hearings were held to consider substantive legislation.

Beginning in the late 1950s, however, Congress turned its full attention to FDA. This time, Congress was primarily interested in oversight. Beginning with the hearings by Representative John A. Blatnick (D-MI) and Senator Estes Kefauver (D-TN) on the pharmaceutical industry in the late 1950s, Congress has spent five decades subjecting the daily work of FDA to detailed oversight scrutiny. Since 1960, there have been far more oversight hearings than legislative hearings regarding FDA. Virtually every aspect of the agency's work has been subjected to intense investigation. For the first two decades of these oversight hearings, on all but one occasion the hearing was conducted to criticize FDA for failing to take adequate regulatory action against a product the committee concluded was unlawful or for approval of a new product the committee thought was unsafe or ineffective. On only one occasion was FDA criticized for not approving a new drug with sufficient speed. On literally hundreds of other occasions the agency was subjected to withering criticism for failing to protect against unsafe and ineffective products.

This congressional criticism had a profound impact on FDA employees at all levels. Already risk averse by nature, they became even more conservative in implementing the FDA premarket approval authority. FDA Commissioner Alexander M. Schmidt summarized the situation as it appeared in 1974:

By far the greatest pressure that the Bureau of Drugs or the Food and Drug Administration receives with respect to the new drug approval process is brought to bear through Congressional hearings. In all of our history, we are unable to find one instance where a Congressional hearing investigated the failure of FDA to approve a new drug. The occasions on which hearings have been held to criticize approval of a new drug have been so frequent in the past ten years that we have not even attempted to count them.

At both the staff level and the managerial level, the message conveyed by this situation could not be clearer. Whenever a difficult or a controversial issue is resolved by approval, the Agency and the individuals involved will be publicly investigated. Whenever it is resolved by disapproval, no inquiry will be made. The congressional pressure for negative action is therefore intense, and ever increasing.

Although Commissioner Schmidt was speaking at perhaps the height of congressional scrutiny, intense critical oversight continued for the next decade.

Amelioration of congressional oversight began to occur only with the gradual unfolding of the AIDS crisis in the last half of the 1980s. Under intense pressure from AIDS activists themselves, Congress began to appreciate the need for prompt and decisive FDA action on important new drugs that are needed by desperately ill patients. This did not, however, blunt continuing criticism of lax FDA programs.

Following the Republican Revolution of November 1994, when the Republican Party regained control of the House and the Senate for the first time in forty years, the situation was reversed. For the forty years before 1994, Congress relentlessly criticized FDA for approving too many new products too quickly. For the two years following 1994, Congress criticized FDA for approving too few new products too slowly. This sea change in congressional approach caught the agency unaware and unprepared. As a consequence, FDA instituted a variety of administrative reforms to speed the premarket approval process and to reduce regulatory burdens on industry.

It is obvious that congressional investigations and hearings relating to FDA programs will change depending upon the political party in power. After such a long time during which Congress focused on the failure of FDA to adequately protect the public from harm, FDA was ill-prepared to respond to charges that the agency was failing to promote the public health by fostering the prompt availability of new products. As we end the first century of FDA, it is apparent that FDA must learn to strike a better balance between these two equally important objectives.

FDA in the World Community

Linda Horton

It is fair to say that the Food and Drug Administration in the United States has won tremendous consumer confidence which is the envy of the world.
—John Bruton

THE YEAR WAS 1997, the speaker the Prime Minister, the audience the Irish parliament when John Bruton reported on a meeting with FDA officials during a St. Patrick's Day trek to Washington. Reeling through the "mad cow crisis," government leaders in many countries were seeking FDA guidance about how to strengthen food safety and consumer confidence.

How did FDA become the international benchmark for science-based regulation, public health-oriented decision-making, transparency, industry responsibility, stakeholder involvement, enforcement, and rule of law? The Irish leader's consultation was not the first time officials abroad had examined the FDA model. Just as FDA in its first century came to be recognized in the United States as the premier domestic consumer protection agency, FDA enjoyed high stature internationally. From the beginning, international influences played a key role in shaping U.S. food and drug law and the agency itself.

Perhaps the most important international influence on U.S. food and drug law has been scientific collaboration. In the last quarter of the nineteenth century, our nation was still a scientific backwater. In a quest for greater knowledge, in 1878, Dr. Harvey Wiley embarked on a trip to Europe to study at leading universities. In his 1930 autobiography, Wiley recounted the influence of this trip on his decision to abandon plans to practice medicine and instead pursue efforts to detect and deter food adulteration. Wiley's studies in the laboratories of Vienna, Berlin, Bonn, Heidelberg, Leipzig, and London expanded his knowledge of analytical chemistry and gave him a network with other pioneers in the field.

After Wiley was appointed Chief Chemist of the Department of Agriculture (USDA) in 1883, he continued these international collaborations, returning to Europe in 1885 to collaborate with French, German, and British scientists and to observe Spanish sugar producers. While President of the American Chemical Society, Wiley organized the first World Congress of Chemists, held in 1892 in Chicago. In 1902 he sought advice from officials of the Imperial Board of Health in Berlin about how to conduct scientific experiments to ascertain the safety of food additives, a consultation that might have influenced his formation of the famous Poison Squad. A year after passage of the 1906 Pure Food and Drugs Act, he assisted the French government in modifying its food law. Two years later he attended an international applied chemistry congress where he addressed the Prince of Wales concerning the benefits of international cooperation.

A second early international influence on U.S. food and drug law involved legislative concepts. Not surprisingly, given our history, British law was a principal source of inspiration. The bedrock legal concepts of "adulteration" and "misbranding" had first appeared in late nineteenth century British legislation and in due course found their way into draft laws in Canada and the United States. In 1881 an Englishman, Professor G. W. Wigner, won $1,000 in a contest sponsored by a U.S. trade association for the best draft food law. Wigner's draft covered drugs as well as

food, an innovation that increased interest in a federal statute that addressed unsafe and fraudulent patent medicines, as well as food. Wiley said this "proposed law had a deep effect on subsequent legislation on the subject."

A third international influence on U.S. food and drug law was concern about the safety of imports, an issue that has carried over into the twenty-first century with enactment of laws such as the 2002 anti-bioterrorism law, the first major strengthening since 1938 of FDA's food authority. The earliest federal food and drug laws—the Drug Importation Act of 1848, the Tea Importation Acts of 1883 and 1897, the Food and Drug Importation Act of 1890, and the Food Importation Act of 1899—applied only to imports. Domestic producers were regulated by states or not at all.

The various import control laws stemmed from the view of some foreign exporters who saw the United States as a dumping ground for inferior products, deemed "good enough for America." An 1848 Congressional Committee Report said that America had "become the grand mart and receptacle of all the refuse merchandise ... not only from European

---

THE MOST IMPORTANT...

The FDA was the first agency in the world to attempt broad scientific review of foods and drugs, and its standards have remained the highest. It is the most known, watched, and imitated of regulatory bodies. Because of its influence outside the United States, it has also been described as the most important regulatory agency in the world.

—Philip J. Hilts, *Protecting America's Health: The FDA, Business, and One Hundred Years of Regulation* (2003).

warehouses but from the whole eastern world." Vast quantities of filthy, sub-potent, and fraudulent pharmaceutical ingredients had overwhelmed U.S. port authorities and undermined the health of soldiers fighting in the Mexican War. A year after the Drug Importation Act was passed, more than 90,000 pounds of inferior drugs were turned back from the Port of New York. Eventually, however, the 1848 drug import law was judged a complete failure. Problems were rampant corruption and statutory neglect of four key needs: an effective enforcement process, a cadre of honest

Inspector John Earnshaw inspected imported food products at the port of Baltimore, circa 1912.

and dedicated scientific and enforcement officials, meaningful standards for pharmaceutical acceptability, and coverage of all drugs, including domestic as well as imported products. The creation of the agency now known as FDA and enactment of the Pure Food and Drugs Act of 1906 began to address these needs.

The Drug Importation Act placed several European pharmacopoeias on the same plane as the U.S. Pharmacopeia (USP), founded in 1820. From 1848 until 1906, the definition of "drug" in federal law included not only products referenced in the USP but also ones listed in the pharmacopoeias of Edinburgh, London, France, and Germany. The 1906 Pure Food and Drugs Act referred only to the USP and the National Formulary. Thus, the provisions in the 1997 FDA Modernization Act (FDAMA) for harmonization of regulatory requirements and mutual recognition arrangements with Europeans had early statutory antecedents going back a century and a half.

The 1899 law that empowered the Bureau of Chemistry to stop imports of adulterated or misbranded foods and drugs

EUROPEAN LEADER ON FDA AND ICH

Fernand Sauer, the European Commission's public health director-general and one of the chief architects of the European drug regulatory system, has "always had a great respect for the capacity of the FDA to mobilize scientific debate." Mr. Sauer's dealings with FDA began in the late 1980s when the commission and FDA initiated bilateral meetings. At the time, Mr. Sauer was in charge of the commission's pharmaceuticals unit, and he met with FDA to figure out whether the European Community was about to become a "fortress Europe" that would saddle producers with Euro-specific requirements as extensive as, yet different from, those of FDA.

From Mr. Sauer's early discussions with Japanese leaders, with FDA officials Elaine Esber, Stuart Nightingale, Carl Peck, and Roger Williams, and with industry representatives, there arose a tripartite commitment to work together toward uniform global standards for drug testing. The International Conference for the Harmonization of the Technical Requirements for the Registration of Pharmaceuticals for Human Use (ICH) was formally inaugurated in 1990.

According to Mr. Sauer, ICH achieved a "spectacular success, given the investment put in, by the end of the 1990s." He believes that "international harmonization should be a by-product of what [regulatory officials] do anyway, not a distinctive activity ... [or an] international diplomatic activity." Furthermore, "since the WHO didn't exercise this function, we offered it to WHO as a contribution of the three main regions where pharmaceutical research is done." The biennial conference to announce progress was "deliberately a public event, with 1,200 delegates to the 1990 conference" and multiples of this number at later ICH biennial conferences.

Industry was at the ICH table from the beginning "to get the best experts" and avoid the "danger that regulators would undertake pet projects that aren't relevant" to product development, according to Mr. Sauer, However, the public interest is paramount, he said, as government representatives from FDA, European authorities, and the Japanese health ministry have controlled the agenda and have taken responsibility for adopting ICH guidelines into their own regulatory systems.

Mr. Sauer said most FDA participants enjoyed their ICH assignment—it added interest and an additional purpose to their work. Also, he believes that the agency gave a lot of recognition to FDA experts who contributed to ICH. Originally they had feared that harmonization meant lowering standards, while the

led it to establish the first district offices and field laboratories to police food and drug imports. Experience gained under this law equipped the bureau for its duties under the 1906 Act. Also in the 1890s, a sister unit in the USDA, the Bureau of Animal Industries—predecessor to today's Food Safety Inspection Service—was authorized to inspect meat imports and exports. Beginning in 1879, the notoriously poor quality of U.S. meat, often infected with trichinae, led other countries to ban U.S. meat. The early export and import control laws must not have been

working, because Upton Sinclair's famous account of disgusting conditions in the U.S. meat-packing industry helped propel into law both the languishing Pure Food and Drugs Act and a meat inspection law covering products for U.S. consumption as well as exports. Both laws were signed on June 30, 1906. The debate leading up to passage of the 1906 Food and Drugs Act included heated arguments—heard again when Congress debated export laws in 1976, 1986, and 1996—as to whether U.S. exports should be required to meet U.S. standards. The 1906 decision was

drug industry feared the opposite. However, the rigorous but sensible ICH output, at a high level of scientific quality, ultimately won over most skeptics, he said.

For Europe, he said, "we had to adjust the regulatory guidance anyway," and ICH "provided the chance to get the best advice from outside" on how this might best be done. "Since each member state had to change its ways, why not do it in harmony with the U.S. and Japan?" Mr. Sauer also credits ICH—and the opportunity it afforded to work with FDA on scientific matters—with helping to pave the way for the intensified technical cooperation effort demanded of European member country experts when the European Medicines Agency (EMEA) began operations in 1995. Despite cooperation since 1975 among European Community experts through a group known as the Committee on Proprietary Medicinal Products, "in the 1986–93 time period, we were not sure we could actually create the EMEA," and ICH helped prove what could be done, he said.

Asked whether FDA and the EMEA are competitors, Sauer said, "The competition was always in a friendly way, not confrontational, and not with the view that anyone had failed." With ICH, the EMEA, and now the new Japanese Pharmaceutical and Medical Devices Agency, FDA is no longer the sole reference point, although he hastened to add that "FDA is still the benchmark."

Fernand Sauer perhaps is a modern European Harvey Washington Wiley. In addition to the key role he played in ICH's birth, Mr. Sauer was chief architect of the EMEA and served as its first Executive Director from 1994 to 2000. He then moved to head the European Community's burgeoning public health responsibilities and was responsible for establishment of the European Centre for Disease Prevention and Control (ECDC). Quite naturally, the ECDC works closely with its larger and older U.S. counterpart.

Looking back on his involvement with FDA, Mr. Sauer said, "What I recollect best are the people in FDA, people who were ready to do things. We always found solutions, and there was always a lot of good will."

Interviewed by Linda Horton
in Brussels, May 17, 2005

that compliance with receiving country requirements would suffice.

In later years, international influences seem to have become less important for a time than they had been during Wiley's era and again at the end of the twentieth century. FDA annual reports recount more or less constant frustration with non-compliant imports during the era in which several of the first international inspections occurred. In 1910 FDA sent an investigator to learn why so many Turkish figs were contaminated with insects and worms. This episode and the efforts that followed may have been the Bureau of Chemistry's first technical assistance project, carried out in parallel with efforts to raise standards in California's fledgling fig industry.

International issues played no discernible role in the enactment of the Federal Food, Drug, and Cosmetic Act of 1938. However, like other U.S. institutions, FDA was

WHEN THE CALL OF DUTY DEMANDS TOO MUCH

I will never forget the morning of Thursday, January 11, 1990, the day that marks the only time FDA employees have lost their lives in the line of duty. Arvin Shroff, Deputy Director of the Office of Enforcement, Office of Regulatory Affairs, walked into my office and told me that the plane carrying my colleague and friend, Jack Harty, and another colleague, Pat Pouzar, was missing. I was the Deputy Director of the International Affairs Staff at the time and Jack was the Director. I immediately wanted to know everything about the situation, and I informed the staff. Needless to say, not much work got done the rest of the day.

During the previous year, an anonymous call to the agency reported that grapes contaminated with cyanide were being shipped from Chile to the United States. After FDA laboratories detected cyanide in grapes at the port in Philadelphia, FDA acted quickly to protect the public health, detaining shipments of all fruit from Chile. Of course, there were tremendous ramifications for the fruit industry in Chile, as consumers became wary of fruit from Chile. The Chilean government responded by trying to ensure that their product was indeed safe and sought FDA's blessing of the process and the security mechanisms they had put in place.

During 1989, John F. Harty, Jr., Director of the International Affairs Staff, Office of Health Affairs, had been an integral part of the negotiations, which culminated in a formal memorandum of understanding between FDA and the Agriculture and Livestock Service of the Ministry of Agriculture of Chile. The government of Chile invited FDA to send a team to Chile to review the procedures it had put in place to ensure the safety of fruit exported to the United States. In response, Jack Harty, FDA's resident diplomat and former investigator, and Pat Pouzar, an accomplished investigator and Acting Director of the Nashville District Office, scheduled a visit.

During the trip to Chile, the FDA team visited several sites that processed fruit for export. To accomplish their mission in an efficient manner, they traveled to at least one site on a small aircraft. Tragically, during their return flight to Santiago, the plane crashed into a mountainside. During the hours and days that passed from the time we learned that the plane was missing until we got word on Saturday night that the wreckage had been found, many dedicated colleagues and friends worked tirelessly to bring the necessary resources to bear on the situation. The Director of the Office of International Health in the Department of Health and Human Services, Linda Vogel, made her office available as a command center for communications with anyone we could think of, including the Secretary of Defense, to make search and rescue aircraft available.

I cannot fully describe the feelings among us in Linda's office that night as we eagerly awaited a call from the Defense Department. Instead, the call came from the State Department to say that the crashed plane had been found and that there were no survivors.

affected by wars. Wartime considerations reportedly influenced the 1940 decision of President Roosevelt to leave the meat inspection program with USDA when he transferred FDA to the new Federal Security Agency, predecessor to today's Department of Health and Human Services. Beef industry interests had argued that, with the war already underway, it was no time to change regulation of a key export commodity needed for the allied effort. On the drug side, supplies of many products were interrupted at the very time demand increased, and the head of the Pharmaceutical Manufacturers Association (now PhRMA) once said that World War II forced the maturation of the U.S. industry. The military's need for reliable supplies of penicillin led to the passage of special legislation to establish a product testing and certification program for this product and later for others.

Both Pat and Jack had long and distinguished careers with FDA—Pat joined the agency in 1964, and Jack in 1965. Both had received several awards, including the FDA Commendable Service Award. They both received the FDA Award of Merit in 1989 "for outstanding dedication and personal sacrifice in conducting foreign inspections to assure the safety of fruit exported to the United States."

The dedication of Jack and Pat to the FDA, their community, and their families was unsurpassed. Attesting the recognition of their contributions to the protection and promotion of the public health of the citizens of the United States, more than 600 persons—including Louis W. Sullivan, M.D., Secretary of the Department of Health and Human Services (DHHS); James O. Mason, M.D., Assistant Secretary for Health; Frank E. Young, M.D., Ph. D., Deputy Assistant Secretary for Health/Science and the Environment; James Benson, Acting Commissioner of Food and Drugs; the Honorable Octavio Errazuiz, Republic of Chile Ambassador to the United States; and Senator Paul Sarbanes of Maryland—attended the joint memorial service in their honor. During the service, Dr. Sullivan presented to both wives the Secretary's Recognition Award "for stalwart, stellar service to all of mankind." Also, during the service, Sen. Sarbanes stated, quoting from Paul Volcker, former head of the National Commission on the Public Service:

> Show me a nation with a mediocre public service and I will show you a mediocre nation. America is not a mediocre nation, and one of the reasons it isn't is because it's been blessed with men like Jack Harty and Pat Pouzar, and women also, who have followed the same high standards and made this a nation of quality and of leadership.

Ambassador Errazuriz, quoting a Chilean poet, ended his remarks saying, "Life is given to us to look for God, death to find Him, eternity to possess Him. Jack and Pat are with God."

Among the many letters of condolences that were received from friends, colleagues, and dignitaries from around the world was a letter from the President of the United States, George Bush, to Mrs. John Harty and Mrs. Patrick Pouzar. The President's letter read in part, "Your husband(s) ... built a distinguished record of public service. (Their) contributions to the Food and Drug Administration will serve as an inspiration to those who will continue (their) important work."

As a testament to the enduring memory of Jack and Pat in the minds of their FDA colleagues, two permanent memorials have been established. The John F. Harty, Jr. Memorial Library was dedicated on October 16, 1992 in the New England District Office where Jack started his FDA career. The Patrick J. Pouzar Investigator of the Year Award is presented annually to FDA's top field investigator.

—Walter M. Batts

After World War II, considerable food and drug production capacity had been destroyed, not only in Germany, Italy, and Japan, but also in occupied countries such as Belgium, France, the Netherlands, Scandinavian countries, and China. Inferior products from war-torn countries that were trying to rebuild production and exports taxed the inadequate import screening resources of FDA. The agency did not simply reject the substandard goods, but it also provided considerable technical assistance to producers in other countries to help them overcome safety and compliance problems.

The birth of the United Nations and its specialized bodies after World War II set the stage for FDA's participation in activities of the World Health Organization (WHO) and the Food and Agriculture Organization of the United Nations (FAO). The last half of the twentieth century saw the re-emergence of U.S. international leadership in new forums involved in setting standards for food, drugs, medical devices, and animal health products. FDA officials participated in a wide range of harmonization programs, collaborations with counterparts in other countries, and enforcement efforts at the U.S. border and in foreign production sites, to assure safety of imports.

For food, important events were the establishment in 1956 of the WHO-FAO Joint Expert Committee on Food Additives (JECFA) and in 1962 of the United Nations Food Standards Programme, also known as the Codex Alimentarius Commission. FDA Deputy Commissioner John L. Harvey served as Codex Chairman its first four years, a leadership role reprised in 1999–2004 by Thomas Billy, a senior U.S. food safety official. The creation in 1995 of the World Trade Organization (WTO) reinforced the role of Codex, as a WTO agreement made Codex the reference body for food safety standards. At the century's end, FDA officials were participating in trade negotiations, WTO committee meetings, and even trade disputes on topics like hormones in beef and genetically modified crops. For pharmaceuticals, the key organizations have been WHO and the International Conference for the Harmonization of the Technical Requirements for Pharmaceuticals for Human Use (ICH).

Since the founding of WHO in 1948, U.S. biologics and drug officials have played major roles in the establishment of international standards for vaccines, multi-source drugs, and current good manufacturing practices (GMPs). In 1982, FDA spearheaded the formation of the WHO International Conference of Drug Regulatory Authorities (ICDRA) with an inaugural meeting in Annapolis. ICDRA meets biennially. The ICH has represented a highly successful effort to harmonize requirements for drugs and biologics among the principal producing regions. Informal discussions about the concept between Fernand Sauer of the European Commission and Elaine Esber of FDA— during the 1989 ICDRA in Paris—and then with the International Federation of Pharmaceutical Manufacturers Associations (IFPMA) led to this unique regulatory-industry initiative, launched in 1990. Participants are representatives of FDA, European and Japanese regulatory agencies, and industry associations of Europe, Japan, and the United States. Harmonization of regulatory requirements had been pioneered by the European Community, but would have done little good without participation by U.S. and Japanese authorities and industry.

For animal drugs, USDA and FDA have participated actively in work of the Office International des Epizooties (OIE), an international organization of veterinary officials aimed at achieving protection of animal health. OIE serves as the secretariat for the Veterinary International Cooperation on Harmonization (VICH), launched in 1996. In addition, the Codex Committee on Residues of Veterinary Drugs in Foods is chaired by the Director of the Center for Veterinary Medicine of FDA.

For medical devices, FDA was a founding member of the Global Harmonization Task Force (GHTF). Formed in 1992, GHTF is an international partnership of device regulatory authorities and the regulated industry aimed at achieving harmonization in medical device regulatory practices. When FDA chaired the organization in 1999, it created the website (www.ghtf.org) and drafted the procedures for adopting standards and broadening GHTF beyond the five founders (Australia, Canada, Europe, Japan, and the United States). FDA officials also have been leaders in fledgling medical device harmonization efforts in the WHO

and Pan American Health Organization, as well as in voluntary consensus standards for medical devices, on such topics as biomaterials standards and the global quality system standard.

Recognition of FDA as the "gold standard" for product approval decisions probably stems from the agency's refusal to approve the drug thalidomide as a sedative, a watershed event that raised FDA's profile internationally while leading to new laws in the United States, Europe, and other countries to strengthen drug regulation. First marketed in West Germany in 1957, thalidomide sales by 1960 had skyrocketed and the product was also on the market in Great Britain, Canada, Portugal, and other countries. The fact that the product was never marketed in the United States, thanks to the heroic efforts of FDA reviewer Frances Kelsey, raised FDA's international stature as a regulatory body.

At FDA approached its 100th anniversary, the agency had become a model for other countries' national legislation. As noted by journalist Philip Hilts, when President Theodore Roosevelt signed into law the Pure Food and Drugs Act, what was groundbreaking about this legislation on an international level was not the law itself, but the institution that, with its enactment, became the world's foremost consumer protection agency. Hilts writes:

Other nations had long since passed laws to control deceptive and adulterated commerce, but the American law was unique in that it didn't just make nasty business practices illegal [but also] established a scientific agency, a small body of researchers and inspectors led by the chief chemist, to report on and, in a limited way, police the dark part of commerce in food and drugs.

Thus, the unique contribution FDA has made to the world is the notion of a public health-oriented, science-based, law-enforcement agency. And if broadly speaking, the United States in the late nineteenth century was a net importer of ideas from other countries about how to regulate food and drugs, a century later it clearly had become a net exporter of regulatory ideas, including the very idea of a national food and drug agency.

Several countries—including the Philippines, Thailand, and China— actually have agencies named "FDA." In the early 1990s, FDA helped the Russian government develop pharmaceutical, food safety, and medical device legislation. After the mad cow crisis, FDA was consulted on the drafting of European laws. By the early twenty-first century, all principal national regulatory agencies in Europe, Japan, Canada, and Australia were following the FDA model of regulation of pharmaceuticals, medical devices, and biological products (including tissue and cell products)—although rarely with food— in a single medical product agency.

By the time FDA's second century had begun, the agency's regulatory policies, food safety regulations, drug and medical device premarket reviews, and inspection techniques were viewed widely as the gold standard, and www.fda.gov became a frequently-visited website. FDA's status as a world-renowned consumer protection agency did not happen overnight but was the result of more than a century of international exchange of ideas, information, and expertise with citizens of other countries struggling to solve the same problems that we have faced in the United States.

The remarkable Dr. Wiley, in his 1909 address to the Prince of Wales in Albert Hall, at the International Congress of Applied Chemistry, said:

There are no means of bringing nations to a better understanding of their mutual hopes and endeavors, no better ways of preserving international peace and amity, than by gathering the fruits of science, borne by its application to all industries.... [D]elegates from all countries of the world... have come to be mutually helpful in the work we are trying to do for the benefit of man. Our purpose is to soften, if possible, the hardships of the poor, to lighten, to some extent, the task of labor by making it more fruitful, to prevent sickness and promote health, to prevent crime and punish wrong-doing, and to eliminate from commerce every species of fraud and misrepresentation.

FDA and 9/11

No one was prepared for the events of September 11, 2001, when two hijacked airliners crashed into the World Trade Center, a third plane crashed into the Pentagon, and a fourth plane thought to be headed for another target in Washington, D.C., crashed into a field in Pennsylvania.

The events of that day not only changed the United States forever, they also changed the FDA.

Virtually everyone at the FDA on that day agrees that the agency, while accustomed to managing disasters and crises, was not prepared for events of the magnitude of what occurred. More than 3,000 innocent people died on U.S. soil that morning.

The agency moved quickly to do what it could: assure that blood could be collected quickly from people living near the disaster sites to help the injured survivors, and assure that safe and effective drugs were available.

The broader challenge for the agency was to see that products, systems, and programs were in place in the event another attack ever occurred.

According to a report in *FDA Consumer* magazine, FDA took action across all of its regulatory responsibilities to assure that the nation would be better prepared for future attacks:

Food: After September 11, FDA conducted food supply vulnerability assessments. FDA issued guidance documents on security measures that the food industry can take to minimize the risk that food will be subject to tampering or other criminal actions.

FDA worked with other federal and state agencies on the Electronic Laboratory Exchange Network, the first integrated, web-based data exchange system for sharing food testing information. It allows multiple agencies engaged in food safety activities to compare and coordinate findings of laboratory analyses.

FDA also has worked closely with other agencies to establish the Food Emergency Response Network — a national network of laboratories ready to respond to a food security emergency.

Imports: The FDA enhanced its efforts to ensure the safety of the nearly six million food shipments that arrive in the United States each year. With additional funding for counterterrorism, FDA hired more than 655 new field inspectors to monitor imports. The addition of these field employees resulted in increased surveillance of imported foods and enhanced laboratory analysis capacity.

The number of ports with an FDA presence more than doubled, from about forty ports in 2001 to about ninety ports by the end of 2002. In addition, the agency increased by more than six-fold the number of food import exams conducted at the border, from 12,000 in fiscal year 2001 to more than 78,000 in fiscal year 2003. The agency also updated its labs to handle the increased number of food samples that may be contaminated by terrorism.

Four Major Regulations: Under the Public Health Security and Bioterrorism Preparedness and Response Act of 2002, FDA developed four new regulations:

1. Registration of food facilities. This regulation requires owners and operators of foreign or domestic food facilities that manufacture or process, pack, or hold food for human or animal consumption in the United States to submit information to the agency about the facility and emergency contacts.

2. Prior notification of imported food shipments. This regulation requires the FDA to receive prior notice of imported food shipments before the food arrives at a U.S. port.

3. Establishment and maintenance of records. Manufacturers, processors, packers, importers, and others are required to keep records that identify the source from which they receive food and where they send it.

4. Administrative detention. The agency gained new authority to detain any food for up to thirty days for which there is credible evidence that the food poses a serious threat to humans or animals.

Drugs: Under a new regulation known as "the animal efficacy rule," FDA can approve medical treatments against terrorist agents based on effectiveness data from animal studies when human studies are unethical and not feasible. Studies demonstrating the safety of the new product in humans are still required.

FDA published a guidance for using medical countermeasures in special groups such as the first responders in an emergency, people in the military, people who live near nuclear facilities, pregnant women, children, and people with compromised immune systems.

FDA also approved a number of drugs intended for use during a national emergency. For example, in January 2002, FDA approved atropine/pralidoxime autoinjector to treat nerve gas intoxication. And in June 2003, new dosage forms of AtroPen (atropine) autoinjectors were approved for use in children and adolescents exposed to nerve agents.

In two instances, FDA located the data on its own, and then called for manufacturers to submit applications. The first example is Prussian blue, a substance that has been used as a pigment for artists since 1704. The substance can treat people exposed to radioactive cesium or radioactive and non-radioactive thallium. Radioactive cesium could be used in a "dirty bomb" or other terror device. On October 2, 2003, this application was approved, giving the nation the first drug that can be used as a medical countermeasure to the threat of radioactive cesium.

The FDA also determined conditions under which pentetate calcium trisodium and pentetate zinc sodium are safe and effective for treating certain kinds of radiation exposure. The agency then encouraged submission of new drug applications for these products. Ca-DTPA and Zn-DTPA are usually given intravenously, and have been used as investigational drugs for forty years.

FDA's focus on countering terrorism continued as it approached its centennial year. In mid-December 2005, FDA issued a final order reaffirming previous conclusions that the anthrax vaccine BioThrax prevents anthrax

resulting from any route of exposure, including inhalation anthrax. As a consequence of FDA's announcement, the Department of Defense continued its policy of vaccinating servicemembers against anthrax.

"The threat of anthrax as a weapon remains real. It is very important to provide our servicemembers with maximum protection against this threat, particularly when operating in certain areas of the world," a Defense Department statement said.

As we enter FDA's centennial year, it is impossible to predict the extent to which the United States and other countries will be vulnerable to terrorist attacks, and what form they will take. In a similar vein, no one can predict how extensive future natural disasters will take place—in the last weeks of August 2005, Hurricane Katrina devastated the U.S. Gulf Coast. The FDA responded to this hurricane to assure that affected residents had safe foods and effective medical supplies.

Whatever the cause of the disaster, it is clear that 9/11/01 and its aftermath enabled FDA to gain new capabilities to protect the public from disaster, whether from terrorists or from natural causes.

—Wayne L. Pines

131

How 9/11/01 Changed FDA

"The world will never be the same again," a senior FDA security expert stated flatly as we began the Commissioner's morning meeting on Wednesday, September 12, 2001. He was right. Struggling to deal with the personal implications of the horror of the day before, FDA's leadership confronted a host of unprecedented problems as we gathered around the Commissioner's conference table.

How much things were changing was immediately clear when somber security guards—wielding flashlights and mirrors on long sticks, designed to inspect the undersides of vehicles for bombs—greeted me as I drove up to the Parklawn Building. Then, before the meeting began, another FDA executive had been distributing blue lanyards inscribed "FDA Emergency Operations," so we could wear our FDA identification in plain sight.

The era of increased security measures had begun for many FDA employees the day before. Even though the Parklawn and other FDA buildings had been closed after the attacks, a host of FDA employees worked throughout that interminable day. Some worked to create an emergency blood-release system so that newly donated blood could be used—with no civilian air traffic, there was no way to send samples of donated blood to testing laboratories. Others worked to help get the Air Force to fly from California skin-grafting materials to be available to treat burn victims at the Pentagon.

The unprecedented catastrophe of September 11 attacks immediately transformed everyone's work rhythms, and at the same time they were dealing with their own feelings of loss, vulnerability, and anger. But FDA employees returning to work on September 12 also faced a new set of challenges—taking stock of our capacity to deal with unknown threats. What vaccines were available or being developed to protect against likely biological agents? What countermeasures were available or needed to be developed to treat victims of such agents as anthrax or smallpox? What biological agents were the most likely to be used in an attack on the nation's food supply, and how could those agents be delivered?

Acting Principal Deputy Commissioner Dr. Bern Schwetz, Secretary of Health and Human Services (HHS) Tommy G. Thompson, and much of the Executive Branch set up new procedures to deal with the attacks' aftermath. Dr. Schwetz, who had manned his post in the Parklawn Building throughout the day of the attacks, began participating the next day in the HHS Secretary's early morning daily conference call to plot the department's responses to the post-9/11 world. Soon, he began holding weekly calls, lasting

ninety minutes or longer, with center directors and executives in the Commissioner's office. These calls, which continued throughout the year, allowed Dr. Schwetz to direct FDA's responses effectively and provided an essential forum for the intra-agency cooperation needed for FDA's coordinated response to the attacks. We discussed everything from the status of HHS contracts for new vaccines, to how to get the word out on administering potassium iodide to children in the wake of an attack on a nuclear power plant or detonation of a dirty bomb containing radioactive material. From September 12 on, FDA employees were being called upon to think about the unthinkable—and to do it every day.

In my own case, as head of FDA's Public Affairs Office, I was handling daily requests for interviews on such topics as protecting the food supply from terrorist attacks, developing countermeasures against biological agents, and (for a few days) whether FDA employees had been exposed to anthrax while handling mail. Anthrax had become more than a theoretical concern for Americans shortly after September 11, when an unknown agent sent letters containing anthrax spores to U.S. Senators and TV news anchors. In addition to creating national concern, the two waves of anthrax mailings involved FDA directly. The Center for Devices and Radiological Health has jurisdiction over tests for screening and confirming the presence of anthrax spores.

Moreover, in a finding that brought the anthrax scare literally to FDA's doorstep, preliminary tests of mail sent in October to Federal Office Building 8 (FOB-8) in southwest Washington, D.C., then the home of the Center for Food Safety and Applied Research (CFSAN), indicated the presence of anthrax. Joseph Levitt, director of CFSAN at that time, held several daily all-hands meetings to keep employees of FOB-8 informed. I have particularly vivid memories of Halloween 2001, the day Dr. Schwetz asked me to draft two versions of an all-hands memo on anthrax in mail sent to FOB-8. The memo would be e-mailed to FDA employees the next day, when confirmatory test results were expected. Fortunately, when the results came back, Dr. Schwetz was able to send the version informing FDA employees that no anthrax had been found in the suspicious FOB-8 letters.

The attacks of September 11 brought other changes, too. In their wake came an atmosphere of unprecedented intensity, more so than ever before, a time when all FDA programs worked more closely with our colleagues at HHS, in greater collaboration and with a single purpose. One HHS team focused on developing a new generation of vaccines against such agents as smallpox and anthrax, drawing heavily on people from the Center for Biologics Evaluation and Research. CFSAN's food security experts engaged extensively and directly with executives from HHS and from Homeland Security on protecting the food supply from terrorist threats. All FDA centers were closely involved in these counterterrorism efforts. Although these efforts deserved the attention they received, they also drew energy and talent away from FDA's more traditional public health work, which itself was increasing.

September 11 brought another legacy: an enormous increase in FDA's already formidable public health responsibilities. For a time, at least, resources grew along with those responsibilities. With the strong support of Secretary Thompson, FDA obtained additional resources that allowed its Office of Regulatory Affairs to hire nearly 700 new employees, many of whom would be deployed to ports of entry, the front lines of new efforts to protect the United States from terrorism. But to many FDA employees—who were reviewing applications, inspecting facilities, or developing a comprehensive set of new measures designed to safeguard the food supply—they simply felt that they were being spread even thinner.

And yet, FDA employees have a century-old tradition of rising to whatever it takes to protect the public's health. That tradition is the key to what, for FDA, is perhaps the most lasting effect of the September 11 tragedy: FDA's continued and expert dedication to fulfill their mission of protecting America's public health. Once again, FDA employees demonstrated their ability to get the job done, in even the most difficult, stressful situations. It is a legacy of which all FDA staff members and leadership, and everyone with an interest in FDA's fortunes, can be justly proud.

—**Lawrence Bachorik**

This is the frontispiece of the popular Puck Magazine from 1884. It marks the beginning of the "pure food" movement in American history in which state chemists and eventually federal chemists in the Bureau of Chemistry began testing all manners of foodstuffs then on the market to see what was really in them.   In some cases, they found less adulteration than had been alleged, and in other cases, they found more. The bib around the chemist's neck signifies the fact that he who tested the food also ate the food being tested. In short, chemists were consumers too.

Keeping America's Food Supply Safe

Joseph A. Levitt

FDA's OVERSIGHT OF THE U.S. FOOD SUPPLY touches every single American, every single day of our lives. This is because we all have to eat, and each day we all eat some kind of food FDA regulates. The breadth of FDA's responsibility is enormous—seafood, fresh fruits and vegetables, milk and dairy products, baby food and infant formula, shell eggs, frozen food, canned food, packaged food, snack food, juice, soft drinks, and more—literally everything in the supermarket except meat, poultry, and processed (liquid) egg products. This constitutes eighty percent of the American food supply.

Like so much of our society, the food supply has gone through incredible change over the past century, since the 1906 enactment of the Pure Food and Drugs Act. There have been changes in technology that make food safer, such as pasteurization of milk. There have been changes in food-testing methods that allow scientists to find chemicals in foods at ever smaller amounts. There have been changes in manufacturing and transport, so that food once purchased locally may now come from anywhere in the world. And there have been changes in availability of food, so that a country once having millions of people who were malnourished now has millions who are overweight or even obese. During the century in which the federal government has regulated food, several themes have recurred: the emergence of new threats, the role of science and law in combating those threats, and the importance of FDA's public credibility.

Great Britain passed its first national food law in 1860, but even before the 1906 Act was passed, food law in the United States was strictly an area of state regulation. Early federal interest was centered in the U.S. Department of Agriculture (USDA), which hired its first chemist in 1862. This was the beginning of the Bureau of Chemistry, the predecessor of the Food and Drug Administration. In 1880, Peter Collier, who was Chief Chemist in the Bureau of Chemistry, first recommended passage of a national food and drug law. The bill was defeated, but during the next twenty-five years, more than 100 food and drug bills were introduced in Congress. With the benefit of this substantial legislative history, when Upton Sinclair published *The Jungle* in 1906, Congress swiftly passed the Pure Food and Drugs Act of 1906. Dr. Harvey W. Wiley led the fight, and it is fitting that the current home of the FDA's Center for Food Safety and Applied in College Park, Maryland, which opened in 2001, is named the Harvey W. Wiley Federal Building.

The food provisions of the 1906 Act were based on two central concepts: adulteration and misbranding. "Adulteration" refers to something being wrong with the food product itself, usually raising a health concern. The food might be decomposed, produced under unsanitary conditions, the product of a diseased animal, or otherwise unfit for consumption. Adulteration could also involve substituting an inferior ingredient, referred to as "economic adulteration." By contrast, "misbranding" concerns how a food product is labeled or otherwise represented for sale. The key to misbranding is that the label or labeling (extensions of the product's label) must be truthful and not misleading to consumers. These twin concepts of adulteration and misbranding carry through until this day.

Although the 1906 legislation was broad in scope, it limited the government's role to being an after-the-fact "policeman" of the marketplace. The law was premised on the belief that food, having been grown, sold, and consumed for thousands of years, was reasonably safe and that the food industry (meat-packers aside) did a reasonably good job. The law made a critical assumption that it should be the food industry's primary responsibility to produce safe and honestly labeled food (i.e., food that was not adulterated or misbranded). It was the government's

FDA Inspector John Earnshaw inspecting a milk bottling operation, 1912.

job, under this paradigm, to oversee and police industry behavior, stepping in when problems arose. This legislative framework set the course of food regulation for a century, in marked contrast to the framework Congress developed at the same time for the meat industry in the Meat Inspection Act of 1906. That legislation called for "continuous" oversight of the meat-packing industry (later extended to the poultry industry), and to this day there is a USDA inspector every day in every slaughterhouse meat processing facility (engaged in interstate commerce) in the country. The USDA inspector oversees industry practices in "real time" and provides a USDA seal to authorize sale.

While the emphasis and concern in 1906 focused more on meat than other food products, it was not very long before food safety scares concerning products regulated by the Bureau of Chemistry came within the public view. In fact, in 1919, two such scares occurred: arsenic poisoning and botulism. In the early twentieth century, arsenic was routinely used as a pesticide. Most of the time, this did not threaten human health because the spraying was done long before picking. In 1915, the Bureau of Chemistry conducted experiments showing that the amount of arsenic that typically remained on fruits and vegetables was innocuous. Yet in 1919, a bureau inspector found arsenic all over pears being sold at a fruit stand in Boston. The bureau reacted quickly: Fruit in storage and on trees was surveyed and tested, shipments from suspected orchards

were reported, and the contaminated barrels were either shipped back for washing or condemned.

The arsenic problem was magnified in 1925, when almost all of Florida's celery crop was embargoed, and again when apples from the Pacific Northwest were embargoed. The affected producers met embargoes of their arsenic-laden produce with hostility. As a result of the apple embargo, one large grower sued the government for taking his property without proving any harm to the public. The government was persuasive in making its case for public health and safety and won the lawsuit. Although it is unclear whether anyone actually suffered from arsenic poisoning as a result

The 1906 Act contained a so-called "distinctive name proviso" which allowed substandard food products access to the marketplace. As the nation's economy spiraled downwards during the Great Depression, such products became increasingly confusing to consumers because, beautifully packaged and widely marketed, they were difficult to distinguish from high-quality products. Salad Bouquet, a diluted vinegar, was labeled "for use like vinegar;" Peanut Spred had fewer peanuts than peanut butter; and Bred Spread was nothing like traditional strawberry jam, consisting only of pectin, artificial colors and flavors, with a few hayseeds thrown in to resemble strawberry seeds. Regulators at all levels rushed into court to protest the deceptive product. The 1938 Food, Drug, and Cosmetic Act helped to correct many of these abuses by providing for the establishment of food standards "in the interests of consumers" and forcing substandard products to call themselves "imitation" on their labels.

of the use of arsenic as a pesticide, the threat was perceived as being real. The bureau's involvement with arsenic began as a responsive action, but soon turned into a preventive one as well, as the bureau launched an intense campaign to get growers to clean their produce before sending it to market. Thus, the government helped minimize the risk whenever arsenic was used as a pesticide. This theme of turning a particular food safety incident into a springboard for improving industry-wide practices is one that would become deeply embedded in FDA's culture over the next century.

The second food scare of 1919 was far more deadly. In 1919 and 1920, dozens of people died from botulism after eating ripe olives. Many of the early incidents of botulism had resulted from home-canned vegetables, but the olives of the 1919–1920 scare had been commercially manufactured, thus jeopardizing the

lives of many more people. There was a cascading effect as incidents occurred first in Ohio (killing six people), then in Michigan, then again in Tennessee. The Bureau of Chemistry launched an investigation and traced the olives to a single batch at a California processing factory, and the poisoned olives from that batch were taken off the market. This is an early example of how, with improved transportation capabilities, food from a single source could be sold relatively far away and in multiple states, making the need for a federal food authority all that more vital. The episode of olives causing botulism continued into 1920, when a fourth tragedy occurred in New York, killing all but the two youngest children in a large family. This time, in addition to removing the tainted lot of olives, the Bureau of Chemistry encouraged California and the olive industry to develop safe processing methods, thereby

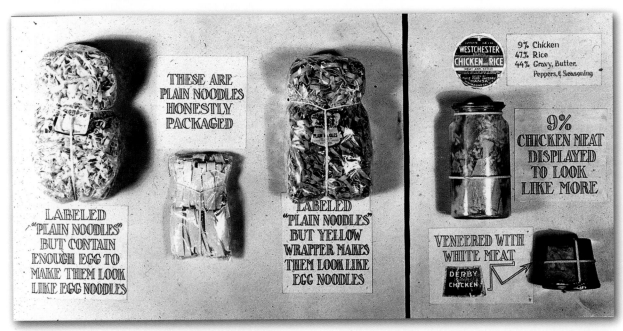

This exhibit from the American Chamber of Horrors shows two of the most common deceptive products on the market in the 1930s. On the left, noodles trying to pass as egg noodles: one by adding a little egg, but not enough to add nutritional value and the other simply wrapping plain noodles in yellow cellophane. On the right, chicken and rice with little chicken—mostly rice and gravy. What little chicken the product did contain was veneered so that the only white meat in the entire jar was carefully positioned to be seen where there was a gap in the labeling.

FDA FIELD OPERATIONS IN ACTION

FDA's field force does amazing work, but none more impressively than when there is a national recall of products that may pose a hazard to the public health. One such mobilization occurred in 1971 and the subsequent two years into 1973. In 1971 a terrible tragedy took place involving canned Bon Vivant Vichyssoise soup that had become tainted with botulism during manufacture. This contamination was not discovered until four cans of the soup had made their way to the dinner table and poisoned those who consumed it.

A couple in Greenwich, Connecticut—a banker and his wife—had been among those unfortunate enough to strictly follow the directions on the label, which instructed the consumer to heat the epicurean delicacy contained within only gently and not let it boil. The banker could not be saved, but his wife survived the ordeal. Interviewed by *The New York Times* from her hospital bed, she said about the soup: "It tasted so bad, we could hardly finish it."

When there is such a need for immediate action, FDA's field offices are at their best—rearranging priorities to assure that the source of the problem is quickly identified and corrected, and more urgently, that tainted products are removed quickly from the shelves. In my capacity as district director, and later headquarters director, of FDA's corps of investigators, I think I felt proudest of my colleagues when they mobilized with a single mission in mind. This was why many of us who served in FDA's regional, district, and resident post offices joined the agency and dedicated our careers to it—in a sense, that's what FDA is all about.

In the Bon Vivant case, FDA investigators traced the botulism illnesses and deaths to underprocessing of the canned vichyssoise (cold potato soup). More than a million cans of food produced by the company under its own and private labels were removed from retailers' shelves.

As a result of this incident, FDA field force began an intensive coverage of other low-acid canned food manufacturers and found other instances of underprocessing, especially involving the canned mushroom industry. Numerous national recalls of canned mushrooms were undertaken. The Bon Vivant tragedy led to industry and government collaboration in preventing or correcting food safety problems. The private and public sectors joined to develop criteria for processing low-acid canned foods. FDA regulations, which were finalized in 1973, now require, among other things, that all commercial processors of low-acid canned foods (such as peas, corn, and mushrooms), as well as acidified foods, register their establishments with FDA and submit processing information (cooking times and temperatures, for example) for each product to the agency. They must also comply with the agency's regulations for good manufacturing practices.

The Bon Vivant tragedy obviously was unfortunate, but thanks to the FDA mobilization, we identified the problem, removed bad products from the market, and fixed the problem, hopefully permanently. That's FDA in action!

—Anthony C. Celeste

leading to the development of improved canning technology.

Canned goods continued to threaten health, often because the contents were spoiled or contaminated. But not until a half century later, in 1971, did the specter of botulism strike again. This was the highly publicized "Bon Vivant Vichyssoise" incident. After eating the cold soup, botulism toxin killed a man named Samuel Cochran, Jr. and paralyzed his wife. The FDA confiscated Bon Vivant's entire stock base, bankrupting the company but preventing further loss of life. As a result, the food-canning industry itself recognized that it needed to have a stricter regulatory scheme to survive, and the industry worked with FDA to develop such a program.

FDA issued new regulations for the control of thermally processed low-acid canned food in an effort to eliminate the threat of botulism. These regulations identified the keys to safe canning and quickly formed the core of industry practices. While no system is foolproof (there was a world-wide recall of Alaskan canned salmon in 1982 when a Belgian citizen died of botulism), such incidents have been extremely rare, and industry standards put into place following the Bon Vivant incident remain today.

Canning was but one food threat FDA has had to deal with. A major advance in food safety came with the enactment of the 1938 Federal Food, Drug, and Cosmetic Act (FD&C Act). It retained the core concepts of adulteration and misbranding, but added the important principle that FDA should be proactive in setting industry standards to prevent harm or deception to the public. In particular, FDA was authorized to set tolerances for added constituents to food whose use was "necessary in the production of a food" or whose occurrence was "unavoidable by good manufacturing practice." FDA later used this authority to set a tolerance for PCBs in fish.

Despite this effort to increase FDA's scope, the agency's authority was still limited to policing the marketplace and acting after the fact, in response to some crisis or perceived crisis. The one issue big enough to change that paradigm—at least for chemicals being added to food— was the fear of carcinogens in the food supply. As the number of people dying from cancer increased in the 1930s and 1940s, public concern about the disease grew exponentially. By 1958, Congress reacted by passing the Food Additive Amendments to the FD&C Act.

With this legislation, FDA's role went from that of policeman to that of gatekeeper. Under this law, companies could no longer add new ingredients to food unless they first received express permission from FDA to do so. To get such permission, food companies (or, just as often, chemical companies) had to conduct extensive testing on laboratory animals to prove to FDA that the ingredient was safe, expressed in the law's legislative history as meaning a "reasonable certainty of no harm." The Food Additive Amendments were a major milestone in federal food regulation. They covered both direct additives to food, such as preservatives or artificial sweeteners, as well as indirect ones, such as packaging materials. The law exempted ingredients generally recognized as safe (GRAS) by qualified experts or those that had received a prior sanction from the government.

The Food Additive Amendments gave FDA considerable authority and discretion to decide what testing was necessary, what scientific methods should be followed, and what levels were considered safe. FDA has always used that authority in a conservative way so as to adhere to established scientific principles and ensure adequate consumer protection. But in one area, Congress gave FDA no discretion at all. In what became known as the "Delaney Clause"—named after a New York congressman—Congress directed FDA to ban, without further analysis, any food additive found to cause cancer in man or animals. This kind of prohibition has enormous public appeal, but also causes FDA great difficulty. This is because advancing scientific knowledge allows the agency to bring sophisticated risk-assessment techniques that enable it to predict, with much greater certainty,

THE CRANBERRY BAN

On what FDA scientists would come to refer to as "Black Monday," November 9, 1959, Secretary of Health Education and Welfare Arthur S. Flemming announced at a press conference that "there should be no further sale of cranberries and cranberry products from Washington and Oregon in 1958 or 1959 because of their possible contamination with aminotriazole," a carcinogenic weed killer. Although many questioned the wisdom of Flemming's dramatic public announcement, including FDA Commissioner George Larrick (who had made it clear that he wished to handle the issue himself), almost no one questioned that Flemming had acted in accordance with the 1954 Miller Pesticide Amendment, which simultaneously allowed USDA to register a pesticide for use while FDA set a "zero tolerance" for residues in the marketed produce. A Wisconsin congressman lamented that "when you live up to the letter of the law, things can get very rough and become very cruel."

'WHENEVER YOU'RE READY!'

Flemming, however, had deliberately decided to act to protect consumers. He genuinely believed that the government "had no right to sit on information of this nature." Flemming supported the basic premise behind what would become the Delaney Clause: animal carcinogens will not be deemed safe for human consumption. Because industry had had several seasons to eliminate its pre-harvest use of aminotriazole, but had not done so, action was indicated, he thought.

During the cranberry crisis, food producers were alerted that pesticide tolerances would be enforced. Flemming's action, for better or worse, set the stage for similar public announcements concerning saccharin and cyclamate. As industry and FDA scientists devised a plan to test the nation's cranberry crop so that holiday traditions would be preserved, the nation's cartoonists had a field day. Politicians from Kennedy to Nixon were photographed consuming cranberries, and FDA chemists started reckoning time by cranberries. Their pesticide work fell either B.C. or A.C.—before or after cranberries. For the first and only time in its history, FDA allowed a product (tested berries) to carry an FDA endorsement, and Congress began a tradition, repeated every decade or so for many years, of asking FDA about the status of the nation's cranberry crop a few weeks before Thanksgiving. No one seemed quite certain whether the queries were humorous.

—Suzanne White Junod

whether test findings in laboratory animals really mean there is a risk to human health.

For example, in the mid-1980s, FDA was presented with a color additive that clearly causes cancer in laboratory animals, but which just as clearly presents a lifetime cancer risk to humans estimated at a mere 1 in 17 billion! If ever there was a negligible or *de minimis* risk to humans, the FDA reasoned, this was surely it, so the agency approved the color additive for use in foods. But a public interest group sued the FDA and won. A U.S. Court of Appeals told FDA that, even though its public policy goal and scientific analysis were reasonable, and even though usually a court would defer to an expert agency's judgment on scientific matters, the Delaney Clause presented that rare instance where Congress intended to be "unduly rigid." So FDA banned the color additive, even though all agreed it presented no real human risk.

Ironically, when FDA followed the Delaney Clause, it could run into trouble as well, as was evidenced in 1977 when FDA reviewed the safety of saccharin, the nation's leading (and, at that time, only) artificial sweetener. Saccharin had been used widely in the United States since before the twentieth century, and became the basis for diet soft drinks and as a table-top sweetener. Following the removal from the market of cyclamates in 1970 (also due to cancer findings in laboratory animals), saccharin was the only artificial sweetener available, something particularly important to the nation's diabetics, among others. When new evidence from a study performed in Canada showed that saccharin caused cancer in laboratory animals, even though the doses used in the animals were very high and the potential human health risk quite low or possibly nonexistent, FDA believed it had no choice but to propose its removal from the

LESSONS FROM RED NO. 2

Red No. 2 once was the most popular red color in foods, drugs, and cosmetics. In 1976, FDA concluded there was not enough scientific data to prove its safety—there was no proof that it was unsafe, just a lack of proof that it was safe. Red No. 2's ban was among the biggest news stories FDA had handled until that time. FDA issued a list of products containing Red No. 2, while explaining that it was not found unsafe.

We were never able to communicate effectively that the color was not necessarily harmful. (I spoke to a mother who was concerned her son would get cancer from eating red M&Ms.) The concept of lack of proof of safety is hard for the public to grasp. The impression is that the product is harmful. My own impression was that the public wanted reassurances when a product was banned. A year later, a Canadian study found that the artificial sweetener saccharin caused cancer in test animals. FDA's announcement to propose a ban, which I wrote, reassured the public that there would not be a cancer epidemic. The public reaction was opposite to that in the Red No. 2 story. The public told us and Congress, they wanted saccharin retained.

I learned from these two episodes that it's awfully hard to predict how the public will react to safety news involving everyday products. The public was more concerned about Red No. 2, which was not shown harmful, than saccharin, which was thought to be a carcinogen. Go figure.

—**Wayne L. Pines**

SUGAR AND SACCHARIN

Shortly after passage of the 1906 Act, James S. Sherman, future Vice President of the United States, then representing Sherman Brothers, a food manufacturing firm in New York, was granted an audience with President Roosevelt to discuss a number of his firm's concerns, which included Harvey Wiley's opposition to his firm's use of saccharin in canned corn. Wiley had concluded from the bureau's "poison squad" studies that saccharin was deleterious to health, and, as well as a health issue, viewed it as both an illegal substitution of a valuable ingredient (sugar) for a less valuable ingredient (saccharin).

When Sherman raised the issue with the President, claiming his firm had saved $4,000 the previous year by employing the substitute sweetener, Wiley did not wait to be cued into the conversation. He recounted:

> I did not wait for the President to ask the customary questions. I was entirely too precipitate in the matter.... I immediately said to the President: "Everyone who ate that sweet corn was deceived. He thought he was eating sugar, when in point of fact he was eating a coal tar product totally devoid of food value and extremely injurious to health."

Roosevelt's answer, Wiley rued, proved his undoing.

"You tell me that saccharin is injurious to health?" I said, "Yes, Mr. President, I do tell you that." He replied, "Dr. Rixey gives it to me every day." I answered, "Mr. President, he probably thinks you may be threatened with diabetes." To this he retorted, "Anybody who says saccharin is injurious to health is an idiot."

This broke up the meeting. Wiley commented, "Had he only extended his royal Excalibur I should have arisen as Sir Idiot."

The following day, the President appointed a Referee Board of Consulting Scientific Experts to reconsider the government's early policies on food additives. Saccharin, as one might have predicted, given the fact that the head of the Board, Johns Hopkins professor Dr. Ira Remsen, had discovered saccharin, received a pardon from the Referee Board. Sugar, therefore, along with Remsen's rebuke of his findings, became the crucible upon which Harvey Wiley's governmental career ultimately fell.

—Suzanne White Junod

market, under the mandate of the Delaney Clause. There was enormous public outcry—political cartoons showed how many hundreds of cans of soft drinks (800) a person would have to consume each day to reach the level fed to laboratory animals. The agency learned that trying to ban a popular product for which there was no substitute was fraught with consequences. Congress stepped in: While not repealing the Delaney Clause itself, Congress passed a moratorium against its application to saccharin so long as the public was warned of the findings and further scientific studies were conducted. Under this fix, all products containing saccharin were labeled with a warning, and all retail stores selling them had to post conspicuous warning signs. Before long, all Americans became familiar with the statement that saccharin "has been found to cause cancer in laboratory animals," but millions continued to consume it anyway. It took more than twenty years for scientific studies to be conducted that would convince the government that, indeed, saccharin did not present a human health risk.

A Commissioner's Initiation

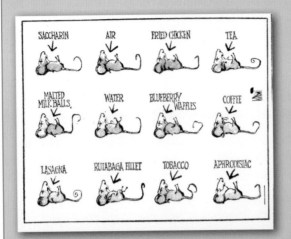

I was still at Stanford as a Commissioner-designate when Acting Commissioner Sherwin Gardner called me to tell me about what became known as the "Canadian rat study" on saccharin. A national furor was developing and, as the time to move my family to Washington drew near, it was getting worse. In its April Fool's issue, the *Stanford Daily's* lead story was "Kennedy Rescinds Saccharin Ban," a headline ignoring the inconvenient fact that FDA had taken no action—yet. When I arrived a couple of days later, a press conference had already been scheduled and I was soon in front of half a dozen TV cameras and a roomful for reporters dying to know what we were going to do.

That was the fun part. The hearings on Capitol Hill were less enjoyable. Sen. Barbara Mikulski (D-MD) wanted to know if we were out of our minds, and at several hearings I was invited to explain the rationale of carcinogenicity testing in animals using high doses. If there is a subject more arcane and challenging to explain, I don't know what it is. And I have the impression that I failed repeatedly.

The core theme of the day was, of course, the phrase "800 cans a day of diet soda." In its initial announcement of the saccharin study, FDA's own press release said that the rats had consumed an amount of saccharin equivalent to 800 cans of diet soda per day for a human. That simplified explanation haunted the FDA for years.

At one hearing, Sen. Richard Schweiker— who later became Secretary of HEW—angrily asked me why I didn't go after tobacco. I unwisely said that if Congress would let me, I'd be glad to. In discussing a statement I had made at this or some other hearing, I told General Counsel Dick Merrill, "I'm not sure I played the right card there." He said, "You played one that wasn't in your hand."

Eventually Congress decided that Americans should have their saccharin as long as it was labeled, and passing legislation prohibiting FDA from banning saccharin, but requiring warning labels, sort of ending the affair. As a souvenir at the time of my retirement, though, my colleagues at FDA gave me 800 cans of diet soda. I am afraid I deserved them.

—Donald Kennedy

What I Learned from Saccharin

From a public relations perspective, March 9, 1977, was a seminal event for FDA. While the agency had, over its then seventy-one year history, been on the front pages many times, no single previous FDA announcement had galvanized public attention as did the proposal to ban the artificial sweetener from soft drinks and as a tabletop sweetener. The saccharin story put FDA on the front pages for weeks, and caused the press to pay more attention than it ever had to FDA activities. The present intense news media coverage of FDA can almost be traced in a straight line back to saccharin.

On March 9, at a 5:30 p.m. press conference in FDA's downtown building, Acting Commissioner Sherwin Gardner announced that a Canadian study had found saccharin to be carcinogenic in rats. Under the terms of the Delaney Clause, which prohibited FDA from permitting the sale of a food additive that causes cancer, saccharin had to be banned, Gardner said.

The public, Congress, the media, and industry all reacted with great emotion. The public started to hoard diet soft drinks. Diabetics panicked. Congress attacked FDA. The media ran multiple stories about the issue—*The New York Times*, for example, on a single day had nine separate stories about saccharin and animal studies. The industry formed a coalition and started advertising, making fun of the statement FDA made that the amount of saccharin consumed by the experimental rats was equivalent to the saccharin in 800 cans a day for people.

Congress later that year enacted legislation prohibiting FDA from banning saccharin, and requiring a warning label to appear on products containing saccharin, as well as signs posted in stores selling such products. Though Congress a quarter-century later rescinded the requirement, to this day some stores and restaurants still carry the signs.

What we in the FDA Public Affairs Office learned was:

- You can never predict how the public will react. A public that at the time feared cancer more than any disease, we learned, feared even more the loss of diet foods.

- Trying to soothe public fears can backfire. The 800 cans a day reference was put into the press release so people who had consumed large amounts of saccharin in the past would not be concerned that they would imminently contract cancer. The tactic backfired, because the public, press, and industry, not understanding how high-dose animal studies work, made a mockery of FDA.

- Don't surprise people with access to the media. FDA failed to notify key members of Congress or even industry, and when they were surprised by the announcement, and without the benefit of our insight, they attacked—quite aggressively.

- Deal with knowledgeable reporters. Coincidentally, on the same day as the FDA announcement, Hanafi Muslims took over the B'nai Brith building in downtown Washington, halting all traffic flow. Reporters were focused on covering that story. Some of the most knowledgeable science reporters, who could have explained high-dose animal studies, did not attend the press conference because of the transportation shutdown. Instead, we had Capitol Hill reporters covering our news, since the FDA's downtown building was nearby. The reporting of a sensitive and hard-to-explain issue was covered by reporters unfamiliar with the topic, leading to stories that lacked perspective.

The saccharin story taught FDA, and me personally, a lot about crisis management and risk communications. One more thing—during the 1970s, as in FDA's previous decades, the relationship between FDA and its parent agency was somewhat distant. I recall Gardner, at some point during the strategy session, asking someone to "notify the Secretary" of the impending announcement. From that episode on, and with each succeeding decade, of course, FDA has become totally integrated into the fabric of its parent agency.

—**Wayne L. Pines**

WHY I DON'T EAT FROG LEGS

It was more than thirty years ago. I was sitting at my desk in the library of the Chief Counsel's Office at FDA awaiting my first assignment. I had visions of prosecuting criminals and protecting the public health. Then a file was dropped on my desk. Much to my chagrin, the caption read: *"United States of America vs. 76,552 Pounds of Frog Legs."* Surely, this must be a joke played on new attorneys! Then I looked up at Arthur Levine; this was no joke. All I could think of was a courtroom full of crippled frogs.

These were not, however, just any frog legs. They had originated in the Ganges River in India, were refused entry into the United States (New York) because of *Salmonella* contamination, shipped under customs bond to Brownsville, Texas, for export to Mexico, then repackaged in boxes marked "Product of Mexico," and shipped to restaurants in Chicago and Detroit, where there had been *Salmonella* outbreaks. The frog legs remaining in Brownsville were seized by Customs, who called FDA in to litigate the seizure action.

The claimant, Manuel Sanchez, argued that FDA had no jurisdiction because the frog legs under seizure remained under customs bond and thus never entered interstate commerce. We argued that the claimant was guilty of fraud, should not be permitted to recondition the frog legs, and that in any event the frog legs had entered interstate commerce for purposes of the FD&C Act and should be condemned.

Our Judge, Reynaldo Garza, Chief Judge of the Southern District of Texas, knew the claimant well and called him "Manny" throughout the trial—not a good sign. But when he told us, halfway through the trial, that he had declined his wife's suggestion of frog legs for dinner, we thought we were making progress.

The Judge found fraud and that FDA had jurisdiction, but refused to destroy the frog legs because they could be reconditioned. Encouraged by the finding of fraud, the U.S. Attorney's office agreed to file several felony counts against Mr. Sanchez and his company. He ultimately pled guilty to two felony counts.

So I did get to protect the public health and prosecute frog legs. But I have never acquired a taste for frog legs.

—**Edward M. Basile**

Despite the outcome of the saccharin episode, fear of cancer has consistently been paramount in the American public's mind. But FDA's scientists knew there were other, more acute dangers lurking from bacteria (pathogens) in the food supply. To the public, food poisoning was uncomfortable, but ultimately, it was just a stomachache. It didn't kill you. That public perception changed dramatically one day in early 1993 when three young children went into a fast-food restaurant (Jack-in-the-Box) in the state of Washington, ordered hamburgers as they had done many times before, and died shortly thereafter. The culprit, a kind of bacteria with a technical-sounding name (*E. coli* 0157:H7), led to more than 700 illnesses in just a few short weeks. And, with that the face of food safety would change forever.

It is worth noting that hamburgers are not regulated by the FDA—their safety instead is overseen by the Food Safety and Inspection Service in USDA—but the problem of bacteria in the food supply was not confined to hamburger. A new wave of bacteria had infiltrated the food supply. Over the next few years, outbreaks of foodborne illness became front-page news. An outbreak of contaminated "fresh" apple juice killed one child and injured

THE PERPETUAL FDA DILEMMA

Sometimes, FDA has been wrong, and in a very public way. An episode that illustrates this occurred in 1989, when FDA investigated two calls to the American Embassy in Chile that grapes headed for the United States had been injected with cyanide. FDA's testing in Philadelphia found cyanide in three grapes.

The agency issued a public warning and embargoed all Chilean fruit shipments. This led to a worldwide alert, affecting Chile's export market. The upshot was that no cyanide was found in any more Chilean fruit. The calls turned out to be a hoax. It was possible, if not likely, that the FDA lab itself had contaminated the three grapes itself. By the time the warning was lifted, however, considerable damage had been done to the Chilean fruit industry.

In retrospect, FDA clearly acted too quickly and perhaps too aggressively. Had the reports proved true, of course, the agency would have been hailed for its rapid deployment of inspectors and scientists to protect the public health. This demonstrates the dilemma FDA has faced since its creation: the need to act to protect the public health based on what inevitably will be incomplete scientific information. Everyone who has worked in positions of responsibility at FDA has faced such a challenge. When do you issue a public warning? When do you recall or withdraw a drug or medical device? How much evidence is enough? What happens if the information proves wrong? Not easy decisions. That's really what FDA is all about.

—Wayne L. Pines

many others. An outbreak of hepatitis A from frozen strawberries in Michigan caused yet another wave of illness. A little-known parasite, *Cyclospora*, contaminated imported raspberries from Guatemala and sickened more than 2,000 American consumers. *Time* magazine ran a cover story headlined, "*E. coli*, the Killer Germ."

Food safety soon became FDA's priority #1. The agency—together with the Centers for Disease Control and Prevention (CDC) and the USDA—developed and implemented a three-pronged strategy to make the food supply safer. This strategy was published in 1997, entitled *Food Safety—from Farm to Table*. The idea was to take a comprehensive approach and attack bacteria wherever in the food supply they occurred. The agency adopted the following plan:

1. Newer Surveillance Systems.

The first step was to get a better understanding of where the problems really were. Through the CDC in Atlanta—which tracks contagious diseases—the government set up a system called FoodNet. This was a network of state and local health departments in nine regions of the country that were charged with actively looking for cases of foodborne illness caused by bacteria, and then reporting the trends. FoodNet started in 1996 and was at full strength by 2001. CDC also conducted a massive review of all data sources and concluded that each year, 76 million cases of foodborne illness occur in the United States, of which 325,000 resulted in hospitalization and 5,000 in death. The most vulnerable populations are the very young, the elderly, the immune-compromised, and the pregnant. These numbers were shocking, and motivated the government to redouble its efforts.

2. Stronger Prevention Programs. FDA had long inspected food manufacturers, its primary attention being on whether the facility looked clean. But since bacteria are not visible to the naked eye, a more sophisticated approach was needed. What emerged was a state-of-the-art system, pioneered at NASA to keep the astronauts' food safe, called Hazard Analysis Critical Control Points (HACCP, pronounced ha-sip). The concept was two-fold: first, identify precisely where in the food production chain bacteria could most readily get into the food (called critical control points); and then apply scientifically validated techniques to either kill the bacteria or reduce their levels as much as possible.

FDA first applied this new strategy to seafood, and USDA quickly followed and applied a similar program to meat and poultry products (with additional testing to verify the meat and poultry program's effectiveness). FDA later extended HACCP to juice products and, while that was being developed, required warning labels on any unpasteurized juice product that did not meet safety standards. The agency also developed "good agricultural practices" for fresh fruits and vegetables and applied

greater attention to inspecting imported food. FDA required safe-handling instructions on cartons of shell eggs, telling consumers to keep the eggs refrigerated and to cook them thoroughly. FDA proposed tighter on-farm controls for eggs, as well. Finally, the agency updated its detailed food safety recommendations—the model food code—to state and local governments, which inspect restaurants and grocery stores nationwide.

3. Faster Outbreak Response. While prevention is paramount, FDA understood that prevention could never be completely successful, and that faster response to actual outbreaks is also necessary. Determining the cause of an outbreak of food poisoning is real detective work, usually led by CDC expert epidemiologists, and it often took weeks before a cause could be identified. With FDA scientists working closely with CDC and USDA, a major scientific breakthrough was achieved whereby bacteria could be "fingerprinted" using DNA technology. What this means is that agency scientists can rapidly identify the bacterium found on one food product and compare it with one from another food product or a human specimen, and see where they match. In this way, the detective work goes much faster, and contaminated food products can be identified and recalled much more

INFANT FORMULA ACT OF 1980

On Thursday July 26, 1979, Dr. Shane Roy of Memphis called FDA's Division of Nutrition. He reported three cases of severe metabolic alkalosis in infants being fed a formula made by the Syntex Corporation. FDA's field investigators were immediately sent to collect data from Dr. Roy and to investigate the manufacturer's processing of the formulas. Chemical analyses showed that Syntex' Neo-Mul-Soy and Cho-Free contained very low chloride levels. Investigators learned that salt was eliminated in the production of these formulas.

Senior managers in FDA's Center for Food Safety and Applied Nutrition, responsible for health hazard analysis, were on leave when Dr. Roy's report arrived. So on Tuesday, July 31, six mid-level managers conducted a health hazard evaluation using data CDC collected. We unanimously agreed that the consumption of the two formulas as the sole source of nutrients presented a life-threatening hazard. We negotiated a class 2 voluntary recall with Syntex, which was initiated on August 2.

Lea Thompson, a reporter for NBC News in Washington, D.C., requested an interview to follow-up the agency's recall press release. FDA spokesman, Wayne Pines, assured her that the recall was ninety-nine percent effective—but, she announced during the interview, she had been able to buy Neo-Mul-Soy from a grocery shelf that very afternoon! She also was concerned about FDA's lack of authority for premarket notification for formula changes. The interview was broadcast nationally on the NBC's "Today Show" and "Evening News," spurring further FDA scrutiny of the recall.

Ms. Thompson's own infant had used Neo-Mul-Soy, and she and other mothers of affected infants continued to pursue the incident. They called for congressional action. Congressman Albert Gore (D-TN), whose infant son also had taken the formula, called hearings on November 1, 1979. He was highly critical of FDA's decision to classify the recall as class 2 rather than class 1 and for not adequately monitoring the recall.

A year later, Congressman Gore's bill, the Infant Formula Act of 1980, passed both houses of Congress and was signed into law by President Jimmy Carter. It provided among other things for premarket notification before formula changes, a significant addition to FDA's legal authority. An alert Memphis doctor (Shane Roy), a concerned mother with media influence (Lea Thompson), and a powerful father with congressional influence (Albert Gore) had changed forever how infant formulas are regulated.

—**John E. Vanderveen**

quickly. CDC scientists estimated that, if this DNA fingerprinting technology (called PulseNet) had been available during the original Jack-in-the-Box incident in 1993, two-thirds of the more than 700 illnesses could have been prevented.

The government's food safety actions were successful in affecting the bottom line in terms of public health. Surveys showed that consumers were more aware of food safety issues and steps they could take to reduce their vulnerability. FDA inspections were finding more and more firms that adhered to the modernized safety standards. Most importantly, by the beginning of the twenty-first century, CDC's tracking of foodborne illness showed a reduction in illnesses from the nine most common pathogens to have been reduced by approximately twenty percent.

Food safety manifests itself in many different ways, not just in terms of contamination. One important example occurred after a major manufacturer of infant formula reformulated two of its soy products by discontinuing the addition of salt. This reformulation resulted in infant formula products that contained an inadequate amount of chloride, an essential nutrient for infants' growth and development. By mid-1979, a substantial number of infants had been diagnosed with hypochloremic metabolic alkalosis, a syndrome associated with chloride deficiency. Development of this syndrome in these infants was found to be associated with prolonged exclusive use

of chloride-deficient formulas. Congress responded in 1980 by passing the Infant Formula Act to provide FDA with greater regulatory control over the formulation and production of infant formula products. This is another example of FDA and Congress addressing new threats that are difficult to predict in advance.

While food safety has always been FDA's dominant mission, an additional major focus has been to ensure truth in labeling of food packages. This dates back to the 1906 Act. From its early days FDA sought to prevent fraud in food labeling. This involved outright falsehoods, such as claims that a food would cure a variety of ailments, as well as label statements that were technically true but which were nevertheless deceptive. Indeed, in a 1924 Supreme Court case involving apple cider vinegar, the court ruled that the 1906 Act made illegal any and all statements on a food label that may mislead or deceive consumers, even if technically true. Nevertheless, limitations of the 1906 Act soon became apparent. The law enabled the government to take action against illegal products once they were on the market, but the government lacked authority to issue affirmative requirements to guide compliance. Thus, profiteers could freely sell products that contained substandard ingredients (such as "fruit" jams made only with water, glucose, grass seed, and artificial color) until the government caught up with them. This undercut the market for authentic products.

Congress sought to fix this problem in the 1938 FD&C Act by authorizing

FDA to issue standards of identity for foods. After its passage, FDA began the long process of establishing standards for scores of food products. These standards provided a clear "recipe" for food products—from milk, cheese, and other dairy products to peanut butter, jellies, and jams. Indeed, one of the largest controversies of the 1970s was FDA's determining how much peanut oil had to be in peanut butter. The food standards provided consumers with increased confidence that the foods they buy are indeed what the labels say they are. Government vigilance continues, evinced by cases periodically brought against individuals or companies that water down their juice despite claiming "100% juice" on the label or against individuals or companies that otherwise substitute cheaper or inferior ingredients.

In 2004, Congress took action to make food labels more user-friendly for persons with food allergies. In the Food Allergen Labeling and Consumer Protection Act, Congress directed that food ingredient lists on product labels clearly identify the eight most common food allergens, using terminology easily understandable to consumers. For example, one of the common food allergens is milk, and whey is a common milk-derived food ingredient, but has been listed on ingredient labels simply as whey. Under the law, the ingredient labels containing must say "whey (milk)" or "contains milk" so milk-allergic consumers can readily identify those products and avoid a potentially serious or even life-threatening reaction.

FDA's role in food labeling extends well beyond food ingredients and general label statements. Because of food's nutritional qualities, it is also FDA's job to be sure that a food product's nutritional qualities are clearly and effectively conveyed. Nutrition information on the food label dates back to the 1970s, with labels containing information on the amount of key nutritional qualities, such as calories, fat, protein, vitamins, and minerals. The original nutritional labels—which were voluntary unless triggered by a nutrition-related claim—were intended to convey relevant information, in a simple format, so that consumers could make better judgments about the foods they buy and consume. In the early 1970s FDA did considerable research to construct a uniform nutrition label that would communicate what the consumer wanted.

The content of the nutrition label has evolved since then. Development of the modern nutrition label was triggered by several events of the 1980s. FDA began that decade, as the link between sodium and hypertension became more clearly established, by issuing new regulations defining "low sodium" and other sodium descriptors. This was followed by a Surgeon General's report that called attention to the dangers of fat, particularly saturated fat and cholesterol, in the American diet. Most of all, food companies responded to the baby boomer generation, which was becoming more health conscious, by flooding the marketplace with health-oriented claims, everything from low cholesterol to high fiber. The most visible such claim was made by a major cereal manufacturer that its bran flake product would help prevent cancer. Government officials responded by calling the food aisle a "Tower of Babel" and vowed to bring order. FDA published a set of proposed regulations, but the issue had become so visible that Congress stepped in and passed the Nutrition Labeling and Education Act of 1990 (NLEA). With that came the modern food label that we see in stores today. Nutrition labeling had three elements: the nutrition facts panel; nutrient content claims (e.g., low fat); and health claims (e.g., reduces the risk of certain cancers).

The nutrition facts panel quickly became the centerpiece of this reform effort. Following the twin mantras of "just the facts" and "keep it simple," FDA developed an easy-to-read label that lists the major nutrients (fat, saturated fat, cholesterol, sodium, carbohydrates, and protein), followed by the amount in the food (usually grams or milligrams). In what became so contentious that it warranted a meeting in the White House Oval Office with the President and two Cabinet Secretaries, FDA also included the percentage of the daily value recommended, based on a 2,000-calorie diet, so consumers could get a sense of proportion of what the quantitative numbers really meant. The nutrition facts panel also has a place for vitamins and minerals, and the percentage of the recommended daily allowance. For the nutrition facts panel to work, especially for comparison shopping, FDA needed

to establish standard portion sizes for different categories of foods. These portion sizes then became the reference point for determining how much of each nutrient was contained per serving in the container. This was one of the most arduous tasks of the entire food-label reform effort, as FDA staff pored through endless reams of government statistics of how much people actually eat of scores of different kinds of food.

FDA also standardized key terms, such as reduced, low, and free for nutrients consumers need to limit (fat, saturated fat, cholesterol, and sodium) and good source or excellent source for nutrients consumers need to increase (calcium, fiber, and protein). The agency calls these nutrient content claims. FDA integrated into these definitions the total content of a food product, so that food companies could not mislead consumers into thinking that a product low in cholesterol was "heart healthy" if that same a product was high in saturated fat. Thus, the 1906 Act's original concept of truthful and non-misleading was still being applied, nearly a century later.

The final element of the new food label addressed so-called health claims. By law, the claim that bran cereal could help prevent cancer made that cereal, legally speaking, a drug according to the FD&C Act. To rationalize this, and apply common sense, Congress created an exception to the drug definition if the food product's claim was backed by "significant scientific agreement" among recognized experts, and the company got approval from the FDA through a formal petition process. The NLEA also directed FDA to review a number of diet-disease relationships that might qualify for a health claim. Most of these claims were related to either reducing the risk of heart disease, certain cancers, or osteoporosis.

In January 1993, FDA published more than 2,000 pages of regulations implementing the full breadth of NLEA. This was one of the largest and most comprehensive sets of regulations FDA had ever published at a single time. Their effect was seen almost immediately, as food companies not only revised their labels, but reformulated their products to present a healthier image on the nutrition facts panel. The most significant area in which this happened was in fat-containing products, and consumers were soon met with a plethora of products that were "reduced," "low," or "free" of saturated fat and cholesterol.

The food label became widely known and read, and remained unchanged for a decade (until FDA required, in July 2003, that the nutrition facts panel also list the amount of trans-fatty acids). The problem that then emerged, however, was that people were not getting any thinner. In fact, the opposite was true. We had gone from a nation that was one-third "ill-housed, ill-clad, and ill-fed" in the 1930s, to a nation where the majority are overweight and a third are obese. This results from a number of factors, including less exercise and an overall more sedentary lifestyle. But in any discussion about obesity, the topic soon turns to

food. In early 2004, CDC reported that diet/exercise was the second leading cause of preventable deaths in the United States (next to smoking), and would soon become the leading cause at current rates. Newspapers and magazines everywhere dubbed obesity the next epidemic.

The agency, again responding to changing times, pledged to reconsider the nutrition label, to provide standardized terms for "low" and "reduced" carbohydrates, and to try to better define portion sizes. The agency advanced the debate by issuing a report called *Calories Count*, and reminding readers of the simple truth that weight control comes down to calories in versus calories out. FDA also liberalized its rules governing health claims. Responding to the desire to get new information to consumers faster, as well as to a string of court cases limiting the agency's authority over commercial speech, FDA adopted a streamlined process for "qualified" health claims. This meant that FDA would review petitions and determine the degree of certainty presented by the science. If the scientific

Testing the contents of canned foods.

153

data were supportive of the claim but still inconclusive, then FDA would require that "qualifying language" to go on the product's label as well. One of the first qualified health claims FDA allowed was for the role of omega-3 fatty acids in reducing the risk of coronary hearth disease.

The regulation of food safety obviously took on international dimensions during the twentieth century, as transportation and communications made trade between countries more common, especially for foods. By the end of the century, the United States had entered into a number of international trade agreements, clearly making the United States part of a global economy and expanding global food system.

The globalization of the food distribution system meant that consumers could go to their local grocery store and, with increasing ease, purchase food that had been grown or packaged literally from anywhere in the world. With that came greater variety, the ability to buy "fresh" fruits and vegetables year round, and a staggering challenge for FDA to monitor a skyrocketing amount of imported food. FDA participated in international standards-setting organizations to promote minimum safety standards and fair trading practices. But FDA's biggest challenge internationally was not in regard to either carcinogens or pathogens, but rather the acceptance (or non-acceptance) of food products developed through biotechnology.

The United States was a world leader in developing new food varieties using biotechnology—a scientific technique whereby a gene with a particular trait is spliced into the DNA of a regular food, like corn or soybeans. While cross-breeding has been used by farmers for thousands of years (such as crossing white corn with yellow corn to get white and yellow corn), new scientific techniques allows more significant kinds of results. For example, using biotechnology, corn can be developed that makes the plant resistant to certain natural pests, thereby obviating the need for farmers to use certain pesticides. FDA developed a new policy and procedure to review such changes before they were used commercially to ensure that there were no ill effects.

By the late 1990s, farmers in the United States, particularly those growing corn and soybeans, increasingly were using biotech-derived seeds. American consumers generally either accepted this technology or were oblivious to it, but many others around the world did not. Europeans, in particular, were highly skeptical of the safety of such products, as well as of the potential environmental repercussions of what they perceived to amount to altering nature, and coined the term Frankenfoods. The European Union banned the growing of crops derived through biotechnology, and effectively banned the importation of such U.S.-grown crops by requiring labeling that American food companies viewed as scary, non-scientific, and altogether unacceptable. The fear of biotech-derived foods was so high in some sectors of the world that certain African countries actually refused American food

Modern food and drug investigation

donations intended to combat widespread food shortages if that food had been derived through biotechnology. The fact that millions of Americans ate the very same food daily was not enough to combat such deep-rooted—even if misguided—fear. FDA was caught in the middle. The agency developed a consensus among the world's scientists of the scientific criteria to be used in reviewing the safety of new crop varieties, but a large gap remained between what the scientists thought and what the public believed. Many believed that public perceptions around the world would not change until foods derived through biotechnology provided a direct benefit to consumers (e.g., more nutritious or less costly food) rather than providing benefits primarily to farmers.

Another way FDA has reacted to external events occurred after the tragic events of September 11, 2001. The threat of terrorism, once reserved for certain regions of the world, had reached U.S.

soil. From new airport security to a new color-coded public threat awareness system, all parts of government faced a new challenge. The new Department of Homeland Security became the focal point for protecting all facets of our society, and each specialized agency, like the FDA, was called upon to do its part. To FDA, it was clear from the start that the food supply was a potential target. This is because food, even from natural sources, can contain bacteria or chemical contaminants that make people sick. If Mother Nature could contaminate food, it was concluded, so could terrorists with a well-thought-out plan. Moreover, the essential nature of food makes it a possible vehicle to inject fear into our society.

Although the agency had relatively little experience in combating terrorism per se, FDA did have experience with product tampering—going back to the highly publicized Tylenol cyanide tampering of the early 1980s and subsequent food-related tamperings, including glass in baby food and a syringe alleged to be in a soft-drink can. Moreover, FDA scientists had nearly a century of experience in combating new and unanticipated threats. The agency put that collective experience to work. FDA took the lessons of food safety from natural sources, together with the lessons from product tamperings on a small scale, and viewed them through a new lens: intentional contamination by an organized, thinking enemy. In a relatively short time, FDA developed its three-part blueprint for combating terrorism:

1. Try to anticipate the enemy. To prioritize where the agency should devote its greatest attention, FDA conducted vulnerability assessments of which types of biological or chemical agents could survive in which types of food. These assessments were augmented by intelligence gathered by the Central Intelligence Agency (CIA) and from law enforcement agencies. The very fact that FDA needed to establish a close working relationship with the CIA spoke volumes of how much the world had changed.

2. Close those gaps and prevent an attack if possible. This was done by providing the food industry with general guidance on enhancing security at their manufacturing facilities, as well as developing more targeted and specialized guidance for those food sectors at greatest risk. FDA also increased its border protection to provide greater scrutiny to the ever-increasing array of imported foods. In this regard, FDA benefited greatly from new funding Congress provided in the wake of September 11 for hundreds of new border inspectors, as well as new legislation that gave FDA greater authority over imported foods, in particular.

3. Devise a response plan. As with natural contaminants, FDA recognized that prevention cannot catch everything, and the agency needed to be able to respond with unprecedented speed should a terrorist event with food ever occur. This response plan involves simulated terrorist attacks that sharpened the agency's responsive actions and public communications. The response plan also included developing a nationwide network of food laboratories at state and federal agencies that could be called upon, in an emergency, to test large volumes of food for potential contamination in a very short period. FDA was painfully aware of the incident, later in the Fall of 2001, when anthrax was found in the U.S. mail, when more than 150,000 samples of white powder over one month overwhelmed many of the nation's public health laboratories.

FDA was also deeply affected by an incident in its own facilities. During the anthrax-in-the-mail episode that occurred shortly after September 11 in and around the nation's capital, the mail room in FDA's own Center for Food Safety and Applied Nutrition in downtown Washington, D.C. was among the first to test "positive" for anthrax. It was just a preliminary laboratory test, the employees were told. For the next six days, while the confirmatory tests waited in the queue at CDC, FDA scientists found out first hand what it felt like to be a consumer rather than the nation's guardian. Although the confirmatory tests came back negative, the fear and uncertainly FDA scientists experienced that week made them redouble their efforts to do whatever was necessary to protect the public from intentionally contaminated food.

In sum, during the course of the twentieth century, consumers rightfully came to have high expectations for the job FDA must do. The food supply is viewed as practically sacred. This is not just for our own well-being, but also in our role as caretakers—for our children, for our parents, for those who are sick or yet unborn. Food is supposed to be good for us and to be nourishing, not make us sick. It is also supposed to be enjoyable, as any child getting an ice cream cone will gladly tell you. Perhaps most importantly, food is essential. Therefore, American consumers take seriously any threat to the food supply—in reality or perception. This makes FDA's job all that much more challenging. Throughout the century, FDA has safeguarded the food supply by responding to this constant change. In doing so, the agency has adhered to its basic goals: keep food safe and wholesome; keep it honestly labeled; and keep its nutritional properties clearly presented. This has been a constant battle, and the agency has not always succeeded. But FDA has succeeded more often than not, to the point where food safety is widely taken for granted. Through it all, FDA has maintained a high degree of public trust. Because of this trust, FDA is rightfully seen as the true and rightful guardian of the nation's food supply.

Humorous cartoon in the editorial section of the *Atlanta Constitution* following enactment of the 1990 Nutritional Labeling and Education Act and the unveiling of the new Nutrition Facts label.

This Humbug Oil was touted to cure diphtheria in both man *or* beast according to its label, which contains directions for both human and animal use. Circa 1906.

FDA's Role in the Pathway to Safe and Effective Drugs

**J. Richard Crout,
William W. Vodra &
Cole P. Werble**

THE REGULATION OF DRUGS FOR HUMAN USE HAS PROFOUNDLY INFLUENCED ALL FORMS OF MEDICAL CARE. A century ago, personal experience determined whether pharmaceutical products worked; today, patients and their doctors throughout the world expect scientific evidence to support the safety and effectiveness of most therapeutic options. Health interventions—such as diet, surgery, and medical devices—are now as likely as pharmaceuticals to be subjected to rigorous clinical trials to prove their beneficial claims.

FDA's implementation of the Federal Food, Drug, and Cosmetic Act served as a major catalyst in this revolution. In 1962, Congress added to the law the requirement that each new drug product be demonstrated to be effective for its intended uses before it could enter the market. Moreover, Congress mandated that effectiveness be shown by "adequate and well-controlled investigations." That phrase has become the cornerstone of FDA's drug regulatory activities and the driver for profound changes in research and clinical practice. Yet, at the time it was inserted into the 1962 legislation, this language was not viewed as momentous, but rather a simple and easy solution to a more vexing legislative dispute over the amount and weight of evidence required to prove effectiveness. Yet this compromise wording has become a landmark in the development of evidence-based medicine. The phrase "adequate and well-controlled investigations" has shaped contemporary medicine and enabled the development of a strong pharmaceutical industry and, much more importantly, of products that keep people alive longer, with a better quality of life.

No one in 1906 would have predicted this outcome. One hundred years ago, unique proprietary formulations of secret ingredients purporting to treat or cure a wide range of diseases dominated the pharmaceutical marketplace. These products often contained addicting substances such as narcotics, alcohol, and cocaine that were not disclosed to the buyer. Other special ingredients—e.g., extracts from animals or plants, chemicals, and similar materials that were not standardized—were added according to private formulas that may (or may not) have been consistently followed from one batch to next. The resulting mixture may have been watered down to yield more bottles to sell.

The Age of Drugs—The saloon-keeper (pictured on the left) is finding it difficult to compete at the turn-of-the-century with the products of the pharmacy, many of which contained high levels of alcohol as well as other ingredients such as opium, which were marketed to all age groups. (*Puck* print courtesy of Larry Halsell)

In the late nineteenth century, Oliver Wendell Holmes, professor of anatomy at Harvard Medical School, wrote that, with few exceptions, all available drugs could be eliminated from medical practice with no loss to patients; indeed, he said, physicians and patients might be better off. At that time, few treatments for diseases were known to work. Anecdotes, first-hand observations, and opinions of experts provided the basis for determining whether a drug was effective. Scientific methods for testing medicines were largely undeveloped.

In developing legislation a century ago, critics of patent medicines were more focused on the disclosure and safety of ingredients and the prevention of adulteration than on claims of therapeutic effectiveness. Quackery was not acceptable, of course, but how could it be prevented? The 1906 Pure Food and Drug Act tried to by prohibiting any statement on a drug label that was "false or misleading in any particular." The government soon sought to outlaw "Dr. Johnson's Mild Combination Treatment for Cancer," which promised to cure cancer painlessly and at home. The Supreme Court ruled, however, that the law did not apply to curative claims. Justice Oliver Wendell Holmes, Jr., son of the Harvard Medical professor, wrote the court's decision, which concluded that therapeutic effectiveness was a matter of opinion. Courts, Holmes said, could not resolve conflicts among practitioners and schools of medicine, nor did the legislation so intend. Congress disagreed and promptly revised the 1906 Act to ban any claim that was "false and fraudulent." Unfortunately, this wording required the government to prove that the seller had intended to deceive the customers, thereby committing fraud. If the seller simply did not know whether the claim was true or false, the government could not act, even if the claim was proven wrong. This burden made the revised statute largely useless to assure drug efficacy.

The 1938 overhaul of the Federal Food, Drug, and Cosmetic Act was enacted as a result of a drug disaster. But, FDA Commissioner Walter Campbell provided the original impetus for the legislation in 1933 during a conversation with a member of President Franklin D. Roosevelt's brain trust, Rexford Tugwell, who was then Assistant Secretary of Agriculture (the department then having oversight of FDA). Over a five-year period, bills were offered, debated, amended, and stalled. Meanwhile, one of the first effective anti-infective drugs was developed, sulfa. Sulfa had drawbacks, however, precluding its use in small children. It was a bulky powder that required large capsules for oral administration and did not go into solution easily, preventing a liquid formulation. In late 1937, a chemist at the Massengill Company discovered that sulfa would rapidly dissolve in diethylene glycol.

Public concerns about the safety and effectiveness of the so-called "soothing syrups" were a major source of support for passage of the 1906 Pure Food and Drugs Act. Marketed to calm colicky and teething babies and toddlers, many contained morphine sulphate. Imitators, however, were also marketed. Who could tell the difference? And which was worse—to contain the addictive morphine or not to contain it? The 1906 Act required that morphine sulfate be listed on the label if it were present and be omitted from the label if it were not present. It was not until 1914 that narcotic ingredients came under stricter controls.

The only premarket testing consisted of a taste test. The product was trade-named Elixir Sulfanilamide and sold in Texas and neighboring states. Within weeks, scores of infants suffered slow, painful death as the diethylene glycol—today's antifreeze—produced irreversible liver toxicity. The resulting press stories aroused public opinion and drove Congress to action. The pending legislation would not have prevented this disaster, however, so a separate provision was inserted to require premarket safety testing of new drugs before release into the market. President Roosevelt signed the legislation on June 25, 1938.

The Elixir Sulfanilamide episode was focused on safety, and little attention was paid to therapeutic effectiveness. The 1938 statute adopted the 1906 standard barring drugs with labeling that was "false or misleading in any particular;" it also required that drug labeling provide "adequate directions for use" to protect users. Finally, new drugs were required to be safe for the uses recommended in labeling. The word "safe" inherently implies some sort of risk/benefit assessment, which leads logically to an assessment of efficacy as well as risk. No one in 1938 thought the safety standard required an extensive effectiveness evaluation. But in 1962, FDA Commissioner George Larrick told Congress that FDA had been reviewing new products for effectiveness under the 1938 safety standard. When a drug presented serious toxicity, he explained, the agency would weigh the advantages of the drug against its disadvantages. Moreover, provisions added to the statute in the 1940s required the agency to evaluate the effectiveness of antibiotics.

Academics would later debate whether FDA could have been even more aggressive in requiring proof of effectiveness under the 1938 Act. During the 1970s, for example, FDA argued that Laetrile—another purportedly painless, nontoxic cure for cancer—was intrinsically unsafe if used in place of an effective treatment. Others have contended that every pharmacologically active substance carries risks (even if not identified), so that, without any therapeutic benefits, an ineffective drug, almost by definition, must be considered unsafe. In support, they could cite one of the rare drug disasters resulting from a lack of effectiveness. Diethylstilbestrol (DES) was a synthetic FDA permitted into the market under the 1938 Act as safe. It was later proposed to prevent miscarriages on the theory that inadequate levels of estrogens caused spontaneous abortions. This hypothesis was not tested scientifically before the practice became widespread. When the drug was tested, it failed. Unfortunately, the medical use continued. In the 1970s, scientists found that the children exposed to DES while in the womb had a high risk of cancer and other adverse health problems that only emerged when they reached puberty.

Interestingly, the political support for proof of drug effectiveness as a condition for marketing did not originally arise from a drug disaster. Rather, it emerged in the

THE ELIXIR SULFANILAMIDE TRAGEDY

In the summer of 1937, a well-established pharmaceutical firm in Tennessee, the S. E. Massengill Company of Bristol, began a project that would change the course of drug regulation. Massengill decided to search for a liquid dosage form of the new wonder drug, sulfanilamide. This would spare children who found it difficult to take the large sulfanilamide tablets, and offer an alternative to any others who preferred a different way of taking their medicine.

Focusing on a group of chemicals known to be good solvents, company chemist Harold Cole Watkins soon found diethylene glycol to be superior in dissolving sulfanilamide. Checking the sulfanilamide preparation for taste, color, and appearance, Massengill began distributing its Elixir Sulfanilamide in September. Watkins did not check to see if the preparation or its components were safe, either in the laboratory or the library. Either approach would have revealed why the firm had made a deadly mistake: diethylene glycol, a chemical analogue of antifreeze, is a powerful poison.

Distribution began on September 4. On October 14, FDA learned that administration of the Massengill preparation had resulted in six deaths in Tulsa; immediately inspectors from Kansas City were dispatched to Tulsa. When they arrived the death toll had climbed to nine, eight of whom were children, and the inspectors found that Elixir Sulfanilamide and severe kidney degeneration were common to all these cases.

With this news, FDA sent its chief medical officer in Washington and one of its best inspectors, located in Cincinnati, to investigate the Bristol plant. Massengill research was nonexistent, and Samuel Massengill, head of the firm, believed the problem was due to idiosyncratic reactions of the patients to sulfanilamide, an opinion he professed steadfastly throughout the ordeal. Nevertheless, the firm issued telegrams requesting return of Elixir Sulfanilamide, without indicating the seriousness of the situation.

FDA launched a massive search around the country for 240 gallons of the drug, unaccounted for by the company. Nearly every one of the 239 inspectors and chemists in the field was marshaled into this service. They also had assistance from some state officials and health professionals. All but about twelve gallons were found, but not in time to save 107 unfortunate patients, many of whom were children. Inexplicably, some patients took the medicine without ill effect.

Massengill could be charged only for violating the proscription in the 1906 Food and Drugs Act against misbranding; an elixir, by definition, had to contain alcohol, yet this product had none. In fact, that was the only basis on which FDA could track down the errant poisons. The firm was fined a paltry sum, though victims' families pursued civil action against the Tennessee firm. But more significantly, from the standpoint of the history of drug regulation, this affair reinvigorated and strengthened a stagnating bill in Congress to reform food and drug regulation. In particular, outrage over this wanton disregard for the public's health ensured that drugs would never again be marketed until a firm proved to FDA its safety.

—**John P. Swann**

Consumption was a nineteenth century term encompassing almost any lung ailment from the common cold to bronchitis; and from tuberculosis to lung cancer. These pre-1906 products reportedly contained strychnine.

course of hearings from 1959 through 1961 chaired by Sen. Estes Kefauver (D-TN). Leading medical thinkers complained that a flood of marketing materials from drug manufacturers, supported by questionable science, were overwhelming the ability of practicing physicians to make intelligent judgments. Dr. Louis Lasagna, a world-renowned pharmacologist, then at the Johns Hopkins Medical School, said, "Modern therapeutics is too difficult and too dangerous for today's doctor to go it alone. He needs help." Thus, it was a desire for reliable information about drugs, not a reaction to some catastrophe, that brought Congress' attention to the clinical trial.

The idea that a controlled experiment could be an accepted scientific method for demonstrating the effectiveness of a drug emerged only in the previous two decades. The actual invention of the randomized medical study is often attributed to Dr. James Lind, a Scottish naval surgeon. In 1747, he divided a dozen sailors ill with scurvy into six groups of two each and treated them respectively with cider, an alcoholic extract, vinegar, seawater, spices, or two oranges plus one lemon. "The consequence was that the most sudden and visible good effects were perceived from the use of oranges and lemons," he observed. In spite of this result, neither the treatment nor the method immediately prospered. It took the British Royal Navy fifty years to give their sailors lemon or lime juice daily to prevent scurvy (creating the nickname of "limeys" for British sailors to this day). The use of the clinical trial as a disciplined scientific method to evaluate new therapies took much longer, emerging only in the mid-1900s.

Until then, the safety and effectiveness of drugs was judged by the methods used since the time of Hippocrates: the observation and testimony of experienced physicians and individual patients. The turning point occurred in the mid-1940s with the work of Prof. Austin Bradford Hill of the United Kingdom. He articulated a comprehensive and cohesive set of principles for the design of clinical trials and their statistical analysis. In 1948, the Medical Research Council of Great Britain published what is considered to be the first modern clinical trial, a study demonstrating that streptomycin reduces mortality in patients with tuberculosis. There quickly followed a series of studies on analgesics that show the importance of randomization, the use of placebos and active controls, and the "double blinding" of subjects and observers to minimize potential bias and improve the usefulness of results.

In 1951, in perhaps the first clinical trial to evaluate an established medical treatment, the investigators showed that high concentrations of oxygen given to premature infants (a common practice of the day) not only failed to reduce mortality but actually caused blindness in a high proportion of treated infants. This shocking result demonstrated the power of the clinical trial to challenge the status quo. In 1955, the ability of the Salk vaccine to prevent poliomyelitis was demonstrated, to great public acclaim, in another pioneering clinical trial. By the

mid-1950s, a sound scientific basis for the design and conduct of controlled clinical trials had developed. Furthermore, use of such trials was growing in special circumstances to evaluate new drugs, vaccines, and medical practices.

The pharmaceutical industry, however, did not apply clinical trials widely to the evaluation of new drugs. Instead, they relied on small studies aimed at elucidating the mechanism of action or demonstrating a short-term pharmacologic effect, such as lowering blood pressure or relieving pain. The medical literature consisted largely of collected series of patients' case reports, a few small clinical studies, and review articles. *The Physician's Desk Reference,* containing the labeling of most prescription drugs, was a small volume about an inch thick. The labeling itself was written in promotional terms.

FDA's role in the evaluation of drugs was also limited. In 1960, the agency had a small handful of medical officers, toxicologists, and chemists (and no statisticians) devoted to the review of drugs. The publicly accepted standard for judging the effectiveness of drugs at the time was the opinion of medical experts. Thus, even had FDA taken a more aggressive interpretation of the 1938 law to imply more evidence of effectiveness, it had neither the popular support nor the resources to implement such an approach.

The drug testing process itself seemed almost casual by today's standards. FDA did not regulate studies on investigational drugs. Protocols, record-keeping, and reporting were neither rigorous nor systematic. Informed consent was not required. Practicing physicians performed most studies. Clinical pharmacology and pharmacokinetics were just emerging as new academic disciplines.

All of that was to change because of another drug disaster. Thalidomide was a minor tranquilizer already marketed in Germany, Japan, and the United Kingdom, for which approval was sought in the United States. One application of the drug was to control morning sickness in pregnant women. While approval of thalidomide was pending at FDA, an epidemic of unusual birth defects emerged in Europe and Japan. Quick and careful detective work revealed thalidomide to be the cause of the tragedy. America was largely spared because of the vigilant work of Dr. Frances O. Kelsey at FDA. Her challenges to the adequacy of the safety testing in the application prevented agency approval of the drug and led to a Presidential citation for her work, a rare acknowledgment of the important work done by FDA employees.

The thalidomide tragedy occurred at a time when drug legislation, developed by Sen. Kefauver as a result of his investigations of pharmaceuticals beginning in 1959, was languishing. The overall thrust of the reform bill was economic: to reduce the cost of medicines through increased competition, stronger antitrust laws, and compulsory patent licensing. Despite a message to Congress from President John F. Kennedy in the Spring of 1962 calling for various forms of consumer protection legislation, including

drug legislation, Kefauver's bill seemed to be going no place. On July 12, 1962, the Senate Judiciary Committee reported out a version of Kefauver's proposal that was so different from what he had advocated that the Tennessee Democrat angrily refused to be the floor manager of his own bill. Prospects for any legislation looked moribund. Three days later, *The Washington Post* published the thalidomide story. The political climate in the country changed overnight, and eighty-six days later, on October 10, President Kennedy signed a bill that had been passed unanimously by both houses of Congress.

Clearly, the period between the *Post* story and the enactment of the Drug Amendments of 1962 (frequently referred to as the Kefauver-Harris Act) involved hectic lobbying and negotiations. Working with congressional leaders, the White House quickly took control of the various drug bills idling on Capitol Hill and began to push for legislation. President Kennedy asked the Senate Judiciary Committee to recall its bill from the floor. Within three weeks of the thalidomide article, Senate legislative drafting had progressed so rapidly that only a few final issues remained. Surprisingly, industry representatives were generally pleased with the progress on the bill, undoubtedly because many of Kefauver's economic proposals, such as those dealing with patents, had been removed. In the political climate of that summer, it is likely that the drug manufacturers acquiesced to public health protections, lest opposition breathe renewed life into Kefauver's economic reforms. By comparison, the changes being crafted by the administration and the Senate Judiciary Committee were a sensible trade-off.

Nevertheless, the drug industry held out for revisions on several key provisions in the bill. One involved new drug approval requirements. Kefauver had a provision in his original bill that a new drug be "efficacious in use" before it could be marketed. Viewed in context of Kefauver's economic agenda, however, the proposed effectiveness requirement might be seen simply as an effort to prevent fraud on the consumer, rather than an attempt to improve therapeutics. In the revision process, the legislators endorsed the idea of therapeutic efficacy, but replaced the phrase "efficacious in use" with "effective for its intended use." Moreover, the committee decided that effectiveness had to be supported by evidence, not merely anecdote, impressions, and opinion. Finally, it adopted the principle that a drug could not enter the market until FDA found that it met the required level of proof of effectiveness. Under the 1938 law, FDA had sixty days to review a new drug application, but it was a default system; if the agency did not object, the drug could be sold on the sixty-first day. Now Congress wanted an affirmative decision from the agency. Clearly these changes would provide FDA with enormous power.

The central remaining issue concerned the amount of evidence that FDA would require to approve a product. Administration proposals called for a "preponderance of evidence." That burden sounded too heavy to persons trained in law, where "preponderance" meant more than fifty percent; some feared it might be read to require a consensus among experts. Opponents offered a substitute legal phrase, "substantial evidence," which courts had long used to signify "more than a scintilla, but less than a preponderance" of evidence. This phrase would not require a majority of experts to agree. Compromise was reached during a late afternoon drafting session on Friday, August 10, 1962. An administration representative demanded that the standard remain "preponderance of evidence," arguing that if only twenty doctors out of 100 who tested the drug considered it effective, it would pass the "substantial evidence" hurdle, but fail the more rigorous "preponderance" standard. To everyone's surprise, Kefauver's top aide, John Blair, sided with the drug industry, saying that innovations frequently meet opposition and take time to gain wide acceptance.

Blair added a condition for his support: substantial evidence must consist of "adequate and well-controlled investigations, including clinical investigations, by experts qualified by scientific training and experience to evaluate the effectiveness of the drug involved." Blair's suggestion of the compromise language creates a nice irony to the codification of this key scientific standard. Blair was not a scientist; he was the economist who had been pushing patent reform as Kefauver's solution to reforming the drug industry. Blocked in

DR. KELSEY'S INTRODUCTION TO FDA

When Dr. Frances Kelsey arrived at FDA in 1960 to join a handful of other medical officers at the agency, she was given a new drug application that, according to her supervisor, would be an easy introduction to the job. The application had been submitted in September, 1960 by the William S. Merrell Company of Cincinnati. Merrell was the American licensee of the German pharmaceutical firm Chemie Grünenthal, which introduced a popular sedative known as Contergan in 1956. Merrell licensed the sedative as Kevadon. It was known generically as thalidomide.

A parallel development in Congress would, along with Kelsey's so-called easy introduction to FDA, fundamentally re-fashion drug controls in America. In December 1959, Sen. Estes Kefauver of Tennessee began a hearing on pricing practices of the pharmaceutical industry. The ten-month-long hearings yielded incendiary information about astronomical drug price increases, but they also investigated the industry's advertising practices, the sort of information firms provide physicians, and the actual value of many medicines on the market. Kefauver distilled these themes into a bill he introduced in April, 1961; it earned swift and substantial opposition.

Believing the evidence for Kevadon was woefully inadequate, Kelsey informed Merrell in November 1960 that the application needed chronic toxicity data to establish its safety over prolonged use. Upon learning early in 1961 of a possible connection between thalidomide and peripheral neuritis (characterized by painful nerve endings in the extremities), she requested studies on Kevadon's use in pregnancy. This was based both on her own work on differential reactions to quinine substitutes by a rabbit fetus and mother, and a concern she shared with some of her FDA colleagues for possible fetal effects. Throughout this process, Merrell increasingly pressured FDA, and Kelsey personally, to approve Kevadon, even bringing in other clinicians to argue for the drug's safety and efficacy.

Drug Detective

● Her skepticism and insistence on having "all the facts" before certifying the safety of a sleep-inducing drug averted an appalling American tragedy — the birth of many malformed infants.

She resisted persistent petitions of commercial interests who presented data supporting claims the inexpensive drug was harmless. The facts finally vindicated Dr. Kelsey, as evidence piled up to show the drug — thalidomide — when taken by pregnant women, could cause deformed births.

Her action won her the President's Award for Distinguished Federal Civilian Service.

FRANCES O. KELSEY, M.D.
Food and Drug Administration

The Federal Civil Service

Four Score Years of Service to America

1883·1963

Little known fact: Frances Kelsey not only worked on the Elixir Sulfanilamide crisis as a graduate student, but she was one of only a few GS-16's in the federal government. This Civil Service Poster pays tribute to her role as a public servant. (FDA History Office)

Meanwhile, a global public health disaster was well underway. Reports began surfacing in the fall of 1961 that thalidomide had produced grave teratogenic effects, and eventually thousands of thalidomide babies were born with flipper-like limbs. The disaster was largely averted in the United States, but not entirely. Merrell had distributed investigational Kevadon to nearly 20,000 patients, including more than 600 pregnant women, without FDA's knowledge of the scope of this study. Seventeen babies were born in the United States with thalidomide-induced birth defects, a few of whom were a result of thalidomide obtained abroad.

The thalidomide disaster imposed an urgency on passing Kefauver's bill and, though stripped of many of the original elements, many other controls remained and still others were added. Drug effectiveness became a criterion for approval along with drug safety. Henceforth, FDA would maintain stricter control over investigations, would exercise authority over prescription drug advertising, and would have greater inspection powers of company records. Moreover, clinical investigators had to secure from patients informed consent that they understand the risks involved in experiments.

For her work, Kelsey was awarded the Presidential Medal, and her role in averting widespread birth defects in the United States remains to this day, one of the best-remembered episodes in FDA history. Kelsey herself remained with FDA the remainder of her career, a public symbol of FDA vigilance.

—**John P. Swann**

THALIDOMIDE AND DR. KELSEY

...[T]wo cases of phocomelia were presented by a German doctor to a pediatric convention. As an American physician later reported the episode, 'Photographs and X-ray pictures showed that the long bones of the infants' arms had almost completely failed to grow; their arms were so short that their hands extended almost directly from their shoulders. Their legs were less affected but showed signs of a similar distortion of growth....

Phocomelia, a name derived from two Greek words meaning 'seal' and 'limb,' had been so rare an affliction that most doctors had never encountered it during a lifetime of practice. But babies by the hundreds began to be born in Germany thus terribly malformed. By November 1961, a German physician suspected the culpable agent to be thalidomide taken during the first three months of pregnancy. Hearing a rumor of this widespread affliction, Dr. Helen B. Taussig, of the Johns Hopkins University pediatrics department, went to Germany immediately for an investigation on the spot and came home to spread the word through letter, public address, and print of thalidomide's horrifying potentiality. Dr. (Frances) Kelsey went to Baltimore to learn first-hand from Dr. Taussig her disquieting intelligence. On March 8, 1962, the American drug company asked Dr. Kelsey that its new drug application be withdrawn.

Dr. Frances O. Kelsey is shown here accepting the highest civilian honor in the federal service, the Civilian Medal of Honor, in 1963 from President John F. Kennedy.

"Had Dr. Kelsey been less adamant and had Kevadon been released, some 10,000 deformed babies would have been born in the United States before the danger was known. That a smaller-scale disaster did not take place was remarkable, considering the widespread distribution of Kevadon by the American company to clinical 'investigators.' Much of the record-keeping by these doctors was non-existent or shoddy, and the FDA had a difficult task making sure that all supplies of the drug had been recalled or destroyed. As it was, only a few cases of phocomelia occurred in America, mostly from thalidomide secured abroad."

—James Harvey Young

The Medical Messiahs—
A Social History of Health Quackery
in Twentieth-Century America (1966)

that goal, Blair suggested the language that would bring a new level of scientific rigor to FDA and the drug industry. The industry representatives, delighted to avoid a "preponderance of evidence" standard, quickly agreed to the addition of an "adequate and well controlled" definition. The compromise was done.

It is not clear who exactly drafted this evidentiary standard. Its roots can be found in the testimony of distinguished figures in the field of drug therapeutics, which included Dr. Lasagna, Dr. Harry Dowling of the University of Illinois School of Medicine, and Dr. Maxwell Finland of Harvard Medical School. These leading academics had argued for good scientific data in support of the efficacy of a new drug if physicians were to practice rational, scientific medicine. They further contended that controlled trials in humans were the best scientific method for establishing proof of efficacy. It is also fair to say that none envisioned the enormous consequences this standard would, in ensuing decades, come to have on the development of new drugs, the pharmaceutical industry, and the practice of medicine. They were seeking to codify in law the best scientific practice of the day, but there is no evidence that they—or Congress—grasped that they were together laying the foundation for a revolution in drug development and medical practice.

The Senate passed the revised bill on August 23, 1962. The House of Representatives held brief hearings and then marked up its bill to conform to the one that had passed the Senate. It was passed on September 27, 1962. Both votes were unanimous.

The 1962 Amendments contained a number of important new provisions in addition to the efficacy requirement. Manufacturers were now required to adhere to current good manufacturing practice (GMP) within the industry. FDA subsequently adopted and updated extensive GMP regulations that have become a model for other national regulatory agencies. They have also been the most frequent basis for enforcement actions against drug manufacturers in the last forty years. Pharmaceutical firms were also required to keep detailed records and make reports to FDA (e.g., of adverse events that occur post-approval). An elaborate regulatory system was established for investigational drugs that specifically includes a requirement that research subjects sign written informed consent forms. FDA was authorized to regulate prescription drug advertising, and FDA's inspectional powers, while in drug manufacturing plants, were expanded.

The agency was initially overwhelmed by the sudden acquisition of new responsibilities. Individual drug firms were equally troubled by the enormity of the new challenges. Both knew that a new era was coming, but its shape was unclear. Indeed, it would be two decades before FDA regulation and pharmaceutical industry practices would evolve to accommodate fully the 1962 Amendments.

The pharmaceutical industry was at the time in the midst of a remarkable growth phase, referred to by some even today as a Golden Age, as the result of a flowering in pharmaceutical R&D following World War II. New antibiotics and new drugs to treat such conditions as high blood pressure, coronary heart disease, mental illness, anesthesia, pain, and inflammation emerged each year. Many would revolutionize the practice of medicine.

In this context, the early years of implementing the 1962 Amendments seemed to portend a major barrier to further progress. FDA began its work by recruiting additional physicians and scientists to its staff and tightening its review standards for new drugs. This latter step had an immediate and dramatic effect on the rate of drug approvals. In 1959, 315 new drug applications were approved, including 63 new chemical entities; in 1966, 82 applications were approved, only 18 of which were new chemical entities. A major reason for the decline in approvals was the lack of properly conducted controlled studies in the applications supporting their effectiveness. For industry, the specter of a permanent reduction in new drug approvals was ominous. Industry and FDA faced a second major challenge. Along with the "wonder drugs" in the 1940s and 1950s, drug firms had also produced a vast number of products of uncertain value, some of them combinations of two active ingredients in a fixed dose. The pharmaceutical marketplace of 1962 thus contained a huge number of products, ranging from the miraculous to the worthless, with a limited number ever having been actually tested for efficacy in controlled clinical trials. One goal of the new law, therefore, was to assure that drug products already being offered for sale were efficacious.

Congress directed FDA to conduct a retrospective review of essentially all the drugs then in the marketplace, applying the new "adequate and well-controlled study" standard for evidence of effectiveness. Little did the authors of the legislation know how tough this job would be and how long it would take. This review, known as the Drug Efficacy Study Implementation (DESI) program, covered both the ingredients in more than 4,000 "new drugs" marketed between 1938 and 1962 and the 16,500 therapeutic claims for use made for these ingredients. The agency lacked the staff to conduct such a burdensome review internally and so contracted with the National Academy of Sciences and National Research Council (NAS-NRC) to establish panels of experts to carry out the initial review.

The results came back at the end of 1968. While virtually all drugs reviewed had ingredients that were pharmacologically active, more than fifty percent of the 16,500 therapeutic claims made for them were unsupported by appropriate scientific studies. Another twenty-four percent of the claims were judged to be "probably effective." Less than one claim in five was found to be unqualifiedly "effective." In addition, many combination drugs were found to lack evidence that all ingredients contributed to the effectiveness of the product. The industry now confronted difficult choices. They could cut back on claims and remove ineffective ingredients in products, reducing the revenues needed to finance future research costs. Alternatively, they could try to prove the effectiveness of the claims and ingredients through new "adequate and well-controlled" studies, diverting resources that could have been used for new research. Finally, they could challenge FDA's legal authority in the courts. The last course was often the most expedient business option.

DESI MODERNIZES THE DRUG MARKET

Few projects have so fundamentally affected medicine as the Drug Efficacy Study Implementation (DESI), which occupied FDA's attention for close to two decades after enactment of the 1962 Kefauver-Harris Drug Amendments. Until 1962, the law required only that drugs be shown to be safe, not that they be demonstrated effective. Once the law was passed, FDA began to require that all new drugs be tested for effectiveness before approval. The larger challenge was what to do about the drugs already on the market, some of which may not have met the new standard.

Recognizing the scope of the challenge, FDA contracted with the National Academy of Sciences (NAS) in July, 1966 to evaluate approximately 4,000 drugs—and their 16,500 claims—that had been approved between 1938 and 1962 on the basis of safety but not efficacy. The NAS formed thirty panels of some 200 experts qualified by training or experience to evaluate the effectiveness of human and animal drugs. FDA solicited evidence from sponsors to support these claims, and forwarded the data to the NAS panels. From October 1967 until April 1969, NAS experts evaluated each drug and each indication as "effective," "probably effective," "possibly effective," "ineffective," or "ineffective as a fixed combination."

In accordance with the Drug Amendments, an "effective" drug had demonstrated by evidence derived from adequate and well-controlled studies that would convince an expert in the field that the drug manifested the effect it was claimed to produce. A drug deemed "probably effective" required more research or a clarification in the labeling. "Possibly effective" meant that the drug required substantially more research to support the claim in question, and "ineffective" indicated a clear absence of evidence that the drug performed as stated. An "ineffective as a fixed combination" conclusion indicated that the drug had at least one effective component, but the combined preparation of two or more active ingredients itself was either unsafe or ineffective. The NAS panels reported that 434 drugs reviewed were effective in all their claims, but fully fifty percent of the claims evaluated lacked substantial evidence of effectiveness.

Implementation of the NAS recommendations took FDA many years to complete. The agency faced lawsuits from companies whose products the agency sought to remove from the market, from those who objected to the process, and from those who believed the agency's progress was too slow, violating the 1962 amendments and posing a threat to the public health. By 1984, in accordance with a court agreement four years earlier, FDA had completed all but forty-two products of the 3,443 drugs reviewed and implemented under DESI, and all but seven by 1987. Thus, over the course of fifteen years, sometimes with strong resistance from business interests, and with immense assistance from NAS, FDA applied modern clinical standards to the therapeutic armamentarium of the 1930s, 1940s, and 1950s to rid the modern medical marketplace of inadequately tested drugs.

—**John P. Swann**

On its part, FDA recognized it was likely to face a wide array of legal battles to complete the DESI program. To handle each case in the traditional way, with a full administrative hearing on each drug, would overwhelm agency resources. Lawyers at FDA thus devised a new and novel "summary judgment" procedure that would avoid such hearings. In essence, when the agency challenged the effectiveness of a drug, the manufacturer would not be entitled to a hearing unless it could demonstrate the existence of adequate and well-controlled studies supporting effectiveness. If FDA could demonstrate that each study offered by the manufacturer failed to meet the "adequate and well-controlled" threshold, there would be no legitimate scientific evidence to consider, and thus no justification for a hearing. In executing this strategy, the agency also needed regulations spelling out in detail the elements of an adequate and well-controlled investigation. With the assistance of Dr. William T. Beaver of the Georgetown University School of Medicine as his primary consultant, William Goodrich, the Chief Counsel of FDA, produced a simple, straightforward statement of the principles for adequate and well-controlled investigations, which has stood the test of time for nearly four decades. These regulations note the need for: a protocol; comparative treatment (usually placebo or another drug); description of the patients to be included and excluded in the study; description of the methods of measurement, randomization, and "blinding;" and proper statistical analysis. These regulations became the first legal battleground over the effectiveness requirement. FDA initially issued them in 1969. The following year, a court set them aside on the grounds that the agency had failed to follow legally required notice-and-comment rulemaking procedures. FDA promptly went through those administrative procedures with the same regulations, and this time the courts upheld them.

The DESI litigation was not over, however. Pharmaceutical manufacturers now urged courts to deny FDA any "new drug" jurisdiction over already marketed products, to decline any deference to the agency on regulatory decisions,

and to block the "summary judgment" mechanism. Each of these requests sought to undercut the agency's fundamental ability to enforce the "adequate and well-controlled" studies requirement. In 1973, the Supreme Court reviewed these issues and ruled in favor of FDA on all points. The court observed that no one disputed that FDA's standards for controlled investigations "express well-established principles of scientific investigation." Interestingly, the court—which had concluded in 1911 that therapeutic effectiveness was a matter of medical opinion that could not be resolved in a court of law—now stated that "impressions or beliefs of physicians, no matter how fervently believed, are treacherous." FDA was freed to use its summary judgment mechanism when the proponent of a drug or claim failed to meet the minimum threshold of evidence of effectiveness. It proceeded, between 1973 and 1984, to complete the DESI process for those products and claims that had been questioned by the NAS-NRC reviewers. As manufacturers submitted requests for hearings supported by numerous clinical studies, FDA meticulously dissected each study for flaws. Frequently, FDA consulted with academic researchers or standing advisory committees for advice on the adequacy of methods. If the agency decided to reject the request for a hearing, it issued a lengthy and detailed explanation as to why the studies, as designed or executed, failed to meet the standards for controlled clinical investigations. It is not an exaggeration to conclude that DESI, more than any other single aspect of implementation of the 1962 Amendments, transformed the broad statutory requirement for evidence of effectiveness into concrete and meaningful standards. As a result of DESI, FDA, academia, and industry all learned a staggering amount about the design and problems of clinical studies in all areas of therapeutics, and the sophistication of clinical research made quantum leaps.

By 1985, when it was largely concluded, the DESI review had directly affected three-fourths of all the prescription drug products that were in the marketplace in 1962, either with withdrawals from the marketplace, removal of ineffective ingredients, or re-labeling of the indications for use. This revolution rationalized the drug therapeutic armamentarium of the United States more than any other single program ever conducted. Though it took three decades to complete, essentially all prescription drug products in the United States met the safety, effectiveness, and manufacturing standards of the 1962 Amendments. This process in turn created an environment in which medicines and medical treatment had credibility to physicians and patients based on real science.

As part of the DESI review, the agency created a new application, known as an Abbreviated New Drug Application (ANDA), to handle the many generic products then in the marketplace that had never been reviewed previously. The purpose of the ANDA was to assure that generic products met the same

manufacturing and formulation standards, and had the same labeling, as the original pioneer product containing the same active ingredient. In 1984, the ANDA and the generic drug process were codified into legislation, completing a long battle to bring all prescription drug products to the same standards. Today, the public can be assured that generic drugs, as well as new chemical entities, meet the same manufacturing standards and deliver the same amount of the same active ingredient to the same site of therapeutic effect in the body.

The effectiveness provisions of the 1962 Amendments also affected the non-prescription or over-the-counter (OTC) drug marketplace. On its own initiative in 1972, the agency began a major review of the ingredients in OTC products, to assure that these products also met modern standards of safety and effectiveness, with instructions for use appropriate for the lay consumer. This project, conducted largely through a series of outside advisory committees and extensive public participation, is still not complete. But it has already accomplished the removal of unsafe or ineffective ingredients from the market, permitted drugs formerly available only by prescription to be sold OTC, and improved dramatically the information available on product labels.

By the 1990s, the once chaotic pharmaceutical marketplace of the mid-twentieth century—a mixture of single entity and combination prescription products approved only for safety, and of generic and OTC drug products never

Following passage of the 1962 Drug Amendments, the size of even routine New Drug Applications began to grow exponentially as illustrated in this photo taken by a drug manufacturer of his NDA. Today, the product submission process is largely electronic making it faster and more environmentally friendly, but certainly less picturesque.

reviewed or approved at all—had been transformed. And a major reason for this transformation was the requirement that drugs be effective for their intended uses, as demonstrated through adequate and well-controlled trials, which was creatively and diligently implemented by FDA.

Despite this effort and obvious progress, by the early 1970s a political backlash developed against the effectiveness requirement, which to some extent continues today. It was originally fueled by a variety of divergent views and interests. Initially, in the early 1970s, medical experts began to observe that, in at least some categories of drugs, FDA was not approving any products at all. For example, no new chemical entity for cardiovascular use was approved in a period of almost five years, from early 1968 to the end of 1972. Moreover, even where FDA did approve new drugs, it was often long after they had been marketed in other advanced countries, a situation that came to be known as the "drug lag." Physicians began to worry that they could not provide their patients the best therapies when they observed that many new drugs were being marketed first in foreign countries, particularly the United Kingdom. This cry was taken up by economists, who argued that physicians and patients were the best arbiters of drug efficacy and that a free market would sort good from bad products. In their view, government regulation made markets inefficient and imposed costs on consumers that exceeded benefits. Another voice in this debate came from libertarians, who contended that the government was protecting people to death. Individuals in a free society should be entitled to take any medicine they wished; Laetrile became a rallying cry for this point of view.

The point of agreement among these disparate interests was that the effectiveness requirement should be

---

FDA SCORES AT THE SUPREME COURT

In the Spring of 1973, the Supreme Court handed down decisions in four cases that paved the way for the FDA's full implementation of the 1962 Drug Amendments. In its initial efforts to implement the Amendments, FDA had lost three important cases in the lower courts. Singly, each loss was problematic, but cumulatively they eviscerated FDA's authority.

When Peter Barton Hutt succeeded William Goodrich as FDA's Chief Counsel, he pursued what he acknowledged to be a risky strategy: a single appeal of all three cases to the Supreme Court, plus a fourth related case. Fortunately, the court was persuaded to take all three cases. Soon after FDA emerged victorious, Hutt explained the significance of the court victory to FDA employees. He was both blunt and succinct: "We went to the Supreme Court and wrote four briefs that basically said, 'Damn it, either give us the authority to be a full-fledged, full-power administrative agency or else tell us we can't do anything and give the job to somebody else.'" Hutt continued with an explanation of the complex legal issues that involved "primary jurisdiction" and the scope of FDA's administrative authority.

Hutt summed up the significance of the decision by telling employees that the Supreme Court had, in essence, "sanctioned the agency as the expert in dealing with foods, drugs, medical devices, and cosmetics." Employees at the briefing say it was one of the high points of their career and seem hard-pressed to say which impressed them more, the victory itself or Hutt's incisive summation of it.

—Suzanne White Junod

---

amended or repealed. Even elements of the medical profession and the drug industry toyed with the idea of joining this movement. The media covered the drug-lag debate extensively, documenting the overseas trips people made to get a drug not available in the United States. Thus, the public was widely aware of this debate. The proponents of Laetrile went so far as to challenge the constitutionality of the effectiveness requirement in court, arguing that the law should not apply to drugs for persons with a fatal illness for which there was no conventional cure. In 1979, the Supreme Court unanimously rejected this argument, observing that:

> Since the turn of the [twentieth] century, resourceful entrepreneurs have advertised a wide variety of purportedly simple and painless cures for cancer, including lineaments of turpentine, mustard, oil, eggs, and ammonia; peat moss; arrangements of colored floodlights; pastes made from glycerin and limburger cheese; mineral tablets; and "Fountain of Youth" mixtures of spices, oil and suet.... Congress could reasonably have determined to protect the terminally ill, no less than other patients, from the vast range of self-styled panaceas that inventive minds can devise.

While this debate was occurring during the 1970s, FDA promulgated a series of landmark requirements and standards that, in conjunction with the "adequate and well-controlled trials" definition, provided a complete regulatory framework for modern clinical research on drugs and biologics. One set, collectively called good clinical practices (GCPs), included requirements for: informed consent of participants in a clinical trial, ethical evaluation by local institutional review boards, monitoring of clinical studies for adherence to protocol and data integrity, timely reporting of adverse events, and periodic reports to FDA. The GCPs, together with FDA's good laboratory practices (GLPs) standards to assure the integrity of toxicology data, have established principles now accepted throughout the developed world.

In 1985, FDA promulgated an updated version of its regulations that prescribe the structure of a new drug application, the kinds of reports required in one, and the processes for reviewing and handling these important applications. Most significantly,

this revision made the first (and to date only) comprehensive restatement of the 1970 definition of "adequate and well-controlled investigation." While adhering to the principles set down fifteen years earlier, the new rule reflects the lessons learned during the DESI program. Since the early 1980s, as well, FDA has been working with its counterpart regulatory agencies in the European Union and Japan, together with the pharmaceutical industry and other governmental authorities in Canada and Australia, in the International Conference on Harmonization (ICH), to reduce inconsistencies and conflicts among national requirements for approval

THE OTC DRUG REVIEW: THE LAWSUIT THAT NEVER WAS

FDA's OTC Drug Review, launched in 1972, was one of the largest undertakings ever for FDA. It was an analysis of drugs in the over-the-counter marketplace, to substantiate the effectiveness of drugs for which "safety only" New Drug Applications (NDAs) had been approved between 1938 and 1962.

The review, however, was not limited to the approximately 400 OTC NDAs approved, but evaluated all then-marketed OTC drugs for safety and effectiveness and proper labeling. The legal premise underpinning the review was based on then-FDA General Counsel Peter Barton Hutt's theory that the Food, Drug, and Cosmetic Act is a "constitution," and that FDA had wide discretion for creating substantive regulations or "monographs" to implement it.

Most food and drug lawyers argued that the regulations exceeded FDA's legal authority, sort of the tobacco fight of its day. Of particular concern was industry's view that FDA was creating a specific narrow standard to control the marketing of future OTC drugs.

Notwithstanding these arguments, a final regulation was published on May 26, 1972. Every day afterwards, we in the Office of General Counsel waited for a lawsuit to be filed by a drug company or the industry trade association, in those days called the Proprietary Association.

Despite the industry's public grumbling, a suit was never filed. I had the honor to be the director of the review.

To those who question the agency's legal wisdom, one needs merely to note that the Supreme Court commented on the wisdom of the OTC Review in *Weinberger v. Bentex Pharmaceuticals*, which was decided about a year after the OTC review started. To this day, no one has ever challenged the legal authority of FDA to promulgate the OTC monograph regulations as substantive rules, nor has FDA ever relied in a court on the substantive rule argument to remove an OTC drug from the market.

—Gary L. Yingling

FIGHTING LAETRILE

The promotion of bogus cancer cures threatens the health of cancer victims who avoid proven therapies, while robbing them of their money. In the 1970s, the almond derivative laetrile was heavily promoted nationally as a cancer cure. Its promoters sought to legalize laetrile, arguing that sick people had the freedom to choose any therapy they wanted.

FDA fought back vigorously: We educated legislators. We issued a laetrile warning poster. We held a hearing in Kansas to air the science and the freedom-of-choice issues. Every time a laetrile story was written, we sought an opportunity to express our skepticism.

The media generally was of two minds. Some editorials denounced laetrile as a hoax. But others in the media argued that people, especially terminal cancer patients, have the right to spend their money any way they want to. They viewed FDA's sole role as educating the public that laetrile does not work, not prohibiting its interstate sale. They argued for the repeal of the efficacy clause in the FD&C Act.

Eventually reality won out. Laetrile disappeared because it did not work. But it took a few years for the public to recognize the deception. The episode underscored the need for FDA to understand the power of the freedom-of-choice argument, which arises frequently in other circumstances. We also learned that FDA must aggressively defend the scientific method and protect patients, especially the most vulnerable, not just from unsafe drugs, but also from cruel hoaxes.

—Wayne L. Pines

FDA's Laetrile Warning Poster and VOCAL's counterposter—This public warning poster, modeled on the FBI's wanted posters from the 1950s and signed by Commissioner Donald Kennedy, alerted the public to the dangers of self treatment with laetrile. Opponents of FDA's laetrile policy saw it differently as illustrated in VOCAL's counterposter, at right.

of new drugs. This effort has led to a series of guidelines and changes in FDA regulations to facilitate drug development and review. Interestingly, throughout this ICH process, FDA's standards have been the benchmark toward which other regulators have moved. Instead of rejecting the rigors of good science to support product approvals, other nations have endorsed them.

Despite the clear contribution of the efficacy requirement to modern medicine, political debates of its value have continued, especially when it is perceived to be a barrier between hope and death for many desperate and dying people. In the mid-1980s, at the start of the AIDS crisis, calls were once again heard that the requirement for scientific proof of efficacy was wrong in the face of an otherwise untreatable disease. Activists staged protests at FDA offices, seeking the right to use whatever medicines they wanted regardless of efficacy, or seeking to set a different standard for AIDS drugs so as to shorten the development period. Members of Congress and the White House staff questioned whether this new and fatal infection justified suspension of the need for adequate and well-controlled investigations.

The agency responded in a number of ways: rushing approval of the first therapies for AIDS, enacting regulations to expedite review of drugs to treat life-threatening conditions, and liberalizing its policy permitting importation of unapproved drugs. FDA did not, however, agree to eliminate proof of effectiveness

as a condition for marketing drugs in the United States. In retrospect, it is clear that despite setbacks and political debate, the broad tide continued to advance in favor of science-based regulation of drug effectiveness. For example, AIDS activists who originally opposed placebo-controlled trials as unethical later came to argue that such studies were the only way to determine which drugs worked in this terrible disease. Less conspicuous were the philosophical and practical changes within the pharmaceutical industry.

As the 1980s progressed, manufacturers became more comfortable with, and better equipped for, the rigors of the drug development and approval process. An industry that once struggled to cope with new regulatory challenges, particularly the effectiveness requirement, became focused on succeeding in a strong regulatory environment. Initially, companies were ill-prepared for the new regulatory requirements. Merck and Lilly, the two largest research spenders in 1961, each spent on R&D about $21 million, between nine and ten percent of their total corporate sales. The entire U.S. research-intensive pharmaceutical industry invested $245 million that year. Without the need for adequate and well-controlled clinical studies, companies did not need physicians and statisticians to design, or numerous experienced investigators to perform, Phase 3 studies.

The changes since 1962 have been astounding. In 2004, pharmaceutical companies spent $38.8 billion on R&D worldwide, according to the industry's trade association. When biotechnology research is added, the total investment is estimated at close to $50 billion. The largest individual pharmaceutical company in 2003, Pfizer, had a $7.1 billion R&D budget—nearly $19.5 million per *day*, compared with the $21 million Merck and Lilly combined spent per year in 1961. In 2001, the Tufts Center for the Study of Drug Development estimated the cost of bringing a new chemical entity to market at $802 million. This figure represents direct cash expenses of $282 million for clinical testing, $121 million for preclinical testing, $80 million for post-approval studies, and the remainder for the opportunity cost of money (that is, how much could have been earned by investing in bonds, not drugs). These estimates also include the cost of the many investigational drugs that fail during the course of development, the pharmaceutical equivalent of dry wells in the oil industry.

The increased investment required to bring new drug products to market has changed the size and structure of the pharmaceutical industry and the rest of the biomedical research community. Those companies with substantial marketing capacity and efficient manufacturing

GENERIC DRUGS: A CRISIS IN CONFIDENCE

In the Summer of 1988, an unforgettably dark chapter in the FDA's otherwise proud history began to unfold. Without warning, a sweeping congressional investigation into the safety of the nation's generic drug supply hit FDA with tornado-like force. The ensuing scandal began with an unannounced raid on FDA's generic drug offices by investigators from Capitol Hill and the Office of Inspector General who sealed off targeted offices and seized custody of agency records. Stunned FDA staffers scrambled to notify the Commissioner and Deputy Commissioner, both of whom were huddled in conference elsewhere in the building. As the lead investigator made his way to the building's exit with armloads of FDA files, an agency official intercepted him and protested the removal of the records. A heated hallway exchange erupted that later in the day mushroomed into a test of wills between the politically powerful committee chairman and senior Executive Branch officials.

The scandal, which quickly deepened and became the object of intense media coverage, lingered for three anguishing years, engulfing the agency in controversy and unprecedented scrutiny. The unfortunate episode stemmed from a serious breach in the integrity of the industry that produces generic medicines, in addition to a breakdown of FDA's regulatory system, designed to protect consumers from unsafe human drugs. Disturbing revelations of corporate misconduct that placed profits above public safety, and unethical ties between drug industry executives and FDA drug reviewers were brought to light after frustrated competitors in the industry privately took their complaints about unfair regulatory treatment to the Congress.

The resulting fallout could have wiped out an industry that only years earlier had been heralded as a much-needed counterbalance to the rapidly escalating costs of prescription drugs, and the virtual monopolistic stronghold brand-name drug firms had on the American pocketbook. The federal government—which had awarded large-dollar procurement contracts for generic drugs to treat military personnel, low-income citizens, and the elderly—worried that collapse of the generic drugs industry could bust the national budget.

Corrupt and deceptive business practices, made worse by poor-quality manufacturing by many unscrupulous generic drug-makers and drug-testing laboratories engendered panic among consumers, causing many to abandon affordable generics and switch to higher-priced brand-name drugs. Doctors

operations have consolidated and increased capitalization to such an extent that movement in their stock is a bellwether for our national economy. While the Dow Jones Industrial Index had no pharmaceutical companies in 1962, it contained three in 2004. At the same time, the emergence of venture capital financing permitted a variety of start-up biotech firms to assume more of the risks and rewards for exploratory drug discovery and early development. They in turn sell, license, or partner with established companies for final development and marketing of successful discoveries.

The clinical trial enterprise has also changed enormously. From the days when practicing physicians did most of the Phase 3 studies on individual protocols in their own offices, it is now common to have large, multisite studies involving hundreds or thousands of subjects. Phase 1 and 2 studies, as well as specialized pharmacokinetic investigations, are often performed in for-profit facilities independent of academic institutions or research hospitals. A specialized field of biostatistics has developed to assist in the design and interpretation of clinical trials. The number of physicians serving as

and pharmacists became reluctant to dispense generic pharmaceuticals. New market clearances from FDA for generic drugs, including versions of innovative drug therapies, came to a virtual standstill. Generics used to treat patients with serious health conditions, such as epilepsy, were recalled. The country's healthcare system faced serious trouble.

FDA leaders clamped down hard on the industry. Tougher industry-wide inspections were conducted to root out "bad actors." The agency's field inspector force was beefed up. In cases when a drug's safety was in question, market approvals were pulled back and government procurement contracts were suspended. Internal FDA procedures were reformed to provide for greater transparency, accountability, and fairness in the drug review process, along with more rigorous pre-marketing requirements. FDA cooperated with Congress and Justice Department attorneys to successfully prosecute scores of malefactors and enact legislation authorizing "debarment" of companies that operate unethically or unsafely. Stern disciplinary action was taken by the agency against some of its own.

Taken together, these actions and the resolve of government leaders to restore eroded public confidence in FDA enabled America's oldest and most vital consumer protection agencies to weather the storm. From near disaster, valuable lessons were learned. The dynamic tension between regulator and regulated industry, the absence of which contributed to the crisis, is now an integral part of FDA's generic drugs evaluation process.

Because of FDA's honest introspection and commitment to systemic change, generic drugs are once again a viable and indispensable part of the armamentarium used to treat the nation's sick and, at the same time, are helping to contain healthcare costs in the United States.

—**James S. Benson &
Robert C. Eccleston**

investigators at any one time is in the tens of thousands, distributed around the world. Patients to serve as research subjects are in such demand that cash payments are part of recruiting incentives.

FDA's requirements have also spawned a significant new service industry to manage the logistics of clinical trials and to assure their integrity and compliance with human protection regulations and good clinical practice standards. Members of this industry include clinical research organizations (CROs), site management organizations, freestanding ethical review boards, biostatistical consulting firms, and other for-profit companies founded specifically to help design, execute, analyze, and report the trials necessary for regulatory approvals. By 2000, more than 500 CRO companies were handling over

---

RESPONDING TO THE CHALLENGE OF AIDS:
ACCESS TO INVESTIGATIONAL DRUGS

FDA's approval process for prescription drugs is based on a straightforward premise: formal approval, based on a positive benefit/risk ratio derived from adequate and well-controlled studies, is needed for widespread use of a new product. However, over the years the agency has permitted access on a broad basis to drugs still being studied. FDA's policy emerged largely from the AIDS crisis of the mid-1980s.

Widespread access to investigational drugs that had a unique medical need first occurred with the large-scale treatment of narcotic addicts with methadone in the early 1970s. When AIDS became such a devastating crisis in the mid-1980s, the highly activist AIDS advocacy community insisted that FDA make investigational drugs available even before they were proven safe and effective, to allow people who had no other hope to grasp any new medicine being developed.

The AIDS community was the most active I ever dealt with in more than three decades of government health service. It also was the most aggressive. Its tactics went far beyond scientific advocacy. The community used the media to attack FDA and even physically came to the FDA headquarters in Rockville to advocate its position in person by "closing down" FDA—in full view of the TV cameras. I remember that day as well as the "die-in" we experienced at a panel presentation in Boston.

Within FDA, we were sympathetic to their cause and concerns and agreed that under the proper conditions drugs that "may be effective" could be the best available therapy and should be made available to patients. At the same time, we wanted to protect the integrity of the new drug application policy that had been built over many years into a successful paradigm for protecting the public health.

Thus, FDA developed a policy for making drugs available on a widespread basis before their formal approval. FDA officially recognized this approach to certain categories of investigational new drugs (INDs) by promulgating the treatment IND regulation in 1985. FDA took full advantage of its excellent relationships with health professional organizations to make health professionals aware of IND drugs that FDA designated as available to physicians for treatment purposes. The *Journal of the American Medical Association* (*JAMA*) announced this new vehicle for practitioners in an invited editorial by FDA.

As specific new drugs were approved for such use, FDA utilized its monthly column in *JAMA*, "From the FDA" (for which I was responsible) and other publications, such as the *FDA Medical Bulletin*, to ensure that physicians and other health professionals were aware of newly available—but not yet approved—drugs for HIV/AIDS, cancer, and other drugs for serious or life-threatening conditions. The

---

twenty-two percent of drug development activities.

FDA has correspondingly grown to regulate this enterprise and review its output. In 2005, the FDA staff reviewing the safety, effectiveness, and quality of drugs and therapeutic biologics numbered in the hundreds and included medical officers, pharmacologists, toxicologists, microbiologists, biologists, immunologists, chemists, biochemists, pharmacists, biopharmaceutical scientists, biostatisticians, epidemiologists, project managers, communications experts, and other professionals. Today, the agency handles roughly sixty to seventy new product approval applications each year (including roughly twenty new molecular entities), 125 to 140 supplements for new clinical uses of approved products,

Office of Health Affairs, which I headed, provided training and technical assistance to physicians whose HIV/AIDS practice was large to assist them in understanding and complying with FDA's good clinical practice regulations. We did this in cooperation with the gay and lesbian physicians' organization.

Recognizing the importance of the principle, we extended the policy to cancer drugs and drugs for other serious or life-threatening conditions. FDA's recognition of the need to make drugs that could help patients with serious or life-threatening diseases prior to approval was a remarkable proactive approach. This use of the IND was novel for drug regulatory agencies worldwide since they were accustomed to looking at the investigational phase of drug development as only a stage leading to marketing approval—with occasional use of the IND drug for a single patient in critical condition—needing case-by-case approval by the company and FDA (the so-called compassionate IND).

The philosophy behind these expanded access initiatives served as a template for other regulatory initiatives, such as the program in 1990 to make investigational drugs and approved drugs used off-label to protect the military during the Persian Gulf War. In fact, the recognition that there will always be drugs in the investigational phase that may provide the best available treatment or prevention is recognized today in the fact that many drugs in our strategic national stockpile are listed as being available for widespread use under "contingency INDs" in emergency situations.

Finally, recognizing the importance of this concept and further refining this approach for national emergencies, legislation Congress enacted in 2004 overcame some of the barriers to providing widespread use of IND products by creating the category of emergency use authorization (EUA) for drug, biologic, and medical device products. These products are either unapproved or approved for indications other than the needed use. The Secretary of Health and Human Services must declare an emergency and the FDA Commissioner must approve the product under the EUA authority.

The AIDS crisis was devastating, but from it emerged a new way of thinking at FDA about making drugs available for serious or life-threatening conditions on a routine or an emergency basis, an approach that has been applied to other crises or potential crises.

—Stuart L. Nightingale

DRUG ADVERTISING

The central feature of the 1962 Drug Amendments was the requirement that drugs be proven effective. But Congress also gave FDA authority to regulate prescription drug advertising, previously the responsibility of the Federal Trade Commission. Alleged marketing abuses, and their relationship to drug prices, were at the core of the congressional hearings that led to that 1962 law. In the nearly half century since, through enforcement practices and policy pronouncements, FDA assumed authority over all aspects of drug promotion financed by companies. FDA had to keep up with the communications revolution and the dramatically changing role of the physician and patient in health care delivery, which has changed how prescription drugs are promoted.

The regulatory road became bumpy from 1995 to 2000, when FDA became embroiled in First Amendment litigation. It ended without clear resolution, but did force the agency to clarify its policies on the regulation of peer-reviewed articles and continuing medical education. Perhaps the most controversial action occurred in 1997, when FDA established rules permitting direct-to-consumer (DTC) advertising on television. The resulting surge in TV advertising for prescription drugs has been controversial as critics tie DTC TV advertising to increased medical costs and inappropriate prescribing.

FDA also played a key role in helping other enforcement agencies initiate action against promotional activities that violated other statutes, such as the anti-kickback law. While the regulation of advertising is a minuscule part of the total FDA budget, the function has become one of the most visible and controversial programs run by the agency.

—Wayne L. Pines

more than 250 abbreviated new drug applications for generic drugs, thousands of applications for clinical studies, and hundreds of thousands of individual reports of adverse drug experiences. Much of FDA's expenses are borne by user fees paid by the pharmaceutical industry. Is the cost of all this activity worth it? Focusing solely on actual out-of-pocket R&D expenses, data suggest that the cost of bringing a new chemical entity to market in 2005 may be approaching $500 million. This number can be viewed in many ways: as the cost of addressing ever more difficult scientific challenges in therapeutics; as the result of overly stringent regulatory burdens; as the unavoidable expense of protecting society from unsafe or ineffective products; as a productive economic investment in

biomedical research; or as a bargain when balanced against the resulting gains in longevity and quality of life.

It is reasonably clear that the more rigorous regulatory standards have not adversely affected the research-based pharmaceutical industry. Initially, the Drug Amendments of 1962 added costs and slowed the development of new drugs while the industry accommodated to the new rules. Over the longer term, however, this law's mandate for scientific quality, and the industry's increased investment in research have led to larger, more creative and more productive drug development programs. Because of the long lead-time necessary for the full development cycle, well more than a decade passed before the first products began to emerge onto the market under the 1962 effectiveness requirements. The new pharmaceuticals reaching the U.S. market in the early 1980s showed the commercial benefits of the more rigorous testing criteria. Whole new classes of medicines passed through the FDA review process, such as nonsteroidal anti-inflammatory drugs (beginning in 1975) and calcium channel blockers (1981). These and other products were successful commercially, in part because their marketing could be supported by solid evidence of effectiveness, not anecdote and endorsement.

Furthermore, the quality of the new products and the persuasiveness of the data showing their benefits enabled drug therapy to gain a central position in the healthcare system. In 1965, drugs were deemed of such low value and cost that

How FDA Clarified the Rules for DTC TV Advertising

It wasn't really an earthquake. It involved no change in regulations nor, really, any change in basic attitude. It certainly did not represent the "relaxation" of rules or enforcement that people attributed to it in subsequent years. What it was, was a draft guidance issued in 1997, entitled "Consumer-Directed Broadcast Advertisements," that removed a major uncertainty confronting anyone then contemplating a consumer-directed broadcast drug advertisement.

Contrary to popular belief, direct-to-consumer (DTC) advertising by the prescription drug industry did not start in 1997. It had been around since the early 1980s, absent only during a moratorium from 1983 to 1985. But, while rapidly growing, the DTC advertising at that time was almost entirely in print because no one knew, and FDA had never said, what would be acceptable for broadcast promotion of prescription drugs. The uncertainty hinged on a single issue: How could "adequate provision" for dissemination of the approved package insert be made in a broadcast advertisement?

For decades, rules for broadcast drug advertisements had required that the "major risks" of the drug be included in the ad, together with either the "brief summary"—that is, all the risk-related information in a product's approved package labeling—or "adequate provision" for the dissemination of the approved package labeling in connection with the ad. But no one knew what that meant in the context of broadcast advertising, and FDA had never described how sponsors could fulfill this requirement.

In the absence of guidance, some very odd promotion took place, mostly in the form of "reminder" advertising. Reminder ads name the product but may not say or suggest what the product is used for. For example, ads showing a woman dancing through fields with the name of an antihistamine mystified consumers. Some ads did say what the drug was used for, and then scrolled the entire package insert at the end of the ad—if you can imagine that. The situation clearly was unsatisfactory. DTC ads were legal and becoming commonplace in print media where it was feasible to include the "brief summary" of risks. But broadcast DTC ads were hamstrung by confusion over the regulatory requirements.

Thus was born the draft guidance on Consumer-Directed Broadcast Advertisements. It ensured that consumers would receive adequate communication of required risk information, and described an approach to doing this. With a workable, permitted approach in hand, drug companies were free to develop DTC ads for TV. The rest is history.

So it wasn't a conceptual revolution. The key to DTC TV promotion of prescription drugs was a rather straightforward draft guidance that set forth for drug companies how to satisfy "adequate provision."

—**Lesley R. Frank & Melissa Moncavage**

they were not included in the coverage of the new Medicare program. It took forty years for Congress and the public to recognize that the contribution of drugs to healthcare demanded their inclusion under Medicare. Another measure of the increasing importance of pharmaceuticals is the share of total healthcare spending on prescription drugs. In 1990, it constituted 6.6% of the national total; by 2000, that figure was nearing 11%. While the climb was aided by enhanced medical insurance coverage and by state Medicaid programs, drug expenditures increased without the support of Medicare. Yet Medicare contributed to the growth of other parts of the healthcare industry in this period. Although some of this change might have resulted from scientific advances alone over the past forty years, it seems unlikely that the enormous investment of the pharmaceutical industry would have occurred without the legal mandate written in 1962. Increased expenditures for R&D led to new and important products supported by persuasive scientific evidence, which in turn led to wider utilization and confidence in the value received, which enabled sustained revenues and profits for the innovator companies.

If the pharmaceutical industry has benefited from the effectiveness requirements, has the rest of the medical community and the public at large? The answer is clearly in the affirmative. One can start by listing entire fields of disease that were either untreated or inadequately handled in 1962 but today have new or vastly improved therapeutic options:

heart disease, cancer, mental illness, reproductive disorders, infectious diseases, diabetes, gastrointestinal diseases, and so on. Another way to state the change is to comment how few drugs on the market in 1962 remain in widespread use; most have been superseded by drugs discovered and developed under the effectiveness requirement.

A second place to see the effects of the controlled-study standard involves the promotion of products. Marketing materials were once a realm for puffery; they now provide meaningful scientific content. This transformation can be illustrated by comparing two advertisements for propriety antibiotics. A 1952 ad for the antibiotic Terramycin® (oxytetracycline) graphically depicts a broken leg, with the headline "Sticks and Stones." The text acknowledges that leverage and pressure are the preferred procedures for broken limbs, and then recommends Terramycin when "infection is a complicating factor in the necessary orthopedic surgery." The ad claims that "Terramycin provides unsurpassed broad-spectrum potency against ever-present bacterial invaders" and "Pure, crystalline Terramycin is well tolerated, widely distributed in the body, and promptly effective." The advertisement did not identify any specific bacteria against which the antibiotic was effective, or name any particular side effects, or give any data on drug absorption, distribution or tissue penetration. By comparison, a 1996 advertisement for the newer antibiotic Biaxin® (clarithromycin) exhibits the

PROTECTING THE INTEGRITY OF DRUGS

One of the key issues FDA faces as it enters its second century is ensuring that the drugs Americans take are safe and effective, and are made in FDA-approved facilities and meet quality standards. Modern-day communications and transportation have undermined the ability of the agency to assure this standard. Consumers who want to bring a personal supply of a medicine into the United States may do so; FDA has a policy under which it will exercise enforcement discretion. However, FDA cannot and does not permit the sale in the United States of either unapproved drugs or drugs made in unapproved facilities.

The importation of drugs from other countries has become a political issue, as consumers faced with the high cost of prescription drug are seeking less expensive supplies. Unfortunately the drugs being ordered via the Internet or those purchased by consumers visiting Canada, Mexico, or other countries may not meet U.S. standards. Counterfeit drugs increasingly have become prevalent, especially when purchased through the Internet. The FDA's strongly held position that drugs must be approved based on adequate and well-controlled studies, made only in approved facilities, and remain under the control of the original manufacturer while being shipped, has been difficult to explain in an era of globalization and worldwide standardization.

There has always been an element in U.S. society that believes the government should not regulate drug efficacy, and that people, especially those with terminal illnesses, should be allowed to buy and take whatever they want. Meanwhile, the public and state government legislators and purchasing officials are seeking ways to get drugs at lower cost. These two philosophies are at odds with good science and good manufacturing practices.

As was true 100 years ago, we still have charlatans who seek to sell sick people a drug that does not work or sell for less a drug that is made poorly or that is an outright counterfeit. It's amazing how some of the same issues facing the country 100 years ago remain in the forefront of public debate, though in a somewhat different guise. People with diseases want to believe that there are miracle cures, and they are willing to forego assured quality in the interests of saving money.

—Wayne L. Pines

emergence of clinical data as a selling tool. After a non-medical image to grab the viewer's initial attention, the marketing piece builds its pitch with clinical data. Columns and charts regarding product attributes and claims are derived from comparative studies, with statistical comparisons, number of subjects participating, and footnotes directing the reader to documentation for the data presented. Complete information is provided on contraindications, warnings, and side effects. This advertisement was clearly written for an audience that expects and demands scientific evidence in support of promotional claims.

A third way to assess the way in which a rigorous standard for scientific proof for drug effectiveness has improved the public health is to examine its extension to other areas of medicine. In 1972, regulatory responsibility for biological products was transferred from the National Institutes of Health (NIH) to FDA. Although the statute regulating biologics was enacted in 1902 and did not mention effectiveness, FDA decided that the standards for pharmaceuticals could be applied to vaccines, blood products, and other biological products. At the time, this decision had limited effect. But with the advent of the biotech revolution, with products made through recombinant DNA, monoclonal antibodies, and gene manipulation—all of which are treated as biologics—it meant that these extraordinary new products would be expected to meet the requirements of controlled clinical investigations.

In 1976, Congress enacted a new regulatory scheme for medical devices, in which it required (for those devices presenting the highest risks or needed to support life) "a reasonable assurance that the device is effective under the conditions of [its] use." In a parallel history to the Drug Amendments of 1962, FDA has had a long struggle to develop and apply standards of evidence. But again, the medical community now expects clinical trial data to substantiate claims for devices such as *in vitro* diagnostics, surgical implants, and imaging techniques. NIH and academic researchers are now routinely applying controlled studies to evaluate other health interventions. Various weight reduction diets have recently been subjected to rigorous randomized studies supported by NIH and conducted in academia. Vitamins, antioxidants, and other dietary supplements have similarly been tested in placebo-controlled trials underwritten by the government. The effects of moderate exercise on cardiovascular health are being compared to greater and lesser (or no) fitness regimens, and surgical procedures

are assessed in relation to alternatives, including drugs. The public recognizes both the costs and the potential benefits of this medical research, and continues to support the U.S. government's long-term commitment to and investment in this area. For example, NIH has had a thirty-seven-fold increase in its appropriations since 1962, from $733 million to more than $27 billion in 2004.

Yet another mirror for the results of the effectiveness requirement can be found in the major medical journals. The bulk of original papers consists of randomized controlled trials; case reports, while still common, are used to generate hypotheses, not prove drug efficacy. And the newest medical literature is frequently reported in daily newspapers and the broadcast media. Thus, the public has become familiar with the kinds of evidence that physicians find reliable. The medical journals are also appearing to approach an FDA-like standard in the peer-review process. For example, several of the most prestigious journals now require submission of the original protocol, to assess the purpose and design of the study as it existed before the authors analyzed the final data.

As the twentieth century ended, the concept of "evidence-based medicine" emerged and took a firm hold. Its goal is to integrate current scientific data so that it can usefully be applied to the day-to-day clinical problems facing the doctor and the patient. Medicine has always been recognized as both an art and a science, and evidence-based medicine does not seek to sacrifice the humanistic

WALKING THE DRUG SAFETY INFORMATION TIGHTROPE

Over the years, FDA has been accused of approving too many drugs too quickly, and of delaying the approval of life-saving drugs by imposing too high a standard. It seems as if the agency teeters perpetually on a tightrope.

In 2004, highly publicized crises involving drugs to treat depression and pain caused FDA to make major innovations on how it manages drug safety, and most particularly in how it communicates safety information to the public. On February 15, 2005, FDA unveiled what it called "a new emboldened vision for FDA that will promote a culture of openness and enhanced oversight within the Agency." FDA's program had two steps. FDA created a Drug Safety Oversight Board to oversee the management of drug safety issues, and started to provide emerging information to health providers and patients about the risks and benefits of particular medicines through a "Drug Watch" page on its website.

The more dramatic of the two actions was the effort to make more information on drug safety available, even as that information was evolving. FDA's new program was part of a continuum that started in the early 1970s, when the agency first recognized an obligation to educate the public about prescription drugs, which until then had been the exclusive province of health professionals.

The new Drug Watch webpage took FDA's commitment to share information to a new level. The webpage provides emerging data and risk information and increased use of consumer-friendly information sheets written especially for healthcare professionals and patients. In 2005, FDA issued more drug safety information than it had in any comparable period in its history.

Walking the drug safety and information tightrope has always been among FDA's greatest challenges. The demand for new and better treatments, especially for terminally ill patients, must be balanced against the need to protect the public from unsafe and ineffective drugs. The communication of drug safety information must be balanced against the legal obligation to protect the confidentiality of trade secret information submitted in drug applications. It's never been an easy tightrope to traverse.

—Wayne L. Pines

art of the profession. Rather, it seeks to provide user-friendly algorithms on how to approach therapy options for specific diseases. The foundation is clinical trial data in the medical literature, which are examined to look for lessons about unique benefits or limitations of application of results. Published studies may also be pooled into a larger statistical analysis, known as a meta-analysis, that increases the sensitivity of the results. The results—produced by government consensus conferences, academic groups, or medical associations—are presented as treatment guidelines, which become available to clinicians, insurers, health maintenance organizations, and the public. Evidence-based medicine has the potential of bringing world-class scientific information to every physician, indeed to every patient, in real time in a clinical context. It would not be possible if the literature did not contain a large number of high-quality controlled clinical investigations. And this literature might not exist but for the effectiveness requirement in the 1962 Drug Amendments.

QUACKERY

"THE EGG"

30 SECOND PUBLIC SERVICE ANNOUNCEMENT

(MUSIC)

ANNCR: Quack products. They're advertised everywhere...

From baldness remedies to cancer cures.

They tease you with the promise of a new beginning...

opening the door to a better, healthier body.

And as you wait to see the promise of a miracle,

you find nothing but empty promises.

Before you put your faith and money into a so called miracle cure, check with your doctor or pharmacist.

Write to:

Quackery
Pueblo, Colorado 81009

A message from the Food and Drug Administration.

Your health could depend on it.

A MESSAGE FROM THE FOOD AND DRUG ADMINISTRATION

Last known public service announcement by FDA concerning medical quackery. By the late 1980's, FDA struggled to know how to educate the public about quackery and experimented with motifs ranging from these fuzzy ducks to black-cloaked thieves to try to protect consumers from ubiquitous fraud. The rise of the Internet, however, has reinvigorated agency efforts to curb quackery.

From whatever perspective, it is clear that FDA's requirements for scientific proof have contributed to a significant channeling of funds, talent, and resources to the understanding of disease states and the causes and treatment approaches to them. FDA's insistence upon adequate and well-controlled investigations as the keystone of regulatory science has thus had a striking effect on the practice of the medical professions, on the biomedical research community, and on society in general.

Entering the second century of federal drug regulation, the science of drug therapeutics is becoming ever more sophisticated. FDA, the pharmaceutical industry, and medical practitioners share a common vision that treatments will be ever more specific to individual patients or sets of patients with common genomic factors. The possibility of predicting drug response—who will benefit from a particular drug and who will not, who will get a serious adverse reaction and who will not—is on the horizon, thanks to the tools of molecular biology, genetics, and pharmacokinetics. But it will also continue to require clinical researchers to evaluate these new approaches and separate the useful from the merely hopeful.

The authors of the 1906 Pure Food and Drugs Act could not have foreseen the scientific and medical advances of the past century. Many of the scientific disciplines essential to the work of today's FDA did not exist then. Nor did the drafters of the 1962 Amendments fully realize the consequences of their words. The adoption and implementation of a rigorous scientific standard as part of government regulation was and very much remains an experiment in American law. Despite its proven gains, the effectiveness requirement is still criticized. The challenge for FDA is to balance the public's insistence on personal access and choice with the public's expectation that the products they have to choose from are safe and effective. Today's FDA is part of a complex public-private relationship among the government, the pharmaceutical and biotech industries, the healthcare professions, and the public at large, all dedicated to improving the health of individuals through the development and wise use of therapeutic drugs. This relationship is truly but forty years old. One can only wonder what the next century has in store.

TYLENOL: THE GRANDADDY OF CRISES

September 30, 1982, started out as a fairly routine day at FDA, but it ended with six, and by the next day seven, tragic deaths in suburban Chicago, and the worst, most public product crisis in FDA's seventy-six-year history. Still unsolved after twenty-three years, someone took several containers of Extra Strength Tylenol, refilled the capsules with lethal amounts of cyanide, and placed the containers on the shelves of several stores in suburban Chicago, within reach of the unsuspecting victims. The Tylenol poisonings became the nation's most widely covered news story of that year and spawned scores of real and contrived copycat tamperings and illnesses. It also became the most studied crisis—until then, management of crises was hardly discussed, but afterward, Tylenol as a product not only regained its position as a prominent pain killer, but "Tylenol" became a code word for a crisis situation that was well-handled by all involved.

The Chicago poisonings and follow-on events robbed consumers of something they took pretty much for granted—unquestioned confidence in the safety of consumer medicines and in countless other routine acts and purchases of daily life. Bob Greene, a syndicated columnist for the *Chicago Tribune*, wrote a week after the deaths:

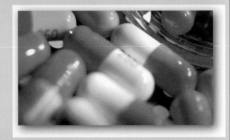

> Every time you order a meal in a restaurant, you have faith that someone in the kitchen didn't put something deadly in your food. Every time you open up a bottle of soda pop, you have faith that someone at the factory didn't decide that a drinker should die. Every time you buy any kind of medicine over the counter, you have faith that what you swallow is what the label says you are going to swallow.... Living itself is an act of faith.

Americans were frightened, confused, and desperately in need of reassurance. And then—as if the local authorities, the manufacturer of Tylenol, the consumer products trade group, and FDA had routinely practiced this scenario—swift, voluntary, and remarkably coordinated actions were taken to prevent further harm, restore confidence, and lay the groundwork for increasing the safety of consumer products.

The loss to the victims' families was indescribable and permanent, but for most of us, in a matter of weeks, the crisis began to fade and, with important changes in place, life returned pretty much to normal. I was Deputy Commissioner at the time and headed the emergency task force Commissioner Hayes organized to manage the crisis. In the face of such a dire threat, I've often thought of what were the most critical factors and actions that restored confidence in Tylenol and in consumer medicine so quickly. For me, they were:

- First, the link of seemingly unrelated, sudden deaths to Tylenol was established with remarkable speed and skill. Action at the national level would not have begun so swiftly had two paramedics and a Chicago medical examiner not observed that tainted Tylenol was a common thread in the first reported deaths. Their recognition also very likely prevented even further deaths in Chicago two more poisoned containers were found on retail shelves during the sweep that followed their discovery.

- The actions that followed have become a case study in responsible crisis management. Major players were: Jim Burke, Chairman of Johnson & Johnson; Dave Collins, Chairman of McNeil, the J&J subsidiary responsible for Tylenol; Joe Chiesa, McNeil President; Tom Gates, MD, its Medical Director; and many other colleagues. If they felt despair and uncertainty, none was apparent. Four decades earlier, J&J had adopted a credo stating the principles on which they would conduct their business. Burke and Collins said the credo told them what to do in the Tylenol crisis and it is impossible to say otherwise.

(Continued)

In 1982 FDA published tamper-resistant packaging regulations to prevent poisonings in the wake of the Tylenol crisis. The Federal Anti-Tampering Act passed in 1983 made it a crime to even threaten to tamper with a product, which swiftly reduced tampering reports nationwide. This Public Service Announcement was designed to make the public aware of the new law.

- J&J involved FDA immediately and continuously. It withdrew the initial lots from which the tampered drugs came and then, in the wake of copycat tamperings, withdrew all Tylenol capsules even though both J&J and FDA had determined that the tamperings did not occur in its plants.

- J&J kept the press and public fully informed and even put its chairman in the unaccustomed role of chief company spokesperson. Some marketing experts pronounced the withdrawal of Tylenol as the end that brand. J&J's early contacts with consumers, however, confirmed what they already knew, that the company was considered just as much a victim as the rest of us, and that there was a remarkable reservoir of brand loyalty. Within six weeks, the company had reintroduced Tylenol capsules in unique triple-sealed packaging, offered replacements for unused product, and set a course for steady recovery.

- The Tylenol poisonings were a shock to other producers of non-prescription medicines. Every company felt vulnerable, and that was equally true of the industry as a whole. On a Sunday, three days into the crisis, Jim Cope, President of the Proprietary Association, which was then the name of the industry's trade association, agreed to a joint effort with FDA to institute safety packaging for consumer products. The association established a Joint Committee on Product Safety with industry, pharmacy, and FDA members. Cope and FDA Commissioner Art Hayes announced the effort at a joint press conference the next day. FDA published implementing regulations in record time, and even then the work was already well under way.

- Paul Hile, FDA's Associate Commissioner for Regulatory Affairs, and Don Healton, Executive Director of Regional Operations, had earlier set up an emergency operations center, including a dedicated closed-circuit conference line linking FDA headquarters to all of the agency's twenty-one district offices. Even in today's communications environment, the agency's conference network was a technological *tour de force* and a miracle of clarity. During this crisis, it was a godsend. Using that facility, for example, FDA launched a nationwide round-the-clock effort to obtain and analyze enough Tylenol capsules to convince itself and the public that the crisis was confined to the Chicago area. With FDA inspectors and technicians working day and night, we were able to report within a few days that more than 1.5 million capsules and other dosage forms had been collected and analyzed nationwide, with no trace of contamination.

- Under Dick Swanson, FDA's Emergency Operations and Epidemiology Branch was organized to deal on-call with unexpected product emergencies. It went immediately to live, round-the-clock staffing to handle the inevitable flood of consumer questions, reports of suspected injuries and the like. Within a month, the number of poisonings alone reported to FDA—real or not—had reached 150. As a sad comment on the intervening twenty-three years, the work of this branch is now institutionalized within FDA as part of an Office of Crisis Management.

- No response was more gratifying than that of local and national media, working with Larry Foster, J&J's Public Affairs Officer and Bill Grigg, then newly appointed to head FDA's public affairs. Just as J&J was considered a victim, so were FDA and other agencies. The efforts made by the company, FDA, the industry, and local authorities to remove the source of danger, to keep the public advised and informed, and to make immediate and long-term changes in safety packaging were followed closely and were generally applauded. The Tylenol crisis not only became required reading for students of business and management, but a critical real-time case study in corporate ethics and conduct.

Halloween of 1982 arrived just a month after the Tylenol poisonings. Everyone involved prepared for a new onslaught of malicious attacks, this time mainly on children. But kids were kids and parents were brave. Trick-or-treating went on as usual, albeit more guarded. Few incidents were reported and a peaceful Halloween seemed to signal that the crisis had begun to run its course.

—**Mark Novitch**

FDA's Role in Regulating Biologics

Daniel A. Kracov

ALTHOUGH IT MAY APPEAR UNNECESSARY TO LOOK BACK TO A STATUTE enacted in 1902 in commemorating the Pure Food and Drugs Act of 1906, the heroic story of regulation under the Biologics Control Act of 1902, the "Virus Act," offers critical insights into the paths not taken in 1906. Indeed, despite the enormous achievements arising from the 1906 statute as amended and interpreted over the last century, in many respects the regulation of biologics as originally framed in 1902—at the time largely concerned with animal-derived vaccines and antitoxins—represents an even more revolutionary model for ensuring medical product safety and efficacy. That approach has endured to this day, converging with the course set by the 1906 Act and shaping the modern FDA.

Both statutes grew out of a dangerous and chaotic era from a public health perspective. Life in the United States in the 1800s made the current age of anxiety over bioterrorism and avian flu look idyllic. Most U.S. citizens could not expect to live into their fifties, and devastating epidemics of cholera, yellow fever, typhoid, smallpox, measles, and diphtheria occurred regularly. Despite important scientific advances, the medical technology available at the time—largely rudimentary vaccination methods—could often be deadlier than the disease. To the extent that such technology was overseen at all, regulation was local, with the federal government having no role.

The 1902 Act was not the first national measure relating to biologics. Efforts to address the availability of vaccines began with the Vaccine Act of 1813, the result of lobbying by James Smith, a crusading Baltimore physician. Smith had seen great success in smallpox vaccination in children, and had established a "vaccine institution" to produce the necessary cowpox material for shipment to other physicians. However, a chronic lack of funding drove Smith to Congress, which designated him the national vaccine agent and required the U.S. Post Office to carry, without postage, mail containing vaccine material.

Within a decade, disaster struck. In 1821, Smith mistakenly mailed smallpox scabs to a physician in Tarboro, North Carolina, resulting in an epidemic in which 10 patients died. A congressional inquiry ensued, including false accusations that Smith had a profit motive or was even intentionally spreading smallpox. In 1822, James Smith was fired, the 1813 vaccine law was repealed, and the notion of federal regulation of the availability of biologics to protect the public health was largely put aside for the next eighty years.

The science relating to biologics did not go into hibernation, however; major developments in bacteriology and immunology in the second half of the nineteenth century included the identification of many disease-causing organisms. Many of these developments took place in Europe, and although lacking systems for the distribution of biologics on a large scale, as early as 1895 Germany, France, Italy, and Russia had taken steps to set up regulatory processes for the inspection and licensing of facilities and accurate labeling of products. In the United States, a handful of state

and local public health agencies did not wait for the federal government to begin the application of these new scientific discoveries and technologies to the production of vaccines, antitoxins, and diagnostics. The New York City Board of Health Laboratories, whose director had traveled to Europe to study the production and testing of diphtheria antitoxin, was particularly advanced, ultimately establishing "culture stations" throughout the city to supply antitoxin for injection and to distribute diagnostic kits for collection of samples for testing.

The U.S. national public health framework remained skeletal. One of its key components was the Department of the Treasury's Marine Hospital Service, which had been established in 1798

In this 1802 cartoon by James Gillray, Edward Jennen inoculates a woman with cow pock, as cows erupt from the pustules of others who have been vaccinated.

to provide medical care for merchant seaman, a role which grew over time to include prevention of epidemics through the examination of passengers arriving on ships for signs of infectious disease. In 1887, Joseph J. Kinyoun, a Marine Hospital Service physician, set up a one-room "Laboratory of Hygiene" in the Marine Hospital in Staten Island, New York, with the objective of applying the emerging sciences of bacteriology and immunology to the activities of the service. Moved to Washington in 1891 and renamed the "Hygienic Laboratory," Kinyoun remained its sole staffer.

Kinyoun traveled several times to Europe, visiting with Dr. Robert Koch and other founders of the field of bacteriology, and shipping diphtheria antitoxin back from the Pasteur Institute. In 1895, the Marine Hospital Service began to immunize horses for the production of diphtheria antitoxin for Marine Hospital Service use and to demonstrate the methods of production for state and local officials.

Entrepreneurs quickly capitalized on these scientific developments. Various companies, largely schooled by the New York Department of Health, saw an opportunity in the diphtheria antitoxin market, including established manufacturers such as H.K. Mulford and Company (later part of Merck) and Parke-Davis & Co. (now part of Pfizer). Various smaller operations, which had been producing smallpox vaccinations, also ventured into the adoption of the techniques necessary for producing

diphtheria antitoxin. A patchwork of local, physician-owned "vaccine farms" emerged across the country, adding to the production "farms" of state and local health departments. Commercial fights and accusations of impure product were common, with claims of sterility becoming a selling point. In 1897, Parke-Davis advertised that "[w]e have never yet had a reported a case of sudden death following the use of our Antitoxin."

As early as 1895, when he was in Europe, Kinyoun had seen the dangers inherent in this unregulated environment. Reporting to the Surgeon General on his study of the production of diphtheria antitoxin, Kinyoun noted:

Many persons will, during the ensuing year, commence to prepare the serum as a business enterprise, and there will, without doubt, be many worthless articles called antitoxin thrown upon the market. All the serum for sale should be made or tested by competent persons. The testing, in fact, should be done by disinterested parties.

Within a few years, Kinyoun's concerns were borne out.

Diphtheria had long been a dreaded disease, with frequent large-scale outbreaks. Children represented the large majority of cases, suffering horribly and often choking to death from the leathery membrane the disease causes in the throat. In 1901, a serious epidemic of diphtheria swept through St. Louis, and rapid production of vaccines was begun, derived from the blood serum of horses immunized against diphtheria. A five-year-old diphtheria patient, Veronica Neill, received two shots of antitoxin in late October of that year, and within days died of a different infectious disease—tetanus. Immediately, contamination of the diphtheria antitoxin was suspected, the St. Louis Health Commissioner suspended distribution, and an investigation begun. The production of diphtheria antitoxin was not a well-characterized process at the time, and required great care to ensure potency and purity. The St. Louis investigation found that a horse—named Jim—used in the production of diphtheria antitoxin for three years had been killed because it had contracted tetanus. Rather than destroying the serum taken from Jim, the St. Louis Health Department had mistakenly distributed the contaminated product. To compound the outrage, it emerged that the janitor had given conflicting statements under oath during the investigation, at first claiming to have discarded the serum and then finally admitting that only a small quantity had been destroyed. By the time the St. Louis incident was over, thirteen children had died from tetanus.

Researchers at the NIH Division of Biologics Standards, which, in 1972, became part of FDA.

That same fall, nine children in Camden, New Jersey, died from contaminated smallpox vaccine, this time produced by private companies. Several rounds of accusations of sale of contaminated vaccines were made among the various producers, with the debate centering around the safety of a new process of using glycerinated lymph to better preserve the vaccines.

These incidents were widely reported, engendering concern that the deaths would be used to undermine the promise of "serum therapy." Echoing many of the controversies today in the vaccine world, an editorial in the *Journal of the American Medical Association* warned that "anti-vaccinationists, anti-vivisectionists … and crotchety persons in general" would use these disasters for "evil purposes." In addition to general calls for regulation by public health officials, the large commercial producers, tiring of competing against local health departments and vaccine farms, saw the possibility of a more orderly and profitable market in regulation.

Yet, despite the controversy, the legislative development of the Biologics Control Act of 1902 occurred very quietly. Prime movers were the Medical Society of the District of Columbia, the Commissioners of the District of Columbia, and the District of Columbia Health Officer, W.C. Woodward. In his report to the House and Senate Committees on the District of Columbia, Woodward enumerated factors that would remain accepted distinctions in the regulation of biologics and drugs for many years to come:

- The purity of these substances is of far more importance than is the purity of ordinary drugs, because the former are ordinarily introduced into circulation directly while the latter are introduced through the digestive tract.

- A dose of an antitoxin … once administered is beyond recall even immediately after administration: a remedy given by mouth can be removed or neutralized by mechanical or therapeutic means.

- The potency of these remedies is of corresponding importance. They are not given in repeated small doses, in which case therapeutic inactivity could be readily discovered and corrected, but are used in full doses, with the expectation, or at least the hope, that it will not be necessary to administer them again. If the first dose prove worthless the loss of time may cost the life of the patient.

- The manner in which these substances are produced and marketed renders it impossible to exercise efficient control over them by any system of inspection which takes cognizance only of the finished product. Efforts to insure their purity must be directed to the establishments where such products are manufactured.

Beginning as a measure to control biologics within the District of Columbia, the drafters quickly realized that the legislation would be virtually worthless if the traffic in biologics between jurisdictions was left unregulated, and the legislative process expanded to "safeguarding from danger liable to arise from interstate or international commerce."

While it took decades to develop the political consensus required for passage of the 1906 Pure Food and Drugs Act, the legislative development of the 1902 Act, titled "An Act to Regulate the Sale of Viruses, Serums, Toxins, and Analogous Products in the District of Columbia, to Regulate Interstate Traffic in Said Articles, and for Other Purposes," occurred with little deliberation. Moreover, the systems for biologics regulation developed in Europe apparently had little or no influence. Introduced in the House of Representatives on April 5, 1902, it was signed into law by Theodore Roosevelt thirteen weeks later, on July 1, 1902, reportedly hastened by support from Dr. Zachariah T. Sowers—physician to the Vice President, the Speaker of the House, and Chairmen of the House and Senate Committees on the District of Columbia. Although W.C. Woodward had consulted with what was now called the Public Health and Marine Hospital Service, there is no indication that the congressional committees had consulted with either the service or the Treasury Department.

Although not a major player in the drafting of the 1902 Act, the Hygienic Laboratory had been growing, albeit slowly. In 1899, its new director, Milton Rosenau, had created divisions of chemistry, bacteriology and pathology, zoology and pharmacology. In 1901, Congress had authorized $35,000 for the construction of a new building in which the lab could investigate "infectious and contagious diseases and matters pertaining to the public health." With this small yet accomplished scientific base, the Public Health Service took on a new role under the 1902 Act as regulator of the nascent interstate commerce in biologics. The 1902 Act set up a board consisting of the Surgeon General of the Army, the Surgeon General of the Navy, and the Supervising Surgeon General of the Marine Hospital Service to oversee the regulation of biologics. Key provisions of the statute included:

- Sale was prohibited unless the biologic had been produced in a licensed establishment.
- The label must bear the "proper name" of article; the name, address, and license number of manufacturer; and an expiration date related to effectiveness.
- Designated agents may inspect licensed establishments.
- Licenses can be suspended or revoked.
- Violations are punishable by fine or imprisonment.

Through these provisions, the philosophy of biologic regulation for many years to come was enshrined into law—"process equals product." It would be decades before many of these regulatory authorities were incorporated into the regulation of other medical products.

The board created under the 1902 Act was also given authority, subject to approval by the Treasury Department, to promulgate biologics control regulations focused on preventing the occurrence of problems rather than the post-marketing detection of violations. The first such regulations were issued on February 21, 1903, and went into effect six months later. The regulations provided that:

- Licenses would be issued and re-issued on the basis of annual inspection; no license would be issued without such an inspection.
- Inspections would be unannounced.
- Licenses could be suspended or revoked on the basis of inspection reports of faulty methods of preparation, faulty construction or administration of establishments, or impurities or lack of potency demonstrated by laboratory examination of samples. Reports would be sent to the Sanitary Board of the Service, which would make recommendations to the Surgeon General and finally the Secretary of the Treasury.
- Inspectors would be professionals with expertise, i.e. commissioned medical officers of the Public Health and Marine Hospital Service above the grade of assistant surgeon.

Regulatory activity began immediately, and within two years, thirteen etablishments had been licensed. The first license was issued to Parke-Davis, and the second to H.K. Mulford, for the sale of smallpox vaccine and diphtheria antitoxin. Regulation was tough under the new regime, and many of the old "vaccine farms" failed to achieve licensure; suspensions occurred fairly regularly. H.M. Alexander and Company was forced to recall contaminated sera from the market, and Parke-Davis and Mulford had their licenses suspended when hoof and mouth disease was discovered in their herds and stables. In addition to inspections, the Hygienic Laboratory began purchasing biologics on the open market and testing them for purity and potency.

However, the Hygienic Laboratory was not wholly transformed into an enforcement authority. The research orientation of the Hygienic Laboratory, which characterizes biologics regulatory entities to this day, remained crucial, and the laboratory played a central role in disseminating scientific developments and training laboratory workers in the private sector. Its science base was put to immediate effect in the promulgation of standards for products, the development of better production methods, and the continued research into agents of infectious diseases.

The newly licensed manufacturers saw significant benefits from the implementation of the 1902 Act, including the elimination of small competitors. The scientific efforts of the Hygienic Laboratory were a particular boon to industry, essentially serving as a public research laboratory for the development of new products and production methods. The government was also a source of essential leadership and expertise in the private sector; e.g., the first Hygienic Laboratory director, Joseph Kinyoun, joined H.K. Mulford, and the third director, John F. Anderson, later directed E.R. Squibb and Sons' Research and Biological

Laboratories. Indeed, from the beginning, the relationship between the Hygienic Laboratory and industry was marked by scientific collaboration rather than conflict, an approach that persisted, albeit diluted over time as the public began to question public-private cooperation. As an industry leader would write in summarizing seventy-five years of biologics regulation in the *Food Drug Cosmetic Law Journal* in 1978, industry and biologics regulators tended to treat each other as "distinct but equally important members of a health providers team cooperating toward the common goal of safe and effective products needed for the public health" and "[t]he relationship that developed was typical of that between scientists, not cozy as has been charged by some in recent years, but mutually respectful albeit with some wariness on occasion."

Although enacted only four years apart, there was little or no relationship between the legislative processes for development of the 1902 Act and 1906 Act. The legislative history shows no indication that the ongoing activities of the Hygienic Laboratory under the newly passed 1902 statute had any significant influence on the drafting or enactment of the Pure Food and Drugs Act. The committees considering the 1906 Act—the Senate Committee on Public Health and National Quarantine, and the House Committee on Interstate and Foreign Commerce—had no apparent role.

The regulatory structure and funding of the biologics regulation changed over time, and the regulatory framework

Bench research, depicted here at an earlier time, has been maintained at the Center for Biologics Evaluation and Research.

became more detailed. In 1912, the Public Health and Marine Hospital Service was reorganized as the Public Health Service, which by 1915 reported that its methods for the standardization of tetanus antitoxin had been "favorably commented upon by English publications" and were "in use in the Colonial Laboratory in Java." The first separate congressional appropriation of funds specifically for the control of biologics occurred in 1917. In 1919, regulations were adopted that included requirements that would be unique to biologics for many years to come, and would eventually be the subject of regulatory modernization efforts, including

provisions mandating:

- Training and qualifications of personnel;
- Maintenance of production and control records for each lot manufactured;
- Inclusion of a manufacturer's name on a distributor's label, and for both manufacturers' names and licenses in the case of a "joint manufacturer";
- Submission of samples of lots of particular products for testing and release prior to distribution; and
- Reporting of changes in equipment, personnel, and manufacturing methods.

By 1921, forty-one establishments had been licensed for the sale of 102 different biologic products. The Public Health Service staff dedicated to administering biologics regulation had grown to 127, including pioneering women scientists such as Dr. Ida Bengston, a bacteriologist noted for her work on bacterial toxins, and Dr. Alice Evans, who would become the first woman to head the Society of American Bacteriologists.

The creation in 1930 of what was then called the National Institute of Health (NIH) as part of the Public Health Service incorporated the Hygienic Laboratory. In 1934, the laboratory promulgated regulations requiring proof of efficacy for new biologic products, a requirement that would not be applied to drug products until the Kefauver-Harris Drug Amendments of 1962. By 1937, the biologics control function had been assigned to a new Division of Biologics Control, later renamed the Biologics Control Laboratory and made part of the new National Microbiological Institute within NIH.

The passage of the Federal Food, Drug, and Cosmetic (FD&C) Act in 1938 introduced statutory ambiguity into biologics regulation. Although the biologics statute clearly defined a regulatory program for biologics, and that program had been in place for thirty-two years, the statutory definition of "drug" introduced in the 1938 Act could also be read as encompassing biologic products. This created the potential for dual jurisdiction, despite a general understanding that the 1938 Act was not intended to include biologics.

The Biologics Control Laboratory played a significant role during World War

II, performing large-scale testing of serums and vaccines needed for soldiers. The laboratory created and revised standards, and developed new methods of production, including methods for novel, unlicensed products needed for the war effort, such as the early flu vaccine. Although the federal government's role in the blood area had previously been constrained by limitations on the preservation and transport of blood in interstate commerce, treating wartime casualties necessitated the mass processing of blood into plasma, which was done by commercial laboratories under the supervision of the Biologics Control Laboratory. As the blood and blood products industry grew in the postwar era, the biologics laws were amended to eliminate confusion in the case law and make clear that blood, blood components, and allergenic extracts are included in federal jurisdiction. Biologics regulators later worked closely with blood banks to address the threat of various infectious agents, and thus ensure a safe blood supply for the entire U.S. population.

In 1944, the laws relating to biologics were revised and consolidated into the U.S. Public Health Service Act, and the Biologics Control Act designated Section 351. Although leaving the basic parameters of biologics regulation intact, the Public Health Service Act also incorporated the developing notion of regulatory standards for product regulation, requiring that licenses be issued only if the establishment and the products meet standards designed to ensure product safety, purity, and

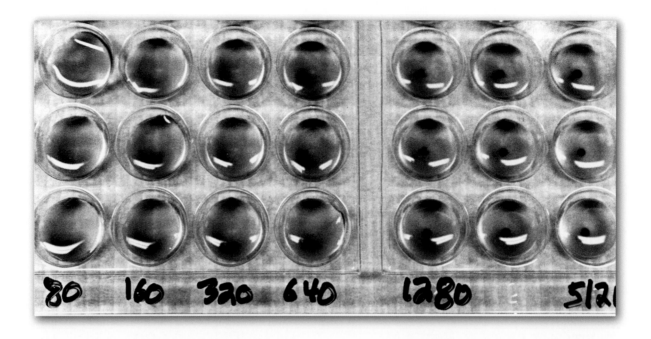

80 160 320 640 1280 512

potency. Again, the dual jurisdiction issue created in 1938 was left ambiguous.

In the postwar era, the development of the Salk polio vaccine was a major relief for the American public. On the day in 1955 that the polio vaccine was cleared, one major city actually signaled the event by air raid sirens, church bells, and turning all traffic lights red for one minute. Tragically, the vaccine also presented a major test for the Laboratory of Biologics Control in the "Cutter Incident" when the new Salk polio vaccine produced by Cutter Labs was found to have caused more than 200 cases of polio, including close contacts of vaccine recipients, and eleven deaths. An investigation determined that the manufacturer had produced a number of batches that contained live virus, causing the suspension of the polio vaccine program and requiring a major effort to change the viral inactivation and testing procedures to ensure a safe vaccine. Despite criticism of the Public Health Service, this national emergency only emphasized the importance

of good biologics regulation. The Biologics Control Laboratory was elevated to the Division of Biologics Standards and given a new building on the NIH campus, as well as additional staff.

In the era that followed, the scientific efforts of the Division of Biologics Standards, undertaken under Director Dr. Roderick Murray, made an enormous contribution to the health of people around the world. In 1963, Murray hired Paul Parkman, M.D., discoverer of the rubella (German measles) virus. The 1964 global rubella epidemic caused 12.5 million cases and resulted in 20,000 infants born with birth defects. By 1966, Parkman and Dr. Harry Meyer, Jr. reported the development of the first effective experimental vaccine for rubella. This proof of principle paved the way for the licensure of the first rubella vaccine in 1969, and ultimately the 2005 announcement by the Centers for Disease Control and Prevention that, while childhood vaccinations should continue, rubella is no longer a health threat in the United States. Both Parkman and Meyer went on to leadership roles in the administration of drug and biologic regulation at FDA.

Despite these achievements, in the early 1970s, the growing consumer movement criticized biologics regulators for failing to review the safety and efficacy of older, licensed products, as FDA's Bureau of Drugs did pursuant to the 1962 Drug Amendments. The solution—the transfer of the Division of Biologics Standards to FDA and the creation of a new Bureau of Biologics—was announced by then-Department of Health Education and Welfare Secretary Elliott Richardson at a 1972 congressional hearing chaired by Sen. Abraham Ribicoff, a frequent FDA critic. Thus, seventy years after the separate creation of statutory regimes for biologics and drugs, biologics were integrated into

---

CREATIVE LAW TO REGULATE BLOOD BANKS

In 1973, the Division of Biologics Standards was transferred from NIH to FDA and became the Bureau of Biologics. At about that time, concern was rising over the spread of communicable diseases, such as hepatitis, through the transfusions of whole blood, red blood cells, and blood plasma. Most blood for transfusion was collected and transfused at local community blood banks. Only a few blood banks that shipped blood products in interstate commerce were regulated, but there were thousands of local blood banks in the United States.

In response to the challenge of how FDA was to get its legal arms around this situation, FDA's General Counsel's Office developed a novel legal theory through the issuance of good manufacturing practice (GMP) regulations. The approach had three parts:

1. FDA relied on the fact that nearly all blood in those days was collected in blood bags that contained anticoagulant that, along with the blood itself, passed to the recipient of the blood. These blood bags were manufactured in Michigan. Therefore, even "local" blood that was transfused into a recipient (at least in forty-nine states, other than Michigan) would consist, in part, of an interstate component. Under accepted FDA law, a blood product containing an interstate component could be viewed as being "in interstate commerce." There was no question that FDA could promulgate GMP regulations for an interstate biological product.

2. FDA relied on a provision in the Biologics Control Act that authorized the federal government to act, usually through a quarantine, in individual states to prevent the spread of communicable disease into interstate commerce. FDA announced that the power to act within a state to prevent the interstate spread of a communicable disease allowed the agency to issue regulations over local blood banks.

3. Finally, FDA noted that the labeling requirement of the Biologics Control Act was not limited to interstate licensed blood but applied to any biological product. FDA lawyers developed an argument that blood not collected in compliance with GMPs would be mislabeled by suggesting that the blood was safe. On that basis, FDA could promulgate regulations to prevent such mislabeling.

Under these legal theories, FDA in 1976 issued the blood GMP regulations, and they have remained unchallenged for thirty years. Importantly, these regulations were in effect in the 1980s to help in the effort to control the spread of HIV. A little creativity went a long way to protect the public health.

—Arthur N. Levine

FDA, although the biologics regulators remained on the NIH campus.

Despite predictions of disaster, over time this transfer resulted in biologics regulators bringing to FDA a unique, research-oriented culture and new regulatory approaches. According to a 1978 article by a Bureau of Biologics employee, the philosophy of regulation at the time was:

"kind of a hybrid of science, that is, research directed toward solving problems unique to biologics, and the more traditional FDA compliance activities.... We also like to think that our style of regulation of vaccines expresses a desire to solve problems, not just create problems for others to solve."

In retrospect, the success of biologics regulation at FDA is not surprising. The concepts we now take for granted as part of drug regulation—demonstration of efficacy prior to marketing, careful regulation of manufacturing processes, etc.—were applied decades earlier in the biologics context.

During this period, FDA also began to assert dual jurisdiction under the Public Health Service Act and the FD&C Act with respect to certain aspects of biologics regulation. A complete integration of drugs and biologics, however, proved less than an ideal approach. In 1982, the two bureaus were briefly merged as the National Center for Drugs and Biologics, creating some degree of friction when the new leadership was largely composed of former Bureau of Biologics personnel, which approached regulation differently. By 1987, the merger was reversed, resulting in the FDA Center

for Biologics Evaluation and Research (CBER).

These bureaucratic changes were a sideshow to the main concerns of biologics regulators and researchers. CBER and industry worked intensely to address urgent concerns of HIV contamination of the blood supply by licensing the first HIV test kits in 1985 and increasing inspections of blood banks to ensure careful screening and processing. CBER also faced the important task of responding to the huge challenge recombinant DNA technology presented, technology that transformed the world of biotechnology and created new ways to manipulate animal- and human-derived biologics for therapeutic and diagnostic use.

Over time, various factors, including scientific advances and commercial pressures, caused a rethinking of long-held provisions of biologics regulation, including some fundamental features of the 1902 Act. These regulatory reforms, largely instituted under the FDA Modernization Act of 1997 (FDAMA), in many respects further increased convergence between biologic and drug regulation. The scope of manufacturing changes requiring FDA approval was narrowed, and the establishment license application, the regulatory vehicle for the traditional process-equals-product biologics approach, and the product license application were combined into one biologics license application that covered both the product and the facility.

In 2003, the tension between CBER's traditional role in regulating biologics and the Center for Drug Evaluation and Research's (CDER's) role in therapeutics, as well as increasing FDA integration of experience from cross-agency reviews of products under varying statutory authorities, shifted therapeutic biologics from CBER to CDER. Products shifted to CDER—generally for regulation under both biologic and drug statutory authorities—included products ranging from monoclonal antibodies for in vivo use to therapeutic proteins to immunomodulators (both non-vaccine and non-allergenic products). Remaining within CBER's review are both the traditional biologic products—vaccines, allergenic extracts, antitoxins, blood and blood products—as well as some of the most innovative and challenging areas of biotechnology, including products composed of human, bacterial, or animal

Technician harvesting egg fluids

cells, such as pancreatic islet cells for transplantation, and gene therapy.

In its various configurations, FDA's biologics regulatory and research expertise has long played an important role in reducing illness and disease throughout the global community. FDA scientists and regulators have helped to harmonize international standards for biologic products, collaborated on the development of frameworks for science-based, regulatory decision-making, and assisted international bodies such as the World Health Organization. These efforts have enhanced regulatory systems and resources around the world, and helped make innovative new biologics, such as vaccines for children, available to meet global health threats.

As biologics regulators continue such work at home and abroad, the pressure for new regulatory frameworks and the convergence of the regulatory approaches descended from the 1902 and 1906 Acts continues, driven by economic pressures relating to the cost of new, life-saving therapeutic biologics. In the coming years we will continue to see a vigorous debate over whether the science has developed to the point where the very rough equivalent of a generic drug process can be created through abbreviated reviews of so-called "follow-on" biologics, while still maintaining safety and efficacy standards.

Despite these continuing calls for change, the core of the Hygienic Laboratory's jurisdiction in 1902—preventing infectious disease—and the scientific and regulatory lessons learned in the long history of the 1902 Act, remain absolutely critical to this nation. Indeed, 185 years after James Smith mistakenly sent smallpox to Tarboro, North Carolina, and 105 years after deaths from contaminated smallpox vaccines in Camden, New Jersey, CBER is now reviewing a new generation of safer smallpox vaccines developed to address the threat of bioterrorism.

OTHER-WORLDLY.

"What is a religious fanatic, Grandpa?"
"Well—it is a woman who has her infant baptized, but forgets to have him vaccinated."

Other-Worldly (43 *Puck* no. 1094 (Mar. 30, 1898)). —Even the grandfather in this family, probably one of its most conservative members, supports vaccination.

The Regulation of Foods and Drugs for "Animals Other Than Man": Distorted Mirror or Mineshaft Canary?

Eugene Lambert

SINCE COMPREHENSIVE FEDERAL REGULATION OF FOODS AND DRUGS BEGAN with the enactment of the Pure Food and Drugs Act of 1906, the definition of "food" and "drug" has covered articles for use by "man or other animals." Darwinism aside, how articles used by "other animals" have been regulated offers insight both into the development of current food and drug issues and how these "other animals" have been both more and less protected than man. The history is complex and does not follow any linear progression; for the half century after 1906, the regulation of drugs used in animals and of foods from animals was either an afterthought or forgotten altogether. Since the 1950s and emerging into the twenty-first century, of course, coordination between the regulation of human foods and drugs became essential because issues such as antibiotic resistance and drug residues in food are critical public health matters.

No one would deny that pet owners sometimes know and care more about what their pets eat than what they themselves eat. The regulatory system that assures the safety of pet foods is little known, recognized, or understood by the public, but that's because, despite the jagged history that brings us to today, the system has worked so effectively, albeit quietly. During the fifty years after 1906, many of the developments in regulating foods and drugs for use by "other animals" took place outside the ambit of the Pure Food and Drugs Act. Drug regulation under the 1906 Act was limited to classic adulteration and misbranding, and few drugs had been developed solely for administration to animals.

In 1913, however, the Virus-Serum-Toxin (VST) Act was passed as part of the appropriations for the Bureau of Animal Industry (the antecedent of the Animal and Plant Health Inspection Service). It created for the first time a comprehensive licensing system for a class of drugs for administration to animals: vaccines. It was patterned on the 1902 Vaccines Act, which then was administered by the Public Health Service. The VST Act was politically driven by the need to assure the quality—safety, purity, and potency—of hog cholera vaccine. Moreover, there was no formal recognition of the VST Act in the laws enforced by FDA until the 1962 Drug

Amendments. In fact, for a quarter century, from 1913 to 1938, one unit of the U.S. Department of Agriculture (USDA) was developing the tools for effective drug licensing, while another unit, FDA, with authority over all other drugs, ignored the activity. Not until the Elixir Sulfanilamide incident in 1937, and the importation of a "vaccine" that was outside the scope of the Vaccines Act, was a quick insertion of a licensing provision made to the pending Food, Drug, and Cosmetic (FD&C) Act draft, giving FDA some nascent parallel jurisdiction over both human and animal vaccines.

The USDA approach to the animal vaccines production was comprehensive. USDA required two licenses for animal vaccines, an establishment license based on a determination that the facility was capable of producing animal vaccines, and, initially issued in conjunction with the first, authorization of production of a particular product, upon demonstration of efficacy, i.e. that it would be safe, pure, and potent. In addition, production batches were submitted to USDA for testing, and could not be sold until released. USDA also regulated the import and export of animal vaccines. Exports required a special license, based on approval of the product in the export destination. Imports required a permit, based on a showing that the product was safe, pure, and potent—the same standards that applied to domestic manufacture. Licensing was conditioned on USDA inspectors having the right to enter manufacturing premises to inspect

and take samples, a mandatory right that FDA did not obtain until 1950 (the FD&C Act having provided initially for factory inspection "after first making request and obtaining permission").

Thus, in the case of "drug" regulation, animal vaccine manufacturers were subject to comprehensive licensing of establishments and products, to proof of safety and efficacy of their products, and to complete mandatory factory inspection. FDA-regulated drugs, both for humans and other animals, would be subject to similar requirements in stages, starting in 1938, but not fully until 1962.

Regulation of food for other animals developed in a somewhat different, but no less circuitous, fashion. In this case, the developments took place largely at the state level, driven by the concern with the adulteration and adequacy of feed for livestock. A system of animal feed licensing, site inspection, and ingredient evaluation developed in major farm states and eventually spread across the country, until now about three-quarters of the states have enacted a uniform feed control statute. The system is supported by either plant or product registrations and tonnage taxes at the state level. The state system of defining feed ingredients remains in place as a parallel means of economic regulation of the composition of food.

By the time Congress in 1938 undertook a comprehensive revision of FDA's authority, spurred by the Elixir Sulfanilamide tragedy, commercial animal food, for both livestock and companion animals, as well as animal vaccines, were

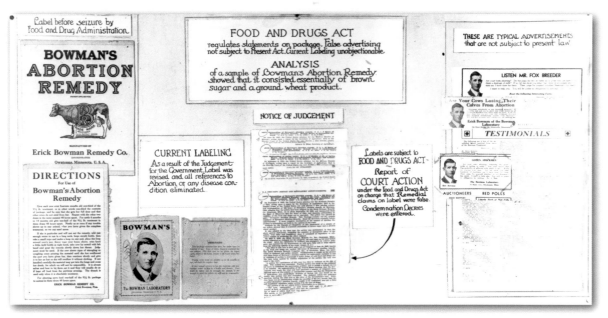

This exhibit is from the American Chamber of Horrors which was instrumental in the passage of the 1938 Food, Drug, and Cosmetic Act. This panel illustrated the adulteration and misbranding problems, as well as the outright quackery that still plagued the animal drug field even as late as the 1930s. Problems had worsened, in fact, as the nation descended into an economic depression.

subject to extensive regulation outside the 1906 Act. What Congress did, and what FDA did with its new authority, initially only marginally changed the landscape of the regulation of food and drugs for other animals.

The adulteration and misbranding provisions of the 1938 FD&C Act added little of a practical nature to the regulatory framework involving foods. The authority to establish mandatory standards of identity, fill of container, and quality for "any food" was not applied to animal feed. FDA's authority to prescribe levels of use of poisonous or deleterious substances that were "unavoidable" in food processing permitted tolerances to be set for pesticide residues, but was not used for animal drug residues in meat, milk, or eggs. On the labeling/misbranding side, FDA acquiesced in the practice that developed under the state feed control acts of listing

classes of ingredients, rather than specific ingredients, on the labels of livestock feed.

The drug side, however, was another story. The FD&C Act contained the new drug licensing provision, and articles intended to be used for other animals were subject to it. For the first time, drugs (defined in the 1906 Act and the FD&C Act to cover "man or other animals"), in addition to animal vaccines, were subject to licensing, but only for safety. Still, developing drugs for veterinary practice was not as important as developing drugs for human medicine, and veterinarians were free to use or prescribe human drugs for their patients.

In the 1950s, a number of developments came together that started to put animal drug regulation in the forefront of developing issues. The first was the discovery that feeding small amounts of antibiotics to animals caused them to grow more efficiently, i.e., to use less feed per pound of body weight gained, and to convert more feed pounds into meat, i.e., muscle. The licensing of antibiotics had developed separately from new drug licensing, because it was based on a system whereby antibiotics were certified, batch by batch.

The second development was the grant to FDA of mandatory establishment inspection authority. This was limited to a physical inspection of the premises, goods in process, ingredients, and labeling. FDA could take samples for analysis, but did not have authority to inspect production or distribution records. The new authority applied to all goods regulated under the FD&C Act, thus reaching animal feed as well as drugs intended for administration to other animals. FDA's authority was starting to catch up to that exercised under the VST Act and by state feed control officials.

The third development created confusion in animal drug regulation. The FD&C Act provision dealing with prescription drugs covered was originally written as any "prescription signed by a physician, dentist, or veterinarian." But this provision did not distinguish between drugs that had to be covered by a prescription, and those that a manufacturer, for marketing reasons, chose to be "prescription drugs." At the urging of a pharmacist member of Congress, Sen. Hubert H. Humphrey (D-MN), the provision was rewritten to define a prescription drug, and to draw a line between prescription and non-prescription status. In doing so, the resulting language provided that "[a] drug intended for use by man… [meeting specified criteria]

ONGOING SAGA OF ANTIBIOTICS IN ANIMAL FEEDS

One of my first orders of business after becoming commissioner was to deal with a *Federal Register* notice proposing to eliminate the use of the antibiotics penicillin, tetracycline, and chlortetracycline as growth-promoting additives in animal feeds. After a quick education from Prof. Stan Falkow of our Advisory Committee, I rewrote the introductory section of the Federal Register notice to describe bacterial susceptibility to antibiotic treatments as "a kind of commons," in this case a public good that was being consumed by private interests. (I do believe that is the only phrase in any *Federal Register* notice that has wound up as the title of an article in *The New Yorker*.)

That approach did us no good at all. We held some hearings, but the House Appropriations Committee produced report language requiring us to await a National Academy of Sciences (NAS) study before proceeding. The NAS labored, but eventually found no "smoking gun" demonstrating the transfer of resistance from animal bacteria to human pathogens, and its report only recommended further study, which gave the meat industry all it needed to prolong delays.

The subsequent steps in this minuet have been well described elsewhere. Eventually these uses of antibiotics dropped off as more and more scientific literature justified our view that the practice was damaging human medicine. Attention in this area now has shifted from livestock to chickens, and from penicillin to chloroquinolenes. I wish today's FDA better luck with this problem than we had with ours!

—**Donald Kennedy**

shall be dispensed only (i) upon a written prescription … or (ii) upon an oral prescription… ." Veterinarians and veterinary drugs were written out of the prescription-drug provision, a point noted in both the House and Senate legislative history. FDA continued to limit certain veterinary drugs to "use by or on the order of a veterinarian," based on an exemption from adequate directions for use. But the scope of the term "prescription drug" would have important consequences in future legislation.

The fourth development was the most far reaching, the Food Additives Amendment of 1958. It covered foods and drugs for use with other animals in a number of ways:

- Traditional ingredients in animal feed were now tested under the generally recognized as safe (GRAS) construct to determine whether licensing was required.

- Drugs added to animal feed were not only regulated as either new drugs or antibiotics, but also as "food additives," requiring approval and the publication of a regulation detailing permitted uses.

- Drugs that left residues in meat, milk, or eggs were also food additives, even if not added through animal feed.

- The efficacy of feed-based drugs had to be established, along with their safety, under the statutory provision that no greater level could be approved than was necessary to achieve the intended technical effect, i.e., the drug benefit.

- Feed-based drugs covered not only those intended for economic production benefits, but also those used to prevent or treat diseases in herds and flocks.

- The Delaney Anti-Cancer Clause applied to all feed-based drugs, as well technical feed ingredients approved as food additives.

Thus, every marketer of a feed-based drug was dealing with two of the three FDA regulatory processes: new drug approval, antibiotic regulation, food additive approval. As a result, applicants for marketing permission faced increasing regulatory complexity. While products intended for use in companion animals underwent a straightforward approval process (either new drug approval or antibiotic batch certification), in the growing market for drugs used in food-producing animals, problems were increasing, stemming primarily from the use of animal feed as the preferred vehicle for administration to many species.

If the drug was administered in feed, or if it left residues in edible tissue, the applicant had to get two separate approvals from FDA, each of which was handled by a different part of the agency without formal coordination, and each of which arose under a law with differing approval requirements and standards. Managing the approval process became correspondingly difficult and complex. In addition, FDA took the position that, when a drug was administered through feed, each feed produced by a local feed mill was the approvable "final dosage form." The sponsor of the drug was simply an active ingredient supplier, supporting the feed mill. This was, of course, a legal fiction, as the drug sponsor simply acted as an agent for feed mills interested in using the newly available drug, but it did mean that the drug sponsor had no administrative rights in the approval, because right was held by its customer. This anomaly applied to only "new drugs." Antibiotic approvals for feed use took the form of regulations providing an exemption from certification, and the permitted products could be sold without further "drug" approval, although of course a food additive approval was required.

By the end of the 1950s, animal vaccines remained subject to comprehensive licensing by USDA, and animal drugs administered through animal feed, or that left residues in edible tissue regardless of the route of administration, were subject to licensing for safety to the animal, efficacy to the animal, and safety to the consumer of meat, milk, or eggs. In addition, the Delaney Clause was creating an uneven playing field for marketers or proposed marketers of the growth-promoting drug diethylstilbestrol (DES), depending on the route of administration and whether it had been approved as a drug prior to the enactment of the Food Additives Amendment.

The changes brought about by the Drug Amendments of 1962 added to the regulatory burden of animal drug manufacturers in the same manner it did to human drug manufacturers. But the amendments also created an ambiguity that has been practically, but not legally, resolved: The scope of FDA's authority to regulate prescription drug advertising. Industry asserted that animal drugs subject to the order of a veterinarian were not prescription drugs, that term having been limited to drugs for human use. FDA disagreed in its prescription drug advertising regulations issued under the amendments, and FDA's position has never been formally challenged.

During the hearings on that pending legislation, the animal drug industry also started a campaign to bring all FDA-jurisdiction animal drug regulation into a single, coherent statutory provision. This took six years to achieve. The resulting law, the Animal Drug Amendments of 1968, was based on the framework of new drug regulation, and its approval of individual licenses that were personal to the drug sponsor.

Appended to that framework were pieces from the antibiotic and food additive systems, including: criteria for assessing human food safety applicable to food additives; a requirement that all approvals be published, similar to food additives; a prohibition on using a new animal drug or feed containing a new animal drug other than in accordance with its approval, as required for food additives; and the application of the Delaney Anti-Cancer Clause to all animal drugs, not just those that were also considered food additives. Finally, drugs added to feed were granted "new animal drug" approvals, while the feeds into which they were incorporated were subject to a new statutory system of licensing feeds.

THE *SALMONELLA* THEORY THAT DIDN'T HOLD UP

As everyone who has worked anywhere at FDA knows, *Salmonella* infections are a major health hazard to the very young and very old and an extremely unpleasant illness to everyone else. Dr. James Goddard, who had been the Centers for Disease Control Director before becoming FDA Commissioner in 1966, had as one of his goals to better control those infections.

He initiated a scientific "circle theory," which posited that *Salmonella* infections went from animal feed to animals, and then to humans—and thus *Salmonella* infections in humans could be significantly reduced if *Salmonella* in animals could be prevented. It was thought at that time that a significant source of *Salmonella* infections in animals was caused by rendered animal feed, which is basically ground-up animal tissue cooked until it is just protein. If that cooked protein could be produced *Salmonella*-free, the theory went, then the animals would be *Salmonella*-free and not pass the organism on to humans. "Breaking the circle" meant that *Salmonella* would not be passed from feed to animals to humans.

So, to put this theory into practice, FDA instituted an enforcement program on the animal rendering industry. It was my privilege to handle most, if not all, of the animal rendering court cases, where FDA sought injunctions to require renderers to produce *Salmonella*-free animal feed. Over a two- or three-year period, I tried two cases and was involved in a number of consent decrees requiring the feed to be Salmonella-free based on the circle theory.

The difficulty was that, as more scientific information became available on *Salmonella*, it became clear that while making *Salmonella*-free animal feed was a noble idea, it would not break the circle and would have only a minor effect, if any, on *Salmonella* contamination of animals. It was a nice theory that was, unfortunately, not scientifically valid. In the end, for those injunctions still in effect, the U.S. Attorney for the District was asked to notify the court that the government did not object to closing the matter.

—Gary L. Yingling

Not until fifteen years later, in 1983, did FDA pull the administrative pieces together so that one bureau (now Center) of Veterinary Medicine controls the entire animal drug approval process. That center also regulates animal feeds, so that cross-cutting issues between foods and drugs for other animals can be dealt with in a single administrative system.

The 1970s brought forth an issue that has remained vibrant and contentious, namely, the significance for human medicine of the use of antibiotics, both low level and therapeutic, in other animals, particularly food-producing animals. The issue arises from the fact that disease organisms mutate and become resistant to certain antibiotics. The resistance mechanism can be transferred to formerly non-resistant organisms. The issue was whether the low-level use of antibiotics (and especially antibiotics used in human medicine) could provoke the growth of resistant organisms in animals fed the low levels, and whether those resistant organisms could be transferred or their resistance transferred to humans, thus impairing the use of those antibiotics in human medicine.

When initially asked by FDA to evaluate the evidence on this subject, the National Academy of Sciences (NAS) in

1980 provided this triple backflip: "The lack of data linking human illness with this subtherapeutic use must not be equated with proof that the proposed hazards do not exist." Or more directly: "The research necessary to establish and measure a definitive risk has not been conducted." FDA tasked industry with conducting the research through an innovative use of the records and reports provision of the new animal drug section of the FD&C Act. NAS weighed in with further reports in 1988 (penicillin) and 1999 (antimicrobials generally).

While Congress had thwarted FDA in its initial attempt to ban a wide range of antibiotics, FDA started to pursue specific drugs, and has recently analyzed therapeutic drugs as well as those used at subtherapeutic levels. But equally important, FDA has also renewed its focus on the excessive use of antibiotics in human medicine, and that contribution to the development of resistant organisms, especially in the hospital environment. Within FDA, a working group among the various centers has been coordinating concerns that apply to both human and veterinary medicine on this important topic.

An additional development in the 1970s was a new means of evaluating human risk. While the Delaney Clause banned the use of a food additive found to "induce cancer in man or other animals," the Drug Amendments added the DES proviso, saying that a carcinogenic animal drug could be added to feed (or approved as an animal drug) if it did not harm the animal, and if "no residue of the drug was found" in meat, milk, or eggs. The question of finding the residue led immediately to the issue of how hard should one look. After initially taking a fixed approach, based on a physiological response model and the limit of detection, FDA found itself challenged by developments in analytical chemistry. Industry was concerned that such developments would lead to a never-ending chase for a smaller and smaller amount. The ultimate resolution, crafted with both rulemaking and litigation, was called the "sensitivity-of-the-method" approach. It provided that a combination of animal testing and a mathematical model would lead to a virtually safe level, and residue testing had only to meet that level, however much chemistry might subsequently improve. While FDA was foreclosed from applying this approach to the basic food additive Delaney Clause, it has been used in to evaluate pesticide residues and contaminants in food and color additives.

In the 1980s, the issue that ran in parallel with human and animal drugs was the development of generic drug approvals and patent term restoration. The enactment in 1984 of the Hatch-Waxman Amendment to the FD&C Act enabled easier approval of generic versions of human drugs. It reflected in part the (continuing) concern with drug costs, and the promise of lower drug prices from generic equivalent drugs. But there are no third-party payers on the animal drug side, at least in the case of food-producing animals. Also in the case of food-producing animals, the drugs used are a cost of production as much as feed and housing, which is a different economic outlook than drugs used to treat humans or companion animals.

Perhaps it is not surprising that the animal drug version of the provision in 1988 not only recognizes the dual markets for drugs used in food-producing and non-food-producing animals, but also contains other "perfecting" amendments to the animal drug provisions. First, the changes to the patent law permitted the applicant to choose between the first approval and the first approval for food-producing animals to trigger patent term extension. Second, the generic approval provisions took into account the need to use other than traditional blood level tests to determine bioequivalence. Third, the superfluous antibiotic certification

provisions were repealed. Finally, a new provision was added to the FD&C Act defining when an animal drug is limited to "use by or on the order of a licensed veterinarian"; this provision essentially parallels the criteria for prescription drugs.

The 1990s were a time of "modernization," including finding new ways to finance the operations of FDA. While animal drugs took the lead initially, human drugs were in the forefront of new financing concepts, and animal drugs only caught up later. The regulation of animal drugs moved further away from the human model that had controlled the Animal Drug Amendments of 1968:

- While the export of unapproved human drugs became more complex, the export of unapproved animal drugs was simplified by making the general export provisions of the FD&C Act applicable.

FDA maintains vigilance over what food-producing animals consume and over the residues they leave.

- The concerns of veterinarians that the prohibition on using animal drugs outside the strict limits of their approvals exposed them to both civil litigation and FDA regulatory action were addressed in the Animal Medicinal Drug Use Clarification Act (AMDUCA).

- The Animal Drug Availability Act (ADAA) expanded the kinds of evidence that could support proof of efficacy, simplified the process for combining two or more animal drugs in a single product or use regimen, provided a process for gaining more certainty in the drug development process, and provided a mechanism for evaluating the safety of drug residues in meat, milk, and eggs from the use of drugs other countries had approved, but not the United States. This latter provision also provided recognition of, and support for, the international procedures for evaluating those residues.

- The 1997 FDA Modernization Act applied some of these ADAA changes to human drugs, but also applied a simplified system for changing the drug manufacturing process to animal drug as well as human drugs.

  While procedural improvements were the animal drug focus in the 1990s, the major innovation on the human side was the passage in 1992 (and its subsequent renewals in 1997 and 2002) of the Prescription Drug User Fee Act (PDUFA). PDUFA provided an infusion of money to FDA through application, establishment, and product maintenance fees. It became the forerunner in 2001 of the Medical Device User Fee and Modernization Act (MDUFMA) and in 2003 of the Animal Drug User Fee Act (ADUFA). But, ADUFA outshines PDUFA by providing four sources of industry funding—sponsor, application, establishment, and product maintenance fees—in addition to the stabilized base funding.

  Thus, as animal food and drug regulation move into the twenty-first century, it can be viewed either as a distorted mirror image of human food and drug regulation, or as a source of insights and warnings of issues that will arise in human regulation. In each of the following areas, the animal food and drug regulation experience offers guidance for human food and drug developments:

- Should human drug exports be simplified to give fuller recognition of other drug regulatory systems?

- Should there be a "no significant risk" approach to the Delaney Clause?

- Should the "substantial evidence" of efficacy be broadened to give statutory recognition to non-clinical endpoints that can be important in speeding drug development?

- If human drug development shifts to the "phased application" approach common in animal drug development, will PDUFA funding sources be broadened to parallel ADUFA to provide a consistent funding pattern?

Dietary Supplements: Populism and Pirandello

Scott Bass

DIETARY SUPPLEMENTS TOOK CENTER STAGE IN THE SECOND HALF OF THE TWENTIETH CENTURY as the category that broke the entrenched food/drug dichotomy under the Federal Food, Drug, and Cosmetic (FD&C) Act. Many themes intersect in an analysis of how dietary supplements became a recognized category, including: self-empowerment, reactions to excessive government regulation, distrust of a healthcare system that began to sink as life expectancy rose, failure of FDA officials to recognize a new paradigm that could have been effectively incorporated, and globalization of both healthcare and treatment philosophies. The confluence of these factors led to the emergence of a category that battered through bureaucratic barricades instead of following a traditional evolutionary path.

During thirty years of contentious battles on judicial and regulatory fronts, Congress twice took the unusual step of pulling back FDA jurisdiction over a category of products that the agency had zealously sought to regulate. The culmination of this struggle, however, leaves this twentieth century category in search of a meaningful twenty-first century position in the food and drug regulatory environment.

The roots of the conflict can be found in a shift in medical practice that began just before enactment of the 1906 law. Many doctors in the late nineteenth century began to adopt allopathic largely sickness-oriented, as opposed to homeopathic largely wellness-oriented, treatment modalities. The former focus on killing disease or excising bodily abnormalities came to dominate U.S. medicine. The successful lobbying effort at the state level for licensure of medical schools and doctors under an allopathic system underlay much of the subsequent legislative treatment of drugs and the exclusion of preventive modalities. The only vestige of the alternative approach is the inclusion of the Homeopathic Pharmacopoeia in the 1938 Federal Food, Drug, and Cosmetic (FD&C) Act's definition of drug, a minor concession to the few remaining adherents of that form of medical practice.

The legislative history of the 1906 and 1938 Acts includes little of note with respect to the nascent vitamin category. Most vitamins were not isolated and identified until the 1920s, and for that reason were not considered in the 1906 Act. Once the nutritional role of vitamins was accepted, government stepped in. The Food and Nutrition Board, a subcommittee of the National Research Council, was authorized to issue recommended daily allowances (RDAs)

Former Louisiana State Senator Dudley LeBlanc was the inventor and flamboyant promoter of Hadacol. Hadacol was promoted in what was perhaps the last of the great American medicine shows. Admission to the show that launched the careers of such mid-century luminaries as Frank Sinatra and Minnie Pearl was by Hadacol box tops: one for a child, two for an adult. LeBlanc and FDA regulators played a game of cat and mouse and LeBlanc tried to escape prosecution by avoiding crossing state lines.

listing minimum levels of nutrients human beings require. In the mid-1930s, FDA established a Vitamin Division to deal with unscrupulous manufacturers and advertisers who sold sub-potent or improperly labeled ingredients.

Economic adulteration was the primary focus of early enforcement efforts. Phony weight-loss supplements were described in the 1933 and 1934 legislative proposals that preceded the FD&C Act, with references to "slenderizers" and products that "can have nutritive ingredients…," but not be sold for drug use. The rarely used term "foods for special dietary use" was included in the FD&C Act, and a reference to the "vitamin, mineral and other dietary properties" of such foods found its way into the Act, as well.

The next notable development occurred in the Judicial Branch. In 1948, Supreme Court Justice William O. Douglas informed the food and drug world that pamphlets distributed to consumers and to vendors touting the health benefits of vitamins, minerals, and herbs constituted "labeling," a holding that has explained much of subsequent drug and dietary supplement law. In the protectionist sentiment of the time, Justice Douglas, speaking for a bare plurality, opined that "the high purpose of the Act to protect consumers who under present conditions are largely unable to protect themselves in this field would then be easily defeated." The enforcement tool handed FDA became the hard core of the enforcement efforts that ensued over the next forty years.

The focus of 1930s America was on nutrition for survival rather than supplementation and disease prevention, but after World War II and the affluence that became America, aggressive judicial and regulatory strategies brought the social conflict over the availability of vitamins and minerals to a head. On June 20, 1962, FDA published a proposal in the *Federal Register* suggesting that only nutrients recognized by "competent authorities" as essential and of significant value in human nutrition could be sold. Maximum and minimum nutrient limits, proposed as RDAs, were included in the proposed regulation.

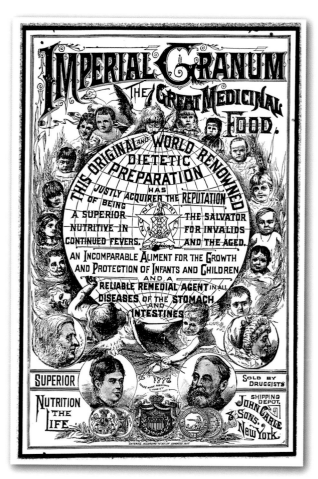

Turn of the century advertisements for health foods such as this blurred the line between foods and drugs. Later, FDA would regulate foods with medicinal value, referring to them as foods "for special dietary use."

> ## COURT VIEW OF VITAMINS
>
> This is the latest but, unfortunately, probably not the last, chapter in the bitter battle between the Food and Drug Administration (FDA) and manufacturers and vendors of pills and liquid containing vitamins and minerals and citizens allied with the latter.
>
> While the manufacturers and vendors have obvious private interests as well, the battle reflects what appears to be a sincere sentiment on the part of many citizens that daily ingestion of a substantial quantity and variety of vitamins and minerals in the form of pills or liquids, in addition to those furnished by ordinary diet, is needed for good health, especially because of the increasing consumption of the modern food fats—sweet drinks, junk foods, heavy sugar diets" and "wheatgerm-free bread and nutritionally inadequate breakfast foods,"... and the FDA's equally sincere belief that the promotion of what, on a previous review, this court called a "dazzling array" of recommended daily dosages and combinations ... is causing consumers to waste millions of dollars annually in the purchase of vitamin and mineral preparations which they either do not need at all or do not need in the potencies or combinations that are being bought.
>
> **—NNFA v. Kennedy (2d Cir. 1978)**

Populist opposition to FDA policies emerged as a significant force at this time; the public felt that FDA was encroaching upon personal freedom by proposing restrictions to vitamin availability in this proposed regulation. As a result, FDA held no hearings on the proposal because of the unexpected waves of public criticism. Four years later, FDA issued standards of identity for vitamin and mineral supplements as "special dietary food products." FDA's effort to impose maximum potency, indirectly this time, failed yet again. On the eve of the effective date of those regulations, in the face of yet more public opposition, FDA published an order staying the effective dates and instead held extensive hearings spanning a two-year period.

Seven years later, in August 1973, FDA issued a final vitamin and mineral regulation stating, most significantly, that any such products with a potency exceeding 150% of the RDA would be deemed drugs, subject to the need to submit substantial evidence of safety and effectiveness. Combinations were prohibited except under very limited circumstances.

Marches on Washington ensued in the manner of the Vietnam War and civil rights protests. The populist push-back brought into this confrontation an unlikely coalition: the Baby Boom generation, growing up from the alternative Woodstock lifestyle whose counter-culture philosophy embraced Eastern herbs and natural products; and far right John Birch Society adherents who believed that the federal government lacked power to restrict the God-given freedom of choice of American citizens. In an unsophisticated, but nevertheless effective, attack on the FDA regulations, this coalition convinced Sen. William Proxmire (D-WI) to introduce what

One of many dietary supplements marketed in the 1950s and 60s for weight loss. (FDA History Office collection)

became Section 411 of the FD&C Act. Section 411 restricts FDA's ability to set maximum potency or prohibit combination products. Proxmire ushered in the passage of Section 411 with an apt metaphor:

What the FDA wants to do is to strike the views of its stable of orthodox nutritionists into "tablets," and bring them down from Mt. Sinai where they will be used to regulate the rights of millions of Americans, who believe they are getting a lousy diet, to take vitamins and minerals.

The real issue was whether the FDA is going to play "God." Religion thus capped the fusion of politically disparate constituents, foreshadowing successful efforts twenty years later, where tenets of the Mormon faith underlay the most

significant legislative battle FDA had ever encountered.

Frustrated by the loss of important appellate court decisions and the passage of Section 411, FDA fought back by turning to the over-the-counter (OTC) drug monograph system in an attempt to impose potency limits for dietary supplements. As part of this effort, FDA introduced the OTC Vitamin and Mineral Drug Product proposal in 1979, but it was withdrawn in 1981 after significant public and industry resistance. By this time, two trade associations had emerged on the judicial and legislative fronts.

FDA then turned to more creative enforcement theories to keep vitamins and minerals in check, even as the dietary supplement market exploded. As a part of the industry's expansion, more and more questionable claims and untested ingredients began to appear in the burgeoning health food trade. Frustrated in its efforts to limit potency, combinations, and therapeutic claims, FDA relied on interpretation of the 1958 Food Additive Amendments, which had been designed to keep unsafe ingredients out of food. The agency filed cases against dietary supplement manufacturers premised upon the argument that a dietary ingredient contained in a capsule or tablet was a "food additive" because the ingredient was added to the tablet or capsule. As a food additive, it was incumbent upon the manufacturer to establish that the ingredient was generally recognized as safe among qualified experts for its intended use.

"Stamp Out the FDA"—Poster illustrating popular sentiment in favor of dietary supplements, and against FDA's regulatory stance against them. The Proxmire Amendment (1976) was the first major statute enacted to limit FDA's jurisdiction over a particular product area. (FDA History Office collection)

Needless to say, it took only one FDA nutrition expert to say that it was not so recognized to dash the efforts of even a Nobel-prize winning panel of experts. No company ever won those cases, even if the ingredient was deemed "safe." It took more than a dozen years before two appellate courts finally put to rest FDA's "unsafe food additive theory" by declaring it an "Alice in Wonderland" construct. But, the battle did not end there. From 1992 to 1994 more letters found their way to Congress on the issue of dietary supplement regulation than on any other issue since the Vietnam War.

Industry and emboldened consumer groups watched warily as the Nutrition Labeling and Education Act (NLEA) passed in 1990. Fearing an unintended effect on dietary supplements, many groups approached Utah Sen. Orin Hatch, a powerful presence in Congress who had led the legislative resolution of the brand name vs generic drug war in 1984. Section 403(r)(6) was added to NLEA, providing FDA the opportunity to evaluate dietary supplement health claims under a more lenient standard than that applied to conventional foods. FDA declined the invitation. Sen. Hatch's view was very clear. He said in 1990:

By their very nature, dietary supplements must be marketed so that the consumer is informed of the health or disease-prevention benefits that may be conferred. Greater flexibility is thus required to permit communication of these benefits. This increased regulatory flexibility is also mandated by the very rapid pace of scientific advances here and abroad linking the prevention of long-term disease to improved nutritional supplementation. For these reasons, a more lenient standard for dietary supplements is envisioned.

In 1991, FDA fired the shot that ultimately provoked the new dietary supplement law. In a proposed health claim regulation, FDA stated that herbs were not eligible for health claims because they were not recognized as nutrients. Utah rose. A month after the 1991 proposal, Sen. Hatch floated a one-page bill that would have permitted

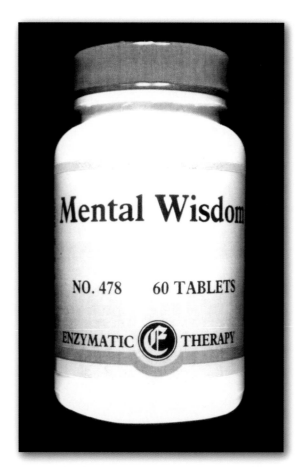

It was unclear from the label whether this was intended to be marketed as a dietary supplement or a homeopathic product when it was purchased in 1999. (FDA History Office collection)

any claims for supplements and no safety requirements. That bill grew into the Health Freedom Act of 1992, a placeholder intended to keep FDA at bay. A potent force fomented in Utah, center of herbal manufacturing, and drew in all the trade associations and citizens' groups. Television ads, including a commercial with actor Mel Gibson reaching for a bottle of vitamin C in front of agents with submachine guns, won a great deal of popular support. Congress was inundated for years with calls, letters, and consumer visits.

It is ironic that the law eventually Congress passed, the Dietary Supplement Health and Education Act of 1994 (DSHEA), grew out of the fact that FDA would not recognize the therapeutic and preventive purposes of herbs. FDA had repeatedly countered earlier efforts to place herbs in "traditional medicine" OTC monographs. Pleas by embassies several years later had met with the same fate. Herbs are not vitamins or minerals, nor, in some sense, are they traditional dietary supplements, as that term was then used. DSHEA was to become the herb tail wagging the vitamin dog.

An Investigation Free from Politics

In November 1983, a drug company began distributing E-Ferol, an intravenous vitamin E formulation intended for use in premature infants (vitamin E being one of the more important nutrients for the premature infant). Vitamin E products, prior to the marketing of E-Ferol, were available in oral as well as intramuscular injection form. But, because the premature infant's stomach could not tolerate the oral dose and the premature infant's muscle mass was too limited for intramuscular injection, neither form was optimal.

E-Ferol was the first vitamin E product designed and marketed for intravenous use in premature infants. Based on the labeling of the product, physicians and pharmacists believed E-Ferol was intended for the treatment of retrolental fibroplasia (a condition that can cause blindness) in premature infants. Physicians and pharmacists also believed that FDA had approved the drug for this use. It hadn't.

Adverse reactions linked to the drug began to be reported very soon after it was first distributed. Before the drug was withdrawn from the market in April 1984, the drug was implicated in the death of thirty-eight premature infants.

Although not only aware of the drug when it was first marketed but also of the fact that the drug was not approved for use in infants, FDA staff nevertheless concluded that E-Ferol was related to a class of injectable products covered by the Drug Efficacy Study (DESI) review. The staff concluded that, since that review was pending, no immediate action against E-Ferol was necessary. When the deaths attributed to E-Ferol and FDA's missed opportunity to regulate the drug became public, the agency was harshly criticized by Congress, the media, and the public for knowing about the marketing of the drug and for failing to take action against it.

At the time, I was an attorney in the Office of General Counsel (OGC) at FDA. I had been in OGC for eight years, splitting my time between litigation and what we referred to as "liaison" work—providing advice and guidance to one of FDA's six centers (in my case, the Center for Foods). Prior to coming to FDA, I had acquired considerable litigation experience while serving as a public defender. I had seen, firsthand, for instance, the devastating effect that an indictment and trial can have on an innocent target. Perhaps because I had this history, my litigation experience at FDA had been almost exclusively on civil matters with the exception of two straightforward misdemeanor cases in which the evidence

FDA's reaction to the new uproar was to dig in its heels. In the face of a growing DSHEA threat, FDA issued the "Dykstra Report" in 1993, blatantly informing industry and consumers that FDA had no intention of recognizing herbal claims or of permitting increased potency of commonly used nutrients like vitamin A. That document provided the last piece of evidence Congress needed to finish its work. Heated hearings, legislative legerdemain and the close of the 1994 congressional session brought forth a unanimous, eleventh-hour vote to pass DSHEA after a fierce fight against Sen. Edward M. Kennedy (D-MA) and Congressman Henry Waxman (D-CA). Senators Hatch and Thomas Harkin (D-IA) effected the passage of a law whose purpose was "to bring some much needed sanity and order to the regulation of the dietary supplement industry... [and to]... encourage good health through the use of nutritional supplements while, at the same time, protecting consumers from unsafe products." Thus, from this social revolution came DSHEA. As some have commented, the "nots" in DSHEA were as significant as its enabling provisions. Under the law, the FDA Commissioner

was so overwhelming that the defendants readily pled guilty. In any event, I was surprised when asked to investigate whether felony violations had been committed in the marketing of E-Ferol. The Center for Drugs and one of the agency's districts, respectively, assigned a compliance officer and a field Investigator to assist in the investigation, and, in time, two lawyers from the Department of Justice joined the investigation team.

Although FDA had suffered considerable embarrassment from its failure to prevent the marketing of E-Ferol, the criminal investigation proceeded at its own pace with no scheduled timetable. In the course of the investigation, we reviewed thousands of documents and conducted scores of interviews across the country. Ultimately, we documented the involvement of the president of the manufacturing company and the president and a vice president of the distributor in the development and marketing of the drug. It was not until July 1987 that the investigation ended and an indictment was returned.

There is, in the parlance of litigators, the adage that once a diligent inquiry is made into the facts, the law generally takes care of itself. And, in the case of E-Ferol, that's what happened. In September 1988, the two corporate presidents were convicted on new drug and drug misbranding felonies and on conspiracy to commit mail and wire fraud. One president was convicted of committing mail fraud. (The other president was acquitted on the mail fraud count, and both presidents were acquitted on counts of committing wire fraud). The vice president pled guilty to two counts of wire fraud and one felony count under the Food, Drug, and Cosmetic Act. Each of the defendants received a fine and a jail sentence and each served time in jail.

The case proved to be a significant judicial victory and precedent for FDA. For me, the case stands out because the agency, although under intense political and public pressure, never questioned the need for and value of a deliberate, painstaking investigation. Rushing to judgment was not an option—a posture, I think, satisfying to the mindset of prosecutor and public defender alike.

—**Fred Degnan**

THE VITAMIN WARS

In February 1992, I entered the glass doors of the Parklawn Building as the newly sworn-in FDA Associate Commissioner for Legislative Affairs, unaware that the battle over dietary supplements was about to explode, and that I would be in the middle. There were no guards in the lobby, no metal detectors. A directory in the lobby pointed me to the commissioner's office on the fourteenth floor.

Not until the dust cleared following almost two combative years of sagebrush rebellion under the battle cry, "Keep your hands off our vitamins," did security in the lobby of Parklawn resembled that of the CIA. During the "war," Commissioner Kessler would receive dozens of death threats, and Congress and FDA would receive hundreds of thousands of hostile letters in the space of several months. Reportedly, the chairman of the House Energy and Commerce Committee, John Dingell, would even encounter pro-vitamin protestors in his home driveway in Dearborn, Michigan. I can personally report that he was not too happy about that.

This "war" started innocently enough. Safety warnings and an import alert were issued for a contaminated batch of the amino acid supplement, L-tryptophan, shipped from Japan. Several American consumers died. Medical journals began investigating a link with exotic symptoms described as refractory eosinophilia myalgia syndrome.

In June 1992, with a deft public relations touch, FDA field investigators joined a task force of approximately two dozen flack-jacket clad federal and local police, guns drawn, entering the Tahoma, Washington, clinic of Harvard-trained physician Dr. Jonathan V. Wright. His crime: ignoring an FDA request to stop using the amino acid and other supplements for which health claims had been made. Dr. Wright had filed a lawsuit against FDA several weeks before; he now alleged retaliation. He had also invited three local Seattle TV stations to record the events, which included officers with bright yellow "FDA" on their backs carting away truckloads of patients' records, injectible B vitamins, and computer equipment.

Like "Remember the Alamo," the tagline "Don't take our vitamins" reverberated into living rooms and health food stores across the country. It struck an anti-government nerve. In certain segments out West, militias had already organized to combat the "black Apache helicopters" swooping down to seize our civil liberties. The West found its voice in Sen. Orrin Hatch (R-UT) who represented a state with a $2 billion dietary supplement industry. Hatch himself took a daily mug of supplement products that kept him alert during mind-

---

is not permitted to declare a dietary supplement product an imminent hazard; only the Secretary of Health and Human Services can do that. FDA may not sue without advance notice. Dietary supplements were explicitly declared not to be food additives. Structure/function claims (health claims without disease mentioned) were explicitly cordoned off and said not to be drug claims.

DSHEA changed the definition of science. The Western empirical-based system of distinguishing truth through adequate investigation was displaced, in part, by more of an Eastern intuitive approach to permitting claims that were proven in part but did not necessarily meet the time-honored drug approval standard of two adequate well-controlled, double-blind, clinical studies. DSHEA changed the definition of drug. It forced a re-thinking of the food/drug dichotomy that has existed so strongly in the century since the 1906 Act was passed:

- "Functional foods" emerged as a new category of standard food products

numbing Labor and Human Resource Committee hearings. He chaired the committee during a period of Republican resurgence. Hatch's health staffer, Anne LeBelle, was inflamed when the commissioner met with her personally and insinuated that she "didn't know how to play the game," when she pushed for FDA flexibility in supplement regulation. She then spent the next six months educating us about the rules of the Senate game; they withheld FDA appropriations and ultimately attached the Dietary Supplement Act of 1992 (DSA) as the price to enact the badly needed Prescription Drug User Fee Act of 1992 (PDUFA).

The DSA provided the framework to force FDA to negotiate a comprehensive long-term compromise in the form of the Dietary Supplement Health and Education Act of 1994 (DSHEA). It prohibited FDA from dictating restrictive new supplement labeling. It required multiple government reports quantifying whether FDA priorities, and the use of limited FDA resources to regulate vitamins and herbs, was justified by the health risks posed by those products. Passage was assured by drug industry support of PDUFA, and a bruising grassroots campaign by supplement interests spearheaded by the Council for Responsible Nutrition.

The homeopathic revolution ignited that June morning in Dr. Wright's Tahoma medical clinic demonstrated the limits of FDA's regulatory reach. It showed federal policymakers that a significant percentage of Americans valued FDA to keep unsafe products off store shelves, but that buyers were the best judges of whether the products worked. DSHEA was ultimately a hard-fought compromise. It bombarded us with product structure and function claims (e.g., creates more energy, increases memory, improves sexual performance) while ultimately establishing industry good manufacturing practices and more truthful ingredient labeling.

On September 19, 1995, Dr. Wright quietly received a registered letter from the U.S. Attorney in Washington state notifying him that the government's case had been closed and that the items seized would be returned. FDA received a message, too: Regulate homeopathic medicine at your own risk.

—Marc J. Scheineson

enhanced with vitamins, minerals or herbs, but for which there was, and is, no FD&C Act category.

- FDA gave away twenty-five percent of the OTC drug market to dietary supplements in its structure/function regulation on January 6, 2000. Dietary supplements are now permitted to carry claims that were traditionally reserved solely to drug products.

- Combination OTC drug/dietary supplement products have begun to emerge, once again without any clear regulatory underpinning.

- Aquaceuticals—water enhanced with vitamins or other nutrients bearing implicit therapeutic claims—have become one of the fastest growing food categories in the world.

- Cosmeceuticals, utilizing functional or "novel" ingredients from the dietary supplement world, and bearing explicit therapeutic claims, continue to challenge the cosmetic/drug paradigm.

- FDA's new time and extent application procedure, applicable to OTC drugs, is in part a concession to the efforts twenty years earlier by the herb industry to place traditional medicines in the OTC Drug Monograph system. Foreign products will now be subject to market access in a matter of months instead of being forced into the several-year, several-hundred million dollar route required for new drug applications.

Finally, DSHEA helped to change the fact that medical schools in America had not been teaching nutrition or preventive health in the twentieth century. The globalization of markets, the increasing influence of Chinese and European herbal products and Chinese medical philosophies, and an inherent distrust of the flat anti-supplement positions taken by the medical establishment, have led to increased nutrition awareness.

DSHEA was, in the end, a law for its time. With life expectancy soaring from the post-World War II era, preventive health has become a mainstay of American life. People cannot afford to be ill, insurance companies do not cover chronic illnesses or long hospital stays, and longevity has brought with it a desire on the part of the "generation that refuses to grow old" a need to remain physically fit and energetic. Dietary supplements are a large part of this paradigm. But the industry has, in the end, failed to deliver fully on its promise.

Many had predicted that the dialectic equation following the passage of DSHEA in 1994 would mirror that of the 1984 Hatch-Waxman Act. Generic drug companies in the 1980s were purchased by larger pioneer manufacturers, and the investment banking field swept through

quickly. What they all discovered was shoddy manufacturing practices and application fraud. Congressman John Dingell (D-MI) held hearings, much of FDA's field force was re-educated to be tough drug inspectors, and many people went to jail. The net result was a strengthened generic drug industry and increasing acceptance of generic drugs in the face of a failing healthcare system. The dietary supplement industry, on the other hand, which propelled freedom of choice into a congressional enactment, was similarly not subjected to a wave of criminal prosecutions or brutal congressional hearings. However, the industry that promised to self-regulate has done so only fitfully. As the twenty-first century begins, the result has been that many products are sub-potent and many product claims lack even the most elemental substantiation.

While several important First Amendment, post-DSHEA court decisions laid the groundwork for increased health-related claims for supplements and foods, all of them require some reasonable basis for the claims. The mainstream players in the dietary supplement industry have made efforts to collect such substantiation and have collectively worked to effectuate responsible legislative and regulatory proposals. However, the explosion of the Internet—an unanticipated development during the drafting of DSHEA—has left consumers "largely unable to protect themselves," in the words of Justice Douglas. The "multiplicity of devices

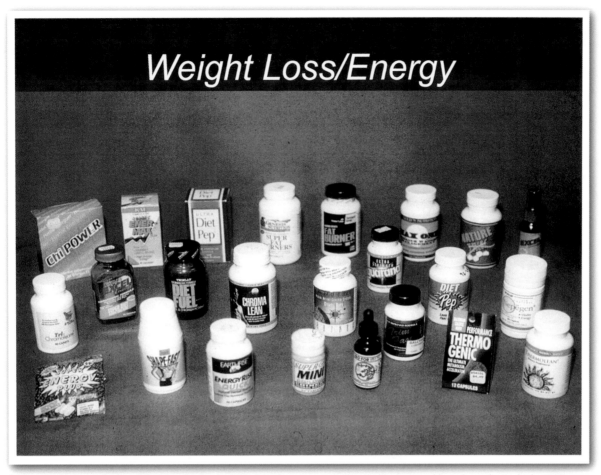

Weight Loss/Energy

FDA continues its earliest tradition of collecting "exhibits" for Congress and others to illustrate problematic products. In the 1990s, FDA became concerned about weight loss claims made for dietary supplements and assembled this collection for Congressional hearings. Most, but not all, of these dietary supplements contained ephedra for weight loss. (Photo courtesy of Lori Love, M.D.)

and... preparations,... many of which are worthless at best and some for which are distinctly dangerous to health," a concern expressed in 1934 by Sen. Stephens, have taken center stage in the press, which has unfairly characterized the industry as "unregulated" and DSHEA as a license to sell unsubstantiated products. The challenge to industry and government will be to contain this category before it dissipates through consumers' lack of confidence.

More responsible players are utilizing dietary ingredients in traditional foods, a direction that can be seen in aquaceuticals and functional foods in Asia, Europe, and the United States. Those traditional food players may ultimately, and ironically, assume control of this category if self-regulatory efforts are not more successful.

Medical schools now teach nutrition, and the FDA defends DSHEA in international harmonization conferences. Industry members who clamored for regulatory freedom now beg for stronger enforcement. Science—albeit an East/West mixture—will ultimately remain the answer to how the next century defines the vitamins, minerals, and herbs that transformed the FD&C Act.

"LIPS THAT TOUCH COAL-TAR SHALL NEVER TOUCH MINE"

LIPSTICK INDUSTRY

Food & Drug Administration

LIPSTICK MAKERS SAY WOMEN EAT LITTLE LIPSTICK ANYWAY!

BUT LOTS of MEN DO!

CRANBERRY

Concerns about Red 19 in cosmetics precipitated this cartoon depiction of FDA and industry wrangling over the language of the Delaney Clause that prohibited colors found to cause cancer "in man or animals." The debate, as highlighted in this cartoon, was how much of the lipstick was actually ingested. How much of it might women (and men) actually consume? Even FDA didn't know the answer to this question.

The Least of FDA's Problems

Thomas Scarlett

NO ONE WHO VISITED THE FDA'S OFFICE IN DOWNTOWN WASHINGTON EVER FORGOT the disturbing photograph of a woman blinded in 1933 by a mascara called Lash Lure. The photo was part of a small historical exhibit that included items from FDA's "Chamber of Horrors," a collection of dangerous and worthless products FDA was unable to control under the 1906 Food and Drugs Act. Assembled in the 1920s and 1930s, the collection dramatized the case for broader FDA product jurisdiction as part of the New Deal's legislative campaign to upgrade the agency's consumer protection authority. At the time, commonly available cosmetics contained potentially toxic ingredients. An aniline dye in Lash Lure could cause dermatitis, leading to corneal ulceration, infection, and in extreme cases, blindness. Many customers were reportedly poisoned by thallium acetate in Koremlu, a depilatory. FDA took no action against Lash Lure or Koremlu because the 1906 Pure Food and Drugs Act did not cover cosmetics, only foods and drugs. Early drafts of the legislation defined "drug" to include cosmetics, but the enacted definition was narrowed to therapeutic products.

Even if cosmetics had been classified as drugs, FDA's ability to move aggressively against regulated products was limited. Undeniably a landmark in consumer protection, the 1906 Act nevertheless promised more than FDA could deliver with the limited regulatory tools the law provided. Continuing fraud and safety incidents after 1906 led to increasingly vitriolic attacks by muckrakers. In 1933, the authors of *100,000,000 Guinea Pigs* indicted federal regulators for "sheer administrative incompetence, shiftiness, and a preference for backstairs methods" stemming from a "marked and growing indifference to the people's interests." From her perspective as an FDA official, Ruth de Forest Lamb rejected the notion that "government officials are incompetent or callous." In *American Chamber of Horrors: The Truth about Food and Drugs*, she conceded that FDA regulation was inadequate, but pointed to the real reason the agency's staff lacked a record of success: "they have no real power."

FDR's administration proposed to fix this. Beginning in 1933, officials used potent images such as the Lash Lure photograph to mobilize support for FDA regulation of cosmetics and medical devices, and for new authority to identify and remedy problems with all FDA-regulated products. Congress resisted at first, but its hand was forced in 1937 by the death of more than

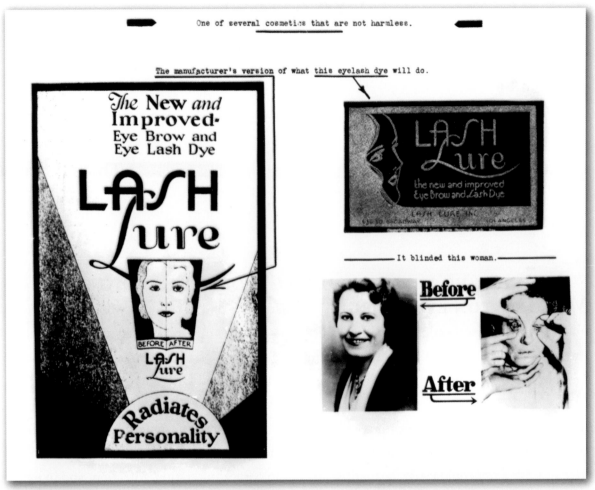

One of several cosmetics that are not harmless.

The manufacturer's version of what this eyelash dye will do.

It blinded this woman.

This panel from the American Chamber of Horrors exhibit illustrates the known problems with Lash Lure, an aniline eyelash dye. Women getting their hair colored in salons often had their lashes and brows tinted to match. This panel shows how the product blinded one woman.

100 people from Elixir Sulfanilamide, leading to rapid House and Senate passage of the Food, Drug, and Cosmetic (FD&C) Act of 1938.

Although it was a drug safety incident that precipitated legislative action, toxic cosmetics played a leading role. From the outset of congressional deliberations, reformers could point to Lash Lure and Koremlu as evidence that real dangers lurked in the underregulated marketplace of consumer products. If the seemingly innocuous decision to visit a beauty shop could blind a woman for life, the federal government obviously needed to step in. Elixir Sulfanilamide moved Congress to take the final step of passing the FD&C

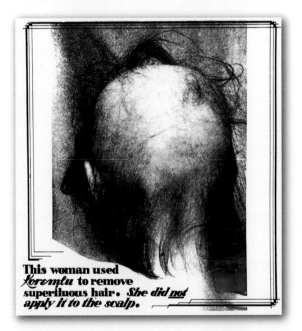

This woman used *Koremlu* to remove superfluous hair. She did *not* apply it to the scalp.

Koremlu was one of the products documented in the American Chamber of Horrors, both in the exhibit and in the book by the same name, written by FDA's Chief Information Officer, Ruth de Forest Lamb, who had worked in the advertising and cosmetics industry prior to coming to FDA. Although used topically, the thallium acetate in the product traveled systemically. Several women who used it as a depilatory were reported to have lost hair on other parts of their body as well, including their head.

Act, but Lash Lure and Koremlu helped push Congress to the brink of action.

Under the 1938 Act, FDA quickly went to court against the more troublesome cosmetics with known toxic ingredients, including mascara and other eye products, lipsticks, and skin-bleach creams. More generally, FDA's close surveillance of the U.S. cosmetic marketplace in the years immediately after 1938 gave the industry an incentive to identify problematic chemicals and reformulate cosmetics with safer ingredients.

During this initial phase of FD&C Act enforcement, the Parfait Powder Puff Company sold hair lacquer pads. The pads were made by Helfrich Laboratories under a 1943 contract. Without notice to Parfait Powder, Helfrich changed the formula; the modified product was harmful. The government filed criminal cosmetic adulteration charges against Parfait Powder under the FD&C Act. In defense,

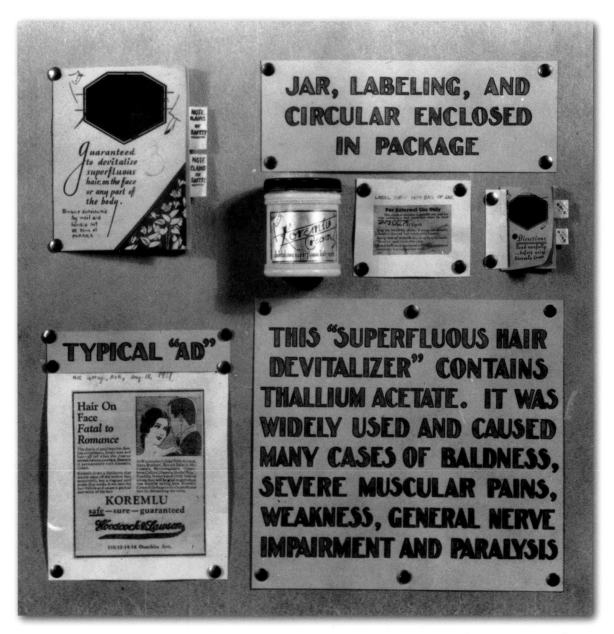

An early depilatory, Koremlu's principal ingredient was thallium acetate. This exhibit is from the American Chamber of Horrors, and dramatically demonstrates the systemic absorption of the product—when a woman used it on her legs, she could lose the hair on her head.

The boom in cosmetics as an industry came in the 1920's—the era of the flapper and the "Gibson girl." Skin "foods," freckle creams, whitening crèmes, and this "obesity crème," Fatoff, were just a few of the cosmetics sporting unsupported claims from 1906–1937 in the absence of regulatory distinctions between cosmetics and drugs.

Parfait Powder argued that since Helfrich changed the formula, Helfrich should be the government's target, not Parfait Powder. The government answered that it was Parfait Powder that chose Helfrich to make Parfait Powder's product, and so Parfait Powder was, in fact, the correct target—not because it made the mistake of adulterating the product, but because it made the mistake of choosing Helfrich as its contractor. In 1947, the lower courts agreed with the government. The Supreme Court declined to review the decision.

The Parfait Powder case reinforced the principle announced in the better-known Dotterweich decision: companies and their officials in FDA-regulated businesses are "strictly liable" as a matter of FD&C Act criminal law for violations they do not directly commit, or even know about. It

is enough that they have a "responsible relationship" to the violation. Parfait Powder, by selecting Helfrich to make cosmetics marketed under Parfait Powder's name, was responsible for ensuring that Helfrich knew what it was doing and properly suffered the consequences of Helfrich's incompetence.

Cosmetics have figured in other FDA judicial milestones. A major Supreme Court administrative law decision, a controversial court of appeals interpretation of the FD&C Act's Delaney Clause, which prohibits cancer-causing substances, and influential findings that any product can be a "drug" if promoted by exaggerated health claims—all began with disputes over cosmetics. Notably, however, these cases were important not because they involved cosmetics, but because they clarified FDA's general legal authority. The cosmetic characteristics of the products that precipitated the litigation were incidental to the principles at stake.

In contrast, it is the distinctive attributes of cosmetics, the properties that make cosmetics different from food, drugs, and devices, that account for another remarkable aspect of the FDA's legal history: Since 1938, Congress has never changed the cosmetic provisions of the FD&C Act. Cosmetics have thus defied the trend in government regulation, especially in the 1950–1980 period, toward more assertive administrative involvement in private sector decisions affecting the health and safety of consumer products and industrial activity. FDA's regulation of drugs and medical devices followed this trend. Drugs were subject to premarket safety review in the 1938 law itself, with effectiveness added in 1962. Devices came under pervasive FDA-administered statutory provisions in 1976. Food ingredients are scrutinized under the procedures and standards of the 1958 Food Additives Amendment. Yet cosmetics in the beginning of the twenty-first century are regulated under the same statutory mechanisms as in 1938: cosmetics must not be adulterated with poisons or contaminants, and they must not be labeled in a false or misleading way.

The reasons for less intense FD&C Act-mandated oversight of cosmetics are directly related to the nature and purpose of cosmetics. Unlike foods and most drugs, cosmetics are used primarily on the outside of the body, thus avoiding a significant route of exposure to toxic elements. Unlike drugs and medical devices, whose therapeutic effectiveness is important to health, cosmetics have a less vital role. How well a lipstick or eyeliner works has never been considered a question FDA should spend its resources answering.

Yet another factor is that cosmetics, unlike drugs, can be made to achieve their desired results through the use of

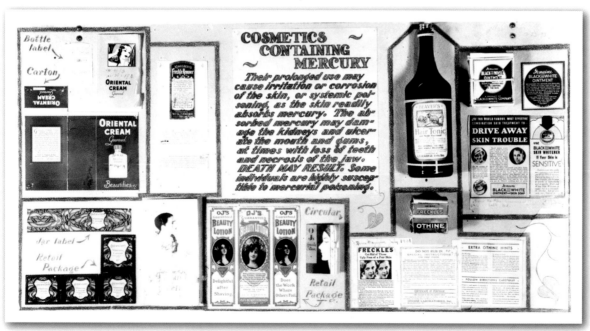

This panel from the American Chamber of Horrors exhibit illustrated the fact that cosmetics containing mercury were still being marketed to consumers and presented a danger to health.

safe ingredients. By definition, a cosmetic is for "cleansing, beautifying, promoting attractiveness, or altering the appearance," not for treating infectious disease or managing diabetes. A product with more ambition than a cosmetic would require more potent ingredients that could have adverse effects. Such a product, however, would not be a cosmetic, but a drug.

An additional explanation for Congress' reluctance to impose stronger controls on cosmetics is that a key cosmetic ingredient—color—is covered by the Color Additive Amendments of 1960. That law subjected color additives in all FDA-regulated products to extensive regulation. Although colors are used in foods, drugs, and medical devices, no FDA-regulated products depend more heavily on them than cosmetics. As a result, beginning in 1960, a key ingredient used by a substantial part of the cosmetic industry came under more demanding regulatory requirements,

In 1955, several New England children were poisoned by popcorn cats that contained excessive levels of orange food coloring. Victims recovered and the "cats" were recalled by the manufacturer. (FDA History Office)

thereby reducing congressional interest in stronger controls over cosmetics as a distinct product category.

The purpose of the Color Additive Amendments was simply to apply more modern toxicity testing standards to colors. Implementing the law became complicated, however, in part because of the so-called Delaney Clause. Like the Delaney Clause in the 1958 Food Additives Amendment, the color additive Delaney Clause prohibited FDA from allowing the continued use of colors found to cause cancer "in man or animal." By the 1980s, it was apparent that an appreciable number of cosmetic colors were in jeopardy of being banned even though theoretical lifetime cancer risks were negligible.

FDA—believing that Congress did not intend the Delaney Clause to prohibit *de minimis* risks—where the risk of cancer over a lifetime based on extrapolation from animal studies was less than one in a million, approved the cosmetic colors Red 19 and Orange 17. Red 19 had a calculated lifetime cancer risk of 1 in 9 million. The risk for Orange 17 was 1 in 19 billion. An advocacy group sued FDA, FDA lost the case, and the cosmetic industry lost Red 19 and Orange 17.

Given the fate of these and other cosmetic colors, it is not accurate to say that cosmetics have entirely escaped the heavy hand of modern safety regulation. It nevertheless remains true that, as a class, cosmetic products have been spared the meticulous oversight FDA exercises over other parts of its jurisdictional territory. In accounting for the cosmetic industry's low

THE ART OF AVOIDANCE

In the 1970s, there was concern about the safety of coal tar hair dyes, widely used for decades. Concern increased when the National Cancer Institute reported that 4-methoxy-m-phenylenediamine (4-MMPD), a hair dye ingredient, was carcinogenic in two animal species. Feelings ran high. Some called for a ban (though coal tar dyes were exempt from the law's adulteration provisions); others feared that the loss of hair dyes would harm national morale. A relative of one FDA official threatened never to speak to him again if FDA banned hair dyes.

FDA Commissioner Donald Kennedy testified before the Oversight Subcommittee of the House Commerce Committee. Although FDA had proposed a warning about 4-MMPD, he was determined to avoid taking a definitive position on whether coal tar dyes were so clearly unsafe that they should be banned. Near the end of his testimony, however, Rep. Clarence Brown (R-OH) asked the question the Commissioner most wanted to avoid: "Just as a final question, Dr. Kennedy, if you were in the position where you were considering dying your hair, with the knowledge, that you now have, concerning the possible risk involved, would you use a coal tar hair dye?" Commissioner Kennedy ducked his head, pointed to his small bald spot, and said, "...I am unmotivated in that direction, Mr. Brown. I do not think it would a do a thing for me." The hearing dissolved into laughter, Mr. Brown's time for questioning expired, and Commissioner Kennedy escaped unscathed, uncommitted, and undyed.

—Richard M. Cooper

profile with FDA, the relatively benign composition and purpose of cosmetics is the most important factor, but the role of sheer good luck should not be overlooked. There have been human injuries from cosmetic products over the years since 1938, probably including some serious ones. But there has been no major, highly visible, extensively publicized incident comparable to Lash Lure and Koremlu, or to Elixir Sulfanilamide or thalidomide or the Dalkon Shield, to provide a catalyst for stronger legislation.

Interest in such legislation is ever present. Comprehensive FDA control of cosmetics has appeared on the congressional agenda often enough to keep the industry on constant alert. One of the earliest attempts to impose greater control on cosmetics, however, did not emerge from Congress but from FDA itself, which in the mid-1960s attempted to require premarket review of

cosmetics, not by asking for new statutory authority, but by expansively interpreting the existing color additive definition to cover not just colorant ingredients, but entire cosmetic products that contained them.

The cosmetic industry challenged FDA's regulation in litigation. FDA insisted that the industry had no right to sue, but should await FDA court action against specific companies, which could then raise any legal objections in defense. Rather than be stalemated, the industry urged the court to entertain its suit for "preenforcement review," arguing that if cosmetic companies took FDA's regulation seriously, as FDA presumably wanted them to, they had to start complying with it now, not later, and therefore needed judicial relief now— not later.

The case was one of several FDA rule-making challenges that went to the Supreme Court, and in a decision announced in 1968, the industry won a solid victory: The court ruled that FDA regulations—including its interpretation of "color additive" as applying to cosmetic products—could be judicially reviewed before the agency tried to enforce them if they met standards of "ripeness." The decision, known under the name of the companion case of *Abbott Labs v. Gardner*, is still the leading Supreme Court case on preenforcement review of federal regulations. In 1969, FDA's broad interpretation of "color additive" was invalidated by the lower courts on remand from the Supreme Court, thus nullifying the threat of administratively imposed premarket review of cosmetics.

Congress, however, throughout the 1960s and 1970s, considered numerous legislative proposals to expand FDA's authority. In 1988 the House of Representatives held hearings on cosmetic safety. As recently as 1997, Sen. Edward M. Kennedy (D-MA) denounced the cosmetic chapter of the FD&C Act as "a dinosaur, an anachronism from the time when drugs didn't have to be effective, when food additives didn't have to be safe, and when medical devices didn't have to be safe or effective." The senator's specific objection was to a provision of the FDA Modernization Act, preempting state cosmetic requirements, and he did not propose to change the FD&C Act. But if there is ever a serious safety incident involving cosmetics, it will quickly revive congressional interest in strengthening FDA cosmetic regulation.

As for the absence of legislation in the 1970s and thereafter, despite repeatedly expressed concerns about cosmetic safety, the cosmetics industry, through its trade association, the Cosmetic, Toiletry, and Fragrance Association (CTFA), can claim much of the credit. Realizing that the issue of inadequate FDA regulation of cosmetics was unlikely to disappear on its own, CTFA successfully petitioned FDA in the early 1970s to establish a voluntary program for cosmetics manufacturer registration, product listing, and reporting of consumer injury complaints. CTFA also created, as an independent organization, the Cosmetic Ingredient Preview, to evaluate the safety of chemicals used in cosmetics. These measures reduced pressure for legislative change in a period of congressional activism. Subsequently, interest in amending the FD&C Act has been checked by a combination of: continued industry self-regulation; ad hoc actions by FDA against specific safety problems (such as irritation from bubble bath products and ingredients that might transmit "mad cow disease"); mandatory cosmetic ingredient labeling; and inclusion of several widely used types of cosmetics (such as antiperspirants and sunscreens) in FDA's comprehensive review of all over-the-counter drugs.

Although assuring safety has always been FDA's main goal in regulating cosmetics, health claims have also attracted the agency's attention. The FD&C Act specifically prohibits misbranding due to "false or misleading" labeling of cosmetics. FDA, however, has a high threshold for

ASSURING COSMETIC SAFETY THROUGH COOPERATION

"Alpha hydroxy acids (AHAs) reverse the signs of skin aging." Over the past ten or more years, it has been impossible to pick up a beauty or fashion magazine and not see such a claim. Truth be told, AHAs have been around since the time of Cleopatra. But what is old is often new again, and skin care products containing AHAs became widespread in the 1990s. In a nutshell, AHAs smooth out the skin surface. Appearance-wise, that's a good thing. FDA and others, however, were concerned that this effect might make the skin more vulnerable to sun damage—a legitimate question, but one without any supporting or opposing data.

In my twenty-two years at FDA in the radiological health and medical devices programs, I've seen my share of scientific questions regarding the safety of a product or procedure, and there are many ways of dealing with them. Given that FDA does not perform premarket reviews of cosmetic ingredients, such as AHAs, how could they address such questions for a cosmetic ingredient? In this case the answer was to turn to a third party, the Cosmetic Ingredient Review (CIR) program, a program I have directed since 1993.

The Cosmetic, Toiletry, and Fragrance Association (CTFA), with the support of FDA and the Consumer Federation of America, established CIR in 1976. CIR retains a panel of independent experts who, in an open, public process, review the safety of ingredients used in cosmetics, and then publish their findings in the peer-reviewed scientific literature. Experienced with reviewing the more than 1,000 individual chemicals used in cosmetics, CIR was well-positioned to address issues of this sort. And, here was a chance to prove it.

How did it actually work? In late 1994, CTFA formally requested that CIR undertake an expedited assessment; FDA agreed that this approach was a good idea; CIR agreed to do it; industry contributed results of unpublished studies it already had done. When CIR requested additional studies, industry and FDA undertook the additional research! Yes—industry *and* FDA! This put a bit of a strain on the "expedited" part of the strategy, because additional studies take time, but the remarkable aspect was that industry and FDA each took responsibility for doing work they do well. For example, FDA's group that conducts skin penetration studies is internationally recognized for its research expertise.

In mid-1997, CIR concluded that using AHAs incurs a small increase in sun damage, but that the risk disappears quickly if use is stopped, and that using a sunscreen (which people should be doing anyway!) eliminates any danger. In 1998, CIR's comprehensive review was published in the *International Journal of Toxicology*. These findings formed the basis for a CTFA petition to FDA to mandate uniform, appropriate user labeling for cosmetic products containing AHAs. In January 2005, in response to the petition, and after proposing a draft and receiving responses, FDA issued guidance for industry on AHA labeling that reflects CIR's findings.

This is an example of a process between industry and FDA that works well, avoids confrontation, and reaches scientifically valid resolution on ingredient issues. It is especially valuable given the limited resources FDA can devote to cosmetics regulation.

—F. Alan Andersen

promotional puffery when it comes to performance claims based on conventional cosmetic properties, such as reddening lips, modifying skin tones, masking skin flaws, and covering gray hair. But the agency draws the line at claims of physiologic effects. An ad that says a skin cream makes a person look younger not by concealing the signs of aging, but by changing the skin itself, does not make a cosmetic claim, in FDA's view, but describes the effect of a drug.

The boundary between "cosmetic" and "drug" is not exact. A product intended to "affect the structure" of the body is, by definition, a drug. A product intended to be "applied to the human body for … altering the appearance" is, by definition, a cosmetic. These two categories would not overlap if it were not for the reality that some products that are undeniably cosmetics, such as antiwrinkle creams, have an effect on the structure of the skin, although only a superficial and temporary one. As a result, several skirmishes between FDA and the cosmetics industry have related to claims for antiwrinkle products.

In the 1960s, major beauty care companies Hazel Bishop, Coty, and Helene Curtis put bovine serum albumin in face creams, and advertised the products as useful for reducing wrinkles. The albumin ingredient forms a film on the skin surface. As the albumin dries, the film shrinks. The shrinking tightens the skin, leaving less surface area and smaller wrinkles. Although it wears off after several hours, the effect is real. The companies advertised the antiwrinkle effect. Ads for the products suggested that consumers think about the effect from a perspective FDA viewed as overly suggestive of drug-like properties. FDA went to court, complaining that the advertising gave such a strong impression that the products—Sudden Change, Line Away, and Magic Secret—were miracle breakthroughs in the science of dermatology that consumers would believe they contained powerful new drugs, despite qualifying language elsewhere in the ad. FDA's cases were made easier by Hazel Bishop's claim that Sudden Change gave a "face lift without surgery," and Coty's

description of Line Away as a "protein" made in a "pharmaceutical laboratory" under "biologically aseptic conditions."

FDA won its cases against Sudden Change and Line Away, but lost against Helen Curtis' more conservatively advertised Magic Secret. The court decisions established an important ground rule for cosmetic promotion: FDA will not challenge optimistic claims about cosmetic benefits, so long as there is no implication that a product alters the human anatomy. FDA's method of enforcing this rule is a powerful one. If a cosmetic claims to alter the body, it is legally a drug and must comply with the rules for drugs. Because no cosmetic can meet those rules, the agency automatically wins, without having to show that the claims are false or misleading for a cosmetic.

Two decades later, skin care products promoted as having anti-aging properties alarmed the FDA. Most objectionable were claims that products slowed or reversed the aging process, repaired the skin, and operated at the cellular level to reduce wrinkles and other imperfections. Threatened with court action in the late 1980s, the companies explained to FDA enforcement officials that although their products contained only traditional cosmetic ingredients, new scientific knowledge demonstrated that the claims were true: moisturizers (to take an example) really did affect the living cells of the skin in ways that opposed the degenerative effects of time. However, whereas the industry's point was that "cosmetic" should be more broadly defined, and that the

1956 photo of Inspector John Cain at work in a white coat at a then-"modern" cosmetic plant.

anti-aging claims were truthful, FDA concluded that if the claims were truthful, the cosmetics were drugs. The stand-off was resolved by a compromise that is still in effect: cosmetic promotion can talk about ingredients that may have drug-like effects, such as alpha-hydroxy acid, but FDA will raise no issue if explicit claims are limited to "temporary" improvement in "the appearance" of "outward signs" of aging.

Cosmetics, unlike foods, do not nourish. Unlike drugs and medical devices, cosmetics do not cure. But cosmetics make us like each other and ourselves, more than we would otherwise—if only superficially and temporarily—and so they are important to our lives. Looking good is not worth feeling bad, however. Cosmetics should not harm us. With a little supervision from FDA, modern cosmetic products usually manage to avoid doing that. If cosmetics are not as central to human existence as bread, aspirin, and pacemakers, they are nevertheless a worthy addition, as well as being the least of the FDA's problems.

Dinshah's Spectro-Chrome

FOOD AND DRUG ADMINISTRATION SEIZURES PROTECT THE PUBLIC FROM FRAUDULENT MEDICAL DEVICES.

Before Congress enacted the 1938 Food, Drug, and Cosmetic Act, Dinshah Ghadiali testified against its passage. In 1946, he himself became subject to the new law as the case against Dinshah Ghadiali and his "Spectrochrome" became the longest trial in FDA's history to date—forty-two days. The device itself was nothing more than a 1,000 watt light bulb passed through a glass tank of water and focused by a crude lens through colored glass slides. Promising "no diagnosis, no drugs, no manipulation, no surgery," the light boxes were labeled to be "for the measurement and restoration of the human radioactive and radio-emanative equilibrium." Testimony showed that Ghadiali himself did not believe in his device. For that matter, neither did the jury which convicted him on January 7, 1947 on twelve counts. Certainly the Ghadiali case was one of the most "colorful" of the hundreds of fraudulent devices prosecuted by FDA in its early days.

FDA Adapts to a New Industry

**Robert C. Eccleston &
John C. Villforth**

The Medical Device Amendments of 1976 eliminate the deficiencies that accorded FDA "horse and buggy" authority to deal with "laser age" problems. It is important not only in what it will do to protect the consumer; it is also important as a symbol for the kind of regulation that I feel is most appropriate to government. It does not represent another expansion of government into affairs we might better manage ourselves. Instead, this is an example of government doing for the individual citizen what he or she cannot do unaided.

—Gerald R. Ford
38th President of the United States

THE WORDS "MEDICAL DEVICES" CONJURE UP ALL SORTS OF CONTRAPTIONS AND GIZMOS IN PEOPLE'S MINDS—from ordinary syringes, scalpels, crutches and bandages, to dazzling, high-tech marvels like magnetic resonance imaging machines and ultrasound imaging devices, implants that automatically sense and correct irregular heart beats and dispense drugs when chemical imbalances occur, and sensory devices that enable severely disabled people to hear, see, walk, speak, and otherwise cope. In today's world of healthcare, medical devices are as ubiquitous as McDonalds' golden arches. We see medical devices—from simple gadgets to exotic machinery—in doctors' offices and out-patient clinics; in hospital emergency rooms, ambulatory surgical centers, and nursing care centers; on counters in neighborhood pharmacies; in Medi-Vac helicopters and ambulances; in our homes, work places, and schools; and even in commercial airliners.

For more than three decades, FDA has served as a national sentry, keeping a watchful eye on this seemingly overnight boom in medical technology and a flourishing industry of small entrepreneurs and international conglomerates alike. At the behest of the U.S. Congress, FDA scientists, engineers, clinicians, and professionals trained in public health have run a regulatory system that, simply put, is designed to keep "bad" devices from reaching the marketplace, get "good" ones in the hands of healthcare providers and consumers, and make sure they function as they should in the real world.

As a backdrop to how this regulatory paradigm came into being, one must travel far back in time. By definition, humans have always inventively used implements of all sorts, and some were used to treat human injury and disease. The lineage of some of today's medical technology is traceable back several centuries. For example, in 1508, Leonardo da Vinci developed the basic principles of the contact lens. Using a large transparent globe to simulate the human eye, he filled it with water and immersed a person's face to demonstrate how "corneal neutralization and replacement" could improve vision.

Following World War II, a surplus of electronic parts found their way on the market as bogus medical devices—which FDA prosecuted. *Look* magazine's Washington correspondent, Jack Wilson, summarized the case cartooned here as follows: "The way it works, you sit in front of the screen and turn on the lights, which glow greenly at your stomach while the smell of the herbs wafts onto your person. This is bio-radiation and you must not keep it up longer than half an hour at a stretch or you will get so young and healthy that the draft board will be after you. This is because the herbs are young herbs, it says in the book, and all you need to do to get young yourself is let them radiate at you. The machine will cure anemia, asthma, constipation, diabetes, epilepsy, goiter, high and low blood pressure, spider bites, tuberculosis, and worms, to mention a few. It is wonderful for loss of memory and leukemia, and better yet for gangrene and gland disorders. You could buy one for $240 if the FDA weren't so nasty about it, and set yourself up as a medicine man to do mankind good. But good." *Look*, October 9, 1951, p. 116.

More than 100 years later, René Descartes, the French philosopher and mathematician, took da Vinci's work a step further. Descartes theorized that by placing a "tube full of water… whose shape is exactly like that of the skin… there will no longer be any refraction at the entry of th[e] eye." The first contact lens prototype was on the record books.

Man's fascination with science and applying its mysteries to treat the sick grew over time. In the late nineteenth century, Germany's Wilhem Roentgen made his serendipitous discovery of X-rays while working with cathode ray tubes in a darkened room. Roentgen's crude image of the bones in his hand evolved into machines that nowadays produce three-dimensional color images of the human anatomy in exquisite detail.

In the early twentieth century, advances in physical science and engineering technology propelled medicine forward in quantum leaps. The pace of medical product innovation and complexity quickened with the introduction of automation and electronics into healthcare. In the 1940s, Wilhelm Kolff—a young, Dutch-born internist and original pioneer in artificial organs—successfully performed the first clinical dialysis on a uremic patient, culminating years of investigational work that ultimately led to present-day hemodialysis treatments. From experiments at major U.S. medical centers in the 1950s emerged the principle of electrical stimulation to maintain regular heart rhythm. This ground-breaking research paved the way for a practical means of inserting pacemakers, which have been implanted in millions of people worldwide who have suffered heart attack or are afflicted with diseases of the heart that interrupt normal pacing.

The 1960s and 1970s saw tremendous proliferation in medical technology. Mechanical heart valves made their way into the clinical arena, as did intraocular lenses, computed tomography imagers, kidney dialysis machines, and total knee prostheses. A decade later, healthcare providers had new-found access to innovative heart assist devices, coronary stents to keep open freshly unclogged arteries, cochlear implants to help hearing-impaired persons discern sounds, lithotripsy machines to eliminate gall stones in lieu

of invasive surgical procedures, specialized laser systems for cataract and other intricate surgeries, and computer-operated radiation therapy machines used to treat cancer.

As the world approached the new millennium, the technological revolution continued at breakneck speed. Transformed into new life-altering medical devices were computerized technologies, micro-electronics and new-age biomaterials, many of which were offshoots from the aerospace and defense industries. Suddenly we seemed to be barraged with cutting-edge products that worked faster with less trauma. Diagnostic results were becoming more reliable, treatment outcomes more favorable, and the quality of people's lives enhanced as never before.

CDRH scientist testing television sets for excessive radiation emission. Circa 1976. Most people don't realize that FDA regulates radiation-emitting consumer goods including televisions and microwave ovens to make sure that they do not emit excess radiation.

The technology boom of the twentieth century inevitably gives rise to unbridled speculation about what lies ahead— telemedicine, virtual reality and robotics, optical biosensor devices, *in vitro* tests that can read a patient's "genetic code" and allow physicians to customize treatment or predict certain diseases before they compromise the person's health, organ replacement and assist devices that utilize hardware and tissue-engineered products to create, in effect, a "bionic" person. All are contenders for the realm of the possible. We also live on the brink of another scientific frontier: nanotechnology, which holds the promise for new-generation medical devices, such as rejection-resistant artificial tissues and organs; sensor systems that detect emerging diseases in the body; and systems for delivering new therapeutic medicines to previously-inaccessible parts of the body.

Whatever the future holds, it seems undeniable that medical devices will continue to have an indispensable role in our healthcare system. In fact, devices have become such a fixture in contemporary medicine that the general public often overlooks their significance. As with airplanes, automobiles, and the myriad other mechanical products found in everyday life, people tend to take for granted that all medical devices are well manufactured and properly serviced, and that the people who use them are adequately trained.

On the whole, public confidence in medical device safety is justified. But as with any human invention, medical devices are not totally risk-free. They have useful life cycles, but they occasionally fail despite the best laboratory and clinical studies to predict their performance before marketing. When one is found to be defective or malfunctions unexpectedly, causing death or injury, the public, the medical community, and the news media legitimately ask questions. And, as with any adverse incident involving pharmaceuticals, food, cosmetics and various other consumer products, they look to FDA for answers.

Unlike FDA's century-long regulation of food and drugs, the agency's regulatory control over the medical devices industry has a much shorter history. In fact, not until the 1960s did interest grow in broader federal regulation of medical device safety. Legislation to strengthen FDA authorities in this area gained traction in the U.S. Congress as part of a broader social reform movement aimed at new protections for the nation's environment, individual civil liberties, and public health.

The "consumerism climate" of those years carried over to later administrations. Within a year after taking office, President Richard Nixon advised Congress of his intention to form a study group to develop new legislative authority to reduce medical device hazards. Nixon's action was a response to growing clamor on Capitol Hill, in the courts, and in the manufacturing and research communities for legislation that would bring clarity and order to inexplicably different regulatory systems for drugs and medical devices. Public watchdog groups added their voice to the chorus of concerns about FDA's limited ability to control a burgeoning, venture-

Inspector Ken Bollinger using a Geiger counter to test for possible radiation exposure in a Washington D.C. Food Fair store with the store manager watching. Concerns about foods having become contaminated with radioactive fallout during the Cold War proved largely illusory but photos such as this one were popular in periodicals around the country during the 1950s.

THE "BANANA" RECALL/WITHDRAWAL

Anyone alive and able to read during the fall of 1980 knew about Rely tampons. They were a product made by Procter & Gamble (P&G) that were associated with a newly identified disease called toxic shock syndrome (TSS).

In September 1980, after twenty-five women died of TSS after using Rely tampons (other women using other tampons also died), FDA met with senior officials at P&G to discuss the situation. There was no hard evidence and no proven theory linking Rely tampons to TSS, but there was enough concern and circumstantial evidence that the FDA felt the need to meet with P&G was urgent.

Literally millions of women had Rely tampons at home, because it was a relatively new product and P&G had distributed millions of samples. Collaborating with the Centers for Disease Control in Atlanta, whose epidemiologists were trying to solve the puzzle, FDA issued its own press release tentatively connecting Rely tampons with TSS, and urging women not to use them. In September and October of that year, the news media provided saturation coverage of the story. One survey showed that 97% of the public knew about the story—a remarkable number seldom achieved by any health situation. The saturation occurred because of the press releases we at FDA were issuing, P&G's own announcement to pull Rely tampons off the market, and P&G's paid TV commercials.

When faced with the evidence, sparse as it was, P&G was aggressive in removing the product. The lone stumbling block in reaching an agreement on the terms of the action came when FDA used the term "recall" to describe the action. P&G insisted that it was a "product withdrawal." The difference is that the term recall meant that FDA had found the product to be legally violative, whereas the term product withdrawal meant it was a voluntary action that did not involve an FDA legal judgment. P&G did not believe there was sufficient scientific evidence for FDA to conclude the product was illegal and wanted to maintain that position for possible litigation purposes.

FDA's General Counsel, Nancy Buc, did not want this legal distinction to stand in the way of forward movement on the program. So we all agreed: we would use the word "banana" to refer to the impending "recall" or "product withdrawal," and leave the legal issue for later resolution. And so it was that FDA and Procter & Gamble collaborated on a "banana" of Rely tampons.

—**Wayne L. Pines**

---

oriented devices industry with its 1,500 manufacturers and $2 billion in shipments. Many worried about the potential for serious health consequences, absent more vigorous federal oversight.

Nixon's establishment of what became known as the Cooper Committee (named after its chairman, Dr. Theodore Cooper, then director of the National Heart and Lung Institute) was a first step in addressing the issue of FDA's make-shift powers over medical devices. At the time, the agency's sole authority was derived from the 1938 Food, Drug, and Cosmetic Act, which did not require new devices to undergo pre-market safety reviews similar to those for human drugs. FDA was even hindered from taking enforcement action except when marketed devices had been shipped across state lines and shown to be dangerous or bogus.

The situation became even more confused when in 1962 Congress passed legislation directing FDA to review effectiveness claims for new drugs before granting market clearance. Again, however, Congress' action did not apply to medical devices. Later court cases further muddied the waters, clouding the distinction between drugs and medical devices and

EIGHT TONS OF POTASSIUM IODIDE

On March 29, 1979, a mishap at the Three Mile Island (TMI) Nuclear Power Plant, near Harrisburg, Pennsylvania, threatened to release radioactive iodine fission products, posing an acute biological hazard to people living in the environs of the plant. The governor and state health officer of Pennsylvania contacted FDA about the availability of drugs to block the uptake of radioactive iodine.

No pharmaceutical company had an adequate supply of potassium iodide (KI) products on hand. The drug had no modern medical use and FDA was asked to provide enough to protect the one million people living within thirty miles of the plant. FDA staff determined that a one-week supply for a family of four required 250,000 1-ounce (30-mL) bottles of a saturated solution of potassium iodide (SSKI). To prepare that quantity required in excess of 16,000 pounds of the drug.

At midnight on March 29, FDA staff contacted Mallinckrodt Chemical Company in St. Louis, Missouri, and requested that 8 tons of KI be formulated into SSKI, packaged in 1-ounce bottles and delivered to Harrisburg as quickly as possible. Supplies of KI were adequate, but the facility to make and bottle SSKI was in Decatur, Illinois. Plant managers in St. Louis and Decatur were directed to ship the drug and prepare the bottling line.

FDA offices provided inspectors to monitor formulation and packaging operations. Exemptions to specific GMP and labeling requirements were authorized to expedite the process. Dropper bottles were unavailable, but there was no time to get them. FDA authorized use of 250,000 1-ounce square glass powder jars, unsuited for liquids and without droppers—the only containers available in quantity. The 250,000 droppers were obtained from Dougherty Brothers in southern New Jersey and shipped to a warehouse in Harrisburg on U.S. Army and company trucks.

The output rate at Decatur was not high enough, so Mallinckrodt personnel suggested that another facility be brought on-line, and Parke-Davis Company in Detroit agreed, but bulk SSKI had to be shipped to Detroit in drums. FDA inspectors were on site at Parke Davis and monitored the packaging and labeling. Parke Davis had 2-ounce dropper bottles. FDA authorized a 1-ounce fill to assure availability for the 250,000 households. FDA staff dictated labeling language via telephone to plant supervisors at Decatur and Detroit.

The first lot of 11,000 bottles was transported to Harrisburg on an Air Force C-130 within 24 hours of the determination to provide the SSKI. Over the next forty-eight hours, a total of 237,000 bottles of SSKI was transported to Harrisburg via chartered civilian aircraft. In the end, the SSKI did not have to be used, but FDA assured that it was there.

—Jerome A. Halperin

leaving FDA in somewhat of a quandary. In an effort to rectify the situation, legislators hurriedly began debating a number of proposals but failed to achieve consensus.

Within a year after it was formed, armed with evidence of some 700 deaths and 10,000 injuries linked to unsafe or defective devices, the Cooper Committee came forward with a litany of sweeping recommendations. At the heart of their proposal, Cooper and his colleagues called for a hierarchical framework of federal regulation—a new paradigm, tailored to a product's potential for harm, with regulatory controls meted out in proportion to the type and degree of risk posed by each medical device.

Devices at the least risky end of the spectrum would be subject to the least stringent regulation. Conversely, devices posing the greatest risk would face the

MERGING DEVICES AND RAD HEALTH

In November 1983 the Bureaus of Medical Devices and Radiological Health (BRH) were merged. The Commissioner decided that because both bureaus required similar technical disciplines (physical science and engineering), they should be combined. My challenge was to merge two different cultures and regulatory responsibilities into a cohesive unit.

Why did this merger work when the effort to merge the Bureaus of Drugs and Biologics was aborted? First, device and radiological health regulators all saw the merger as an opportunity to work on the many exciting new technologies being developed. Second, they used similar approaches to minimize the consequences of products, particularly capital equipment products, that would be in use for many years and which required constant attention.

BRH had dealt with products such as medical X-ray machines where unnecessary radiation exposure could result not only from defective machines, but also the from machine operator's improper settings, or from over-prescribed use. Minimizing radiation exposure depended on performance standards for the machines and educational programs for the operators.

This approach was translated through the merger to include medical devices such as kidney dialysis equipment and anesthesia machines. Using standards—both voluntary and mandatory—and education, coupled with enforcement where necessary, was a common approach. The combined technical staff, with expertise in science, engineering, training, and education, could work competently on either device or radiation products. It was primarily this public health approach to regulation that made this merger work and led to a cohesive Bureau (now Center) for Devices and Radiological Health.

—**John C. Villforth**

greatest regulatory scrutiny. For high-risk and breakthrough devices, the committee colleagues took a page from FDA's time-tested pre-market evaluation system for pharmaceuticals. Wanting to give the public full assurance of the safety and medical effectiveness of newly emerging medical technologies, the committee pushed for authorizing FDA to assess the benefits and

risks of products before companies were allowed to introduce them into commerce.

Yet, despite the apparent urgency, Congress took some five and a half years to come up with a legislative answer. While waiting for Congress to act, the agency seized the initiative and began to "regulate" certain products as medical devices and erected an administrative infrastructure to

IUD's were a viable alternative to the birth control pill, but the wicking string on the Dalkon Shield increased a users' risk of getting Pelvic Inflammatory Disease nearly five fold, posing an unreasonable risk. PID can result in life-threatening infections and sterility. First marketed in 1971, distribution of the IUD was stopped in 1974, and recommendations that it be removed from even asymptomatic women were issued in 1984. (gift to the FDA History Office from Dr. Marlene Haffner).

support its foray into legislatively uncharted territory.

A major stimulus for congressional action came after public hearings in the early 1970s on the dangers of a widely used contraceptive device, the Dalkon Shield, and other intrauterine devices. Both congressional houses settled on a final bill in May 1976. That same month—on May 28—President Ford signed the landmark legislation into effect.

Now, thirty years later, through the prism of history, it is clear that the public health has benefited substantially. As with other medical products, program leaders at FDA faced the challenge of finding an appropriate balance in the constant tension between product innovation and product safety. Great care had to be taken not to impede technological innovation on the one hand; on the other hand, the agency could not afford to prematurely move innovative products from research laboratories to the medical arena before safety and effectiveness testing was satisfactorily completed.

There was also the necessity for an operational culture in which the law's regimented procedures were balanced with a practical-minded business approach. The norm had to be solid risk assessment and sensible remediation of problems, instead of reflexively applied "one size fits all" solutions. This was—and is—crucial given the fundamental differences between medical devices and drugs. Viewed against

UNINTENDED CONSEQUENCES

I attended hundreds of meetings while at FDA and after I left, but the one I remember best occurred in 1990 when I represented Pfizer on the Bjork-Shiley heart valve. This valve was sold from 1979 to 1986. In a few cases, it could and did fracture, possibly leading to death. Lawyers filed many cases seeking damages because, they said, their clients felt anxious. The litigation led to a major class action settlement.

FDA's Center for Devices and Radiological Health (CDRH) and the Commissioner's office felt strongly that valve patients should be warned of the potential danger. Pfizer went about the process systematically, conducting focus groups with actual valve patients as it drafted letters, and hiring and training nurses to talk with patients in need of counseling. FDA, however, thought the process was going too slowly. So it issued its own information, via public statements, warning patients that their implanted valves could break. The warning led to many patients having their valves removed and replaced, an extremely delicate and medically dangerous surgery; some patients died while undergoing the procedure.

At the meeting I recall so vividly, a senior CDRH official stood up and observed, clearly from his heart, that never before had an FDA action actually killed people, namely patients whose valves were functioning well, but who were so frightened by the FDA-generated publicity that they sought surgery. I think CDRH learned from the experience that warnings, even those that seem to be in the best interests of the public health, can have unintended consequences. In dealing with similar situations involving other implanted products later in the decade, I could see a more sensitive approach. There was a new respect for the power FDA holds over the public, that a warning about a potentially unsafe implanted product must be balanced against the risks associated with its unnecessary removal.

—Wayne L. Pines

THE BREAST IMPLANT SAGA

In December 1990, shortly after Dr. David Kessler's arrival as FDA Commissioner, I rode with him to a series of congressional briefings. On one occasion, he asked me what I thought government policy for breast implant evaluation should be. My response was that, unlike most devices, the risk/benefit evaluation for breast implants was unique. Specifically, with virtually all devices, the agency must determine that the benefits of the product outweigh its risks. However, with breast implants, the agency's role should be to require companies to study and articulate the risks associated with implants and so label the products. But the benefit-side of the equation could only be quantified by the woman who was seeking implants in consultation with her physician.

Kessler disagreed. He thought that it was, in fact, government's responsibility to evaluate both risks and benefits for implants. Needless to say I lost the argument and, from that time forward, FDA has been trying not only to determine risks, but also benefits for implants. This continues to be an extremely difficult, if not impossible, task because the benefit is so personal to the individual considering implants.

But the story begins much earlier. The Medical Device Amendments were enacted in 1976. The law calls for the classification of all medical devices on the market into one of three categories: class I, low-risk products requiring general controls; class II, moderate-risk, including mandatory standards in

The National Organization for Women (NOW) and Ralph Nader's Public Citizen sponsored a rally in front of HHS in 2003 to protest any approval of the re-marketing of silicone gel breast implants following the moratorium on the use in 1991.

the near-monolithic pharmaceutical business, many devices are products of a "cottage" industry. Unlike drugs, device types number in the thousands, with huge variation in complexity that pose much greater opportunities for malfunctions in design, manufacture, and use that can profoundly affect product performance.

That leadership challenge was put to the test in the mid-1980s when anesthesia machines operated at hospitals in Denver, Detroit, and Jackson, Mississippi, were linked to the death of four patients undergoing surgery. The

news media instantly spotlighted these tragic incidents, and the newspaper stories spawned congressional oversight hearings in Washington. The public was understandably on edge.

FDA's intervention in the crisis began soon after the first two deaths. Device experts from the agency teamed up with the manufacturer and Denver hospital representatives to trouble-shoot the problem. Independent tests at FDA's laboratories in Maryland uncovered the source: a rubber "O" ring inside the machine had become swollen from

addition to general controls; and class III, high-risk and new products, which would require pre-market approval or, if the product was already on the market, a premarket approval application (PMA). Silicone gel breast implants were on the market before 1976. Struggle though it did with advisory committees, manufacturers, and plastic surgeons, the agency was unable to come up with a final classification until 1988, when the products were finally placed in class III. One of Kessler's first initiatives at FDA was to bring the production of breast implants under stringent agency control.

I recall vividly during the period immediately following his appointment, while I was Deputy Commissioner, a briefing by Center for Devices and Radiological Health (CDRH) leaders suggesting a two-year time table for requiring PMAs for silicone gel implants. The center believed this timeframe was the minimum companies would need to develop clinical data and submit a PMA. But, Kessler insisted on a much shorter period. Two years is a relatively short time for clinical data to be collected and the PMA submitted, but, Kessler argued, manufacturers had known since 1976 that they might ultimately be required to submit PMAs, and clearly since 1988 when the classification was finalized. He further argued that all the efforts to postpone final classification were simply a ruse to put off indefinitely the PMA requirement.

Kessler seemed greatly distressed by the agency's failure to stringently regulate breast implants. The holiday season of December 1991 and January 1992, after I had returned to my duties as CDRH Director, was memorable. A group of twenty or more of us, including Kessler, endlessly reviewed breast implant data looking for potential misinformation from companies and adverse events in an attempt to build a database to help in the evaluation of expected PMAs and, as it turned out, to declare a moratorium on the sale of implants.

The outcome is history. FDA held advisory committee hearings to evaluate the data in the PMAs and concluded that insufficient data existed. The story was on the front page of the newspaper. Women with the implants sued, and eventually there was a settlement. Breast implants remained big news for years. Now, almost fourteen years later, the story is back. CDRH approved one manufacturer of silicone gel breast implants, opening the door again to ready availability of the product.

—**James S. Benson**

exposure to high concentrations of anesthetic, preventing the machines from delivering a properly concentrated flow of anesthesia and instead causing patients to receive massive overdoses. Based on this forensic analysis, FDA ordered an immediate product recall and an alert to all equipment users with instructions on how to correct the defect in the same model machines in use nationwide.

The horrific and preventable nature of these fatal mishaps commanded news headlines, obscuring a comparatively much larger anesthesia problem, most of which was unrelated to equipment failure. Statistics told the larger story. An estimated 2,000 to 10,000 deaths were occurring each year from the 20 million surgical procedures in which anesthesia was used, of which only four percent were attributable to mechanical problems. The bulk of the problem was caused by complications from the way the machines were operated. This revelation made clear the need for a broad-based strategy. It required a working partnership among FDA, the anesthesia community, and industry stakeholders. For the partnership to succeed, mutual trust among the parties was paramount. So, too, was the need for constructive solutions that forthrightly addressed the problem's root causes and avoided gratuitous regulatory action.

The anesthesia situation was strikingly similar to what many of the same FDA leaders had faced in the 1970s with the well-publicized issue of medical X-ray overexposure. Excessive radiation exposure from routine diagnostic examinations was a multi-dimensional public health problem, and thus was not conducive to a single solution. One of the many causative factors was varying radiation output levels due to differences in manufacturing and assembly of X-ray machines. FDA issued a regulatory standard based on in-house science and engineering that prescribed uniform manufacturing specifications. The standard's signature feature was a requirement for positive beam limitation (PBL) hardware in every machine. Pioneered by the agency's radiation scientists, the revolutionary PBL concept enabled X-ray personnel to mechanically conform X-ray beam sizes to anatomical areas being radiographed. This single action significantly reduced or eliminated unwanted radiation exposure without compromising diagnostic information.

Yet, as helpful as the X-ray equipment standard was, it was only a partial solution. Like the anesthesia situation, the greater contributor to the problem had a human face. Many X-ray examinations were unnecessary, and the amount of radiation used in X-ray studies often exceeded what

was needed for a high-quality diagnostic result. Some technologists performing the tests lacked critical knowledge on radiation protection techniques used to safeguard patient groups, such as children and women of child-bearing age, who are highly sensitive to radiation. In light of the substantial consequences X-ray professionals had on patient safety, educational programs directed at changing their behavior occupied a central place in FDA's overall strategy. The agency's radiological health experts enlisted national physician and radiology organizations to participate in outreach programs that defined for doctors in the field the clinical circumstances justifying certain X-ray examinations, especially those capable of delivering high doses of radiation.

Relying on consensus-building and peer-reviewed literature, this collaborative initiative dramatically curtailed the number of X-ray exams (some by half or more) being ordered as a matter of clinical routine or a defense against medical malpractice lawsuits. The new X-ray guidelines became accepted standards of medical care and, apart from radiation savings, lowered healthcare expenditures and physicians' fears of malpractice suits. Complementary programs to sensitize radiologists and technologists, both in practice and in training, to radiation hazards produced equally remarkable results.

Separate quality assurance programs encouraging use of lower-dose imaging techniques also appreciably reduced exposure. Additionally, FDA leveraged the radiological expertise in state health agencies to conduct joint demonstration projects in U.S. dental offices and mammography facilities to induce health professionals to change outmoded or unsafe X-ray practices. These programs accounted for as much as a fifty percent reduction in patient radiation doses and, for mammography, helped quell growing worries that breast X-rays might themselves increase the risk of breast cancer, causing some women to forego the life-saving procedure.

But FDA didn't stop there. Recognizing that consumers were eager to assume a greater role in decisions about their own healthcare, the agency joined forces with consumer advocacy groups to launch a national public education campaign aimed at educating American consumers on the benefits and risks of diagnostic X-rays. A more enlightened and empowered public began asking probing, well-informed questions of doctors and X-ray personnel. This new wave of activism expanded the physician-patient dialogue. X-ray prescribers began thinking more carefully about whether an X-ray procedure was really necessary and service providers paid closer attention to protecting patients from unnecessary exposure.

Taken together, this integrated program of regulatory and non-regulatory actions, coupled with development of new low-

Radiological Health Mobile Training Laboratory. This mobile training lab took advanced training to radiological health workers in the states.

dose imaging technologies, has provided American consumers with protection that might not have been possible without FDA acting as a catalyst for change. FDA's actions also fulfilled the intent of the Radiation Control for Health and Safety Act of 1968, a legislative achievement of the Lyndon Johnson era. Unlike the medical devices law that followed eight years later, the Radiation Safety Act was written in a way that gave administrators broad discretion and flexibility in meeting the national radiation protection goals outlined in the legislation. Careful to avoid micro-

---

THE "CROWN JEWEL" OF ENFORCEMENT ACTIONS

It was July 1993 and the age of enforcement under FDA Commissioner David Kessler. I was in Minneapolis waiting for the jury to return a guilty verdict in the research fraud case against Dr. Barry Garfinkel, then a tenured professor at the University of Minnesota School of Medicine and one of the nation's foremost child psychiatrists. I had called Rick Blumberg, FDA's Deputy Chief Counsel for Litigation, to update him, but he wanted to discuss his immediate concern—staffing for three new injunction recommendations forwarded by the Center for Devices and Radiological Health's (CDRH's) Office of Compliance. It proposed injunctions against three large medical device companies based on alleged violations of FDA's good manufacturing practice (GMP) regulations. Blumberg briefly described the nature and background of each case and wanted to know which one I wanted to handle.

The case involving Siemens Medical Systems stood out. Siemens AG was a huge multinational conglomerate based in Germany that manufactured everything from automotive parts to telephones and computer systems. It was also one of the largest medical device manufacturers in the world. The injunction recommendation extended to eleven of Siemens Medical Systems' manufacturing facilities (six foreign, five domestic) that produced patient monitors, ventilators, ultrasound equipment, linear accelerators, pacemakers, and other devices. I volunteered to take the Siemens case because it clearly presented the greatest challenge. It was also intriguing to me because of my German heritage and language skills. Little did I know just how complex and challenging the case would prove.

During September and October 1993, with considerable help from FDA's foremost device GMP experts, I helped orchestrate the final phase of the investigation, which focused on evaluating compliance at three of Siemens' domestic manufacturing facilities. Agency investigators completed strategic factory inspections and gathered "fresh" evidence putting FDA in position to try to negotiate a favorable injunction through a consent decree.

The first direct contact with the company occurred in early November 1993 during a tension-filled teleconference with numerous Siemens officials and its legal counsel. Ron Johnson, CDRH's Director of Compliance, told the company that the center had decided to pursue a "corporate-wide injunction" against Siemens based on evidence collected at its facilities during the last year. I then outlined the general terms FDA would require in a settlement.

Siemens officials expressed disappointment with the decision, but wanted to know more about the specific terms. I agreed to provide a draft consent decree for their consideration. Due to the number of domestic and foreign facilities and the wide range of issues involved, it took me nearly two weeks to develop a draft consent decree and obtain the necessary approval from various agency officials and the Department of Justice.

Over the course of the next few months, I devoted virtually all of my time to preparing the agency's formal injunction recommendation, negotiating an agreement, and, in the event negotiations proved unsuccessful, preparing to file for a preliminary injunction. The negotiating sessions with Siemens' legal counsel were complex, often lasting several hours and covering numerous unique issues. To me, an army of lawyers appeared to be representing Siemens. (We later estimated that there were

management of the program, congressional lawmakers exercised legislative restraint by setting forth only general targets and parameters for a federally-run electronic product radiation reduction program. The job of implementing it was delegated to FDA, using a broad assortment of regulatory enforcement, educational and federal-state partnering authorities conferred by the statute.

In many respects, the 1968 Act served as an ideal template for other radiation protection laws. In the early 1990s, for example, congressional legislators

about thirty outside and in-house lawyers representing the company, including former Solicitor General and Judge Kenneth Starr, later of fame for his role as the Independent Counsel investigating President Clinton.)

One of the issues was whether the agency could impose restrictions on Siemens' foreign manufacturing facilities, which shipped products and components to the United States. We had received a thirty-five-page letter from one of the lawyers arguing that our proposed decree violated various international laws and treaties. Another issue related to specific requirements for Siemens' domestic service and repair operation relating to complaint handling, complaint investigation, and failure investigation. One of the most discussed provisions authorized FDA to simply issue a letter shutting down certain manufacturing and distributing operations if the agency later found additional evidence of GMP violations. (That provision, then in its infancy, has since become one of the agency's favorite consent decree provisions.)

A year and a day after he left the Justice Department, Judge Starr appeared in person at one of the negotiating sessions and attempted to persuade us to include an alternative dispute resolution mechanism in the decree. My Justice Department co-counsel and I rejected his request. His appeal to our supervisors was also unsuccessful.

Finally, in February 1994, after three months of intensive negotiation, we reached a mutually agreeable consent decree of permanent injunction. The thirty-page decree featured the following:

- Three domestic manufacturing facilities were immediately shut down and could not resume operations until FDA authorized their resumption;

- Siemens was banned from importing devices from one of its foreign facilities;

- Four other domestic and foreign facilities were required to correct GMP problems and certify compliance;

- All other Siemens AG facilities around the world that exported devices to the United States were required to certify compliance with FDA's GMP regulations within eighteen months.

The Siemens case captured the attention of the entire medical device industry. Based on the number of facilities and range of medical devices involved, it is regarded by many as the largest medical device enforcement action ever undertaken by FDA. One Justice Department official later told me that he thought it was one of the largest civil actions brought by the federal government. At the time, FDA officials referred to it as the "crown jewel" in the agency enforcement initiative to bring "corporate-wide" injunctions against companies with GMP violations at multiple facilities. Although it proved to be a difficult experience for Siemens, the company rebounded from the action and rehabilitated its image with the agency as a result of improved communication and a proven commitment to compliance.

—**Mark S. Brown**

mandated that FDA ensure that all U.S. mammography facilities meet high-quality operating standards. The genesis of Congress' action was First Lady Betty Ford's candid admission of her bout with breast cancer, which sent huge numbers of women to mammography centers around the country for mammographic examinations. Then, as now, mammography was heralded as a clinically useful adjunct to physical self-exams in detecting early-stage breast cancer, a devastating disease that remains the second leading cause of cancer mortality in women. So overwhelming was the public's response to the news of Mrs. Ford's condition that healthcare providers and women's advocacy groups raised concerns about uniform access to these services, as well as the potential for variability in the quality of breast X-ray exams and concomitant rise in population exposure to radiation. Together, they succeeded in getting these issues on the national agenda and lobbied for federal oversight of facilities providing these life-saving procedures. Legislative victory came in 1992 with passage of the Mammography Quality Standards Act.

As with its approach to excessive radiation doses, FDA sought the assistance of others in tackling Congress' new assignment relating to mammography. With technical and administrative support from states and health professional groups, the agency's mammography quality assurance program had, in two major respects, a salutary effect on the national goal of reducing breast cancer incidence. First, an independent federal study concluded that FDA's efforts in this area improved the overall quality of mammography services without restricting access to such services. Study data showed that in the mid-1990s, roughly one-third of mammography facilities in the United States were operating free of any violations; today, the level of compliance has more than doubled. Second, FDA's mammography quality assurance program has given women greater peace of mind as they exert greater control over their personal health and medical care. And due in part to FDA's efforts to enhance mammographic quality, breast cancer mortality rates steadily declined by fifteen percent between 1990 and 2000.

The lesson from both radiation protection programs was clear. Sensible integration of science-driven regulation, targeted education, and leveraging of public and private sector experts worked well in addressing national public health issues. FDA administrators were determined to institutionalize the same "business model" in the agency's medical device program.

The situation calling for improvements in the safety of anesthesia services would prove to be an early test of their resolve. One fact was clear: product regulation alone could not achieve desired reductions in anesthesia mortality and morbidity. Real results would come only if the anesthesia community were engaged in a dialogue fostering broader awareness of the problem and direct involvement in remedial strategies to avert human error mishaps. To this end, FDA entreated experts from nationally recognized anesthesiology and nurse anesthetist

Ed Seagle, Divison of Radiological Health engineer, State Assistance Branch Medical X-ray Program, demonstrates one phase of conducting a survey of a medical X-ray unit. The block of wood on the table was used as a so-called "phantom" patient.

organizations and anesthesia equipment manufacturers. As a consortium, the group by consensus developed an easy-to-use, pre-operative checklist—analogous to pre-flight checklists used by airline pilots—to enable anesthesia providers to confirm proper functioning of their equipment before surgery. Clinical validation of the checklist led to formal endorsement from the anesthesia community, followed by dissemination to all practitioners and hospital risk managers throughout the United States. As a follow-up, the agency and its consortium partners produced an instructional videotape to educate and motivate anesthesia providers on use of the checklist. In short order, the checklist became a universal standard of care. Medical malpractice insurance carriers

lowered liability premiums for healthcare institutions that incorporated the checklist into their routine anesthesia delivery practices, resulting in annual cost savings estimated at $300 million.

Building on these successes, the FDA-led consortium next produced a series of educational videotapes covering assorted topics relating to anesthesia safety, such as human errors and management of adverse events. This series is still being used for in-service training and continuing education programs nationwide, providing continual reinforcement of optimal anesthesia practices.

Collectively, these efforts, which grew out of the patient tragedies at the Colorado, Michigan, and Mississippi hospitals, also gave rise to establishment of a non-profit foundation whose mission was prevention of anesthesia mishaps through information-sharing, incident investigations, and research projects. Started in 1984, the Anesthesia Patient Safety Foundation brought together anesthesiologists, surgeons, other physicians, nurse anesthetists, hospitals, equipment manufacturers, and FDA anesthesia experts to develop innovative strategies and programs designed to cut down on preventable events. A notable output of the foundation has been development of first-of-a-kind anesthesia training simulators to give anesthesia providers "hands on" experience before treating actual patients in the operating room.

The much-publicized incidents in Colorado, Michigan, and Mississippi also underscored the fact that besides sub-standard manufacturing, device failures occur because of inadequate equipment design and a workable interface between users and medical technologies. There was also a greater appreciation of the fact that manufacturers of anesthesia machines—for that matter, all medical devices—have the technical capacity to eliminate intrinsic design flaws at pre-production stages in the manufacturing process. Recognizing this, FDA policy-makers set out by regulation tighter quality assurance checks, or design controls, at critical points during production. At the same time, the agency initiated a human factors program to prevent medical errors through improved ergonomics design and better product labeling. These dual actions have better enabled device-makers to ferret out inferior products before they leave the assembly line and arm health professionals with essential information on the safe use of products that make it to the market.

As for tangible gains in anesthesia safety, published evidence reveals that patient mortality rates have declined by more than ninety percent, from one or two deaths per 10,000 anesthesia administrations in 1984 to the current rate of one death per 100,000-200,000. This public health achievement should be a comfort to people scheduled to undergo surgery (one in ten Americans will do so in their lifetime), knowing the risk of an anesthesia-caused accident is negligible.

While the anesthesia and radiation case studies amply illustrate how FDA has exercised its regulatory, research, and educational authorities—often synergistically—to fulfill its ever-important role of protecting and promoting public health, they are hardly isolated examples—there are countless others. Each of following examples demonstrates how FDA has kept faith with public trust and offers evidence of how the agency, by meeting its public health obligations, has made a real difference in people's lives:

- In the mid-1980s, FDA ordered a halt to the marketing of two critical, life sustaining devices: certain mechanical heart valves due to metal fatigue-induced stress fractures that compromised the structural integrity of the valves; and cardiac pacemaker leads whose insulation covering electrical pacing wires eroded after implantation. In both instances, the premature failures seriously endangered patient lives.

- At about the same time, the agency aggressively responded to the spiraling trend of toxic shock syndrome cases and their association with high-absorbency tampons. FDA required tampon makers to re-design package labeling to better assist women in selecting tampon products that met their personal needs and provide clearer information about the relationship between the risks of contracting toxic shock syndrome and standard indicators of tampon absorbency across different commercial brands. FDA's action was based on absorbency test methods developed in its own science laboratories.

- In the earliest stages of the AIDS pandemic, as the world raced to find ways to control and cope with the deadly disease, "barrier" protection became the hallmark of public health advice on how individuals could keep themselves safe from harm. FDA rallied behind government health leaders to ensure that their public health pronouncements were scientifically credible. FDA tested so called barrier products, such as condoms and medical gloves, to validate claims that they could control human-to-human transmission of HIV. Among FDA's findings was that natural membrane condoms were not as effective as latex condoms. FDA research also produced universal test methods for detecting leaks and high-quality manufacture of safe and effective latex products. And later, as reports surfaced about latex allergic reactions, FDA scientists provided national advice on how latex

barrier products could continue to be used to combat HIV while at the same time reducing the risk of latex-borne allergies.

- In cooperation with other Public Health Service agencies, federal health reimbursement agencies, and the renal dialysis community, FDA reduced the incidence of life-threatening infections from widely varying cleansing and disinfection practices in hospital-based hemodialysis centers and freestanding clinics. This result was achieved by a combination of service provider educational programs, agency promulgated dialysis practice guidelines, national medical practice reforms relating to multiple use of dialysis treatment system components, and improvements in manufacturing and labeling of dialysis equipment.

- Based on leading-edge research by FDA scientists, the agency compelled manufacturers of motorized wheelchairs, pacemakers, and other electrically powered medical devices to re-engineer their products to make them less vulnerable to electromagnetic interference, which had caused some products to spontaneously malfunction, posing serious health threats to the millions of people who rely on them.

- Working in conjunction with the medical device and healthcare industries, as well as academia, FDA reduced patient entrapment injuries involving bed rails used in hospitals, senior living facilities, and home healthcare settings through a nationwide public education

A SIDE EFFECT OF WORKING AT FDA

Working at FDA provides its employees with many insights into how to protect themselves. I saw this as a benefit even before I officially joined the agency. I spent a summer at FDA in 1984, before being hired full-time. That summer, one of my tasks was to file in the historical files some materials on the agency's current efforts to limit the exposure of patients to unnecessary radiation.

One of the recommendations was that hospitals eliminate requirements for a pre-admission chest X-ray, a requirement that probably originated out of public health concerns—tuberculosis or lung cancer—but it had long outlived its usefulness, according to the Center for Devices and Radiological Health (CDRH) officials quoted in my filing materials.

When I returned to Atlanta to complete a teaching requirement at Emory for my Ph.D., I discovered that I needed to have my tonsils removed. Emory required a pre-admission chest X-ray. I argued vehemently that this was unnecessary and against FDA recommendations, but all to no avail. I did at least have the presence of mind to remember that FDA had recommended that patients request lead "shielding" in cases where X-rays were necessary or at least in my case, inevitable. The technician seemed a bit annoyed, as I recall, but the shielding was provided to me. It was a good thing, too, because the first image did not come out properly and the procedure had to be repeated.

As a mother, when my injured son required head X-rays as a toddler, I requested shielding for him as well. He too required a second set of films. The people at FDA are not necessarily healthier but at least they do have unique access to information that helps protect them and their loved ones.

—**Suzanne White Junod**

campaign and manufacturer re-designs of these products.

- The agency halted a rash of incidents involving accidental electrocution of people, including toddlers and young children, by getting manufacturers of infant apnea monitors to make retrofit changes to electrical plugs so that wall-socket connections were safer and less prone to improper handling of the products' electrical wires.

- FDA radiation safety and computer experts intervened when certain radiotherapy machines used to treat various cancers had malfunctioned because software controls had gone awry, causing a few patients exposure to more radiation than clinical treatment called for. Agency expertise and

oversight of corrective actions by the manufacturer spared thousands of cancer patients from unintentionally being massively overdosed with radiation.

More generally, FDA has a long history of leading the way, through pioneering research on development of innovative test methods—including accelerated life testing—for experimental medical devices. These testing methods are adopted by the industry, enabling manufacturers and FDA product reviewers to better identify, predict, and correct performance problems with new devices before mass production begins. The agency also remains vigilant over scores of clinical trials involving investigational medical devices to be sure studies are conducted ethically and study participants are treated humanely, as well as to terminate or modify product studies found to cause participants unacceptable health risks. Finally, FDA maintains rigorous surveillance over thousands upon thousands of marketed devices to pinpoint problems that may arise so that timely corrections can be made before isolated incidents escalate into major disasters.

By any just measure, the compact President Ford made with the American people in 1976—to have government do for its citizens what they are unable to do for themselves—has been kept. His prophetic message to the nation upon signing the public law giving FDA expansive new powers over medical devices was, over the 30 years that followed, borne out by the agency and its corps of public servants.

Technology will continue to flourish; it will add to the vibrancy of our national economy and secure America's future role in globalization. Medical devices, for the foreseeable future and beyond, will be developed and used for the prevention of disease, correction of disease, and rehabilitation from disease. The scores of dedicated men and women at FDA who are responsible for the safety of medical products will continue to keep public health protection as their number one priority.

The distinguished, award-winning

Mr. Omar V. Garrison

exposes the corruption existing in many
federal bureaus, and especially in

Our Food and Drug Administration: The Sleeping Giant

(asleep to the "Big Boys," that is!)

"The thing that bugs me is that people think the FDA is protecting them; it isn't. What the FDA is doing and what the people think it's doing are as different as night and day." — by a former FDA commissioner as quoted in *The New York Times* 12:31:69.

At a time when our natural foods and environment need special attention, the FDA plays cops-and-robbers by harassing the very people who are dedicated to good health through natural foods. Is this a protective smoke screen created by an FDA-william for good, rich food processors who could care less about your health?

Omar V. Garrison says it is. In his new book, THE DICTOCRATS, he minces no words when he reveals his findings to you.

Why, for example, did FDA allow the sale of cyclamates for over 20 years when it had reason to believe they were harmful? Who was paying whom? How much hanky-panky was involved in the $287,000.00 windfall raked-in by one FDA official — under the table, of course?

The author of THE DICTOCRATS spent five years scaling the invisible walls that surround our federal agencies — and tearing apart, bit by bit, the bureaucratic machinery that virtually runs our everyday lives.

The result is a dramatic story of legalized corruption, blackmail and bribery in federal bureaus. The arrogance and high-handed crookedness that exist in many government offices, the deception and dirty tricks in the bureaucrats' arsenal, will make you wonder what has become of our human values and cherished Constitutional rights.

Raw, naked, unchecked power is demonstrated by the countless vendettas FDA conducts against individuals whose only "crimes" were to exercise their freedom to question the bureaucrats' dogma.

Reading THE DICTOCRATS may cause you a few sleepless nights—but it will also open your eyes to a bad situation that needs correcting. Get your copy of THE DICTOCRATS today. If unavailable locally, send $1.25 to:

**BOOKS FOR TODAY — Room 314
325 W. Huron St., Chicago, Ill. 60610**

Trade inquiries: Arco Books, Inc., or your wholesaler

Laws Affecting FDA

Significant amendments to the Federal Food, Drug, and Cosmetic Act (FD&C Act) since 1980; date shown is when the law was approved:

- Infant Formula Act of 1980 (Oct. 26, 1980)
- Orphan Drug Act (Jan. 4, 1983)
- Drug Price Competition and Patent Term Restoration Act of 1984 (Sept. 24, 1984)
- Prescription Drug Marketing Act of 1987 (Aug. 18, 1988)
- Generic Animal Drug and Patent Term Restoration Act of 1988 (Nov. 16, 1988)
- Nutrition Labeling and Education Act of 1990 (Nov. 8, 1990)
- Safe Medical Devices Act of 1990 (Nov. 28, 1990)
- Medical Device Amendments of 1992 (June 16, 1992)
- Prescription Drug User Fee Act (PDUFA) of 1992 (Oct. 29, 1992)
- Animal Medicinal Drug Use Clarification Act (AMDUCA) of 1994 (Oct. 22, 1994)
- Dietary Supplement Health and Education Act of 1994 (Oct. 25, 1994)
- Food Quality Protection Act of 1996 (Aug. 3, 1996)
- Animal Drug Availability Act of 1996 (Oct. 9, 1996)
- Food and Drug Administration Modernization Act (FDAMA) of 1997 (Nov. 21, 1997)
- Best Pharmaceuticals for Children Act (Jan. 4, 2002)
- Medical Device User Fee and Modernization Act (MDUFMA) of 2002 (Oct. 26, 2002)
- Animal Drug User Fee Act of 2003 (Feb. 20, 2003)
- Pediatric Research Equity Act of 2003 (Dec. 3, 2003)
- Minor Use and Minor Species Animal Health Act of 2004 (Aug 2, 2004)
- Food Allergen Labeling and Consumer Protection Act of 2004 (Aug. 2, 2004)

Other laws affecting FDA; date shown is when the law was approved, but the law may have been amended since:

- Federal Food and Drugs Act of 1906 (repealed)
- Federal Meat Inspection Act (March 4, 1907)
- Federal Trade Commission Act (Sept. 26, 1914)
- Filled Milk Act (March 4, 1923)
- Import Milk Act (Feb. 15, 1927)
- Public Health Service Act (July 1, 1944)
- Trademark Act of 1946 (July 5, 1946)
- Reorganization Plan 1 of 1953 (March 12, 1953)
- Poultry Products Inspection Act (Aug. 28, 1957)
- Fair Packaging and Labeling Act (Nov. 3, 1966)
- The National Environmental Policy Act of 1969 (Jan. 1, 1970)
- Controlled Substances Act (Oct. 27, 1970)
- Controlled Substances Import and Export Act (Oct. 27, 1970)
- Egg Products Inspection Act (Dec. 29, 1970)
- Lead-Based Paint Poisoning Prevention Act (Jan. 13, 1971)
- Federal Advisory Committee Act (Oct. 6, 1972)
- Government in the Sunshine Act (Sept. 13, 1976)
- Government Patent Policy Act of 1980 (Dec. 12, 1980)
- Federal Anti-Tampering Act (Oct. 13, 1983)
- Sanitary Food Transportation Act (Nov. 3, 1990)
- Mammography Quality Standards Act (MQSA) (Oct. 27, 1992)
- Bioterrorism Act of 2002 (June 12, 2002)
- Project BioShield Act of 2004 (July 21, 2004)

The Authors

F. Alan Andersen joined FDA in 1971, in radiological health and medical devices, later heading the research and testing laboratory and briefly, the Office of Device Evaluation, before becoming director of the independent Cosmetic Ingredient Review in 1993. At FDA, he developed radiation product standards and regulations for toxic shock syndrome warning labels on tampons. His work earned the PHS Superior Service Award and the FDA Award of Merit. He received his PhD from Penn State.

Lawrence Bachorik, PhD, is senior advisor for International Policy and Communications in FDA's Office of International Programs. Before joining that staff in March 2005, he served for six years as FDA's Associate Commissioner for Public Affairs and was the agency's principal advisor on media relations and strategic communications. Previously, he was director of public relations for a large not-for-profit healthcare system in the Washington, DC, area.

Edward M. Basile is a senior partner in the FDA/Healthcare Practice at King & Spalding LLP, and serves as national FDA counsel for numerous medical device manufacturers. From 1975 to 1985, he served as associate chief for Drugs & Biologics and Enforcement in FDA's chief counsel's office. From 1985 to 1987, he served as deputy general counsel for AdvaMed, a national medical device trade association. He received his BSME from Lafayette College and JD from George Washington University Law Center.

Scott Bass heads Sidley Austin Brown & Wood's International Food and Drug Law Practice. He was adjunct professor at Georgetown University's Graduate School of Public Policy, is co-chair of the ABA Food and Drug Law Committee, and chaired the New York State Bar Association Section on FD&C Law. He co-authored two books on The Dietary Supplement Health and Education Act, which he had a major role in drafting. He received his JD from the University of Michigan Law School.

Walter M. Batts is deputy director of FDA's Office of International Programs. He provides policy and program direction for FDA with foreign governments, international and regional organizations, and domestic agencies. He has held several positions since joining FDA in 1972, including leadership positions in the Bureau of Drugs and, since 1986, in International Affairs. He is the recipient of numerous FDA awards, including the Award of Merit, and awards from other agencies.

James S. Benson served at FDA from 1972 until 1992. From 1988 to 1991, he was deputy commissioner, including one year as acting commissioner. His last post at the agency was director of the Center for Devices and Radiological Health. After retiring from FDA, he was executive vice president of AdvaMed, until 2002. Currently he serves on several boards of directors and is president of his home owners' association. He also does limited consulting.

Walter R. Benson, PhD, served at FDA from 1963 to 1986, the last ten years as director, Division of Drug Chemistry. He has been project leader at the International Organization for Chemical Sciences in Development since 1992. He won FDA's Award of Merit for training pesticide petition reviewers in regulatory chemistry. He has led research groups in pesticide and drug analysis, published sixty-five papers, and established a WHO drug-testing and training laboratory for sixteen African countries.

Mark S. Brown is a partner with King & Spalding LLP. He served as an associate chief counsel with FDA from 1990 to 1994, and as an attorney with the FTC Bureau of Consumer Protection from 1985 to 1989. He received his AB from the University of Michigan (1982) and JD from St. Louis University (1985).

Anthony C. Celeste, beginning his FDA career as a chemist in New York, served at FDA for twenty-five years. His last post was director of the Office of Regional Operations. He also served as district director in the Cincinnati and Boston Districts, and laboratory director in Detroit. He is now senior vice president, AAC Consulting Group Inc./Kendle Intl.

Richard M. Cooper was FDA's chief counsel during 1977-1979, and is a partner at Williams & Connolly LLP, where his clients have included manufacturers of pharmaceuticals, medical devices, and foods; research organizations; and clinical investigators. He has written extensively on food and drug law and practice, has edited one FDLI book and co-edited another, has chaired the *Food & Drug Cosmetic Law Journal* editorial board, and has served on committees of the Institute of Medicine.

J. Richard Crout, MD, served as director of the Bureau of Drugs (now Center for Drug Evaluation and Research) from 1973 to 1982. He is a clinical pharmacologist whose career also includes roughly a decade each in academic medicine, the pharmaceutical industry, and consulting. He has been awarded an honorary Doctor of Medicine from Uppsala University and the Distinguished Service Award of the U.S. Public Health Service for his FDA service.

Fred Degnan is a partner in King & Spalding's Washington office where, since 1988, he has specialized in food and drug law. Prior to joining King & Spalding, he served for eleven years in FDA's Office of General Counsel. Since 1989, in addition to his responsibilities at King & Spalding, he has taught food and drug law at The Catholic University of America's Columbus School of Law, where he serves as a distinguished lecturer.

Robert C. Eccleston began his career in 1973 in FDA's radiological health program, where he held policy coordination and congressional and intergovernmental relations posts. Eccleston has served as executive assistant to FDA's acting commissioner, congressional fellow, World Health Organization medical devices consultant, and Executive Secretary to the Global Harmonization Task Force. He currently is a senior public health advisor at the Center for Devices and Radiological Health and is a FDA Alumni Association co-founder.

Lesley R. Frank has served at FDA for sixteen years, as a chemist in the Center for Drug Evaluation & Research and the Center for Veterinary Medicine, and as regulatory counsel, acting group leader, and currently senior advisor-regulatory counsel in the Division of Drug Marketing, Advertising, and Communications. She graduated with high honors from the George Washington University School of Law and was an associate with Arnold & Porter. She has a PhD in medicinal chemistry from the University of Maryland.

Jerome A. Halperin served as a U.S. Public Health Service officer from 1958 to 1983. He served as deputy director of the FDA Bureau of Drugs and acting director of the Office of Drugs. Following retirement from government, he joined the CIBA-Geigy pharmaceutical company. In 1989, he was elected executive vice president and CEO of the U.S. Pharmacopeia Convention, Inc. In July 2001, he was elected president and CEO of the Food and Drug Law Institute.

Linda R. Horton began her FDA career as its first management intern and later was legislative director, trial attorney, devices counselor, and deputy chief counsel for regulations and international policy director (1968-2002). She retired from FDA, became a Hogan & Hartson partner, and heads its European life sciences practice in Brussels. In 1999 she received the first FDLI Leadership Award for a government official. Her law degrees are from George Washington (JD) and Georgetown (LLM).

William Horwitz began his FDA career at Minneapolis in 1939, and transferred to Washington to serve in various technical administrative positions dealing with food and the AOAC. He received the HEW Distinguished Service Award and the AOAC Wiley Award. The Royal Society of Chemistry (UK) awarded him the Boyle medal for his discovery and application of the "Horwitz Horn" to analytical chemistry. He retired from FDA in 2000 and now edits *AOACI Official Methods*.

Peter Barton Hutt is a senior counsel in the Washington, DC, law firm of Covington & Burling, specializing in food and drug law. He served as chief counsel for the Food and Drug Administration during 1971-1975. He is the co-author of the casebook used to teach food and drug law and teaches a full course on this subject each year during the winter term at Harvard Law School.

Suzanne White Junod has been a historian at FDA since 1984. She received her PhD in medical history at Emory University under James Harvey Young and has received a number of agency and professional awards for her scholarly publications. She is the immediate past president of the Society for History in the Federal Government and a member of FDLI. She writes the History Corner for FDLI's *Update*.

Donald Kennedy was FDA commissioner from April 1977 to June 1979. He returned to Stanford to serve first as provost and then, from 1980 to 1992 as president. For the past six years he has been editor-in-chief of *Science*, the weekly journal of the American Association for the Advancement of Science. With Richard Merrill, he co-chairs the National Academies program on Science, Technology and Law.

Daniel A. Kracov is a partner at Arnold & Porter and is co-head of its pharmaceutical and device practice. He concentrates on the regulation of drugs, biologics, and medical devices, and related policy and legislative matters. He assists clients in negotiating the legal requirements relating to the development, approval, marketing of, and payment for biomedical products. He is the author of numerous articles and has lectured widely on topics relating to FDA and health care law.

Eugene Lambert joined Covington & Burling in 1961, and embarked on food and drug law through the Drug Amendments of 1962 and the peanut butter standard. Since working on the passage of the Animal Drug Amendments of 1968, he has been intimately involved in the legislative and regulatory issues confronting the animal drug and pet food industries. This is his eighth essay on animal drug or feed issues.

Arthur N. Levine has practiced food and drug law for thirty-five years. He is a partner at Arnold & Porter, where he counsels drug, device, and biologics clients on FDA compliance, regulatory, and enforcement issues. Before beginning private practice, he served in FDA's General Counsel's Office for twenty years, thirteen of those as the deputy chief counsel for litigation. He regularly lectures and publishes on FDA issues, often in FDLI-sponsored forums.

Joseph A. Levitt is a partner in the Washington, DC, office of Hogan & Hartson, LLP. He is a twenty-five-year veteran of FDA. From 1998 through 2003, he was Director of FDA's Center for Food Safety and Applied Nutrition. Prior to that, he held senior positions in the Commissioner's Office, Center for Devices and Radiological Health, and Office of General Counsel. He has received numerous honors and awards, including three Presidential Executive Rank Awards.

Richard A. Merrill is professor of law and former dean at the University of Virginia School of Law. He served as FDA's chief counsel from 1975 to 1977, and received the FDA Award of Merit and, on two occasions, the Commissioner's Special Citation. With Peter Barton Hutt, Merrill is the author of the leading text on food and drug law.

Abbey S. Meyers is president of the National Organization for Rare Disorders. She is considered the primary consumer advocate responsible for passage of the Orphan Drug Act of 1983. She has served as the consumer representative on the National Commission on Orphan Diseases, the NIH Human Gene Therapy Subcommittee, the NIH Recombinant DNA Advisory Committee, the FDA Biological Response Modifiers Committee, and the National Human Research Protections Advisory Committee.

Nancy Bradish Myers, JD, is a Washington-based attorney with expertise in health care law and regulation, policy development, government relations and political analysis for investors. She has served as a senior strategic advisor in FDA's Office of the Commissioner; special counsel for science policy for PhRMA; political analyst for Lehman Brothers; reimbursement counsel for BIO; and lobbyist for the Blue Cross Blue Shield Association. She assists organizations meet regulatory, reimbursement, and political goals.

Melissa Moncavage has served at FDA for twenty-five years in FDA's Office of Management and in the Center for Drug Evaluation and Research. She has been in the Division of Drug Marketing, Advertising, and Communications since 1992 and is currently the leader of its Direct-to-Consumer Review Group. She has an MPH degree from the Johns Hopkins University.

Stuart L. Nightingale, MD, served at FDA from 1976 to 1999, the last seventeen years as associate commissioner for Health Affairs. He was assistant to the director, Bureau of Drugs from 1976 to 1980, before joining the Office of Health Affairs. Currently, he serves as deputy assistant secretary for Public Health Emergency Preparedness, HHS. At FDA, he promoted close collaboration with health professional organizations and the human subject protection community, and greatly expanded FDA's international activities, especially international harmonization.

Mark Novitch, MD, was at the FDA from 1971 to 1985, last serving as deputy and acting commissioner. After FDA, he spent nine years at the Upjohn Company, retiring in 1993 as vice chairman and chief compliance officer. He also served as president of the U.S. Pharmacopeia and chairman of the Food and Drug Law Institute. He is a member of several corporate and voluntary boards of directors.

Wayne L. Pines served at FDA from 1972 until 1982, the last four as Associate commissioner for Public Affairs. He was founding editor of *FDA Consumer*, and twice won the Award of Merit. He is a crisis, regulatory, and media consultant at APCO Worldwide. In 2004 he was named an FDA Alumnus of the Year, and helped found the FDA Alumni Association. This is the tenth book he has written or edited on FDA-related issues.

William M. Rados is program manager of FDA's website. Previously, he was director of the FDA Communications Staff, editor of *FDA Consumer* and an FDA press officer. He also worked in FDA's Centers for Devices and Radiological Health and for Veterinary Medicine. Before joining FDA, he was a public affairs specialist for Eisenhower Army Medical Center in Georgia, and a business reporter and editor. He has a BA from Notre Dame and an MA from Ohio State.

Thomas Scarlett was Chief Counsel of FDA from 1981 to 1989. He was an associate with White & Case, 1969-1971, and staff attorney in HEW's Social and Rehabilitation Services Division, 1971-1973. He joined the FDA Counsel's Office in 1973, later becoming deputy chief counsel for regulations and hearings. He was at Morgan, Lewis & Bockius from 1979 to 1981. Since 1989 he has been a principal at Hyman, Phelps & McNamara. He graduated from Columbia University and Yale Law School.

Marc J. Scheineson is a partner in the Washington, DC, office of Alston & Bird. He heads its food and drug practice. He previously served as associate commissioner for Legislative Affairs at FDA. He is co-chairman of the American Bar Association's Committee on Food and Drug Law. He received his BA and JD from the University of Cincinnati and its College of Law and his LLM from the Georgetown University Law Center.

William B. Schultz is a partner at Zuckerman Spaeder. He was previously deputy assistant attorney general, Civil Division, Justice Department (1999-2000), deputy commissioner for Policy, FDA (1994-1998), counsel to the House Subcommittee on Health and the Environment (1989-1994), and attorney at Public Citizen Litigation Group (1976-1989). He taught civil litigation and food and drug law at Georgetown Law Center. He graduated from the University of Virginia Law School (JD, 1974) and Yale University (BA, 1970).

John P. Swann, a historian at FDA since 1989, received his Bachelor's degree in chemistry and history from the University of Kansas, and his PhD in the history of science and pharmacy from the University of Wisconsin. He was awarded a post-doctoral fellowship at the Smithsonian Institution, and later was senior research assistant at the University of Texas Medical Branch. His publications have focused on the history of drugs, biomedical research, the pharmaceutical industry, and regulatory history.

Joseph G. Valentino served at U.S. Pharmacopeia for thirty-five years as executive associate and secretary, senior vice president and general counsel. He was the official liaison to the FDA for twenty-five years and co-founded the USP/FDA Drug Product Reporting Program. Prior to joining USP he was a Food and Drug Officer in the FDA's Bureau of Regulatory Compliance. He is a *cum laude* graduate of Rutgers College of Pharmacy, and received his JD from Rutgers School of Law.

John E. Vanderveen joined FDA in 1975 as director, Division of Nutrition, and later served as director, Office of Plant and Dairy Foods and Beverages. He retired in 1998 and has since served as an Emeritus Scientist. He earned a BS at Rutgers University and a PhD at the University of New Hampshire. From 1961 until 1975, he was a scientist with the Air Force. He received many awards including the 2000 FDA Distinguished Alumni Award.

John C. Villforth, RADM (Ret.), was director of FDA's Bureau of Radiological Health from 1969 until 1982 and, until retiring from government in 1990, headed the Center for Devices and Radiological Health. He was also a U.S. Public Health Service assistant surgeon general and chief engineer. He later became president of the Food and Drug Law Institute. He currently sits on corporate boards and serves several non-profit organizations, including the FDA Alumni Association which he helped establish.

William W. Vodra served as FDA's associate chief counsel for drugs from 1974 to 1979. He helped draft many major regulations (GMPs, GLPs, GCPs, bioequivalency, Orange Book) and the Drug Regulation Reform Act of 1978, in which FDA provided a roadmap for the future of pharmaceutical regulation. He received four FDA Awards of Merit. He is now a partner at Arnold & Porter, where he counsels clients on regulatory compliance and crisis management.

Andrew C. von Eschenbach, MD, is acting commissioner of Food and Drugs and director of the National Cancer Institute. Dr. von Eschenbach's four-decade career as a nationally recognized urologic oncologist, medical educator, and cancer advocate includes twenty-five years at the University of Texas M.D. Anderson Cancer Center in Houston. He is also a three-time cancer survivor. A native of Philadelphia, Dr. von Eschenbach earned his medical degree from Georgetown University School of Medicine in 1967.

Cole P. Werble is editor-in-chief of *The Regulation Policy Market Access (RPM) Report*. He was an independent consultant on the Medicare Modernization Act and vaccine policy. From 1974 until 2002, he was president, editorial director, and owner of *FDC Reports*, publisher of *The Pink Sheet* and other FDA-related publications. He serves on several boards including Children's Research Institute at the Children's National Medical Center. His BA is from Williams College and his MA from the University of Chicago.

Gary L. Yingling is a partner at Kirkpatrick & Lockhart Nicholson Graham LLP. He has a pharmacy degree from the University of North Carolina and a law degree from Emory. He transferred from the Centers for Disease Control to FDA's Office of General Counsel where he was a trial attorney and later deputy chief counsel for administration. He received FDA's Award of Merit as director of the *OTC Drug Review*. He is past president of the Food and Drug Law Institute.

Contributors to Chapter 5 include Michael Taylor, Resources for the Future; Meg McKnight, Associate at Hogan & Hartson; and Darvin Williams, Katherine Bierlein, and Nicole LaGrande, 2004 summer associates at Hogan & Hartson.

Contributors to Chapter 11 include Peter B. Carstensen, a Center for Devices and Radiological Health systems engineer; Charles A. Finder, MD, a radiologist in the CDRH mammography standards program; Joanne K. Choy, a staff member in the CDRH mammography standards program; and F. Alan Andersen, PhD, a former senior CDRH manager and scientist, now with the Cosmetic, Toiletry, and Fragrance Association.

Endnotes

1. Louis Filler (ed.), *The World of Mr. Dooley* 144, 148 (1962).

2. See Mark T. Law & Gary D. Libecap, *Corruption and Reform? The Emergence of the 1906 Pure Food and Drug Act and the 1906 Meat Inspection Act* (ICER Working Paper No. 20) (2003).

3. Sean D. Cashman, *America in the Gilded Age From the Death of Lincoln to the Rise of Theodore Roosevelt* 23 (3d ed. 1993).

4. The percentage of the U.S. population living in towns of 2500 people or more was: 6% in 1800, 15% in 1850, 37% in 1890, and 46% in 1910. Paul Starr, *The Social Transformation of American Medicine* 69 (1982).

5. U.S. Dep't of Commerce, Bureau of the Census, *Historical Statistics of the United States Colonial Times to 1957* at 74 (1961).

6. *Id.* at 7.

7. *Id.* at 72.

8. *Id.* at 544-45, 546-47.

9. *Id.* at 281.

10. Cashman 284.

11. John W. Chambers II, *The Tyranny of Change: America in the Progressive Era, 1890-1920* at 38 (2d ed. 2000).

12. R. James Kane, *Populism, Progressivism, and Pure Food*, 38 Agricultural History 161, 166 (1964).

13. James Harvey Young, *Pure Food Securing the Federal Food and Drugs Act of 1906* at 107-08 (1989).

14. Susan Strasser, *Satisfaction Guaranteed The Making of the American Mass Market* 6-7 (1989).

15. Thomas J. Schlereth, *Victorian America Transformations in Everyday Life, 1876-1915* at 60 (1991).

16. *Id.* at 182.

17. *Id.* at 157.

18. Law & Libecap 21.

19. John Higham, *Writing American History: Essays on Modern Scholarship* 93 (1970).

20. Schlereth 141.

21. Schlereth 141.

22. Clayton A. Coppin & Jack High, *The Politics of Purity Harvey Washington Wiley and the Origins of Federal Food Policy* 26 (1999).

23. For example, "[c]ans and boxes concealed colors and odors and prevented shoppers from tasting food before they bought it." Strasser 35. In more formal economic terms, technological advances in food processing and distribution led to asymmetries between sellers and buyers as to information about product identity and quality, and thereby created opportunities for processors to reduce costs through deception. Thus, the market could not be relied on to deliver pure high-quality food. Consequently, there was a need for regulation of food quality and labeling by scientific experts, who, with respect to those matters, had a comparative advantage over consumers. Law & Libecap 8.

24. Coppin & High 30.

25. Reports of a number of contemporaneous studies of adulteration are summarized in F. Leslie Hart, *A History of the Adulteration of Food Before 1906*, 7 Food Drug Cosm. L.J. 5 (1952).

26. Mitchell Okun, *Fair Play in the Marketplace The First Battle for Pure Food and Drugs* 67 (1986).

27. Even where adulteration or fraud could be detected, consumers could not take protective action unless they could identify the producer of the adulterated or fraudulent product. The greatly increased use of brand names in the late 19th century helped to address that problem, but did not address the need to be able to detect actual adulteration or fraud.

28. Advances in food technology "increased the range of products available, [but] they also increased uncertainty about product quality, because consumers now knew less about where their food was from and what was added to it. Thus, consumer anxieties about quality – specifically, about food adulteration – were increasingly common." Marc T. Law, *The Origins of State Pure Food and Drug Regulation*, 63 J. Econ. Hist. 1103, 1105 (2003) (footnote omitted).

29. Most of the state laws prohibited the coloring of oleomargarine to look like butter, Okun 277; yet, in most months, dairies added annatto to butter to imitate its color at midsummer, id. at 266.

   The federal statute, among other things, imposed taxes on manufacturers, wholesalers, and retailers of oleomargarine and a tax of 2¢/lb. on oleomargarine, itself, to be paid by its manufacturer. 24 Stat. 209 (1886). In 1902, the tax on oleomargarine was quintupled to 10¢/lb. 32 Stat. 193 (1902). The 1902 oleomargarine legislation removed dairy interests' opposition to a general pure-food law. Oscar E. Anderson, Jr., *The Health of a Nation Harvey W. Wiley and the Fight for Pure Food* 143 (1958).

30. Quoted in Okun 129-30.

31. Id. at 169. In 19th century terminology, "ethical" drugs were those advertised solely to physicians (in accordance with the 1847 code of ethics of the American Medical Association); "proprietary" drugs where those advertised to the general public, and included "patent medicines"; the term "patent" in this context referred to a secret formula, not to a patent (which required disclosure of ingredients). Peter Temin, *Taking Your Medicine Drug Regulation in the United States* 3 (1980); Young, Pure Food 26.

32. Okun 180.

33. *Id.* at 172.

34. Temin 22.

35. Id. at 24.

36. *Quoted in Young, Pure Food* 19 (emphasis in original).

37. *Id.* at 117.

38. *Id.* at 120.

39. Richard H. Shyrock, *quoted in* Robert M. Crunden, *Ministers of Reform The Progressives' Achievement in American Civilization*, 1889-1920 at 175 (1982).

40. Okun 244-45.

41. Starr 18.

42. Starr 128.

43. Schlereth 283.

44. James Harvey Young, *The Toadstool Millionaires: A Social History of Patent Medicines in America before Federal Regulation*, ch. 7, at 6 (1961), *available at* http://www.quackwatch.org/13Hx/TM/07.html.

45. Starr 129.

46. Schlereth 284.

47. Young, *Toadstool Millionaires*, ch. 9, at 3, *available at* http://www.quackwatch.org/13Hx/TM/09.html.

48. "Although this court has refrained from any attempt to define the limits of that power, yet it has distinctly recognized the authority of a State to enact . . . 'health laws of every description;' indeed, all laws that relate to matters completely within its territory and which do not by their necessary operation affect the people of other States. According to settled principles the police power of a State must be held to embrace, at least, such reasonable regulations as will protect the public health and public safety." *Jacobson v. Massachusetts*, 197 U.S. 11, 25 (1905). *See also* Mortyn Keller, *Affairs of State Public Life in Late Nineteenth Century America* 410 (1977).

49. U.S. Const., art. II, § 2.

50. Daniel P. Carpenter, *The Forging of Bureaucratic Autonomy Reputations, Networks, and Policy Innovation in Executive Agencies, 1862-1928* at 38 (2001). Carpenter characterizes the 19*th* century federal bureaucracy as a regime of clerks. *Id.*

51. 1 Alexis de Toqueville, *Democracy in America* 125 n.17 (Phillips Bradley ed. 1945) (originally published 1835).

52. U.S. Dep't of Commerce 7.

53. *Id.* at 710. The numbers under "Executive Branch" are of civilian employees, excluding those in the Post Office.

54. "In 1901, the President's staff consisted of a secretary, two assistant secretaries, two executive clerks, four lesser clerks or telegraphers, and a few doorkeepers and messengers." Keller 298.

55. Carpenter 42-43, 48-50.

56. Nathaniel Hawthorne, *Novels* 124 (Library of America ed. 1983).

57. Carpenter 30, 39, 60. "Year after year in the mid-nineteenth century congressional committees heard an ever-growing litany of complaints about the performance of executive departments: piles of undelivered mail, sloth and graft in duties collection and land distribution, the glacial pace of naval construction." Id. at 63.

58. Robert H. Wiebe, *The Search for Order[,] 1877-1920* at 37 (1967).

59. Keller 245.

60. 22 Stat. 403 (1883).

61. Carpenter 46.

62. *Id.* at 191. The Department had been established in 1862. 12 Stat. 387 (1862). In 1889, it had attained Cabinet rank. 25 Stat. 659 (1889).

63. Charles Darwin, *The Origin of Species by Means of Natural Selection* 51 (Modern Library ed. undated) (originally published 1859).

64. *Bartlett's Familiar Quotations* 514:15, 579:20 (15th ed. 1980).

65. *Id.* 621:6.

66. "If by saying 'that it is the duty of the state to adopt measures for protecting the health of its subjects' it is meant (as it is meant by the majority of the medical profession) that the state should interpose between quacks and those who patronize them, or between the druggist and the artisan who wants a remedy for his cold — if it is meant that to guard people against empirical treatment the state should forbid all unlicensed persons from prescribing – then the reply is that to do so is directly to violate the moral law. Men's rights are infringed by these, as much as by all other trade interferences. The invalid is at liberty to buy medicine and advice from whomsoever he pleases; the unlicensed practitioner is at liberty to sell these to whomsoever will buy. On no pretext whatever can a barrier be set up between them without the law of equal freedom being broken; and least of all may the government, whose office it is to uphold that law, become a transgressor of it." Herbert Spencer, *Social Statics* 333 (Robert Schalkenbach Foundation ed. 1995) (originally published 1851) (emphasis in original).

67. Richard Hofstadter, *Social Darwinism in American Thought* 4-5 (rev. ed. 1955).

68. U.S. Dep't of Commerce 139.

69. *Quoted* in Alvin M. Josephy, Jr., *On The Hill A History of the American Congress* 248 (2d ed. 1979).

70. 1 *Holmes-Pollock Letters* 58 (Mark De Wolfe Howe ed. 1941), *quoted* in Hofstadter 32.

71. Nevertheless, the doctrine of *laissez faire* coexisted with federal governmental support for railroads, state occupational licensing laws and laws regulating public utilities, and some other forms of economic regulation by the States. *See* Lawrence M. Friedman, *A History of American Law* 453-60 (2d ed. 1985).

72. *See generally* David W. Noble, *The Progressive Mind, 1890-1917* (1970).

73. A Member of Congress stated in 1885: "In ordinary cases the consumer may be left to his own intelligence to protect himself against impositions. By the exercise of a reasonable degree of caution, he can protect himself from frauds in under-weight and in under-measure. If he can not detect a paper-soled shoe on inspection, he detects it in the wearing of it, and in one way or another he can impose a penalty upon the fraudulent vendor. As a general rule the doctrine of laissez faire can be applied. Not so with many of the adulterations of food. Scientific inspection is needed to detect the fraud, and scientific inspection is beyond the reach of the ordinary consumer. In such cases the Government should intervene." *Quoted* in Law & Libecap 8.

74. George E. Mowry, *The Era of Theodore Roosevelt and the Birth of Modern America 1900-1912* at 19 (1958).

75. *Lochner v. New York*, 198 U.S. 45, 61 (1905).

76. *Id.* at 75 (Holmes, J., dissenting).

77. Matthew Josephson, *The President-Makers: The Culture of Politics and Leadership in an Age of Enlightenment, 1869-1919* at 10 (1940).

78. Chambers 151-52.

79. Upton Sinclair, *The Jungle* unnumbered page (Signet ed. 1960) (originally published 1906).

80. *Id.* at 349 (afterword by Robert B. Downs, quoting Sinclair).

81. Cashman 360.

82. 24 Stat. 379 (1887).

83. Friedman 451-52; Cashman 359-60.

84. 34 Stat. 584 (1906).

85. Young, *Toadstool Millionaires*, ch. 4, at 7, *available at* http://www.quackwatch.org/13Hx/TM/04.html. In the last third of the 19th century, however, there was a resurgence of such laws. See Hofstadter 4-5.

86. Keller 412.

87. Young, *Toadstool*, ch. 4 at 7.

88. Starr 100. So, too, did the Supreme Court in *American School of Magnetic Healing v. McAnnulty*, 187 U.S. 94 (1902) (holding that statute authorizing Post Office to reject letters to persons engaged in fraudulent scheme did not reach scheme involving therapeutic claims, which the Court treated as opinions incapable of being proved true or false).

89. Cashman 364.

90. Starr 80-81.

91. *Id.* at 90, 92, 109. In 1900, the U.S. had about 110,000 physicians, of whom only about 33,000 belonged to any medical society (local, state, or national), and only 8,000 belonged to the AMA. By 1910, the AMA had 70,000 members, about half the profession. Id. 109-10.

92. Keller 300.

93. *Id.* at 310, 381. Over half of federal revenue during 1876-1904 came from taxation of alcohol. Young, *Pure Food* 165.

94. 26 Stat. 209 (1890).

95. Josephy 263.

96. *United States v. E.C. Knight & Co.*, 156 U.S. 1 (1895).

97. Josephy 278.

98. Robert A. Caro, *The Years of Lyndon Johnson: Master of the Senate* 9 (2002).

99. *Id.* at 33.

100. Okun 75-82.

101. *Id.* at 89.

102. *Id.* at 82-87.

103. *Id.* at 100

104. *Quoted in id.* at 104.

105. *Quoted in id.* at 105.

106. *Id.* at 167.

107. Young, *Pure Food* 4.

108. Law 1106.

109. *Id.*

110. *See* Law 1117.

111. *Id.* at 1104 (footnote omitted). Law also concludes that "proxies for the importance of consumer groups are closely correlated with cross-state variation in state pure food and pure dairy laws." *Id.* What he calls "consumer groups" were organizations with broader purposes, such as the Women's Christian Temperance Union and the General Federation of Women's Clubs, who also campaigned for pure food laws. *Id.* at 1123.

112. During floor debate in 1906, Senator Heyburn referred to "decisions of the Supreme Court of the United States that the jurisdiction of the United States under the interstate-commerce clause of the Constitution continues so long as the goods are in unbroken packages, and the State's jurisdiction does not attach so long as they are in unbroken packages . . . ." 40 Cong. Rec. 2723 (Feb. 20, 1906); *see also* S. Rep. 56-516, at 529-30 (1900). *In Leisy v. Hardin*, 135 U.S. 100 (1890), for example, the Court held under the Commerce Clause of the Constitution, that, unless authorized by Congress, a State could not ban the sale from an unbroken original package of an otherwise legitimate article of commerce imported from another State, in that case intoxicating liquors. The Court also explained, however: "Articles in such a condition as tend to spread disease are not merchantable, are not legitimate subjects of trade and commerce, and the self-protecting power of each State, therefore, may be rightfully exerted against their introduction, and such exercise of power cannot be considered a regulation of commerce, prohibited by the Constitution . . . ." *Id.* at 113. In *Plumley v. Massachusetts*, 155 U.S. 461 (1894), the Court upheld against a challenge under the Commerce Clause a statute banning the sale of oleomargarine except "in a separate and distinct form, and in such manner as will advise the consumer of its real character, free from coloration or ingredient that causes it to look like butter." The Court viewed the statute as directed against fraud. *Id.* at 468. "If there be any subject over which it would seem the States ought to have plenary control . . . , it is the protection of the people against fraud and deception in the sale of food products." *Id.* at 472. Also, *compare Powell v. Pennsylvania*, 127 U.S. 678 (1888) (statute totally banning sale of oleomargarine upheld, against Fourteenth Amendment challenge, as applied to oleomargarine manufactured in State where sold) *with Schollenberger v. Pennsylvania*, 171 U.S. 1 (1898) (identical statute held unconstitutional under Commerce Clause as applied to oleomargarine imported from another State into State where sold). In *Schollenberger*, the Court stated: "The general rule to be deduced from the decisions of this court is that a lawful article of commerce cannot be wholly excluded from importation into a State from another State where it was manufactured or grown. A State has power to regulate the introduction of any article, including a food product, so as to insure purity of the article imported, but such police power does not include the total exclusion even of an article of food." *Id.* at 12; *see also id.* at 14. Also, in *Austin v. Tennessee*, 179 U.S. 343 (1900), the Court made clear that original packages could not be manipulated to evade state-law restrictions.

113. *See* Law & Libecap 9.

114. Law 1122. Federal regulation gave a competitive advantage to national firms over regional or local firms. Coppin & High 6.

115. 9 Stat. 237 (1848).

116. Young, *Pure Food* 6-7.

117. *Id.* at 29.

118. 34 Stat. 768 (1906).

119. Young, *Pure Food* 16-17.

120. The appropriation was for chemical analyses by the Patent Office, then part of the Department of State. 9 Stat. 284, 285 (1948).

121. Young, *Pure Food* 32-33.

122. *Quoted* in Young, *Pure Food* 51.

123. *Id.*

124. Okun 127.

125. *Quoted in id.* at 137.

126. Young, *Pure Food* 51-57.

127. *Id.* at 60.

128. Okun 166.

129. Young, *Pure Food* 60-61.

130. *Id.* at 50.

131. Harvey W. Wiley, *An Autobiography* 13, 14, 18, 67-73, 97, 122, 159, 288 (1930).

132. 2 Mark Sullivan, *Our Times The United States 1900-1925[,] America Finding Herself* 520 (1927).

133. Coppin & High 44-45.

134. Young, *Pure Food* 92.

135. *Id.* at 103.

136. Carpenter 203-04.

137. Young, *Pure Food* 103.

138. Quoted in Young, *Pure Food* 96.

139. 26 Stat. 414 (1890). It was expanded in 1891. 26 Stat. 1089 (1891); *see also* 28 Stat. 727, 731-33 (1895). An earlier statute had directed the establishment in the Department of Agriculture of "a Bureau of Animal Industry" with a Chief "whose duty it shall be to investigate and report upon the condition of the domestic animals of the United States, their protection and use, and also inquire into and report the causes of contagious, infectious, and communicable diseases among them, and the means for the prevention and cure of the same, and to collect such information on these subjects as shall be valuable to the agricultural and commercial interests of the country . . . ." 23 Stat. 31 (1884).

140. The 1891 act was also intended to provide some protection for cattlemen and eastern butchers against "dressed" meat prepared in Chicago. Law & Libecap 9.

141. Young, *Pure Food* 96-97.

142. *Id.* at 98.

143. Carpenter 268.

144. *Quoted in Young, Pure Food* 98-99.

145. *Id.* at 99.

146. Law & Libecap 15.

147. Wiley 202-03.

148. Law & Libecap 16.

149. Young, *Pure Food* 110.

150. *Id.* at 112.

151. Quoted in Young, Pure Food 138-39.

152. Id. at 135-39.

153. *Adulteration of Food Products*, S. Rep. 56-516 (1900).

154. Wiley commented in his autobiography that, until Mason became Chairman of the Committee, "[pure food bills in the Senate had been regularly committed to the Committee on Manufactures, much as an infant would be left to starve in a barren room." Wiley 224.

155. *E.g., Adulteration of Food Products*, S. Doc. 56-141, (1901); *Adulteration, Etc. of Foods, Etc.*, S. Rep. 57-972 (1902).

156. Lorine Swainston Goodwin, *The Pure Food, Drink, and Drug Crusaders*, 1879-1914 at 17-23 (1999).

157. *Id.* at 30-34.

158. *Id.* at 65-72.

160. Chambers 32.

161. Carpenter 261. 162. Id. at 261.

162. *Id.* at 261.

163. Young, *Pure Food* 129.

164. Josephson 128.

165. Quoted in *id.* at 99-100.

166. David W. Noble, *The Progressive Mind, 1890-1917* at 159 (1970).

167. Wiley 221-23.

168. Josephson 174.

169. Mowry 201.

170. 32 Stat. 728 (1902).

171. Young, *Pure Food* 148-49.

172. McCumber had been chosen for the Senate by a political machine dominated by railroads. Kane 165. In North Dakota, Edwin Ladd, the state chemist, had exposed widespread fraud in processed foods sold in the State, which he attributed to eastern economic interests. He obtained enactment of a pure-food law in 1901. He was active in the AOAC and was a close ally of Wiley. Young, *Pure Food* 181-82. "[W]hen he argued that North Dakota was the docile victim of Eastern commercial interests, he struck a raw nerve and the resulting reflex exceeded all expectations. 'North Dakota is the "dumping ground" of spurious products' became his strident battle cry." Kane 163 (footnote omitted).

173. 32 Stat. 286, 296 (1902). The bill also authorized the Secretary of Agriculture, in collaboration with the AOAC, to set standards for the purity of foods and to define "adulteration" "for the guidance of the officials of the various States and of courts of justice." The locus of standard-setting authority was very controversial. Among food processors, Wiley was feared as an excessively zealous regulator. Initial standards under the 1902 law were issued in 1903. Young, *Pure Food* 161-62. By 1906, standards had been issued for many foods. *Id.* at 180.

174. Wiley 216, 219.

175. Young, *Pure Food* 152-55.

176. Wiley 216-17.

177. Wiley's opposition to preservatives whose safety was not supported by long use was based on scientific theories that had no validity. Coppin & High 55.

178. Wiley 217-18.

179. Carpenter 2.

180. 30 Stat. 947, 951-52 (1899); 32 Stat. 1147, 1157-58 (1903)

181. Young, *Pure Food* 164.

182. *Id.*

183. Josephy 280-81.

184. Goodwin 226-27.

185. *Quoted in id.* 227.

186. Young, *Pure Food* 170; Coppin & High 59-60, 61. A group of publishers lobbied Heyburn against regulation of patent medicines for fear it would reduce advertising revenues. Coppin & High 60.

187. Chambers 96.

188. Young, *Pure Food* 185.

189. Id. at 198; Michael McGerr, *A Fierce Discontent The Rise and Fall of the Progressive Movement in America, 1870-1920* at 161 (2003).

190. Crunden 178-79; Young, *Pure Food* 198.

191. Crunden 179; Young, *Toadstool Millionaires*, ch. 13, at 5.

192. Young, *Pure Food* 195.

193. Goodwin 219.

194. Young, *Pure Food*. 195-96.

195. *Id.* at 194.

196. Mowry 206.

197. Crunden 95.

198. Young, *Toadstool Millionaires*, ch. 13, at 2.

199. Goodwin 219-20.

200. Wiley characterized him as a "militant proponent of pure food." *Wiley* 228.

201. Goodwin 163; Sullivan 530.

202. Young, *Pure Food* 178. Heinz used benzoate of soda, a preservative, in catsup until 1905. Coppin & High 30. Once it developed technology that made benzoate of soda in catsup unnecessary, it favored banning it. *Id.* at 65-66. Similarly, Frederick Pabst also supported pure food and drugs legislation, to prevent others from using chemical preservatives or additives in beer after technological developments made them unnecessary and to enhance the public image of beer as pure and safe. Donna J. Wood, *The Strategic Use of Public Policy: Business Support for the 1906 Food and Drug Act*, 59 Bus. Hist. Rev. 403, 420-21 (1985). Heinz and Pabst reflect the effect of technological advances on competition and efforts by companies benefiting from such advances to have their competitive advantage written into law. Id. at 428.

203. Sullivan 530; Goodwin 163-64.

204. Crunden 188.

205. On that alliance, *see* Sullivan 526.

206. Thomas A. Bailey, *Congressional Opposition to Pure Food Legislation, 1879-1906*, 36 Am. J. Sociology 52, 63-64 (1930).

207. Young, *Pure Food* 182-83.

208. Bailey 52.

209. *E.g.*, 24 Stat. 209 (1886).

210. 29 Stat. 253 (1896).

211. Laws were enacted in 1883 "to prevent the importation of adulterated and spurious [t]eas," in 1890 in part to "prohibit[] the importation of adulterated articles of food or drink," and in 1897 "[t]o prevent the importation of impure and unwholesome tea." 22 Stat. 451 (1883); 26 Stat. 414, 415-17 (1890); 29 Stat. 604 (1897). Enactment of the Tea Adulteration Act of 1883 was supported by importers and wholesalers. Okun 289-90.

212. 26 Stat. 414, 414-15 (1890). Meatpackers sought the 1890 inspection law to help exports. Okun 290-91.

213. Laws were enacted in 1888 "to prevent the manufacture or sale of adulterated food or drugs in the District of Columbia," and in 1898 "[t]o prevent the adulteration of candy in the District of Columbia." 25 Stat. 549 (1888); 30 Stat. 398 (1898).

214. 32 Stat. 728 (1902).

215. In 1902, a law was enacted "[t]o prevent a false branding or marking of food and dairy products as to the State or Territory in which they are made or produced. 32 Stat. 632 (1902).

216. Temin 29; Wood 422-27.

Sometimes, in the struggle for advantage, Wiley's position on an issue (*e.g.*, regulation of whiskey) was supported by one side (straight-whiskey interests) and opposed by the other (rectified-whiskey interests). Coppin & High 54. Wiley, who oversaw the purchasing of whiskey for the Cosmos Club in Washington D.C., favored straight whiskey. *Id.* He considered rectified whiskey adulterated, Wiley 203-04, and mislabeled, Coppin & High 57. Wiley's placing of himself in the middle of such controversies between economic competitors helped him gather support for the legislation (*e.g.*, attacks on rectifiers may have increased support for the bill among advocates of temperance, *id.* 62), but also made him personally a target of some of its opponents, *id.* 56, 66, 67-68, and probably enhanced some opposition. In the end, of course, Wiley gained enough support for enactment.

217. Young, *Pure Food* 181.

218. This analysis goes somewhat beyond Crunden 182-83.

219. See in this connection Carpenter 261; Crunden 185-86; Wood 409.

220. Young, *Pure Food* 229.

221. Crunden 173.

222. Young, *Pure Food* 230.

223. Young, *Pure Food* 229.

224. Crunden 192.

225. Coppin & High 81-82.

226. Young, *Pure Food*, 166-68; Pub. L. No. 59-384, § 8, 34 Stat. 768, 770-71 (1906).

227. The AMA also lobbied Aldrich on behalf of the bill in mid-February. Sullivan 533. For some hypotheses as to why Aldrich permitted the bill to proceed, see Coppin & High 76.

228. 40 Cong. Rec. 2720 (Feb. 20, 1906) (statement of Sen. Lodge).

229. It survived in the final legislation. *See* Pub. L. No. 59-384, § 7, fifth, proviso, 34 Stat. 768, 770 (1906).

230. It, too, survived in the final legislation. *See* Pub. L. No. 59-384, § 7, first proviso, 34 Stat. 768, 769 (1906).

231. Young, *Pure Food* 208; 40 Cong. Rec. 2724-28 (Feb. 20, 1906). The Supreme Court later held that the 1906 Act did not reach false therapeutic claims. *United States v. Johnson*, 221 U.S. 488 (1911) (Holmes, J.).

232. 40 Cong. Rec. 2773 (Feb. 21, 1906).

233. Law & Libecap conducted an empirical analysis comparing the votes of 57 Senators who voted both on a procedural motion on a food and drugs bill in 1903 and on the Senate bill on February 21, 1906. They concluded that the analysis roughly supports the view that muckraking about patent medicines aroused consumer interest in food and drugs legislation, which weakened politicians' opposition, changed votes, and thereby broke the political stalemate. Law & Libecap 28-29. The Law & Libecap analysis is not refined enough, however, to separate the effects of muckraking

about patent medicines from other muckraking about drugs and food from 1904 to early 1906.

234. Wiley 228. In the 57th Congress, Mann had strongly opposed granting enforcement powers to the Department of Agriculture. Repeated visits from Wiley evidently changed his mind. Carpenter 268.

235. Young, *Pure Food* 211.

236. *Id.*

237. In the House, the patent-medicine provision was championed by Rep. Edwin Y. Webb of North Carolina, who during the February 1906 hearings quoted from Samuel Hopkins Adams's series in *Colliers. Id.* at 218. The muckrakers' attacks on patent medicine also won Wiley's support for their inclusion in the bill. Coppin & High 70.

238. This provision survived in the final legislation. See Pub. L. No. 59-384, § 3, 34 Stat. 768, 768-69 (1906).

239. This provision did not survive in the final legislation.

240. 2 Sullivan 534.

241. *Id.*

242. Young, *Pure Food* 220.

243. *Id.*

244. *New York Times,* June 4, 1906, at 9.

245. *New York Times,* June 5, 1906, at 9.

246. *New York Times,* June 8, 1906, at 8. Coppin & High found no evidence that Cannon delayed the bill. They note that he later attributed the delay to normal House procedures. Coppin & High 81.

247. Young, *Pure Food* 236-37.

248. *Id.* at 240.

249. *New York Times,* May 28, 1906, at 1.

250. *New York Times,* May 29, 1906, at 1.

251. *New York Times,* June 5, 1906, at 1.

252. Young, *Pure Food* 235-51.

253. *Id.* at 254.

254. Sullivan 549.

255. Young, *Pure Food* 254.

256. *Id.* at 261.

257. Wiley 231.

258. Sullivan 550.

259. Law & Libecap explain the role of such crises as "rais[ing] the perceived benefits of enacting federal food and drug regulation and lower[ing] the cost of bringing diverse interest groups together." Law & Libecap 2.

260. 188 U.S. 321 (1903); Keller 418.

261. Crunden 165.

262. 32 Stat.728 (1902).

263. 34 Stat. 669, 674 (1906).

264. Temin 31.

265. *Id.* at 30-31.

266. Carpenter 179. Wiley wrote of Wilson: "There was no questioning his ability, his political sagacity and to a certain extent his tact. But I look back upon the fifteen years I spent as his subordinate in the Department of Agriculture and can not withhold the conviction that he had the greatest capacity of any person I ever knew to take the wrong side of public questions, especially those relating to health through diet." Wiley 190-91.

267. Carpenter 212.

268. *Id.* at 179-211, 213-14.

269. *See generally* Carpenter. See also, e.g., Senator Heyburn's rationale for delegating enforcement authority under the 1906 Act to the Department of Agriculture, stated in debate on the bill. 40 Cong. Rec. 2733 (Feb. 20, 1906). Wiley's assessment of the food adulteration problem was also moderate and politically credible. A Senate report in 1901 summarized his view:

Dr Wiley has stated that probably 95 per cent of all food products have been adulterated at some time in some country; but he estimates that scarcely 5 per cent of the food products bought at random, other than spices and ground coffee, would now be found to be adulterated. Moreover, the adulteration which is injurious to health is much less extensive than that which is merely more fraudulent.

S. Doc. 56-141 at 2 (1901) (footnote omitted).

270. Anderson 105.

271. It is striking that, although Wiley was located in the Department of Agriculture, pure food legislation was viewed as serving the interests of farmers generally, and during the 1880s the Grange supported pure-food legislation, Gabriel Kolko, *The Triumph of Conservatism A Reinterpretation of American History, 1900-1916* at 108 (1963), farm groups were not prominent in Wiley's coalition, Carpenter 257. Nor were working-class urban consumers of adulterated and misbranded food and drugs. Coppin & High 31. Moreover, although before 1900 food and drugs legislation was considered by the Agriculture Committees in the House and Senate, after 1900 neither committee was involved in such legislation. Carpenter 266.

272. On the importance of the diversity of a coalition supporting a government official's desired course of action, *see* Carpenter 30-32.

273. Coppin & High 87.

274. *Id.* at 17; Carpenter 30-35.

275. *Cf.* Wiebe xiv, 159-60, 191.

276. *Id.* at 159-60.

277. Wood argues that U.S. food exporters supported the legislation for this reason. Wood 421. The business firms that would support regulation as a means to increase public confidence would tend to be those large enough to care about public perception of a product category, not merely public perception of their own products.

278. Gabriel Kolko points out that the long history of relations between the federal government and the railroads had been highly beneficial to the railroads. Kolko 59

279. See generally Wood; Kolko 108-10. Kolko characterizes as "conservative" legislation that "preserve[s] the basic social and economic relations essential to a capitalist society." *Id.* at 2.

280. Keller 398.

281. *Id.* at 409.

282. Coppin & High 36, 54, 56, 58-59, 62, 66-67, 73.

Index